Korean Vocabulary Practice for Foreigners

English Version

Beginning Level

초급

외국인을 위한
한국어 어휘 연습

연세대학교 한국어학당 편

연세대학교 출판문화원

Preface

The Korean Language Institute of Yonsei University celebrated its 54rd anniversary this year. Throughout the years, the Korean Language Institute has published teaching materials for conversational Korean, practice workbooks, and much more. However, as the number of students that are learning Korean increases, their demands became more diverse. As a result of a rise in demands to practice Korean vocabulary, it became necessary to increase teaching materials for practicing vocabulary words.

'Korean Vocabulary Pratice for Foreigners' is divided into three books: Beginner, Intermediate, and Advanced. This book was published in order to build the vocabulary of Korean language students while increasing their proficiency in the language. Also, this book was written to prepare students for the various kinds of Korean Proficiency Examinations that currently exist. Vocabulary words that form part of the text book and that may appear on the Korean Proficiency Examinations have been carefully chosen and along with each word an explication of its meaning and example sentence have been provided. Also, a section of various practice problems is included so that students can make good use of the words they have learned.

'Korean Vocabulary Pratice for Foreigners' can be used as a complimentary textbook at the Korean Language Institute for learning vocabulary or can be used by students who are studying Korean on their own. We hope that 'Korean Vocabulary Pratice for Foreigners' can be used to efficiently teach vocabulary to students of the Korean language while improving their proficiency.

Yonsei University Language Research and Education Center
Korean Language Institute Compilation Committee

머리말

연세대학교 한국어학당은 올해로 창립 54주년을 맞이했습니다. 연세대학교 한국어학당은 그동안 회화 교재, 언어기능별 교재, 활용연습용 교재 등 많은 교재를 집필, 출간하였습니다. 그러나 한국어를 배우는 학습자들이 늘면서 그들의 요구도 다양해졌습니다. 특히 한국어 어휘 학습에 대한 학습자들의 요구가 높아져 어휘 학습용 교재가 필요하게 되었습니다.

'외국인을 위한 한국어 어휘 연습'은 초급, 중급, 고급의 3권으로 구성되었습니다. 이 책은 한국어를 공부하는 학습자들의 어휘력을 향상시켜 한국어 숙달도를 높이기 위해서 출간하게 되었습니다. 특히 '외국인을 위한 한국어 어휘 연습'은 현재 시행되고 있는 다양한 한국어능력 평가 시험에 대비하도록 구성되었습니다. 한국어 교재와 한국어능력 평가 시험에서 다루어지고 있는 어휘를 등급에 맞게 선정하여 각 어휘의 의미를 설명하고 예문을 제시하였습니다. 또한 다양한 문제를 통해 학습한 어휘를 활용할 수 있도록 구성하였습니다.

'외국인을 위한 한국어 어휘 연습'은 한국어교육기관에서 어휘 학습을 위한 부교재로 활용할 수 있으며 혼자서 공부하는 학습자는 자습용으로 활용할 수 있습니다. '외국인을 위한 한국어 어휘 연습'이 한국어 학습자들이 효율적으로 어휘를 학습하여 한국어능력을 향상할 수 있도록 하는 데 기여할 수 있기를 바랍니다.

연세대학교 언어연구교육원 한국어학당 교재편찬위원회

Introductory Remarks

01   This book is designed for students who will be learning Korean at a beginner's level.

02   This book is separated into 15 sections.

03   The book is separated into 50-100 subjects including vocabulary words to enhance the learning of these subjects. The vocabulary words include headwords, synonyms, antonyms, related words that add up to about 1,300 total.

04   Each word is explained through pronunciation, parts of speech, translation, detailed explanation for the word when needed, usage, expression, synonyms, antonyms, related words, and examples.

05   The examples are written in grammar that can be understood by a beginner.

06   The vocabulary is ordered in counter-subject, sections, and 가나다 order.

07   Each subject is separated into vocabulary explanation and practice questions. First the vocabulary explanation section includes detailed vocabulary definition when needed, word usage, word expression, synonyms, antonyms, related words, and examples to further explain the word, and the practice question section is created for the learner to be able to apply the vocabulary words learned, and to be able to verify that they have learned it.

08   The vocabulary practice section is divided into different categories. We took into consideration the needs for the students who will be taking the Korean Language Test (TOPIK), and designed this book so that the examples and practice questions could reflect what could appear on these tests.

09   The vocabulary index includes different headwords, synonyms, antonyms, related words and they're all included in 가나다 order. Index includes the amount of vocabulary words and the page numbers with the words.

일러두기

01 외국인을 위한 한국어 어휘 연습(초급)'은 한국어를 배우는 외국인 학습자를 위한 어휘집으로 초급 단계에서 알아야 할 어휘를 소개하였다.

02 이 책은 주제별 총 15과로 되어 있다.

03 이 책은 주제별로 약 50개~100개 정도의 어휘를 제시하여 설명하였다. 총 어휘 개수는 표제어, 유의어, 반의어, 관련어 등을 모두 포함하여 1,300여 개이다.

04 각 어휘 설명에는 발음, 품사, 번역, 어휘 의미에 대한 상세 설명, 활용 구문, 활용 표현, 유의어, 반의어, 관련어, 예문 등이 포함되어 있다.

05 예문에는 초급 단계의 학습자가 이해할 만한 문법을 사용하였다.

06 어휘 제시의 순서는 대주제, 소주제, 가나다순이다.

07 각 과는 크게 어휘설명과 연습문제의 두 부분으로 구성되어 있다. 먼저 어휘 설명 부분에서는 어휘 정의에 대한 상세 설명, 활용 구문, 활용 표현, 유의어, 반의어, 관련 어휘, 예문을 통해 학습자들이 어휘에 대해 충분히 이해할 수 있도록 했고, 어휘 연습 문제 부분에서는 어휘문제들을 통해 앞서 배운 어휘를 정확하게 이해했는지 확인할 수 있도록 했다.

08 어휘 연습 문제는 다양한 유형으로 제시하였다. 특히 한국어능력시험(TOPIK)을 준비하는 학습자들을 고려하여 한국어능력시험의 문제 유형과 같거나 유사한 문제들을 수록하였다.

09 단어 색인에는 각 과에서 주요하게 다룬 표제어는 물론 표제어의 유의어, 반의어, 관련 어휘도 모두 포함하여 가나다순으로 제시하였다. 단어 색인에는 단어가 제시된 페이지와 과도 같이 제시하였다.

Subject Map

chapter	Counter-subject	Sections	Number of Vocabulary words
1	Position and Location	1. position 2. location	54
2	Object	1. clothing 2. general merchandise, jewels, accessory 3. stationary 4. home appliances, home electronics 5. kitchen appliances, bathroom appliances 6. furniture 7. object properties	104
3	Time I	1. number 2. time, hour 3. date	41
4	Time II	1. order 2. length of time 3. time	43
5	People I	1. family, close relatives 2. relationship 3. name, age, gender 4. appearance, personality	61
6	People II	1. emotion, thought 2. occupation 3. posture, movement	61
7	Daily Life I	1. everyday living 2. contact	56
8	Daily Life II	1. meeting 2. shopping	45

chapter	Counter-subject	Sections	Number of Vocabulary words
9	**School and Work**	1. personal relationship 2. study and work 3. school life 4. work life	93
10	**Leisure**	1. exercise 2. sensibility, view/watch 3. travel 4. hobby	51
11	**Food**	1. taste 2. drink, snack 3. ingredient, sauce 4. cooking 5. food 6. meal	96
12	**Transportation**	1. means of transportation and places to ride the transportation 2. get on, boarding 3. road, driving	58
13	**Nature and Season**	1. animal life, plant life 2. color 3. nature, scenery 4. weather 5. season	66
14	**Residence**	1. building 2. house 3. moving 4. house life	57
15	**Health**	1. physical 2. illness, symptom 3. hospital, treatment	75

내용구성

과	대주제	소주제	어휘개수
9	학교와 직장	1. 대인관계 2. 학업과 업무 3. 학교 생활 4. 직장 생활	93
10	여가	1. 운동 2. 감상 · 관람 3. 여행 4. 취미	51
11	음식	1. 맛 2. 음료 · 간식 3. 재료 · 소스 4. 요리 5. 음식 6. 식사	96
12	교통	1. 탈것 · 타는 곳 2. 승차 · 탑승 3. 길 · 운전	58
13	자연과 계절	1. 동식물 2. 색깔 3. 자연 · 경치 4. 날씨 5. 계절	66
14	주거	1. 건물 2. 집 3. 이사 4. 집안일	57
15	건강	1. 신체 2. 병 · 증상 3. 병원 · 치료	75

차례 Contents

위치와 장소

01

Position and
Location

001
걸다

[걸다] 동사 to hang

to attach something from the top to a hook, a piece of string, ect, ㄹverb

[Usage] N에 N을/를 걸다

[Expression] 벽에 그림을 걸다 to hang the picture on the wall

옷걸이에 옷을 걸다 to hang the clothes on the hanger

[Example] 옷을 옷걸이에 거세요. Hang the clothes on the hanger please.

가족사진을 벽에 걸었어요. I hung the family picture on the wall.

002
근처

[근처] 명사 near

[Usage] N 근처

[Synonym] 주변 surroundings

주위 close proximity

[Example] 병원 근처에는 약국이 많습니다.

There are lots of pharmacies near the hospital.

저는 학교 근처에 있는 하숙집에 살아요.

I live in a boarding house near my school.

003
넣다

[너타] 동사 to put in

[Usage] N에 N을/를 넣다

[Expression] 지갑에 돈을 넣다 to put the money in the wallet

커피에 설탕을 넣다 to put the sugar in the coffee

[Example] 가방에 책을 넣었어요. I put the book in the bag.

삼계탕에 소금을 넣어서 드세요.

Put salt in the samgyetang soup and eat it.

004
놓다

[노타] 동사 to lay

[Usage] AV어/아/여 놓다

N에 N을/를 놓다

[Expression] 넣어 놓다 to lay inside

걸어 놓다 to place by hanging

책상 위에 책을 놓다 to place the book on the table

[Synonym] 두다 to place

[Example] 식탁 위에 수저를 놓았습니다. I laid the eating utensils on the table.

바닥이 더러우니까 가방을 놓지 마세요.

The floor is dirty, so do not place bag on the floor.

005
두다

[두다] 동사 to place

[Usage]　　AV어/아/여 두다

　　　　　N에 N을/를 두다

[Expression]　놓아두다 to put in place

　　　　　넣어 두다 to put inside

　　　　　걸어 두다 to hang in place

[Synonym]　놓다 to lay

[Example]　지갑은 서랍 안에 잘 넣어 두었어요.

　　　　　I placed the wallet in the cabinet carefully.

　　　　　오늘은 회식이 있어서 차를 집에 두고 출근했어요.

　　　　　Today there is an office dinner so I left my car at home.

006
밑

[밑] 명사 under

　　　　　below, underneath

[Usage]　　N 밑

[Synonym]　아래 below

[Antonym]　위 above

[Example]　제일 밑에 있는 책이 뭐예요?

　　　　　What is the book underneath all of the others?

　　　　　나무 밑에서 할아버지들이 바둑을 둡니다.

　　　　　The grandfathers are playing chess under the tree.

007
사이

[사이] 명사 1. distance　2. between time　3. relationship

　　　　　1. distance

[Usage]　　N과/와 N 사이

[Example]　학교와 병원 사이에 은행이 있습니다.

　　　　　There is a bank between the school and hospital.

　　　　　2. between time

[Usage]　　N과/와 N 사이

[Example]　한 시에서 두 시 사이에 전화하세요.

　　　　　Call between one o'clock and two o'clock.

　　　　　3. relationship

[Usage]　　N 사이

　　　　　N과/와 N 사이

[Expression]　친구 사이 friend relationship

　　　　　부부 사이 married relationship

　　　　　부모와 자식 사이 parent and child relationship

선생님과 학생 사이 teacher and student relationship

[Example] 부부 사이에는 비밀이 없어야 한다고 생각해요.
I think there should be no secrets in a married relationship.

008
속¹

[속] 명사 inner side

[Usage] **N** 속

[Expression] 물 속 under water

숲 속 inside the forest

산 속 inside the mountain

봉투 속 inside the envelope

상자 속 inside the box

[Synonym] 안 inside

[Antonym] 겉 outside

[Example] 봉투 속에 돈을 넣으세요. Put the money inside the envelope.

주머니 속에 아무것도 없어요. There is nothing inside the pocket.

009
안

[안] 명사 inside

[Usage] **N** 안

[Expression] 집 안 inside the house

학교 안 inside the school

건물 안 inside the building

가방 안 inside the bag

안으로 들어가다 to go inside

[Synonym] 속¹ inner

[Antonym] 밖 outside

[Example] 가방 안에 만화책이 있어요. There is a comic book inside the bag.

교실 안에서 음식을 먹으면 안 됩니다.
You cannot eat inside the classroom.

010
앞

[압] 명사 front

[Usage] **N** 앞

[Antonym] 뒤 back

[Example] 선생님 앞에 학생들이 앉아 있어요.
There are students sitting in front of the teacher.

12(열두)시에 학교 앞에서 만납시다.
Let's meet at twelve o'clock in front of the school.

'안' and '속' can usually be interchanged.

가방 안 inside bag (O) / **봉투 안** inside envelope (O)

가방 속 inner part of bag (O) / **봉투 속** inner part of envelope (O)

Sometimes the words cannot be interchanged. When referring to a place, '안' (inner) is usually used rather than '속'.

학교 안 inside school (O) / inside the office **회사 안** (O)

공항 안 inside the airport (O)

학교 속 inner side of school (X) / **회사 속** inner side of office (X)

공항 속 inside of airport (X)

In these cases we don't use '안' but '속'.

산 안 inside the mountain (X) / **숲 안** inside the forest (X)

물 안 in the water (X) / **사람 안** inside the human (X)

산 속 within the forest (O) / **숲 속** inside the forest (O)

물 속 within the water (O) / **사람 속** within a human (O)

011
어디

[어디] 대명사 where

[Example] 어디로 가면 버스를 탈 수 있어요? Where can I go to ride the bus?

나는 서울에서 왔는데 너는 고향이 어디야?
I am from Seoul, where is your hometown?

012
옆

[엽] 명사 side

[Usage] **N** 옆

[Example] 우리 집 옆에 공원이 있습니다. There is a park next to my house.

한국에서는 어른과 술을 마실 때 고개를 옆으로 돌리고 마셔요.
When drinking with an elder in Korea, you should turn your head to the side and drink.

013
올려놓다

[올려노타] 동사 to put above

[Usage] **N**에 **N**을/를 올려놓다

[Expression] 책상 위에 가방을 올려놓다 to place the bag on top of the desk

[Antonym] 내려놓다 to put below

[Example] 가스레인지 위에 주전자를 올려놓았다.
I placed the kettle on top of the gas range.

아침에 학교에 오면 선생님 책상에 숙제 공책을 올려놓으세요.
When you come into the classroom in the morning, please put your homework book on top of the teacher's desk.

014
위

[위] 명사 above, up

[Usage]	<u>N</u> 위
[Expression]	위로 올라가다 to go above
[Antonym]	밑 bottom
	아래 under
[Example]	양말은 침대 위에 있어요. The socks are on top of the bed.
	숙제 공책을 책상 위에 놓았어요.
	I placed the homework book on top of the table.

015
위치

[위치] 명사 position, location

[Expression]	건물 위치 the location of the building
[Related word]	장소 place
[Example]	책상을 놓을 위치를 알려 주세요. Tell me where to place the table.
	우리가 묵을 호텔의 위치를 지도에서 확인해 보자.
	Let's check the location of the hotel we'll be staying at by looking at the map.

016
있다

[일따] 형용사 to have, to exist

[Usage]	<u>N</u>이/가 있다
[Antonym]	없다 don't have
[Example]	우리 반에 미국 사람이 있어요. There is an American in my class.
	저는 한국어 교과서가 3(세)권 있습니다.
	I have three Korean textbooks.

017
가게

[가게] 명사 store

[Usage] N 가게

[Expression] 옷가게 clothing store

신발 가게 shoe store

[Example] 집 근처에 가게가 있어서 편해요.
There is a store close to my house so it is very comfortable.

설탕을 사러 집 앞에 있는 가게에 갔다 왔어요.
I went outside and bought sugar at a store in front of my house.

018
경찰서

[경찰써] 명사 police station

[Example] 제일 가까운 경찰서가 어디에 있어요? Where is the closest police station?

길을 잘 모르면 경찰서에 가서 물어보세요.
If you cannot find the right direction, go and ask inside the police station.

019
공원

[공원] 명사 park

[Expression] 놀이 공원 play ground

[Example] 저는 주말마다 공원을 산책해요. Every weekend I take a walk in the park.

일요일에 가족과 같이 공원에 놀러 갔어요.
On Sunday, my family and I went to the park to play.

020
극장

[극짱] 명사 theater

[related word] 영화관 movie theater

[Example] 저녁 6(여섯)시에 극장 앞에서 만납시다.
Let's meet in front of the theater at 6pm.

수업이 끝난 후에 영화를 보러 극장에 갈 거예요.
After class I will be going to the theater to watch a movie.

021
꽃집

[꼳찝] 명사 flower shop

[Synonym] 꽃가게 flower store

[Example] 요즘은 꽃을 배달해 주는 꽃집이 많아요.
These days there are many flower shops that deliver the flower to your home.

저는 요즘 꽃집에서 아르바이트를 합니다.
These days I work part-time at the flower shop.

022
노래방

[노래방] 명사 karaoke

[Expression] 시험이 끝난 후에 친구들과 같이 노래방에 갔어요.
After finishing the exam, my friends and I went to a karaoke.

제가 자주 가는 노래방은 비싸지만 깨끗하고 넓어서 항상 사람이 많아요.
The karaoke that I go to is expensive but it is clean and large, so there are always a lot of people there.

023
대사관

[대사관] 명사 embassy

[Usage] N 대사관

[Expression] 미국 대사관 American embassy
일본 대사관 Japanese embassy
한국 대사관 Korean embassy

[Example] 중국 대사관은 어디에 있어요?
Where is the Chinese embassy?

비자를 받으려면 대사관에 가야 해요.
In order to receive a visa you need to go to the embassy.

024
문방구

[문방구] 명사 stationary store

[Synonym] 문구점 stationary shop

[Example] 학교 근처에 문방구가 많아요.
There are many stationary stores near the school.

문방구에서 연필, 지우개, 종이, 자, 가위 등을 살 수 있어요.
Stationary stores sell pencils, erasers, paper, rulers, scissors and many other supplies.

025
미술관

[미술관] 명사 art gallery

[Example] 미술관에서 사진을 찍으면 안 돼요.
Photos cannot be taken in the art gallery.

경기도 과천에 국립현대미술관이 있어요.
There is a national modern art gallery in Gyeong-gi-do Gwa-chan.

026
박물관

[방물관] 명사 museum

[Example] 한국의 국립중앙박물관은 서울 용산에 있습니다.
There is a national central museum at Yong-san in Seoul, Korea.

박물관에 가서 유물들을 보면서 역사 공부를 했어요.
I went to the museum and looked at the artifacts and learned a lot about history.

027
밝다

[박따] 형용사 1. to be bright 2. to be bright (the feeling of the color)

3. to be bright (emotionally happy)

1. to be bright

[Usage] N이/가 밝다

[Antonym] 어둡다 to be dark

[Example] 불을 켜니까 방이 밝아졌어요.
After turning on the lights, the room became bright.

2. to be bright (the feeling of the color)

[Usage] N이/가 밝다

[Antonym] 어둡다 to be dark (feeling of the color)

[Example] 미선 씨는 밝은 색 옷이 잘 어울려요.
Misun looks good in bright colored clothing.

3. to be bright (emotionally happy)

[Usage] N이/가 밝다

[Example] 밝은 목소리 bright and positive voice

표정이 밝다 to have a happy expression

밝게 웃다 to smile cheerfully

[Antonym] 어둡다 to have dark, negative, pessimistic personality

[Example] 우리 사무실에 재미있는 사람들이 많아서 항상 분위기가 밝아요.
There are many funny people in our office, so the mood is always happy and positive.

028
방송국

[방송국] 명사 broadcasting station

[Example] 방송국에 가면 연예인을 많이 볼 수 있어요.
If you go to the broadcasting station, you can see many celebrities.

저는 졸업 후에 방송국에서 기자로 일하고 싶습니다.
After graduation, I would like to work in a broadcasting station as a reporter.

도움말

There are broadcasting stations like the ones below.

한국방송(KBS)　　　문화방송(MBC)　　　서울방송(SBS)　　　교육방송(EBS)

029
백화점
    [배콰점] 명사 department store
    [Example]   백화점 물건은 비싸기는 하지만 질이 좋아요.
    The products in the department store are expensive, but the quality is good.

    세일 기간에는 백화점에 사람이 많아서 복잡해요.
    During sales season there are many people in the department store so it is very busy.

030
병원
    [병원] 명사 hospital
    [Usage]   병원에 입원하다 to be hospitalized in the hospital
    병원에서 퇴원하다 to be discharged from the hospital
    [Example]   남편이 병원에 입원했어요.
    My husband is hospitalized right now.

    많이 아프면 병원에 가세요.
    If you are really sick, go to the hospital.

031
빵집
    [빵찝] 명사 bakery
    [Synonym]   제과점 bakeshop
    [Example]   저는 아침마다 빵집에서 빵을 사요.
    Every morning I buy bread at the bakery.

    학교 안에 있는 빵집은 값이 싸고 맛있어서 학생들에게 인기가 많아요.
    The bakery in the school is very popular because the bread is inexpensive and delicious.

032
서비스센터
    [서비스센터] 명사 service center
    [Example]   휴대전화가 고장이 나서 서비스센터에 갔습니다.
    My cell phone broke so I went to the service center to get it fixed.

    서비스센터에 사람이 많아서 1(한)시간 동안 기다렸어요.
    There were many people at the service center so I had to wait an hour to get service.

033
서점
    [서점] 명사 bookstore
    [Synonym]   책방 bookshop
    [Example]   오늘 서점에 가서 책을 많이 사 왔어요.
    I bought many books from the bookstore.

    큰 서점에는 오랫동안 서서 책을 읽는 사람이 많습니다.
    In the larger bookstores there are many people that read books standing up for a long time.

034
세탁소

[세탁쏘] **명사** laundromat

[Expression] 세탁소에 맡기다 to leave clothes at the laundromat

[Example] 봄이 되어서 겨울옷을 세탁소에 맡겼어요.
Spring is here, so I left the winter clothes at the laundromat to be cleaned.

이 옷은 드라이클리닝을 해야 하니까 세탁소에 맡기세요.
This clothing needs to be dry-cleaned, so leave it at the laundromat.

035
수영장

[수영장] **명사** swimming pool

[Expression] 실내 수영장 inside pool

야외 수영장 outside pool

[Example] 저는 아침마다 수영장에 가서 수영을 해요.
Every morning I go to pool and swim.

지금은 날씨가 추워서 야외 수영장을 이용할 수 없습니다.
Right now it is cold, so the outside pool cannot be used.

036
술집

[술찝] **명사** drinking bar

[Example] 오늘은 회사 근처 술집에서 회식을 합시다.
Let's go to a bar near the office and have an office party.

이번 주말에 집 근처에 있는 술집에서 친구들을 만나기로 했어요.
I promised my friends this weekend that I would meet them at a bar near my house.

037
슈퍼마켓

[슈퍼마켇] **명사** supermarket

[Synonym] 마트 market, mart

가게 store

편의점 convenient store

[Example] 지금 집 앞 슈퍼마켓에서 세일을 한다고 해요.
There is a sale going on right now at the supermarket in front of my house.

슈퍼마켓에서 쌀이나 병맥주 등 무거운 것을 사면 주인 아저씨가 집까지 배달해 줍니다.
If you purchase heavy merchandise like rice or bottled beer, the owner will deliver it to your home.

038
스키장　　　[스키장] 명사 ski resort

[Example]　　　영수는 겨울이 되면 주말마다 스키장에 가요.
　　　　　　　　Young-soo goes to the ski resort every weekend during the winter.

　　　　　　　　저는 밤에 스키장에서 스키를 타는 것을 좋아해요.
　　　　　　　　I like skiing at night at the ski resort.

039
시골　　　　[시골] 명사 country

[Expression]　　시골 생활　country life
　　　　　　　　시골 풍경　country scenery

[Antonym]　　　도시　city

[Example]　　　시골은 공기가 좋아요.　The air is clean in the country.

　　　　　　　　시골에는 차가 많지 않아요.　There are few cars in the country.

040
시장　　　　[시장] 명사 market

[Usage]　　　　N 시장

[Expression]　　수산 시장　fish market
　　　　　　　　동대문 시장　Dongdaemoon market

[Example]　　　남대문 시장에는 여러 가지 물건이 많아요.
　　　　　　　　There are many different products at Namdaemoon market.

　　　　　　　　바다 근처 수산 시장에 가면 싱싱한 회를 사서 먹을 수 있어요.
　　　　　　　　You can eat fresh fish if you buy fish at fish markets near the ocean.

041
식당　　　　[식땅] 명사 restaurant

[Synonym]　　　음식점　food place
　　　　　　　　레스토랑　restaurant

[Example]　　　이 근처에 싸고 맛있는 식당이 있어요?
　　　　　　　　Is there a restaurant close-by that sells cheap but delicious food?

　　　　　　　　수업이 끝난 후에 식당에 가서 식사합시다.
　　　　　　　　Let's go eat after we finish class.

042
약국　　　　[약꾹] 명사 pharmacy

[Related word]　약사　pharmacist

[Example]　　　큰 병원 근처에는 약국이 많아요.
　　　　　　　　There are many pharmacies near large hospitals.

　　　　　　　　머리가 아파서 약국에서 약을 사 먹었어요.
　　　　　　　　I had a headache, so I bought medicine from the pharmacy and ate it.

043
우체국

[우체국] 명사 post office

[Related word] 편지 letter

우표 postage stamp

소포 package

[Example] 우체국에서 소포를 보냈어요. I sent a package at the post office.

국제우편을 부치러 우체국에 가는 길이에요.
I am on my way to the post office to send an international parcel.

044
운동장

[운동장] 명사 sport stadium, schoolyard

[Example] 우리 아버지는 토요일 아침마다 운동장에서 축구를 하십니다.
Every Saturday morning my father plays soccer at the schoolyard.

요즘은 집 근처에 있는 초등학교 운동장에 가서 운동을 합니다.
These days I exercise at the schoolyard near my house.

The words underneath are words used to express a place with the ending '-장'.

운동장, 축구장, 야구장, 농구장, 배구장, ……
Exercise stadium, soccer field, baseball field, basketball court, volleyball court, ……

045
은행

[은행] 명사 bank

[Expression] 은행원 bank clerk

[Related word] 통장 bankbook

저축 saving, deposit

송금 remit, send money

현금자동인출기 ATM machine

[Example] 돈이 없어서 은행에 가서 돈을 찾았어요.
I didn't have any money, so I went to the bank and withdrew money.

은행에 가서 달러를 한국 돈으로 바꾸려고 해요.
I'm going to the bank to exchange money from U.S. dollars to Korean won.

046
조용하다

[조용하다] 형용사 1. to be quiet in atmosphere 2. to be quiet in personality

1. to be quiet (in atmosphere)

[Usage] N이/가 조용하다

[Expression] 주위가 조용하다 the surroundings are quiet

교실이 조용하다 the classroom is quiet

[Antonym] 시끄럽다 to be noisy

[Example] 도서관에서는 조용히 해야 합니다. In the library, you must be quiet.

13

2. to be quiet (in personality)

[Usage] **N**이/가 조용하다

[Expression] 조용한 말 quiet words

조용한 목소리 quiet voice

성격이 조용하다 quiet personality

[Antonym] 시끄럽다 to be noisy

[Example] 어머니는 조용한 목소리로 이야기하셨다.
My mother talked in a very soft voice.

047
주유소

[주유소] 명사 gas station

[Example] 주유소마다 기름 값이 달라요. The price of gas varies at every gas station.
우리 집 근처에 있는 주유소에서는 기름을 넣으면 휴지를 줍니다.
The gas station near our house gives us tissue paper if we put gas in at that station.

048
집

[집] 명사 house

[Expression] 예쁜 집 pretty house

집 한 채 one house

집이 넓다 the house is big

집을 짓다 to build a house

[Example] 이사 간 집이 어디예요? Where is the house that you moved to?
집이 넓고 밝아서 참 좋아요.
The house is bright and large, so I like it a lot.

049
카페

[카페] 명사 café

[Related word] 커피숍 coffee shop

[Example] 카페에서 친구를 만나기로 했어요.
I promised my friend that I would meet him at the café.

요즘 카페에서 공부하는 사람이 많아요.
There are many people studying at cafés nowadays.

050
편의점

[퍼니점] 명사 convenient store

[Example] 편의점은 24(이십사)시간 문을 열어요.
The convenient store is open 24 hours.

요즘 밤에 편의점에서 아르바이트를 해요.
Recently I've started to work at the convenient store at night.

051
학교

[학꾜] 명사 school

[Expression]
초등학교 elementary school

중학교 middle school

고등학교 high school

대학교 college, university

학교생활 school life

학교를 졸업하다 to graduate from school

[Example]
우리 학교에는 여러 나라에서 온 학생들이 있습니다.
There are many students at my school who have come from different countries.

요즘 친구들을 많이 사귀어서 학교생활이 재미있어요.
I've met many friends, so school life is really fun.

052
학원

[하권] 명사 private educational institute

[Usage]
N 학원

[Expression]
영어 학원 English institute

미술 학원 art institute

태권도 학원 tae-kwon-do institute

학원에 다니다 to go to a private education institute

[Example]
저는 요즘 운전 학원에 다니고 있어요. I attend a driving institute.

제 여자 친구는 피아노 학원 선생님입니다.
My girlfriend is a piano teacher at an institute.

053
회사

[회사] 명사 office

[Expression]
회사원 office worker

무역회사 trade office

회사를 그만두다 to quit working at the office

회사에 다니다 to work at an office

회사에 출근하다 to go to work at an office

[Example]
우리 아버지는 컴퓨터 회사에 다니십니다.
My father works at a computer office.

회사 일 때문에 오늘 부산으로 출장을 가요.
Today I'm going to Busan for a business trip.

054
PC방

[피시방] <u>명사</u> computer room

[Example]　PC방에는 게임을 하는 사람이 많아요.
　　　　　　There are many people who play computer games in the computer room.

컴퓨터가 없어서 PC방에서 숙제를 했습니다.
I don't have a computer, so I did my homework in the computer room.

Different words that end with '-방' and refer to places are at the bottom.

노래방, PC방, 찜질방, 공부방, ……

Karaoke, computer room, sauna, study room, ……

[1~15] 다음 단어를 한국어로 바꿔 쓰십시오. Change these words into Korean.

1. side ( ) 2. under ( )

3. near ( ) 4. bakery ( )

5. hospital ( ) 6. department store ( )

7. museum ( ) 8. swimming pool ( )

9. embassy ( ) 10. to hang ( )

11. to place ( ) 12. to be bright ( )

13. to be quiet ( ) 14. to place on top ( )

15. to be loud ( )

[16~20] 그림을 보고 (   )에 알맞은 것을 고르십시오.

Look at the picture and choose the correct word.

16.

가 : 책이 어디에 있어요?

나 : 침대 (   )에 있어요.

❶ 밖　　　　❷ 안

❸ 옆　　　　❹ 위

17.

가 : 여기가 어디예요?

나 : (   )이에요/예요.

❶ 학교　　　　❷ 은행

❸ 서점　　　　❹ 문방구

18.

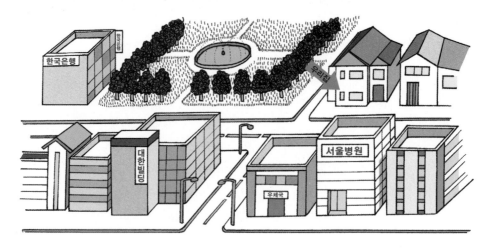

가 : 집 옆에 무엇이 있어요?

나 : 우리 집 옆에는 (   )이/가 있어요.

❶ 공원   ❷ 은행   ❸ 우체국   ❹ 병원

19.

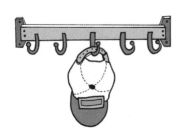

가 : 이 모자를 어떻게 할까요?

나 : (   )어/아/여 놓으세요.

❶ 넣다   ❷ 개다

❸ 열다   ❹ 걸다

20.

가 : 아무것도 안 보이는군요.

나 : 네, 너무 (   )어요/아요/여요.

❶ 어둡다   ❷ 복잡하다

❸ 시끄럽다   ❹ 재미없다

[21~30] 다음 문장을 읽고 알맞은 어휘를 골라 쓰십시오. 어휘는 한 번만 쓰십시오.
Read the following sentence and choose the right word. Use the words once.

안	밖	위	밑	앞
뒤	근처	밝다	있다	없다
놓다	넣다	걸다	어둡다	시끄럽다

21. 학생증을 책상 위에 (   )으세요/세요.

22. 우리 집 (   )에 지하철역이 없어서 좀 불편해요.

23. 미선 씨 지우개가 책상 (   )으로/로 떨어졌어요.

24. 오후에 시간이 (   )으면/면 같이 쇼핑하러 갈까요?

25. 그것은 밖에 놓지 말고 냉장고 안에 (   )으세요/세요.

26. 이 옷걸이에 코트를 (   )어/아/여 놓았는데 어디로 갔지?

27. 제 (   )에 키가 큰 사람이 앉아 있어서 영화가 잘 안 보여요.

28. 어제 밤에 (   )은/ㄴ 소리 때문에 잠을 잘 잘 수 없었어요.

29. 영희 씨가 기분이 나쁜가 봐요. 표정이 (   )어요/아요/여요.

30. 이 방은 햇빛이 잘 들어와서 다른 방보다 훨씬 (   )군요/는군요.

[31~35] (   ) 안에 알맞은 것을 고르십시오. Choose the correct one.

31. 영화가 재미있나 봐요. (   )에 사람이 많아요.

    ❶ 극장   ❷ 은행   ❸ 시장   ❹ 병원

32. 일이 많아서 주말에도 (   )에 갑니다.

    ❶ 집   ❷ 바다   ❸ 시골   ❹ 회사

33. 편지를 부치러 (   )에 갔다 왔어요.

   ❶ 은행   ❷ 편의점   ❸ 백화점   ❹ 우체국

34. 안경을 서랍 안에 (   )어/아/여 놓았어요.

   ❶ 끄다   ❷ 넣다   ❸ 닫다   ❹ 걸다

35. 방이 너무 (   )어서/아서/여서 불을 켰어요.

   ❶ 덥다   ❷ 밝다   ❸ 어둡다   ❹ 따뜻하다

[36~40] 밑줄 친 부분과 반대되는 뜻을 가진 것을 고르십시오.
Choose the word that is the opposite of the underlined word.

36. **가 :** 미국 친구가 <u>있어요</u>?

   나 : 아니요, (   )어요/아요/여요.

   ❶ 많다   ❷ 싸다   ❸ 없다   ❹ 적다

37. **가 :** 가방이 의자 <u>위</u>에 있어요?

   나 : 아니요, 의자 (   )에 있어요.

   ❶ 밖   ❷ 안   ❸ 옆   ❹ 아래

38. **가 :** 집 <u>안</u>에만 있으니까 답답하지 않아요?

   나 : 그럼, 잠시 (   )에 나갔다 올까요?

   ❶ 밖   ❷ 옆   ❸ 근처   ❹ 아래

39. **가 :** 교실이 <u>조용해요</u>?

   나 : 아니요, 아주 (   )어요/아요/여요.

   ❶ 넓다   ❷ 밝다   ❸ 깨끗하다   ❹ 시끄럽다

40. **가 :** 방이 어두워요?

    나 : 아니요, (   )어요/아요/여요.

    ❶ 밝다　　　　❷ 더럽다　　　　❸ 비싸다　　　　❹ 편하다

[41~45] 밑줄 친 부분과 의미가 가장 가까운 것을 고르십시오.
Choose the word that is most similar to the underlined section.

41. **가 :** 미선 씨 집이 여기서 가까워요?

    나 : 네, 이 (   )이에요/예요.

    ❶ 안　　　　❷ 밖　　　　❸ 근처　　　　❹ 위치

42. **가 :** 상자 속에 뭐가 있어요?

    나 : (   )에 뭐가 있는지 알고 싶으면 직접 열어 보세요.

    ❶ 밑　　　　❷ 안　　　　❸ 밖　　　　❹ 위

43. **가 :** 어? 볼펜이 아래로 떨어진 것 같아.

    나 : 기다려 봐. 내가 책상 (   )에서 찾아볼게.

    ❶ 밑　　　　❷ 위　　　　❸ 밖　　　　❹ 옆

44. **가 :** 학생들이 아무 말 없이 앉아 있네요.

    나 : 곧 시험을 보니까 (   )게 기다리고 있는 거예요.

    ❶ 시끄럽다　　❷ 조용하다　　❸ 재미있다　　❹ 편안하다

45. **가 :** 보석은 어디에 넣어 놓았어요?

    나 : 옷장 제일 아래 서랍의 안쪽에 넣어 (   )었어요/았어요/였어요.

    ❶ 있다　　　　❷ 두다　　　　❸ 신다　　　　❹ 주다

[46~50] 밑줄 친 단어의 쓰임이 잘못된 것을 고르십시오. Choose the one that is incorrectly used.

46. ❶ 제 공책은 집에 있어요.　　　　　　　　　　(　　　)
　　❷ 밥그릇을 식탁 위에 있어요.
　　❸ 교실에 시계와 달력이 있어요.
　　❹ 저는 한국 친구가 한 명 있어요.

47. ❶ 안은 깨끗한데 밖은 더럽네요.　　　　　　　(　　　)
　　❷ 비가 오니까 밖으로 들어가세요.
　　❸ 좀 답답하네요. 잠깐 밖에 나갑시다.
　　❹ 밖에 누가 왔나 봐요. 무슨 소리가 들려요.

48. ❶ 이 색깔은 너무 어두운 것 같아요.　　　　　(　　　)
　　❷ 방이 어두워서 책을 읽을 수가 없어요.
　　❸ 표정이 어두워요. 안 좋은 일이 있나 봐요.
　　❹ 공기가 아주 어두우니까 기분이 상쾌하네요.

49. ❶ 벽에 달력을 놓았어요.　　　　　　　　　　(　　　)
　　❷ 교실에 사람이 없어요.
　　❸ 침대 위에 옷이 있어요.
　　❹ 지갑 안에 카드를 넣었어요.

50. ❶ 여기에는 외국인들이 참 많아요.　　　　　　(　　　)
　　❷ 색깔이 좀 어두운데, 밝은 색은 없어요?
　　❸ 사람들이 모두 큰 소리로 말하니까 조용하군요.
　　❹ 오늘은 시간이 별로 없는데요. 내일 만나는 게 어때요?

물건

02

Object

02-1 | 의류

001
멋지다

[먿찌다] 형용사 to be fabulous

(person, object, work) to be desirable for a person because it is pretty to look at, or is just wanted by a person

[Usage] 멋진 **N**

N이/가 멋지다

[Expression] 멋진 자동차 a fabulous car

옷이 멋지다 the clothing is fabulous

[Synonym] 멋있다 to be wonderful

[Example] 그거 정말 멋진 생각이다. That is a wonderful idea.

양복을 입으니까 정말 멋지구나! You look wonderful in a suit!

002
바지

[바지] 명사 pants

[Example] 반바지 short pants

청바지 jeans

바지를 입다 to wear pants

[Related word] 치마 skirt

[Example] 바지가 길어서 조금 줄였습니다.

The pants were long, so I shortened them.

날씨가 추우니까 치마보다 바지를 입는 것이 좋겠어요.

Since the weather is cold, it is better to wear pants rather than a skirt.

003
벌

[벌] 명사 pieces

the unit used to count clothes

[Expression] 옷 한 벌 one piece of clothing

[Example] 백화점에서 세일을 해서 옷을 세 벌 샀어요.

There was a sale at the shopping mall, so I bought 3 pieces of clothing.

곧 겨울이 될 테니까 겨울 코트를 한 벌 더 준비하세요.

Winter is coming closer, so prepare another (piece) coat.

004
블라우스

[블라우스] 명사 blouse

[Expression] 블라우스 한 벌 one blouse

[Example] 어머니 생일 선물로 블라우스를 한 벌 샀어요.

For my mother's birthday, I bought her a blouse.

지금 입은 까만 치마에는 이 블라우스가 어울리겠다.

The black skirt that you're wearing will look great with this blouse.

005
속옷

[소곧] **명사** undergarment

clothing that you wear under outer clothing

[Expression] 속옷 한 벌 one piece of undergarment

[Synonym] 내의 underclothing

[Example] 한국에서는 첫 월급을 받으면 부모님께 속옷을 선물한다.
In Korea, people buy parents undergarments after they receive their first paycheck.

하얀 색 옷을 입을 때에는 속옷도 하얀 색을 입는 것이 좋아요.
When wearing white clothing, it is best to wear white undergarments as well.

006
스웨터

[스웨터] **명사** sweater

[Expression] 스웨터 한 벌 one sweater

[Example] 스웨터를 입으니까 춥지 않고 따뜻해요.
I feel warm because I am wearing a sweater.

여자 친구가 선물해 준 스웨터를 입었다.
I am wearing the sweater that my girlfriend gave me for a present.

007
양복

[양복] **명사** suit

western style formal clothing for men

[Expression] 양복 한 벌 one suit

양복을 맞추다 to get a fitting for a suit

[Example] 결혼식에는 양복을 입고 가야 해요.
You need to wear a suit for the wedding.

이 양복에 어떤 넥타이가 어울릴까?
What kind of tie will go well with my suit?

008
여성복

[여성복] **명사** women's clothing

[Example] 올해에는 밝은 색깔의 여성복이 유행할 거예요.
This year bright colored clothing will be the trend for women.

여성복 매장은 백화점 2(이)층과 3(삼)층에 있어요.
The departments that have women's clothing are located on the second and third floors.

도움말

Other words that end in '복' and represent clothing.

남성복, 여성복, 아동복, 수영복, 등산복, ……
men's clothing, women's clothing, children's clothing, swimwear, hiking clothing, ……

25

009
옷

[온] 명사 clothing

something that one wears to cover oneself in the winter, to protect in the summer, and to look fabulous

[Expression] 옷장 closet

옷 한 벌 one piece of clothing

옷이 작다 the clothing is small

옷이 맞다 the clothes fit

옷을 입다 to wear the clothes

[Example] 너에게는 밝은 색 옷이 잘 어울린다.
You look good in bright colored clothing.

요즘 살이 많이 빠져서 입던 옷들이 모두 커요.
I lost a lot of weight recently, so all of my clothes are big for me.

010
원피스

[원피스] 명사 one-piece

a type of clothing that is made with a shirt and skirt being put together, it is worn by women

[Expression] 원피스 한 벌 one one-piece

[Example] 하얀색 원피스를 입은 아이가 제 딸이에요.
The child who is wearing the white one-piece is my daughter.

지금 제가 입고 있는 원피스는 어머니가 직접 만들어 주신 거예요.
The one-piece that I am wearing was made by my mother.

011
입다

[입따] 동사 to wear

to put or wrap clothes on the body

[Usage] N을/를 입다

[Related word] 끼다[1] to put body parts into something, ex: gloves

신다 to put on shoes

쓰다[1] to use

[Antonym] 벗다 to take off

[Example] 오늘 모임이 있는데 뭘 입고 나갈까?
I have a meeting today, what should I wear?

한국의 중·고등학생들은 교복을 입어요.
Korea middle and high school students wear uniforms.

012
잠옷

[자몯] 명사 night gown

clothing that is worn when going to sleep

[Expression] 잠옷 한 벌 one night gown

[Example] 이제 잘 시간이니까 잠옷으로 갈아입어라.
It's time to sleep, so change into your night gown.

언니가 생일 선물로 예쁜 잠옷을 선물해 주었어요.
My older sister bought me a pretty night gown for my birthday present.

013
찢어지다

[찌저지다] 동사 to get ripped

to get torn and unraveled or parted

[Usage] 찢어진 **N**

N이/가 찢어지다

[Expression] 찢어진 옷 ripped clothing

종이가 찢어지다 the paper is ripped

[Related word] 찢다 to rip

[Example] 물건이 무거워서 물건을 담은 비닐봉지가 찢어졌어요.
The objects in the plastic bag were so heavy that the bag ripped.

요즘 젊은 사람들 사이에서 찢어진 청바지가 유행이다.
The trend among youngsters now-a-days is the ripped jeans.

014
치마

[치마] 명사 skirt

[Expression] 치마 한 벌 one skirt

[Related word] 바지 pants

[Example] 그 치마는 너무 짧은 것 같아. It seems that that skirt is too short.

저는 바지보다 치마가 더 잘 어울려서 치마를 자주 입어요.
I look better in skirts rather than pants, so I wear skirts more often.

015
코트

[코트] 명사 coat

a thick type of clothing worn to protect against the cold

[Expression] 반코트 a half-coat

겨울 코트 winter coat

코트 한 벌 one coat

[Example] 반코트를 입어서 다리가 추워요. I wore a half-coat so my legs are cold.

여름에는 겨울 코트를 싸게 살 수 있어요.
I can buy winter coats for much cheaper during the summer.

016
티셔츠

[티셔츠] 명사 t-shirt

[Expression] 티셔츠 한 벌 one t-shirt

[Related word] 와이셔츠 dress shirt

[Example] 청바지에 하얀색 티셔츠를 입고 나갔다. I wore jeans and a white t-shirt.

내일 운동회에 우리 반은 파란색 티셔츠를 입기로 했어요.
Tomorrow my class decided to wear blue t-shirts for field day.

017
한복

[한복] 명사 Korean traditional clothing
traditional Korean clothing

[Expression] 한복 한 벌 one Korean traditional clothing

[Example] 한복은 한국의 전통 옷입니다. '한복' is a traditional Korean clothing.

한국 사람들은 설날이나 추석 같은 명절에 한복을 입는다.
Korean people wear traditional clothing on lunar new year's day and during national holidays.

02-2 잡화 · 보석 · 액세서리

018
가방

[가방] 명사 bag

[Expression] 책가방 book bag

서류 가방 bag for documents

여행 가방 vacation bag

가방을 들다 to hold the bag

가방을 메다 to carry the bag

[Example] 학교에 가려고 가방에 책과 공책을 넣었다.
I put books and notebooks in the bag for school.

할머니 가방이 무거워 보여서 버스 정류장까지 들어 드렸어요.
Grandmother's bag looked heavy, so I carried it to the bus stop for her.

019
가지다

[가지다] 동사 to have

to carry in one's hand or body

[Usage] N을/를 가지고 가다

N을/를 가지고 다니다

[Example] 교과서를 안 가지고 왔어요. I didn't bring my textbook.

수학여행을 갈 때 미선이가 카메라를 가지고 가서 우리 반 친구들의 사진을 찍기로 했다.

Misun is going to bring a camera to take a picture of our class during the field trip.

020
구두

[구두] 명사 formal shoes, dress shoes

western style shoes made out of leather, plastic, and other material

[Expression] 구두 한 짝 one dress shoe

구두 한 켤레 one pair of dress shoes

구두를 신다 to wear dress shoes

[Example] 새 구두 때문에 발이 아파요.

My feet hurt because of the new dress shoes.

구두를 벗고 방 안으로 들어오세요.

Take off your dress shoes and come inside.

021
귀걸이

[귀거리] 명사 earrings

[Expression] 귀걸이 한 쌍 a pair of earrings

귀걸이 한 짝 one earring

귀걸이를 하다 to put on earrings

[Synonym] 귀고리 earrings

[Example] 요즘 유행하는 귀걸이가 뭐예요? What earrings are trendy right now?

남자 친구에게서 선물로 받은 귀걸이 한 짝을 잃어버렸다.

I lost one of the earrings that my boyfriend bought me.

022
끼다[1]

[끼다] 동사 to put on

(usually on the body) to place on to hang

[Usage] (N에) N을/를 끼다

[Expression] 안경을 끼다 to put on glasses

손에 장갑을 끼다 to put hands in the glove

손가락에 반지를 끼다 to put the ring on the finger

눈에 콘텍트렌즈를 끼다 to put contact lenses in the eyes

[Antonym]	빼다 to take out
	벗다 to take off
[Example]	날씨가 추우니까 장갑을 끼세요. It is cold outside so put on gloves.
	저기 안경을 낀 분이 우리 어머니이십니다.
	The lady who is wearing glasses is my mother.

023
넥타이

[넥타이] 명사 neck-tie

[Expression]	넥타이 한 개 one neck-tie
	넥타이를 매다 to tie on the neck-tie
	넥타이를 풀다 to loosen the neck-tie
	넥타이를 하다 to put on the neck-tie
[Example]	양복 색깔과 넥타이 색깔이 잘 어울려요.
	The color of the suit and the tie look great together.
	아버지한테서 넥타이를 매는 방법을 배웠어요.
	I learned how to wear my tie from my father.

024
들다

[들다] 동사 1. to hold 2. to lift

1. to take in one's hand, ㄹverb

[Usage]	N을/를 (N에) 들다
[Expression]	가방을 들다 to carry the bag
	꽃을 손에 들다 to carry the flowers in one's hand
[Example]	꽃을 들고 사진을 찍는 것이 좋겠어요.
	It will look nice if you take the picture while holding the flowers.

2. to hold an object and lift upwards

[Usage]	N을/를 (N에) 들다
[Expression]	손을 머리 위로 들다 to put hands above the head
[Example]	질문이 있으면 손을 들고 질문하세요.
	If you have a question, raise your hand.

025
로션

[로션] 명사 lotion

one type of cosmetic that is used on the face, hands, and body to make it more smooth and soft

[Expression]	로션을 바르다 to lather on lotion
[Example]	세수한 후에 로션을 바릅니다. I put on lotion after I wash my face.
	겨울에는 손에 로션을 자주 바르는 것이 좋아요.
	It is good to put on hand lotion frequently during the winter.

026
매다

[매다] 동사 to tie

an action that is done in order to fasten to things together so that they will no come undone, or unfasten

[Usage] (**N**에) **N**을/를 매다

[Expression] 넥타이를 매다 to tie the neck tie

스카프를 매다 to put on the scarf

신발 끈을 매다 to tie the shoe string

[Antonym] 풀다 to untie

[Example] 나는 뛰기 전에 운동화 끈을 다시 맸다.
I tied my shoe strings before running.

오빠는 거울을 보면서 넥타이를 맵니다.
My older brother is tying his tie while looking into the mirror.

027
메다

[메다] 동사 to carry

to put on the shoulder, or on the back

[Usage] (**N**에) **N**을/를 메다

[Expression] 어깨에 가방을 메다 to carry the bag on the shoulder

[Example] 아이는 책가방을 메고 학교에 갔다.
The child carried his backpack all the way to school.

배낭 하나만 메고 여행을 가려고 해요.
I plan on carrying one bag for my vacation

028
모자

[모자] 명사 hat

[Expression] 모자를 쓰다 to wear the hat

[Example] 교실에서는 모자를 쓰고 있으면 안 됩니다.
You cannot wear a hat in the classroom.

이 사진에서 하얀 모자를 쓰신 분이 우리 할아버지이십니다.
The person wearing the white hat is my grandfather.

029
목걸이

[목꺼리] 명사 necklace

[Expression] 목걸이를 하다 to be wearing a necklace

[Example] 진주 목걸이가 아주 잘 어울리는군요!
You look great with that pearl necklace on!

지금 하고 계신 목걸이가 참 예쁜데 어디에서 사셨어요?
The necklace that you have on right now is very pretty, where did you buy it?

31

030
목도리

[목또리] 명사 scarf, muffler

an object used to wrap and protect the neck from the cold, used to look cool

[Expression] 목도리를 하다 to put on a scarf

목도리를 두르다 to wrap the muffler around the neck

[Example] 날씨가 추워져서 오늘은 코트도 입고 목도리도 했다.
The weather was very cold today so I wore a coat and a muffler.

목에 목도리를 두르지 않아서 바람이 불 때마다 좀 추워요.
I didn't put on a scarf, so every time the wind blew I felt cold.

031
반지

[반지] 명사 ring

[Expression] 결혼반지 wedding ring

반지를 끼다 to put/wear on the ring

반지를 빼다 to take the ring off

[Example] 한국에서는 아기의 첫 번째 생일에 금반지를 선물합니다.
In Korea the baby is given a gold ring on his/her first birthday.

손을 씻으려고 반지를 뺐는데 어디에 두었는지 기억이 나지 않는다.
I took off my ring to wash my hand, and now I don't know where I put them.

032
보석

[보석] 명사 jewel

a very strong beautiful rock that is used on necklaces, rings, and other accessories, it sparkles and is very expensive

[Example] 여자들은 보통 무슨 보석을 좋아해요?
What kind of jewel do women like?

결혼반지에 많이 쓰이는 보석은 다이아몬드예요.
Diamonds are the most common jewel used on wedding rings.

033
선글라스

[선글라스] 명사 sunglass

[Expression] 선글라스를 끼다 to put on sunglasses

선글라스를 쓰다 to wear sunglasses

[Example] 실내에서는 선글라스를 벗어라.
Take off your sunglasses while you're inside.

미선이는 외출할 때 항상 검은색 선글라스를 써요.
Misun always wears black sunglasses when she goes outside.

034
손수건

[손쑤건] 명사 handkerchief

[Expression] 손수건 한 장 one handkerchief

손수건으로 닦다 to wipe with the handkerchief

[Example] 땀이 나서 손수건으로 닦았어요.
I wiped off my sweat with my handkerchief.

손수건을 꺼내서 우는 아이의 눈물을 닦아 주었다.
I took out my handkerchief and wiped off the tears of a crying child.

035
스카프

[스카프] 명사 scarf

[Expression] 스카프를 하다 to have on a scarf

스카프를 매다 to tie on a scarf

스카프를 두르다 to wrap the scarf around

[Example] 이 물방울무늬 스카프는 얼마예요?
How much is this scarf with the bubble design?

그 원피스에 하늘색 스카프를 하면 더 예쁠 것 같아.
That one piece will look really great with a sky blue scarf.

036
스타킹

[스타킹] 명사 stocking

[Expression] 스타킹 한 켤레 one pair of stockings

스타킹을 신다 to wear stockings

[Example] 저는 치마를 입을 때 보통 스타킹을 신습니다.
Usually when I wear a skirt I wear stockings.

요즘에는 여러 가지 색깔과 디자인의 스타킹이 있어요.
Now-a-days there are many types of stockings with different colors and designs.

037
슬리퍼

[슬리퍼] 명사 slippers

[Expression] 슬리퍼 한 켤레 one pair of slippers

슬리퍼를 신다 to wear slippers

[Example] 바닥이 차가우니까 슬리퍼를 신어라.
The floors are cold, so wear your slippers.

신발을 벗고 슬리퍼로 갈아 신고 들어오세요.
Take off your shoes and wear the slippers and come inside.

038
시계

[시계/시게] 명사 watch, clock
an object that tells time

[Expression] 벽시계 wall clock

손목시계 watch

시계가 느리다 the clock is slow

시계를 보다 to look at the clock

시계를 차다 to put on the watch

[Example] 시계를 보니까 벌써 점심시간이 되었다.
I looked at the clock and it was already lunch time.

요즘은 휴대전화가 있어서 시계를 안 차고 다니는 사람이 많아요.
Now-a-days everyone has cell phones so few people wear watches.

039
신다

[신따] 동사 to wear (to do with feet)

to put feet inside shoes or socks

[Usage] N을/를 신다

[Expression] 양말을 신다 to wear socks

신발을 신다 to wear shoes

[Antonym] 벗다 to take off

[Example] 내일 등산할 테니까 등산화를 신고 오세요.
Tomorrow we'll go hiking so please wear your hiking shoes.

제가 지금 신고 있는 신발은 아주 편해서 좋아요.
The shoes that I'm wearing are very comfortable so I like the shoes.

040
신발

[신발] 명사 shoes

an object that is used for walking, and for going outside

[Expression] 신발장 shoe closet

신발 한 짝 one shoe

신발 한 켤레 a pair of shoes

신발을 신다 to wear shoes

[Example] 집에 오면 신발을 벗어서 신발장에 넣어라.
When you come home, take off your shoes and place them in the shoe closet.

이 신발이 좀 큰데 한 치수 작은 것으로 주세요.
These shoes are big so, please give me one size smaller.

041
쓰다¹

[쓰다] 동사 1. to wear on head 2. to put on eyes 3. to use over head

1. hats and such used to cover the head, 으 verb

[Usage] (N에) N을/를 쓰다

[Expression] 모자를 쓰다 to wear the hat

[Antonym] 벗다 to take off

[Example] 교실에서는 모자를 쓰고 있으면 안 됩니다.
You cannot wear the hat inside the classroom.

2. glasses and such used to hang on face, 으 verb

[Usage] N을/를 쓰다

[Expression] 안경을 쓰다 to put on glasses

[Antonym] 벗다 to take off

[Example] 우리 반에는 안경을 쓴 학생이 많아요.
There are many students who wear glasses in my class.

3. to use umbrellas for rain and sun over the head, 으 verb

[Expression] 우산을 쓰다 to use an umbrella

[Example] 두 사람은 우산을 같이 쓰고 갔다. The two people shared an umbrella.

042
안경

[안경] 명사 glasses

[Expression] 안경을 닦다 to clean glasses

안경을 끼다 to wear glasses

안경을 쓰다 to wear glasses

안경을 벗다 to take off glasses

[Example] 안경을 닦으니까 아주 잘 보여요.
I can see clearly after cleaning my glasses.

저는 눈이 너무 나빠서 안경을 벗으면 아무것도 보이지 않아요.
My eyes are so bad that if I don't wear my glasses I can't see anything.

043
액세서리

[액쎄서리] 명사 accessory

[Expression] 액세서리를 하다 to put on accessories

액세서리를 달다 to hang accessories on something

[Example] 옷에 액세서리를 달았어요. I attached an accessory on my clothing.

액세서리 가게에서 친구에게 줄 선물을 골랐다.
I bought a present at the accessory store for my friend.

044
양말

[양말] 명사 socks

[Expression] 양말 한 짝 one sock

양말 한 켤레 a pair of socks

양말을 신다 to wear socks

[Example] 저는 집에 오면 양말부터 벗어요.
When I come home, the first thing I do is take off my socks.

날씨가 너무 추워서 양말을 두 켤레 신었습니다.
The weather is so cold that I wore two pairs of socks.

045

우산

[우산] 명사 umbrella

[Expression] 우산을 쓰다 to use an umbrella

우산을 펴다 to open an umbrella

우산을 접다 to fold an umbrella

[Related word] 양산 umbrella used to cover from the sun

[Example] 비가 오니까 저와 같이 우산을 쓰고 갑시다.

It is raining so let's share this umbrella and go together.

날씨가 흐리니까 우산을 가지고 가는 것이 좋을 것 같아요.

The weather is a bit cloudy so it would be safe to take an umbrella.

046

운동화

[운동화] 명사 running shoes

shoes that are used for exercise

[Expression] 운동화 한 짝 one running shoe

운동화 한 켤레 a pair of running shoes

운동화를 신다 to wear running shoes

[Example] 이 운동화는 달리기 선수들이 신는 운동화라고 해요.

These running shoes are used by runners.

운동화를 신으면 발이 편해서 운동을 하지 않을 때도 많이 신어요.

The running shoes are comfortable, so I wear them even when I'm not exercising.

047

잃다

[일타] 동사 to lose

something that one used to have but now is lost

[Usage] N을/를 잃다

[Expression] 잃어버리다 to lose

지갑을 잃다 to lose the wallet

[Example] 친구가 사업에 실패해서 많은 돈을 잃었다.

My friend failed in his business, so he lost a lot of money.

버스에서 지갑을 잃어버렸는데 어떻게 하죠?

I lost my wallet in the bus, what should I do?

048

장갑

[장갑] 명사 gloves

an object that protects the hand, protects from the cold, or just worn to be fashionable

[Expression] 털장갑 fur gloves

장갑 한 짝 one glove

장갑 한 켤레 one pair of gloves

장갑을 끼다 to put on the gloves

[Example]	스케이트를 탈 때에는 꼭 장갑을 껴야 한다.
	When you are skating, you must wear gloves.
	날씨가 추우니까 장갑을 끼는 것이 좋겠어요.
	Since it is cold outside, it would be wise to wear gloves.

049
지갑

[지갑] 명사 wallet	
[Example]	거스름돈을 받아서 지갑에 넣었어요.
	I took the change and put it in the wallet.
	여행을 가면 지갑을 잃어버리지 않게 조심하세요.
	When you're on vacation, make sure that you don't lose your wallet.

050
차다¹

[차다] 동사 to wear or put on	
	to place objects on the waist or wrist
[Usage]	(**N**에) **N**을/를 차다
[Expression]	팔에 팔찌를 차다 to wear bracelets on the arm
	손목에 시계를 차다 to wear a watch on the wrist
[Example]	아내는 금으로 만든 팔찌를 찼다.
	My wife is wearing a bracelet made out of gold.
	오늘 시계를 차는 것을 깜빡 잊어버렸어요.
	I forgot to wear my watch today.

051
켤레

[켤레] 명사 a pair	
	a unit used to count pairs of things such as shoes, socks, gloves and other things
[Expression]	신발 한 켤레 one pair of shoes
	양말 두 켤레 two pairs of socks
	장갑 세 켤레 three pairs of gloves
[Example]	이 핸드백은 지금 입고 있는 청바지에 어울리는 것 같지 않아요.
	This handbag does not seem to look good with the jeans.
	현관에 신발이 여러 켤레 있는 걸 보니까 손님들이 오신 모양이에요.
	There are many pairs of shoes out in the entrance, so we must have company.

052
핸드백

[핸드백] 명사 handbag or purse	
	an object used to carry by hand or on shoulder, it is usually small, and carries objects
[Example]	요즘 유행하는 핸드백이 어떤 거예요?
	What is the trendy style of handbag this season?
	지갑하고 휴대폰을 핸드백에 넣었어요.
	I put my wallet and my cell phone in my purse.

37

053
향수

[향수] 명사 perfume

[Expression] 향수를 뿌리다 to spray perfume

[Example] 외출하기 전에 향수를 뿌렸어요.

I sprayed on perfume before I left the house.

여자 친구 생일 선물로 향수를 샀다.

I bought perfume for my girlfriend's birthday present.

054
화장품

[화장품] 명사 cosmetics

the word used to refer to lotion, toner, lipstick, and other makeup materials

[Expression] 화장품 가게 cosmetic store

화장품을 바르다 to put on makeup

[Example] 이 화장품을 발라 보세요. 아주 좋아요. Try this makeup. It is really nice.

이 근처에 싸고 좋은 화장품 가게가 있어요?

Is there a cosmetic store nearby that is good quality and cheap?

02-3 | 문구류

055
가위

[가위] 명사 scissors

[Expression] 가위로 자르다 to cut with scissors

[Example] 엄마는 아이의 머리를 가위로 잘랐다.

The mother cut the child's hair with scissors.

가위나 칼은 아이에게 위험한 물건이니까 잘 넣어 두세요.

Scissors and knives are dangerous, so keep them away from children.

056
공책

[공책] 명사 notebook

an empty book used to write in and to draw

[Expression] 공책 한 권 one notebook

[Synonym] 노트 notebook

[Example]   문방구에 가서 공책을 열 권 사 와라.
Go to the stationary store and buy 10 notebooks.

수업 내용을 공책에 써 놓으면 집에서 공부할 때 다시 볼 수 있어서 좋아요.
If you take notes in class, you can take it home and study later.

057
볼펜

[볼펜] 명사 ball point pen

[Expression]   볼펜 한 자루   one pack of ball point pens

[Example]   시험을 볼 때 까만색 볼펜으로 쓰십시오.
At the test, write with a black ball point pen.

볼펜을 안 가지고 왔는데 좀 빌려 주세요.
I didn't bring a ball point pen, please let me borrow one.

058
봉투

[봉투] 명사 envelope, bag, sack

a pocket that one can use to put letters, documents and other materials

[Expression]   서류 봉투   document envelope
편지 봉투   letter envelope
쓰레기봉투   trash bag
봉투 한 장   one envelope
봉투에 넣다   to put in the bag

[Synonym]   봉지   bag, sack

[Example]   이 서류를 넣을 수 있는 봉투를 좀 주세요.
Please give me an envelope that I can place these documents inside.

한국 사람들은 쓰레기를 버릴 때 가게에서 파는 쓰레기봉투를 사서 거기에 넣어서 버려요.
Korean people buy trash bags from the store and throw away trash using those bags.

059
수첩

[수첩] 명사 daily planner

a small notebook that is carried around and can be used to jot notes and other things at any time

[Example]   수첩에 해야 할 일을 적어 놓으면 잊어버리지 않아서 좋아요.
If I write down what I need to do, it allows me not to forget what I need to do.

나는 수첩에 단어를 적어 놓고 시간이 날 때마다 보고 외웠다.
I wrote down vocabulary in my daily planner and at every spare moment I reviewed and memorized the words.

060
연필

[연필] 명사 pencil

[Expression] 연필 한 자루 one pencil

[Related word] 지우개 eraser

[Example] 저는 보통 연필로 숙제를 해요. I usually do my homework in pencil.

연필로 쓰면 틀렸을 때 지우개로 지울 수 있어서 저는 연필로 쓰는 것을 좋아해요.

I like writing with a pencil because even if I make a mistake I can erase the error.

061
자루

[자루] 명사 piece

a counting unit used for counting writing utensils

[Expression] 연필 한 자루 one pencil

볼펜 열두 자루 12 ball point pens

[Example] 볼펜이 있으면 한 자루만 빌려 주세요.

If you have a ball point pen, please let me borrow one.

아이들에게 연필 세 자루씩 선물해 주었다.

I gave each of my children 3 pencils as a present.

062
지우개

[지우개] 명사 eraser

a tool that is used to rub off mistakes made by pencil or chalk

[Expression] 지우개 한 개 one eraser

지우개로 지우다 to rub off with the eraser

[Example] 칠판을 지우개로 깨끗하게 지웠다.

I erased the chalk board cleanly with the eraser.

틀린 글씨를 지우개로 지우고 다시 쓰세요.

Please erase the mistakes with the eraser and write is again.

063
필통

[필통] 명사 pencil case

[Expression] 필통 한 개 one pencil case

필통에 넣다 to put in the pencil case

[Example] 필통 안에 볼펜이 몇 자루 있어요?

How many ball point pens do you have in your pencil case?

그 학생은 필통에서 연필을 꺼내서 적기 시작했다.

That student took out a pencil from the pencil case and started to write.

064
가전제품

[가전제품] 명사 home appliances

electronic equipment used in households, such as the washing machine, refrigerator, television and other appliances

[Example] 좋은 가전제품이 많이 나와서 집안일이 편해졌다.
There are many good home appliances that make home living more comfortable.

요즘 신혼부부에게 가장 인기 있는 가전제품은 로봇청소기입니다.
The most popular type of home appliance for newlyweds is the robot vacuum cleaner.

065
고장

[고장] 명사 breakdown

equipment that no longer does its job

[Expression] 고장이 나다 to be broken
고장을 내다 to break

[Example] 휴대전화가 고장이 나서 서비스센터에 맡겼다.
My cell phone is broken, so I left it at the repair center to get it fixed.

컴퓨터가 고장인가 봐요. 화면에 아무것도 나오지 않아요.
My computer must be broken. Nothing is coming out on the screen.

066
고치다

[고치다] 동사 1. repair   2. amend

1. to fix something so that it can be used again

[Usage] N 을/를 고치다

[Related word] 수리하다 to fix
수선하다 to repair

[Example] 고장이 난 자동차를 고쳤어요. I fixed the car that was broken.

2. to fix a wrongdoing or a mistake

[Usage] N 을/를 고치다

[Expression] 버릇을 고치다 to fix a bad habit
발음을 고치다 to fix pronunciation
문장을 고치다 to fix a sentence

[Example] 나쁜 버릇은 고치기가 힘들어요. It's hard to fix a bad habit.

067
냉장고

[냉장고] 명사 refrigerator

[Expression] 냉장고 한 대 one refrigerator
냉장고에 넣다 to put in the refrigerator

[Example]   우유가 상하지 않게 냉장고에 넣어라.
    Put the milk in the refrigerator so that it doesn't go bad.

    냉장고에 시원한 맥주가 있으니까 꺼내서 드세요.
    There is a cool beer in the refrigerator, so go ahead and drink the beer.

068 노트북

[노트북] 명사 notebook

a small computer that can be carried around, a shorter word for notebook computer

[Related word]   컴퓨터 computer

[Example]   노트북은 점점 작아지고 기능도 다양해져서 사용하기가 편리해졌어요.
    The notebook computer is becoming smaller and has a lot more functions and it makes it easier to use.

    요즘에는 비행기 안에서 노트북으로 일을 하는 사람을 많이 볼 수 있다.
    You can see many people in the airplane using the notebook to do work.

069 대

[대] 명사 for machine

a counting unit that is used to count cars, and big equipment

[Expression]   자전거 한 대 one bicycle

    컴퓨터 스무 대 20 computers

[Example]   우리 집에는 컴퓨터가 네 대 있어요.
    There are four computers in my home.

    주차장에 자동차가 한 대밖에 없어요.
    There is only one car in the parking lot.

070 디지털 카메라

[디지털 카메라] 명사 digital camera

[Expression]   디지털 카메라로 찍다 to take pictures with the digital camera

[Example]   요즘 디지털 카메라가 없는 사람이 없어요.
    Everyone has a digital camera now-a-days.

    디지털 카메라로 찍은 사진은 모두 컴퓨터에 저장할 수 있어서 좋다.
    It's nice to use a digital camera because I can save all of the pictures on my computer.

071 비디오

[비디오] 명사 1. video (videotape) 2. VCR

1. tape that is used to store movies, a shortened word for videotape

[Expression]   비디오를 보다 to watch a video

[Example]   심심해서 비디오를 빌려다가 친구와 같이 봤어요.
    I was bored so I borrowed a movie and watched it with my friend.

2. an equipment that is used to watch a videotape

[Expression]   비디오 한 대 one VCR

비디오를 켜다 to watch a video

[Example] 비디오 좀 켜 주세요. Please turn on the video.

072
사용하다

[사용·하다] 동사 to use

to apply a product that is correctly applied for the right situation

[Usage] N을/를 사용하다

[Related word] 쓰다³ to use

이용하다 to utilize

[Example] 어른에게 존댓말을 사용해야 합니다.
You must use the honorific form when talking to an elder.

서양 사람들은 식사할 때 젓가락을 사용하지 않아요.
Western people do not use chopsticks when eating food.

073
선풍기

[선풍기] 명사 fan

[Expression] 선풍기 한 대 one fan

선풍기를 켜다 to turn on the fan

[Example] 방에 에어컨은 없고 선풍기만 있어요.
I don't have air conditioning but I do have a fan.

날씨가 너무 더워서 선풍기를 켜도 시원하지 않아요.
The weather is so hot that even if I turn on the fan it does not become any cooler.

074
세탁기

[세탁끼] 명사 washing machine

[Expression] 세탁기 한 대 one washing machine

세탁기를 돌리다 to wash clothes in the washing machine

[Example] 건조 기능이 있는 세탁기는 아주 편리하다고 해요.
The washing machines with the dry function are convenient to use.

세탁기를 돌릴 때 빨래의 색깔에 따라 따로따로 돌려야 한다.
When washing clothes, you should separate the colors and wash them separately.

075
에어컨

[에어컨] 명사 air conditioner

[Expression] 에어컨 한 대 one air conditioner

에어컨을 켜다 to turn on the air conditioner

[Example] 날씨가 더운데 에어컨을 켤까요?
The weather is hot, shall I turn on the air conditioner?

에어컨을 켰으니까 금방 시원해질 거예요. 조금만 기다리세요.
I turned on the air conditioner, it will become cooler very soon. Please wait a little bit.

076
청소기

[청소기] 명사 vacuum cleaner

[Expression]
진공청소기 a vacuum cleaner

청소기 한 대 one vacuum cleaner

청소기를 돌리다 to turn on the vacuum cleaner

[Example]
밤에 청소기를 돌리면 시끄러우니까 낮에 청소하세요.
The vacuum cleaner is loud at night, so please clean during the day.

청소와 걸레질을 한 번에 하는 청소기가 나왔다고 한다.
There is a new vacuum cleaner that cleans as well as wipes the floor at the same time.

077
컴퓨터

[컴퓨터] 명사 computer

[Expression]
컴퓨터 한 대 one computer

컴퓨터를 켜다 to turn on the computer

[Example]
저는 컴퓨터로 보통 인터넷을 합니다.
I use the internet on the computer.

수업이 끝나고 집에 오면 바로 컴퓨터부터 켭니다.
After school, I go home and turn on the computer.

078
텔레비전

[텔레비전] 명사 television

[Expression]
텔레비전 한 대 one television

텔레비전 프로그램 television program

텔레비전을 보다 to watch television

텔레비전을 켜다 to turn on the television

텔레비전을 끄다 to turn off the television

[Example]
아침을 먹은 후에 텔레비전을 봤다.
After eating breakfast I watched television.

어제 밤에 텔레비전을 보다가 잠이 들었어요.
Yesterday night I fell asleep watching television.

079
그릇

[그른] 명사 bowl, plate, dishes

an object that holds food, a unit that counts food

[Expression]
밥그릇 rice bowl

반찬 그릇 side dish bowl

그릇 한 개 one bowl

음식 한 그릇 one bowl of food

그릇을 씻다 to wash the dishes

[Example]
자장면 세 그릇 배달해 주세요.
Please deliver three bowls of black noodles.

한국 사람들은 밥그릇을 들고 먹지 않습니다.
Korean people do not hold onto their bowls when they eat.

080
냄비

[냄비] 명사 pot

a cooking appliance that is used to boil or cook food

[Example]
냄비가 뜨거우니까 조심하세요. The pot is hot, so be careful.

먼저 큰 냄비에 물을 붓고 끓이세요.
First, put water into the big pot and boil the water.

081
비누

[비누] 명사 soap

[Expression]
세수 비누 face soap

빨래 비누 laundry soap

[Example]
아이는 비누로 얼굴을 씻었다. The child washed his/her face with soap.

언니는 빨래 비누로 와이셔츠를 빨았다.
My older sister washed dress shirt with laundry soap.

082
샴푸

[샴푸] 명사 shampoo

[Example]
너 무슨 샴푸를 쓰니? 향기가 참 좋다.
What kind of shampoo do you use? It smells really good.

샴푸가 눈에 들어가면 아프니까 조심해라.
If the shampoo gets in your eyes, it will hurt so be careful.

083
수건

[수건] 명사 towel

[Expression]
수건 한 장 one towel

수건으로 닦다 to wipe off with a towel

[Example] 땀이 나서 수건으로 닦았다. I was sweaty, so I wiped it off with a towel.

세수를 한 후에 이 수건으로 얼굴을 닦으세요.

After washing your face, wipe it off with this towel.

084
수저

[수저] 명사 spoon and chopsticks

[Expression] 수저를 놓다 to place the spoon and chopsticks

수저를 들다 to lift the spoon and chopsticks

[Related word] 숟가락 spoon

젓가락 chopsticks

[Example] 수저를 양손에 들고 먹으면 안 된다.

It is not good to eat with a spoon and chopsticks in both hands.

윗사람이 수저를 먼저 들 때까지 식사를 시작하지 말고 기다려야 합니다.

You must wait for the elder to lift the spoon and chopsticks first before you eat.

085
접시

[접씨] 명사 plate

a flat type of bowl

[Expression] 접시 한 개 one plate

접시에 담다 to place on the plate

[Example] 접시에 과일을 예쁘게 담았어요. I placed the fruits beautifully on the plate.

설거지를 하다가 접시를 깨뜨렸어요.

I broke the plate while washing the dishes.

086
칫솔

[칫쏠] 명사 toothbrush

[Expression] 칫솔 한 개 one toothbrush

칫솔로 이를 닦다 to brush teeth with a toothbrush

[Related word] 치약 toothpaste

[Example] 여행갈 때 칫솔과 치약을 꼭 가져가세요.

Remember to take a toothbrush and toothpaste when going on vacation.

이를 튼튼하게 하려면 칫솔을 잘 사용하는 것이 중요합니다.

In order to make your teeth strong you need to know how to use a toothbrush.

087
칼

[칼] 명사 knife

[Expression] 칼 한 자루 one knife

칼로 썰다 to chop with a knife

칼로 자르다 to cut with a knife

[Example] 칼로 과일을 깎았어요. I cut fruit with a knife.

당근을 썰다가 칼에 베었어요. I cut myself while cutting a carrot.

088
컵

[컵] 명사 cup

an object used to hold water and other liquids as well as used as a counting unit for cups of drinks

[Expression] 물 한 컵 one cup of water

컵 한 개 one cup

우유 한 컵 one cup of milk

컵에 따르다 to pour into the cup

[Related word] 잔 glass, cup

[Example] 아주머니, 컵 하나 갖다 주세요. Please give us a cup.

우유를 한 컵 마셔서 배가 그렇게 고프지 않아요.
I drank a cup of milk, so I am not that hungry.

02-6 | 가구

089
가구

[가구] 명사 furniture

[Example] 가구가 너무 많으면 집이 좁아 보여요.
If there are too much furniture, the house will look very small.

아이 방에 놓을 가구를 사려고 왔어요.
I came to buy furniture for the baby room.

090
소파

[소파] 명사 sofa

[Example] 동생은 소파에 누워서 텔레비전을 보고 있다.
My younger sibling is laying down on the sofa and watching television.

편하고 디자인도 예쁜 소파를 하나 사고 싶어요.
I want to buy a sofa that has a pretty design and is comfortable.

091
식탁

[식탁] 명사 dining table

[Related word] 밥상 eating table

테이블 table

[Example] 어머니께서 식탁에 저녁을 차려 놓으셨어요.
My mother has placed the dinner on the table.

밥을 먹기 전에 행주로 식탁을 깨끗하게 닦았다.
I washed the table before eating at the table.

092
의자

[의자] 명사 chair

[Expression] 의자 한 개 one chair

의자에 앉다 to sit on the chair

[Example] 의자에 똑바로 앉아라. Sit upright on the chair.

책상은 높은데 의자가 낮아서 불편해요.
The desk is high, but the chair is low, so I feel uncomfortable.

093
책상

[책쌍] 명사 desk

a steady piece of furniture used to study on, read or used for working

[Expression] 책상 한 개 one desk

[Related word] 의자 chair

[Example] 책상 위에 책이 쌓여 있다. There are books stacked on the desk.

공부하려고 책상 앞에 앉기만 하면 잠이 와요.
Every time I try to study at the desk I end up falling asleep.

094
책장

[책짱] 명사 bookshelf

[Expression] 책장에 책을 꽂다 to place the books in the bookshelf

[Synonym] 책꽂이 bookcase

[Example] 책장에서 읽고 싶은 책을 골라 보세요.
Take a look at the shelf and take a book you would like to read.

다 읽은 책은 책상에 쌓아 놓지 말고 책장에 꽂아라.
After you finish reading a book, don't stack it on the table but place it in the bookshelf.

095
침대

[침대] 명사 bed

[Expression] 침대에 눕다 to lay on the bed

[Example] 너무 피곤해서 침대에 누웠다. I was so tired that I lay down on the bed.

옛날 한국 사람들은 침대에서 자지 않고 바닥에 이불을 깔고 잤습니다.
A long time ago Korean people did not sleep on beds, but slept on the floor with blankets.

096
그렇다

[그러타] 형용사 to be a certain state

(to state the condition of the word used at the beginning) state, shape, personality verb, ㅎ verb

[Usage]
그런 **N**
그렇게 **AV**

[Expression]
그런 사람 that type of person
그렇게 하다 to do it that way

[Related word]
이렇다 to be this way
저렇다 to be one that way

[Example]
그렇게 자주 결석을 하면 안 돼요. You can't be absent so often.
영수는 맡은 일을 성실하게 해요. 저는 그런 사람과 일하고 싶어요.
Young-soo does his work sincerely. I want to work with a person like that.

097
다르다

[다르다] 형용사 to be different

to compare the shape, size, and personality and notice the differences, 르 verb

[Usage]
N이/가 다르다

[Antonym]
같다 to be the same

[Example]
쌍둥이도 성격이 달라요. Twins have different personalities.
나라마다 문화와 사고방식이 다릅니다.
Every country has different cultures as well as different ways of living.

098
두껍다

[두껍따] 형용사 to be thick

to have more layers than normal, ㅂ verb

[Usage]
두꺼운 **N**
N이/가 두껍다

[Expression]
두꺼운 옷 thick clothing
책이 두껍다 the book is thick

[Antonym]
얇다 to be thin

[Example]
영어 사전이 두꺼워서 무거워요.
The English dictionary is thick, so it is heavy.

강의 얼음이 두껍게 얼어서 사람들이 강 위에서 낚시를 하고 있어요.
The water in the lake has frozen thickly, so people are fishing on top of the lake.

099
무겁다

[무겁따] 형용사 to be heavy

to weigh a lot, ㅂverb

[Usage] 무거운 <u>N</u>

<u>N</u>이/가 무겁다

[Expression] 무거운 짐 heavy objects

가방이 무겁다 the bag is heavy

[Antonym] 가볍다 to be light

[Related word] 무게 weight

[Example] 이 책상은 너무 무거워서 혼자 옮길 수 없어요.

This desk is so heavy that I can't move it alone.

할머니께서 무거운 짐을 들고 가시는 것을 보고 도와 드렸다.

I saw a grandmother holding very heavy things, so I helped her carry the object.

100
물건

[물건] 명사 object, stuff

something that people made, and an item that has a certain shape

[Example] 저는 물건을 자주 잃어버려요. I lose my objects frequently.

남대문 시장에 가면 물건을 싸게 살 수 있어요.

If you go to Nam-dae-moon, you can buy stuff for cheaper.

101
비슷하다

[비스타다] 형용사 to be similar

to compare things according to shape, size, and personality and can see that it is not the same thing but not different

[Usage] <u>N</u>이/가 <u>N</u>과/와 비슷하다

[Related word] 같다 to be similar

[Example] 우리 고향 날씨는 한국과 비슷해요.

My homeland's weather is similar to that of Korea.

부부가 성격이 비슷하면 잘 싸우지 않을 것 같아요.

If the married couple has similar personalities, I don't think they will fight often.

102
어떻다

[어떠타] 형용사 to be this kind of……

the condition, and view of something, ㅎverb

[Usage] 어떤 <u>N</u>

[Expression] 어떤 사람 what kind of person

어떻게 하다 to do something this way

어떻게 지내다 to be in a condition of being

50

[Example]	건강은 좀 어떠세요? How is your health?
	요즘 어떻게 지내니? How are you these days?

103
좋다

[조타] 형용사 1. to be good-natured   2. to be good, fine, nice

1. attitude or substance, health of body, also used when the character, personality, manner, or way of speaking is soft and kind

[Usage]	N이/가 좋다
[Expression]	질이 좋다 the quality is good
	성격이 좋다 personality is good
	태도가 좋다 attitude is good
	건강이 좋다 health is good
[Antonym]	나쁘다 to be bad
[Example]	오늘 본 영화는 내용이 정말 좋았다.
	The movie I watched today had a good theme.

2. something that is liked by a person and also a person's emotion or feeling is happy

[Usage]	N이/가 좋다
[Expression]	요리가 좋다 I like cooking.
	기분이 좋다 I feel good.
[Antonym]	싫다 I don't like it.
[Example]	저는 지금 하고 있는 일이 정말 좋습니다.
	I really like the job that I have right now.

104
크다

[크다] 형용사 to be big

length, width, thickness, size is larger than normal, 으 verb

[Usage]	N이/가 크다
[Expression]	큰 인형 big doll
	눈이 크다 eyes are big
[Antonym]	작다 to be small
[Example]	잘 안 보이니까 글씨를 크게 써 주세요.
	I can't really read your writing, Can you write it bigger?
	어제 산 옷이 커요. 작은 옷으로 바꿔야겠어요.
	The clothing I bought yesterday is too big. I will have to get an exchange for a smaller size.

[1~15] 다음 단어를 한국어로 바꿔 쓰십시오. Change these words into Korean.

1. clothing	(	)	2. knife	(	)
3. cup	(	)	4. notebook	(	)
5. undergarment	(	)	6. pencil	(	)
7. chair	(	)	8. desk	(	)
9. bed	(	)	10. toothbrush	(	)
11. air-conditioner	(	)	12. computer	(	)
13. to be big	(	)	14. to be different	(	)
15. to be heavy	(	)		

[16~20] 그림을 보고 (   )에 알맞은 것을 고르십시오.
Look at the picture and choose the correct word.

16.

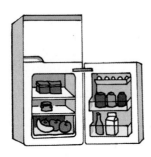

가 : 이 음식은 어떻게 하지요?

나 : (   )에 넣으세요.

❶ 옷장   ❷ 냉장고

❸ 노트북   ❹ 텔레비전

17.

가 : 뭘 신을 거예요?

나 : (   )을/를 신을 거예요.

❶ 구두   ❷ 양말

❸ 슬리퍼   ❹ 운동화

18.

가 : 무엇으로 쓸까요?

나 : (   )으로/로 쓰세요.

❶ 볼펜   ❷ 연필

❸ 칫솔   ❹ 지우개

19.

가 : 오늘 결혼식이 있는데 뭘 입고 가야 할까요?

나 : 결혼식 때 남자들은 보통 (   )을/를 입어요.

❶ 양복   ❷ 코트

❸ 스웨터   ❹ 블라우스

20.

가 : 뭘 하고 있어요?

나 : 사진이 (   )어서/아서/여서 테이프로 붙이고 있어요.

❶ 찍다   ❷ 자르다

❸ 찢어지다   ❹ 잃어버리다

[21~30] 다음 문장을 읽고 알맞은 어휘를 골라 쓰십시오. 어휘는 한 번만 쓰십시오.
Read the following sentence and choose the right word. Use the words once.

컵	가위	냄비	물건	봉투
들다	매다	메다	잃다	차다
가지다	고치다	그렇다	멋지다	어떻다

21. ( )으로/로 잡지의 사진을 잘랐다.

22. 라면을 먹으려고 ( )에 물을 끓였어요.

23. 아버지는 파란색 넥타이를 ( )고 출근했다.

24. 책이 무거운데 교실까지 ( )어/아/여 주세요.

25. 시장은 백화점보다 ( )도 많고 값도 싸서 자주 가요.

26. 휴대전화를 ( )고 오지 않아서 하루 종일 불편했어요.

27. 아이는 교과서와 필통을 넣은 가방을 ( )고 학교에 갔다.

28. 편지 ( )에 받는 사람의 주소와 이름을 정확하게 쓰세요.

29. 고장이 난 노트북을 ( )으려고/려고 서비스센터에 갔어요.

30. 경기장에서 열심히 뛰는 선수들이 정말 ( )어요/아요/여요.

[31~35] ( ) 안에 알맞은 것을 고르십시오. Choose the correct one.

31. 날씨가 추우니까 ( )을/를 하고 나가세요.

❶ 모자 ❷ 반지 ❸ 목도리 ❹ 스타킹

32. 먼저 손을 씻고 ( )으로/로 깨끗하게 닦아라.

❶ 물 ❷ 샴푸 ❸ 수건 ❹ 향수

33. 동생은 잠을 자려고 (　　　)으로/로 갈아입었다.

   ❶ 잠옷　　　　❷ 치마　　　　❸ 여성복　　　　❹ 원피스

34. 이사를 가게 되어서 침대, 소파, 식탁 등 (　　　)을/를 새로 사려고 해요.

   ❶ 가구　　　　❷ 보석　　　　❸ 화장품　　　　❹ 가전제품

35. 오늘은 시계를 (　　　)지 않고 학교에 갔어요.

   ❶ 매다　　　　❷ 쓰다　　　　❸ 잃다　　　　❹ 차다

[36~40] 밑줄 친 부분과 반대되는 뜻을 가진 것을 고르십시오.
Choose the word that is the opposite of the underlined word.

36. **가 :** 가방이 <u>무거워요</u>?
   나 : 아니요, 무겁지 않아요. (　　　)어요/아요/여요.

   ❶ 고치다　　　　❷ 가볍다　　　　❸ 그렇다　　　　❹ 멋지다

37. **가 :** 한국의 문화는 중국의 문화와 <u>달라요</u>?
   나 : 다른 것도 있고 (　　　)은/ㄴ 것도 있어요.

   ❶ 같다　　　　❷ 들다　　　　❸ 매다　　　　❹ 좋다

38. **가 :** 이 옷은 좀 <u>얇은</u>데요.
   나 : 그래요? 그럼 (　　　)은/ㄴ 옷을 드릴게요.

   ❶ 가지다　　　　❷ 두껍다　　　　❸ 멋지다　　　　❹ 무겁다

39. **가 :** 신발이 좀 <u>크지</u> 않아요?
   나 : 아니요, (　　　)어요/아요/여요.

   ❶ 신다　　　　❷ 메다　　　　❸ 작다　　　　❹ 차다

40. **가** : 질이 좋아요?

    나 : 아니요, 질이 (   )어요/아요/여요.

    ❶ 나쁘다   ❷ 다르다   ❸ 어떻다   ❹ 고장나다

[41~45] 밑줄 친 부분과 의미가 가장 가까운 것을 고르십시오.
Choose the word that is most similar to the underlined section.

41. **가** : 이 케이크를 어떤 <u>그릇</u>에 담을까?

    나 : 이 (   )에 담자.

    ❶ 수저   ❷ 물건   ❸ 접시   ❹ 냉장고

42. **가** : 신발을 사야 하는데 어떤 것이 좋을까?

    나 : 저 (   )은/는 어때? 한번 신어 봐.

    ❶ 장갑   ❷ 시계   ❸ 우산   ❹ 운동화

43. **가** : 이 넥타이를 한 번 <u>해</u> 보세요.

    나 : 네, 한 번 (   )어/아/여 볼게요.

    ❶ 끼다   ❷ 매다   ❸ 들다   ❹ 입다

44. **가** : 이 청소기를 <u>써</u> 본 적이 있어요?

    나 : 아니요, 한 번도 (   )은/ㄴ 적이 없어요.

    ❶ 가지다   ❷ 고장나다   ❸ 사용하다   ❹ 찢어지다

45. **가** : 빨간색 치마와 노란색 치마 중에서 어느 것이 <u>마음에 들어요</u>?

    나 : 저는 노란색 치마가 더 (   )어요/아요/여요.

    ❶ 밝다   ❷ 좋다   ❸ 가볍다   ❹ 예쁘다

[46~50] 밑줄 친 단어의 쓰임이 잘못된 것을 고르십시오. Choose the one that is incorrectly used.

46. ❶ 목도리를 <u>신으면</u> 더 따뜻할 거예요. ( )
    ❷ 오늘 네가 <u>신은</u> 스타킹이 정말 예쁘다.
    ❸ 양복을 입을 때에는 보통 구두를 <u>신어요</u>.
    ❹ 오늘 등산을 가려고 하니까 운동화를 <u>신어라</u>.

47. ❶ 공부를 열심히 <u>하세요</u>. ( )
    ❷ 이 많은 요리를 혼자 다 <u>했어요</u>?
    ❸ 오늘은 귀걸이하고 목걸이를 <u>하고</u> 나갔다.
    ❹ 날씨가 춥지 않은데 왜 장갑을 <u>하고</u> 왔어요?

48. ❶ 음식 맛이 좀 <u>쓴데요</u>. ( )
    ❷ 어머니께 편지를 <u>썼다</u>.
    ❸ 바람이 차서 목도리를 <u>썼다</u>.
    ❹ 이 세탁기는 어떻게 <u>쓰는</u> 거예요?

49. ❶ 이 양말 세 <u>켤레</u>에 얼마예요? ( )
    ❷ 책상 위에 필통 세 <u>자루</u>가 있어요.
    ❸ 동대문 시장에서 원피스를 두 <u>벌</u> 샀어요.
    ❹ 어머니는 냉장고를 한 <u>대</u> 더 사고 싶어하십니다.

50. ❶ 시계를 <u>차고</u> 왔어요? ( )
    ❷ 가방을 <u>메고</u> 학교에 갔다.
    ❸ 이 신발을 한번 <u>껴</u> 보세요.
    ❹ 혼자 이 가방을 <u>들</u> 수 있겠어요?.

시간 I

03

Time I

001
만

[만] 수사 ten-thousand

[Expression] 만 원 10,000 won

사람 만 명 10,000 people

[Related word]

10,000	20,000	30,000	......	100,000	1,000,000	10,000,000
만	이만	삼만	......	십만	백만	천만

[Example]

나는 지난달에 교통비로 5(오)만 원을 썼다.
Last month I used 50,000won for transportation.

축구를 보러 경기장에 온 사람이 만 명쯤 된다.
There were about 10,000 people that came to the stadium to watch soccer.

002
많다

[만타] 형용사 to have a lot

to be more than the regular amount

[Usage] N이/가 많다

[Antonym] 적다¹ to be small

[Example] 이번 연휴에는 여행을 가려고 하는 사람들이 많다.
For this holiday, there are many people who want to go on vacation.

한국에서 여러 가지 많은 경험을 할 수 있어서 참 좋았다.
I had a good time in Korea because there are many things to experience.

003
몇

[면] 수사 1. some, several, a few 2. how many, how old, what time

1. an amount that is not a lot

[Usage] 몇 N

[Example] 한국어 공부를 시작한 지 몇 달 되었습니다.
It's been a few months since I've started to study Korean.

2. (asked as a question) word used to ask the amount of the word that comes after '몇'

[Usage] 몇 N

[Example] 오늘이 몇 월 며칠이에요?
What is the month and day today?

004
백

[백] 수사 one hundred

[Expression] 백 원 100 won

장미 백 송이 100 roses

[Related word]

100	200	300	......	900	1,000	10,000,000
백	이백	삼백	......	구백	천	천만

[Example] 지난 시험에서 백 점을 받았다.
I received a one hundred on the last test.

이번 동창회에는 동창들이 백 명쯤 왔다.
For the reunion we had about a hundred people attending the event.

005
수

[수] 명사 amount

objects that can be counted and can tell the size of something

[Expression] 수가 적다 the amount is small

[Example] 매년 태어나는 아이의 수가 점점 적어지고 있다.
Every year there are less amounts of babies being born.

경기장에 온 사람이 너무 많아서 얼마나 왔는지 그 수를 알 수 없다.
There are so many people in the stadium that we cannot calculate the amount.

006
스물

[스물] 수사 twenty

[Usage] 스무 **N**

[Synonym] 이십 twenty

[Related word]

10	20	30	40	50	60	70	80	90	100
열²	스물	서른	마흔	쉰	예순	일흔	여든	아흔	백

[Example] 스무 살에 결혼을 하셨다고요?
You got married when you were twenty?

한 반의 학생이 모두 열 명이고 두 반이 함께 가기로 했으니까 선생님과 학생 모두 스물 두 명이다.
There are ten students in each class, so since we decided to go with two classes the total amount including the teachers is twenty-two people.

007
십

[십] 수사 ten

[Expression] 십 원 ten won

십 쪽 ten pages

십 층 tenth floor

[Synonym] 열² ten

[Related word]

10	20	30	……	100	1,000	10,000
십	이십	삼십	……	백	천	만

[Example] 십 주 동안 한 시간도 빠지지 않고 출석했다.

For ten weeks I attended every class without missing even an hour.

십 년이 지나도 너는 하나도 달라지지 않았구나.

Ten years have passed and you haven't changed a bit.

008
억

[억] 수사 one hundred million

[Expression] 일억 원 one hundred million won

[Example] 몇 년쯤 돈을 벌면 일억 원을 모을 수 있을까?

How many years will it take for me to save up a hundred million won?

이렇게 큰 집을 사려면 몇 억 원은 필요할 거예요.

In order to a buy a house as big as this, it will cost a few hundred million.

도움말

'10, 100, 1000, ……' when reading these numbers you don't need to say one in front of them, just refer to them as ten, hundred, and thousand, but in front of '100,000,000' you must use 'one' hundred million.

Example: 10,000원(만 원) ten thousand won

111,110원(십일만 천백십 원) one hundred and eleven thousand and hundred ten won

111,111,111원 (일억 천백십일만 천백십일 원)
one hundred million eleven million a hundred eleven thousand and a hundred eleven won

009
일¹

[일] 수사 one

[Expression] 일 번 number one

일 원 one won

[Synonym] 하나 one

[Related word]

1	2	3	4	5	6	7	8	9	10
일[1]	이	삼	사	오	육	칠	팔[2]	구	십

[Example] 요즘 일 원짜리 동전은 찾아보기 어렵다.
Now-a-days it's hard to find the one won coin.

일 년쯤 한국어를 배우면 한국말을 얼마나 잘 할 수 있을까요?
If I learn Korean for about a year, how much will I learn?

010 천

[천] 수사 a thousand

[Expression] 천 원 a thousand won

책 천 권 a thousand books

[Related word]

1,000	2,000	3,000	......	10,000	100,000
천	이천	삼천	......	만	십만

[Example] 천 원이면 아이스크림을 하나 사 먹을 수 있겠다.
With a thousand won I can buy an ice cream.

우리 대학교에 다니는 외국인 학생 수가 삼천 명쯤 된다고 한다.
There are about three thousand international students that go to the university.

011 하나

[하나] 수사 one

[Usage] 한 N

[Expression] 한 사람 one person

한 마리 one animal

[Synanym] 일[1] one

[Related word]

1	2	3	4	5	6	7	8	9	10
하나	둘	셋	넷	다섯	여섯	일곱	여덟	아홉	열[2]

[Example] 요리할 준비를 다 끝낸 줄 알았는데, 중요한 재료 하나가 빠져 있었다.
I thought I had everything ready to cook, but I forgot one important ingredient.

학생 한 명이 질문을 하니까 다른 학생들도 여러 가지 질문들을 하기 시작했다.
One student asked questions and now many students are asking questions as well.

도움말

There are different ways of saying and using the numbers in Korean, Korean numbers and Chinese numbers are also used. For the Korean numbers '하나, 둘, 셋, 넷, 스물' are the regular numbers but they have different forms like '한, 두, 세, 네, 스무'. So be cautious of these differences of usage.

Number	Chinese Numbers	Korean Numbers	Different Form
1	일	하나	한 살
2	이	둘	두 살
3	삼	셋	세 살
4	사	넷	네 살
5	오	다섯	다섯 살
6	육	여섯	여섯 살
7	칠	일곱	일곱 살
8	팔	여덟	여덟 살
9	구	아홉	아홉 살
10	십	열	열 살
⋮	⋮	⋮	⋮
20	이십	스물	스무 살
21	이십일	스물하나	스물한 살
22	이십이	스물둘	스물두 살
23	이십삼	스물셋	스물세 살
24	이십사	스물넷	스물네 살
⋮	⋮	⋮	⋮
30	삼십	서른	서른 살

012
낮

[낟] 명사 1. day 2. afternoon

1. from sunrise to sunset

[Expression]	낮이 짧다 the day is short
[Antonym]	밤 night
[Example]	봄이 되니까 낮이 점점 길어진다. Since it is spring the days are becoming longer.

2. past the morning and before it is night

[Expression]	낮잠 nap 낮 두 시 2pm
[Synonym]	오후 afternoon
[Example]	아침에 내리던 비가 낮이 되니까 그쳤다. The rain that started in the morning has stopped in the afternoon.

013
늦다

[늗따] 형용사 to be late, to be tardy

to come later than the time promised

[Usage]	N이/가 늦다
[Expression]	늦은 시간 late time of the day 늦게 오다 to be late at coming to something 늦게까지 일하다 to work until late
[Antonym]	이르다 to be early
[Example]	이렇게 늦은 시간에 무슨 일로 전화하셨어요? For what reason did you call so late in the afternoon? 일찍 도착할 거라고 생각했는데 늦게 도착했다. I thought I was going to arrive early, but I arrived later than expected.

014
반

[반] 명사 a half

[Expression]	한 시 반 1:30 반으로 나누다 to split into half
[Example]	일을 반밖에 못했는데, 벌써 퇴근할 시간이 됐어요. I completed only half of my work, but it's already time to go home. 벌써 1(한)시 반이다. 밤이 늦었으니까 이제 자야겠다. It's already 1:30am. It is late in the night, I better go to sleep.

015
분[1]

[분] 명사 minute

[Expression]   한 시 오십오 분 1:55

[Related word] 시 hour

            초 second

[Example]   지금 3(세)시 15(십오)분이다. It is 3:15.

            시험 시간은 60(육십)분이에요. 시험 잘 보세요.
            You will receive 60 minutes in the test. Good luck on the test.

016
새벽

[새벽] 명사 early morning, break of dawn

            before the sunrises and before it is completely bright

[Expression]   이른 새벽 early morning

[Related word] 아침 morning

            오전 the forenoon

[Example]   새벽에 우유를 배달하는 아르바이트를 하고 있어요.
            I have a part time job where I deliver milk in the early morning.

            회사가 멀기 때문에 새벽에 일어나서 첫차를 타고 출근해야 한다.
            My office is far, so I have to wake up early in the morning and take the first
            subway to get to work.

017
시

[시] 명사 hour

[Expression]   열 시 십 분 10:10

[Related word] 분[1] minute

            초 second

            시간 time

[Example]   벌써 아홉 시야. 빨리 일어나! It's already 9am. Hurry up, wake up!

            일곱 시가 조금 지났으니 아버지께서 곧 퇴근해서 집에 오시겠다.
            It's a little past 7pm, so father should be getting off work and on his way home.

018
아침

[아침] 명사 1. morning 2. breakfast

            1. the time that is from early sunrise until breakfast time

[Expression]   아침 운동 morning exercise

            아침 아홉 시 9am

            아침이 밝다 the morning has come

[Synonym]   오전 morning

[Example]   어제 늦게 자서 그런지 오늘 아침에는 일어나기가 힘들었어.
            Yesterday I slept late, so it was hard to wake up this morning.

2. breakfast

[Expression] 아침을 먹다 to eat breakfast

[Related word] 점심 lunch

저녁 dinner

[Example] 아침을 꼭 먹어야 건강을 지킬 수 있어요.
We must eat breakfast in order to be healthy.

019
언제

[언제] **부사** when

(used when asked a question)not knowing exactly when, and asking when

[Example] 언제 시간이 되니? 시간이 될 때 우리 꼭 만나자.
When do you have time? When you have time, let's meet.

제가 언제 전화를 드릴까요? 편한 시간을 말씀해 주세요.
When should I call you? Please tell me when you're free.

020
오전

[오전] **명사** 1. a.m. 2. morning

1.the time in between midnight and noon

[Expression] 오전 네 시 4am

[Antonym] 오후 afternoon

[Example] 일이 다 끝났을 때가 오전 한 시였다.
I finished all of my work and it was 1am.

2. the time when the sun rises to noon

[Expression] 오전 열한 시 11am

[Synonym] 아침 morning

[Example] 오늘 저녁에는 시간이 안 되니까 내일 오전에 만납시다.
Tonight I don't have much time let's meet tomorrow morning.

도움말

'morning' and 'afternoon' have two different meanings. you label '오전' 'AM', and '오후' 'PM'.

02:10 오전 두 시 십 분 am 02:10

23:50 오후 열한 시 오십 분 pm 23:50

Usually when speaking, early morning is '새벽' and the time where it is close to breakfast time is '오전'. Noon to dinner time is '오후'.

오전 9(아홉)시에 수업이 시작된다. My classes start at 9am.

오후 4(네)시에 친구를 만나기로 했다. I will meet my friend at 4pm.

021
일찍

[일찍] 부사 early

a time earlier than the set time

[Usage] 일찍 AV

[Expression] 일찍 출발하다 to leave early

일찍 일어나다 to wake up early

[Antonym] 늦게 late

[Example] 오늘은 일찍 일어나서 오랜만에 아침 운동을 했다.
I haven't exercised in a long time, but I woke up early and exercised this morning.

수업이 일찍 끝나서 친구들하고 차를 한 잔 하고 집에 왔다.
The class ended earlier than usual, so my friends and I had some tea and went back home.

022
저녁

[저녁] 명사 1. evening 2. dinner

1.the time when the sun is about to set and about to be night

[Expression] 저녁 일곱 시 7pm

[Related word] 밤 night

[Example] 저녁이 되니까 날씨가 선선해졌어요.
It is becoming cooler because it is night.

2. dinner food/last meal of the day

[Expression] 저녁을 먹다 to eat dinner

[Related word] 아침 breakfast

점심 lunch

[Example] 다이어트를 위해서 저녁을 먹지 않기로 했다.
I decided to not eat dinner for my diet.

023
지나다

[지나다] 동사 to pass

time passes and that time escapes.

[Usage] N이/가 지나다

[Expression] 지난해 last year

지난 수업 last class

시간이 지나다 time has passed

[Example] 네 시가 조금 지났다. It is a little past 4.

지난 시간에 배운 것을 복습해 봅시다.
Let's review what we learned last time.

68

024
쯤

[쯤] 접사 about

(to fix behind a noun) meaning similar to '정도'(degree)

[Usage]　　　**N**쯤

[Expression]　반년쯤　about half a year

　　　　　　세 시쯤　about 3 o'clock

　　　　　　열 명쯤　about 10 people

[Example]　　이번 일은 한 달쯤 걸릴 것 같다.　This work will take about a month.

　　　　　　오늘 수업은 다섯 시 십 분쯤에 끝났어요.　Today's class ended at 5:10pm.

025
초

[초] 명사 second

[Expression]　육십 초　60 seconds

[Related word]　시　hour

　　　　　　분¹　minute

[Example]　　일 분 일 초가 급하다. 빨리 병원으로 가자.

　　　　　　One minute one second is precious. We have to hurry and go to the hospital.

　　　　　　지금 4(네)시 22(이십이)분 35(삼십오)초를 지나고 있습니다.

　　　　　　It is passing 4 o'clock 22 minutes and 35seconds right now.

 도움말

When talking about time, we say the hour in Korean numbers and minutes and seconds in Chinese numbers.

3:20:56 (세 시 이십 분 오십육 초) 3 hours 20 minutes and 56 seconds

6:10:05 (여섯 시 십 분 오 초) 6 hours 10 minutes 5 seconds

026
날

[날] 명사 day

the time when the earth is rotating once during a 24 hour period

[Usage]   <u>N</u> 날

<u>AV</u>는/은/을 날

[Expression]   어느 날 someday

[Related word]   일² day

날짜 date

[Example]   우리는 첫눈이 오는 날에 만나기로 약속했다.

We promised to meet when the first snow comes.

언니는 어느 날 갑자기 아무 말 없이 여행을 떠났다.

My older sister left for vacation without telling anyone.

027
날짜

[날짜] 명사 date

saying which day it is

[Expression]   결혼 날짜 wedding date

출국 날짜 date of departure

날짜가 지나다 to pass the date

[Related word]   날 day

[Example]   결혼식 날짜는 언제로 정했어요?

What date did you decide to get married?

시험 날짜와 시험 시간을 다시 한 번 확인해라.

Check the date of the test as well as the time of the exam.

028
내일

[내일] 부사 tomorrow

[Related word]   어제 yesterday

오늘 today

[Example]   내일 운동회가 있는데 비가 오면 어떻게 하지요?

There is a sports competition tomorrow, but what if it rains tomorrow?

오늘은 너무 피곤하니까 우리 내일 만나서 얘기하자.

I'm too tired today, let's meet tomorrow and talk.

029
년

[년] **명사** year

[Expression] 일 년 one year

이천십 년 year 2010

[Synonym] 해 a year

[Example] 저는 2010(이천십)년 9(구)월 1(일)일에 결혼했어요.
I got married September 1, 2010.

4(사)년 동안의 대학 공부가 끝나고, 이제 졸업할 날만 남았다.
I have studied for 4 years at the university, now all I need to do is graduate.

030
어제

[어제] **부사** yesterday

[Related word] 오늘 today

내일 tomorrow

[Example] 어제 영수 씨에게 계속 전화했는데 받지 않았어요.
Yesterday I kept calling Young-soo, but he didn't pick up.

어제 너무 피곤해서 화장도 지우지 못하고 자 버렸다.
I was so tired yesterday that I fell asleep without taking off my makeup.

031
연휴

[연휴] **명사** holiday

a vacation that lasts longer than 2 days

[Related word] 휴일 vacation

[Example] 이번 연휴에는 오랜만에 해외로 여행가자.
Let's go overseas this vacation period.

설날 연휴가 되면 사람들은 가족들을 만나기 위해 고향으로 간다.
During the Lunar New Year people go to their hometowns to visit their families.

032
오늘

[오늘] **부사** today

[Related word]

5월 18일 May 18th	5월 19일 May 19th	5월 20일 May 20th	5월 21일 May 21st	5월 22일 May 22nd
그저께/그제 the day before yesterday	어저께/어제 yesterday	오늘 today	내일 tomorrow	모레 the day after tomorrow

[Example] 오늘 손님들이 몇 시쯤 오신다고 했지요?
What time did you say the guests are arriving today?

오늘 해야 할 일은 오늘 안에 다 끝내야 한다.
We need to finish everything we need to finish for today.

033
올해

[올해] 명사 this year

[Synonym] 금년 this present/current year

[Related word]

2010년	2011년	2012년	2013년	2014년
재작년 2 years ago	작년 last year	올해 this year	내년 next year	내후년 in 2 years

[Example] 올해 날씨가 좋지 않아서 채소 값이 많이 올랐다.
This years weather was not so good, so the price of vegetables went up.

5(오)년 동안 사귄 여자 친구와 올해 결혼하기로 했다.
I will get married this year to the the girl that I've dated for 5 years.

034
요일

[요일] 명사 day of the week

each day of the week

[Expression]

일요일	월요일	화요일	수요일	목요일	금요일	토요일
Sunday	Monday	Tuesday	Wednesday	Thursday	Friday	Saturday

[Example] 오늘이 무슨 요일이에요? What day is it today?
월요일부터 금요일까지 날마다 네 시간씩 한국말 수업이 있어요.
I have 4 hours of Korean lesson Monday through Friday.

035
월

[월] 명사 month

[Expression]

1(일)월 January	2(이)월 February	3(삼)월 March	4(사)월 April	5(오)월 May	6(유)월 June
7(칠)월 July	8(팔)월 August	9(구)월 September	10(시)월 October	11(십일)월 November	12(십이)월 December

[Related word] 개월 month

달 month

[Example] 생일이 몇 월 며칠이에요?
What is the month and day of your birthday?

시월이 되면 단풍이 예쁘게 드니까 단풍구경을 갑시다.
In October the leaves change into pretty colors, so let's look at leaves during that period.

036
일²

[일] 명사 day

(use Chinese numbers) unit to count the day

[Expression]

1(일)일	2(이)일	3(삼)일	4(사)일	5(오)일	......	30(삼십)일
1st day	2nd day	3rd day	4th day	5th day	......	30th day

[Example] 이번 달 7(칠)일이 남편 생일이다.
The 7th day of this month is my husband's birthday.

중간시험은 다음 주 월요일부터 금요일까지 5(오)일 동안 본다고 한다.
The midterm exams will be 5 days from Monday through Friday next week.

037
작년

[장년] 명사 last year

[Related word] 내년 next year

올해 this year

[Example] 작년 3(삼)월에 대학에 입학했다. I entered college last March.

올해 여름은 작년 여름보다 더 길고 더 더울 거라고 한다.
This year's summer will be longer and hotter than last year's.

038
주

[주] 명사 1. week 2. week

1. the days from Monday to Sunday, 7 days

[Expression] 지난주 last week

이번 주 this week

다음 주 next week

[Example] 지난주에 새 학기가 시작되었다. The new semester started last week.

2. the unit used to count weeks

[Expression] 한 주 one week

일 주 one week

십 주 10 weeks

[Synonym] 주일 a week

[Example] 한 주만 더 지나면 방학이 끝나요.
After one week our vacation period will end.

039
주말

[주말] 명사 weekend

[Expression] 주말을 보내다 to spend the weekend

[Related word] 평일 weekday

[Example] 이번 주말에 날씨가 좋으면 놀러 가자.
If the weather is good this weekend, let's go out.

73

주말에 시간이 있으면 보통 때 만나지 못했던 친구를 만난다.
If I have time during the weekends, I meet friends that I haven't been able to meet.

040
평일

[평일] 명사 weekday

word to express normal days, the exceptions include Saturday, Sunday, and holidays

[Related word] 주말 weekend

[Example] 평일에는 출근하고 주말에는 쉰다.
I work during the weekdays and rest during the weekend.

식당 근처에 회사가 많으면 평일에 손님들이 많다.
If there are many restaurants near the office, there are many customers during the weekday.

041
휴일

[휴일] 명사 legal holiday

days of rest, like Sundays and vacation periods

[Expression] 공휴일 national holiday

[Example] 우리 아버지는 휴일마다 늦잠을 주무신다.
My father sleeps late during the holidays.

휴일이 되면 가족과 함께 가까운 곳으로 소풍을 가야겠다.
During the vacation period I should take my family to a nearby place and have a picnic.

[1~15] 다음 단어를 한국어로 바꿔 쓰십시오. Change these words into Korean.

1. night	( )	2. hundred	( )
3. minute	( )	4. date	( )
5. next year	( )	6. October	( )
7. yesterday	( )	8. when	( )
9. long weekend/holiday	( )	10. morning	( )
11. 7	( )	12. hundred million	( )
13. 1	( )	14. Friday	( )
15. Wednesday	( )		

[16~20] 그림을 보고 (   )에 알맞은 것을 고르십시오.

Look at the picture and choose the correct word.

16.

가 : 장미꽃이 몇 송이 있어요?

나 : (   ) 송이 있어요.

❶ 네　　　　❷ 다섯

❸ 여섯　　　❹ 일곱

17.

가 : 지금 몇 시예요?

나 : (   )시 (   )분이에요.

❶ 이, 삼십　　　❷ 둘, 반

❸ 두, 반　　　　❹ 두, 삼십

18.

가 : 아침을 몇 시에 먹어요?

나 : (　　　) 아홉 시에 먹어요.

❶ 낮　　　　　❷ 점심

❸ 오전　　　　❹ 새벽

19.

가 : 오늘이 몇 월 며칠이에요?

나 : (　　　)월 (　　　)일이에요

❶ 열, 열　　　　❷ 일, 열

❸ 십, 십　　　　❹ 시, 십

20.

가 : 언제 한국에 왔어요?

나 : (　　　) 왔어요.

❶ 그저께　　　　❷ 어제

❸ 내일　　　　　❹ 내일

[21~30] 다음 문장을 읽고 알맞은 어휘를 골라 쓰십시오. 어휘는 한 번만 쓰십시오.
Read the following sentence and choose the right word. Use the words once.

낮	밤	어제	오늘	내일
올해	내년	주말	오전	오후
아침	저녁	늦다	많다	지나다

21. (   )에 일어나면 먼저 운동부터 합니다.

22. (   )마다 잠이 잘 오지 않아요. 어떻게 하지요?

23. (   )이/가 며칠 남지 않았어요. 새해 계획은 세우셨어요?

24. 우와! 책이 진짜 (   )네요! 정말 이 책들을 다 읽으셨어요?

25. 아직도 공부하니? 시간이 많이 (   )었다/았다/였다. 빨리 자라.

26. 점심을 먹기 전까지 (   )에는 보통 도서관에서 공부를 합니다.

27. 벌써 한 시가 (   )었네요/았네요/였네요. 이제 수업을 끝냅시다.

28. 벌써 날이 어두워졌어요. 가을이 되니까 (   )이/가 점점 짧아지네요.

29. 이번 (   )에 뭘 하실 거예요? 시간이 있으시면 저하고 같이 영화를 보러 갑시다.

30. 밤이 늦었어요. 지금 이 시간에는 택시를 잡기도 어려우니까 그냥 여기에서 주무시고
    (   ) 가세요.

[31~35] (   ) 안에 알맞은 것을 고르십시오. Choose the correct one.

31. 이번 시간에는 (   ) 시간에 공부한 것을 다시 복습하겠습니다.

   ❶ 그　　　　❷ 몇　　　　❸ 지난　　　　❹ 다음

32. 저는 서른 살(   ) 결혼할 생각입니다.

   ❶ 쯤　　　　❷ 세　　　　❸ 부터　　　　❹ 나이

33. 오늘이 무슨 (   )인데 어머니가 음식을 이렇게 많이 하셨어요?

    ❶ 일   ❷ 날   ❸ 날씨   ❹ 날짜

34. (   ) 12월에 유학을 와서 한국말을 공부한지 벌써 여섯 달이 되었습니다.

    ❶ 작년   ❷ 올해   ❸ 내년   ❹ 지난달

35. 이번 추석 (   )은/는 5일이에요. 그래서 친구들하고 여행을 갈 계획이에요.

    ❶ 날   ❷ 방학   ❸ 날짜   ❹ 연휴

[36~40] 밑줄 친 부분과 반대되는 뜻을 가진 것을 고르십시오.
Choose the word that is the opposite of the underlined word.

36. **가 :** 공원에서 산책하는 사람이 <u>많아요</u>?

    나 : 아니요, (   )어요/아요/여요.

    ❶ 작다   ❷ 적다   ❸ 길다   ❹ 짧다

37. **가 :** 어제 <u>일찍</u> 집에 들어왔어요?

    나 : 아니요, (   ) 왔어요.

    ❶ 늦게   ❷ 짧게   ❸ 느리게   ❹ 천천히

38. **가 :** 오늘은 <u>오전</u>에 수업이 있어요?

    나 : 아니요, (   )에 있어요.

    ❶ 새벽   ❷ 아침   ❸ 점심   ❹ 오후

39. **가 :** 비행기가 <u>밤</u>에 도착했어요?

    나 : 아니요, (   )에 도착했어요.

    ❶ 낮   ❷ 저녁   ❸ 오후   ❹ 평일

40. **가** : 평일에는 바쁘시죠?

    나 : 아니요, (   )에 더 바빠요.

    ❶ 주말   ❷ 방학   ❸ 일요일   ❹ 공휴일

[41~45] **밑줄 친 부분과 의미가 가장 가까운 것을 고르십시오.**
Choose the word that is most similar to the underlined section.

41. **가** : 보통 <u>아침</u> 몇 시에 식사하세요?

    나 : 저는 보통 (   ) 8시에 아침을 먹어요.

    ❶ 낮   ❷ 오전   ❸ 오후   ❹ 저녁

42. **가** : 돈이 <u>조금</u>밖에 없는데, 이걸로 엄마 선물을 살 수 있을까?

    나 : 그럼, (   )은/ㄴ 돈으로도 살 수 있는 선물이 있을 거야.

    ❶ 작다   ❷ 적다   ❸ 짧다   ❹ 싸다

43. **가** : <u>이십</u> 명쯤 집에 초대하려고 해요.

    나 : (   ) 명이면 음식을 많이 준비해야겠어요.

    ❶ 열   ❷ 십이   ❸ 열두   ❹ 스무

44. **가** : 지금 세 시 <u>삼십 분</u>이에요?

    나 : 네, 세 시 (   )이에요.

    ❶ 반   ❷ 번   ❸ 분   ❹ 방

45. **가** : <u>지난해</u>에 한국에 오셨다고 했지요?

    나 : 네, (   ) 5월에 왔어요.

    ❶ 작년   ❷ 올해   ❸ 내년   ❹ 후년

[46~50] 밑줄 친 단어의 쓰임이 잘못된 것을 고르십시오. Choose the one that is incorrectly used.

46. ❶ 지금 몇 시예요? ( )

     ❷ 오늘이 몇 요일이에요?

     ❸ 오늘이 몇 월 며칠이에요?

     ❹ 학생 몇 명이 아직 안 왔어요.

47. ❶ 지난 일은 다 잊어버리세요. ( )

     ❷ 시간이 벌써 이렇게 지났네요.

     ❸ 지난 시간에는 여기부터 하겠습니다.

     ❹ 힘들었던 시간이 다 지나면 좋은 날이 올 거예요.

48. ❶ 오늘이 무슨 날이에요? ( )

     ❷ 한국에 처음 온 날 뭘 했어요?

     ❸ 이번 달 1날은 어머니 생신이다.

     ❹ 이번 주 토요일은 우리 오빠가 결혼하는 날이다.

49. ❶ 사람이 한 명도 없어요. ( )

     ❷ 육 월 육 일은 일요일이에요.

     ❸ 삼 일 동안 쉬지 않고 일만 했어요.

     ❹ 열 달 동안 열심히 한국말을 공부했습니다.

50. ❶ 낮 열 시에 아침을 먹어서 배가 좀 고파요. ( )

     ❷ 휴일에는 놀러 가는 차들이 많아서 길이 복잡해요.

     ❸ 아침에는 날씨가 좋았는데 오후가 되니까 날씨가 흐려졌다.

     ❹ 이렇게 밤늦게까지 일했는데, 내일 새벽에 일어날 수 있겠어요?

시간 Ⅱ

04

Time Ⅱ

001
나중

[나중] 명사 1. after 2. later

1. completing one work and doing the next

[Antonym] 먼저 first

[Example] 중요한 일을 먼저 하고 그렇지 않은 것은 나중에 하자.
Let's complete the important work first, and leave the rest for later.

2. after sometime has passed

[Example] 요즘은 좀 바쁘니까 나중에 시간이 되면 한 번 보자.
I've been busy these days, so how about we meet when I have some free time.

002
다음

[다음] 명사 1. the following 2. next

1. the following order

[Usage] 다음 N

[Example] 다음 시간 next time
다음 문제 next question

[Related word]

지난 N	이번 N	다음 N
last N	this N	next N

[Example] 이번 시간에는 10(십)쪽까지 공부했으니까 다음 시간에는 11(십일)
쪽부터 하겠습니다.
This time I studied up to page 10, so next time I will start studying from page 11.

2. after finishing a task

[Usage] AV 은/ㄴ 다음

[Example] 물건 정리를 다 한 다음에 방 청소를 하자.
Let's clean up the objects and then clean the room.

003
마지막

[마지막] 명사 last

the final time or end of an order

[Usage] 마지막 N

[Expression] 마지막으로 in conclusion

[Antonym] 처음 first

[Related word] 중간 middle

[Example] 오늘이 선생님과의 마지막 수업이라고 생각하니까 너무 슬프다.
It is sad to think that this is the last class with my teacher.

배워야 할 내용을 모두 공부했으니까 시험을 보기 전에 마지막으로
한 번 복습해 보자.
We have learned everything for the topic so let's review the material for the exam.

004
먼저

[먼저] 부사 first of all

the beginning in time as well as in order

[Antonym] 나중 later

[Example] 먼저 제 것부터 계산해 주시면 안 될까요?
Can you calculate my material first?

한국에 도착한 후에 제일 먼저 부모님께 전화부터 했다.
After arriving in Korea, the first thing I did was contact my parents.

005
째

[째] 접사 order

(used to tell the amount or length of time and is placed after nouns
and numerals) talking about order

[Expression]

첫째	둘째	셋째	넷째	다섯째	…	열째
first	second	third	fourth	fifth		tenth

사흘째 for the third day

두 잔째 second drink

[Example] 오늘로 한국 생활 반 년째이다.
Today is the half year mark of my life in Korea.

제 옆에 있는 아이는 제 둘째 동생이에요.
The child next to me is my second younger sibling.

006
처음

[처음] 명사 the begining

the starting point of time or order

[Expression] 처음부터 since the beginning

처음으로 for the first time

[Antonym] 끝 the end

마지막 last

[Example] 문제를 처음부터 끝까지 잘 읽어야 해요.
You must read the question carefully from beginning to end.

처음에는 일이 재미있었는데 지금은 재미없어졌어요.
The work was fun in the beginning but now it's not fun.

007
첫

[천] 관형사 first

the beginning

[Usage]   첫 <u>N</u>

[Expression]   첫사랑 first love

첫 시간 first time

[Example]   첫 문제부터 너무 어려우면 학생들이 힘들어해요.
If the first question is too difficult, the students will have a hard time.

오늘은 첫 수업이니까 서로 인사하고 소개하는 시간을 갖겠습니다.
Since this is the first class, we will have time to greet and introduce each other.

04-2 | 시간의 길이

008
개월

[개월] 명사 month(s)

(used to label after Chinese numbers) unit used for counting months

[Usage]   <u>Num</u> 개월

[Expression]   일 개월 one month

[Synonym]   월 month

달 month

[Example]   한국에 온 지 6(육)개월이 지났다.
Six months have passed since I've been in Korea.

3(삼)개월 동안 고향 음식을 한 번도 먹지 못해서 너무 먹고 싶다.
Since I haven't had food from my hometown for 3 months, I want to eat it a lot.

009
걸리다

[걸리다] 동사 to take

to take time

[Usage]   <u>N</u>이/가 걸리다

[Expression]   시간이 걸리다 it takes time

[Example]   집에서 학교까지 몇 시간 걸려요?
How long does it take to get from home to school?

버스로 한 시간 걸려서 학교에 도착했다.
It took an hour for me to arrive at school.

010
길다

[길다] 형용사 1. to be long 2. to be long 3. to be long

1. taking a long time, ㄹverb

[Usage] **N**이/가 길다

[Expression] 시간이 길다 to have a long time

[Antonym] 짧다 to have a short amount of time

[Example] 긴 시간 동안 제 이야기를 들어주셔서 감사합니다.
Thank you for listening to my story for such a long time.

2. the large distance between one end to the last end of an object, ㄹverb

[Usage] **N**이/가 길다

[Expression] 긴 머리 long hair

다리가 길다 legs are long

[Antonym] 짧다 to be short

[Example] 긴 머리를 짧게 잘랐다.
I cut my long hair and now it's short.

3. having many words in speaking or writing, ㄹverb

[Usage] **N**이/가 길다

[Expression] 긴 말씀 long words

이야기가 길다 the story is long

[Antonym] 짧다 to have minimum words

[Example] 어떻게 된 일인지 다 말하려면 얘기가 복잡하고 길어.
If I tell you everything that happened, it will be a confusing and long story.

011
달

[달] 명사 1. month 2. moon

1. word used for dividing a year into 12 months, and used to refer to 1
of those sections which are usually 30 days

[Usage] **Num** 달

[Expression] 열두 달 12 months

[Synanym] 월 month

개월 month

[Example] 한 달 동안 한국 여기저기를 돌아다니며 구경했다.
I explored Korea by walking around and wandering the streets for a month.

2. the moon

[Expression] 달밤 moonlit night

달빛 moonlight

보름달 full moon

[Related word] 별 star

해 sun

85

밤 night

[Example]   달이 밝고 둥글다.
The moon is bright and round.

012
동안

[동안] 명사 during that time, the length of time from the beginning to the end

[Usage]   **N** 동안

AV는 동안

[Expression]   방학 동안 during the break

이틀 동안 for two days

잠시 동안 for a short time

공부하는 동안 while studying

[Example]   엄마가 설거지를 하는 동안 나는 방 청소를 했다.
While mom was doing the dishes, I cleaned my room.

며칠 동안 밖에 나가지도 않고 집에서 공부만 했어요.
For a few days I stayed inside and only studied.

013
며칠

[며칠] 명사 a few days, several days, can also be used to refer to the day of the date

[Expression]   몇 월 며칠 what month and day

[Example]   몇 월 며칠에 한국에 가요?
What month and day do you leave for Korea?

일 때문에 바빴으니까 며칠 여행을 다녀오는 게 어때?
You were busy with work, so why don't you go on vacation for a few days?

014
보내다

[보내다] 동사 1. pass time 2. to send

1. to let time by

[Usage]   **N** 을/를 보내다

[Expression]   시간을 보내다 to spend time

[Synonym]   지내다 to spend time doing something

[Example]   어제는 친구와 이야기하며 즐거운 시간을 보냈어요.
Yesterday I spent the day talking and having a good time with my friend.

2. to send a person or object to another place

[Usage]   **N** 에게 **N** 을/를 보내다

[Synonym]   부치다 to mail

[Example]   열심히 일해서 번 돈을 고향에 계신 부모님께 보내 드렸다.
I sent my hard worked money to my hometown to my parents.

015
보름

[보름] 명사 1. half a month 2. 15th day of the lunar month

1. 15days

[Example]	보름 동안 여행을 다녀왔다.
	I traveled for 15 days.

2. 15th day of the lunar month

[Expression]	보름날	day of full moon, 15th day of the lunar month
	보름달	full moon
	정월 보름	the 15th of January

[Example]	어제 추석이었는데 보름달을 보면서 소원을 빌었니?
	Yesterday was Thanksgiving and the full moon was out, did you wish for something while looking at the moon?

016
사흘

[사흘] 명사 three days, 3 days

[Related word]

하루 1 day	이틀 2 day	사흘 3 day	나흘 4 day	닷새 5 day	엿새 6 day	이레 7 day
여드레 8 days	아흐레 9 days	열흘 10 days	......	보름 15 days	......	한 달 1 month

[Example]	비가 사흘 동안 계속 내렸다.
	The rain has been coming for 3 straight days.
	이번 연휴는 사흘이라서 가족들과 함께 설악산에 갔다 오려고 해요.
	This time the holiday is for 3 days, so I've decided to go to Sul-ak mountain with my family.

017
시간

[시간] 명사 1. hour, time 2. time

1.the time from beginning to end, time passing

[Usage]	**Num** 시간
[Expression]	스물네 시간 24 hours
	시간이 빠르다 time is so fast
	시간이 흐르다 time is passing
	시간이 지나다 time has passed
	시간을 보내다 spending time
[Example]	시간이 지나면 다 괜찮아질 거야.
	Everything will be fine once time has passed.

2. time, when one is doing something

[Usage]	**N** 시간
	AV을/ㄹ 시간이 되다
[Expression]	수업 시간 class time
	약속 시간 promised meeting

87

[Example]   아침을 먹을 시간이 다 됐는데, 왜 아직도 안 일어나니?
It's time to eat breakfast, why are you still not up?

018
오래

[오래] 부사 for a long time

[Expression]   오랫동안 for a long time

오랜 시간 a long time

오래 걸리다 to take a long time

오랜만에 만나다 to meet in a long time

[Example]   고향 친구들을 오랫동안 만나지 못해서 너무 보고 싶다.
I haven't met my hometown friends in a long time, I really miss them.

남자 친구와 오래 사귀었지만 아직 결혼할 생각은 없다.
I've dated my boyfriend for a long time, but I have no intentions of marrying him yet.

019
주일

[주일] 명사 week, a word used to wrap all 7 days into one

[Usage]   **Num** 주일

[Expression]   일주일 one week

[Synonym]   주 week

[Example]   올해가 몇 주일이 안 남았다. There are not many weeks left for this year.

3(삼)주일만 더 공부하면 이번 학기가 끝나요.
If I study 3 more weeks, the semester will be finished.

020
해

[해] 명사 1. the total of earth's rotation around the sun   2. sun

1. the total of earth's rotation around the sun

[Usage]   **Num** 해

[Expression]   한 해 one year

지난해 last year

[Synonym]   년 year

[Example]   12(십이)월이 되면 한 해 동안 있었던 일들을 정리한다.
When December comes around, I organize everything I did for the year.

2. the sun

[Expression]   햇빛 sunlight

[Related word]   낮 day

[Example]   낮 12(열두)시가 되니까 해가 머리 바로 위에 있다.
The sun is right above my head because it's noon.

도움말

When telling time is Korean we use Korean numbers as well as Chinese numbers. The tables below show the difference in usage.

(1) 해/년 year

일 년	이 년	삼 년	사 년	오 년	……	이십 년
한 해	두 해	세 해	네 해	다섯 해	……	스무 해

(2) 달/개월 month

일 개월	이 개월	삼 개월	사 개월	오 개월	……	이십 개월
한 달	두 달	세 달	네 달	다섯 달	……	스무 달

(3) 일 day

일 일	이 일	삼 일	사 일	오 일	육 일
하루	이틀	사흘	나흘	닷새	엿새
칠 일	팔 일	구 일	십 일	십오 일	삼십 일
이레	여드레	아흐레	열흘	보름	한 달

The Chinese numbers are used in different contexts such as length of time and the date, so pay attention to these differences.

한 달은 삼십 일이다. (the length of time) One month is 30 days.

오늘은 삼 월 삼십 일이다. (date) Today is March 30th.

04-3 | 시간

021
가끔

[가끔] 부사 sometimes once in a while

[Related word] 자주 often

항상 always

[Example] 저는 시간이 나면 가끔 집 근처에 있는 공원을 산책해요.
When I have time, I walk at the park near my home.

술을 좋아하지 않지만 친구들을 만나면 가끔 술을 마신다.
I don't like alcohol but I drink it sometimes when I'm with friends.

022
갑자기   [갑짜기] 부사 all of a sudden

[Example]   갑자기 일이 생겨서 약속을 지키지 못했다.
                     Something came up all of a sudden, so I couldn't keep my promise.

                     친구의 전화를 받고 갑자기 뛰어 나갔어요.
                     I got a call from a friend, so I went out on short notice.

023
계속   [계속/계속] 부사 continuously

[Expression]   계속되다 to be kept going
                     계속하다 to keep doing

[Example]   쉬지 않고 계속 일을 하니까 너무 피곤해요.
                     I am so tired because I kept working without stopping.

                     며칠 동안 계속된 비로 빨래가 잘 마르지 않아요.
                     My laundry is not drying because it's been raining for a few days.

024
곧   [곧] 부사 soon

[Synonym]   바로 right after

[Example]   수업이 끝나면 곧 집에 들어가겠습니다.
                     I will go home right after my lesson.

                     조금 더 기다리면 곧 어머니가 오실 거야.
                     Wait a little bit longer, your mother will be here soon.

025
금방   [금방] 부사 1. right before   2. right after

                     1. right before speaking

[Synonym]   방금 just a moment ago

[Example]   금방 밥을 먹었는데 뭘 또 먹자고 그러니?
                     We ate just now, and you want to eat something else already?

                     2. right after speaking

[Synonym]   곧 soon

[Example]   금방 갈게! 조금만 더 기다려 줘!
                     I will leave soon! Please wait a little longer!

026
때   [때] 명사 the time or moment

[Usage]   **DV/AV** 을/ㄹ 때

[Expression]   그때 that time
                     방학 때 during the vacation time

[Example]   시간이 있을 때 아무 때나 오세요. Come whenever you have time.

가족이 보고 싶을 때 부모님께 전화를 한다.
Whenever I miss my family, I call my parents.

027
바로

[바로] 부사 1. soon (time)   2. the very, the exact

1. pretty quickly

[Synonym] 곧 before long

금방 soon

[Example] 이 약은 밥을 먹은 후에 바로 드셔야 합니다.
You must take the medicine right after eating.

2. a certain specific thing

[Example] 이게 바로 내가 사고 싶었던 옷이야.
This is the exact clothing that I wanted.

028
벌써

[벌써] 부사 already

[Synonym] 이미 before/already

[Antonym] 아직 not yet

[Example] 벌써 이 일을 다 끝냈어요? Did you already finish all of this work?

네가 벌써 대학생이 되었구나. You have already become a college student.

029
빠르다

[빠르다] 형용사 to be quick
르 verb

[Usage] N이/가 빠르다

[Expression] 말이 빠르다 words are quick

걸음이 빠르다 walks really fast

시간이 빠르다 the time is going by so quickly

[Antonym] 느리다 to be slow

[Example] 내 친구의 한국말은 너무 빨라서 알아듣기가 어려워요.
My friend talks so quickly in Korean that it's hard for me to understand.

시간이 참 빠르다! 한국에 온 게 엊그제 같은데, 벌써 1(일)년이 지났다.
Time is so quick! It feels like I arrived in Korea a few days ago, but it's already been a year.

030
서두르다

[서두르다] 동사 to hurry up
to work in a rush to get something else, 르 verb

[Usage] N 을/를 서두르다

서둘러서 AV

[Example] 준비를 서둘러라. 기차 시간에 늦겠다.
Hurry up and get ready. You will be late for the train.

서둘러서 가면 영화가 시작되기 전에 도착할 수 있을 거야.

If you hurry up and go, you will be able to make the movie.

031
아직

[아직] 부사 1. still 2. still

1. the need for longer time to finish a task, and an extended time needed for something to be complete

[Usage] 아직 안 **AV**

아직 못 **AV**

[Antonym] 벌써 already

이미 already done

[Example] 죄송합니다. 아직 다 끝내지 못했습니다.

I'm sorry. I haven't completed it yet.

2. something is not complete and is going on

[Usage] 아직 **AV**

[Expression] 아직도 still

[Antonym] 벌써 already

이미 already

[Example] 아직 시험을 보고 있으니까 좀 조용히 해 주세요!

I am still taking the exam so please be quiet!

032
어서

[어서] 부사 welcome or hurry

[Synonym] 빨리 quickly

얼른 rapidly

[Example] 어서 오세요! Welcome!

시간이 다 됐습니다. 어서 시험지를 내세요.

It is already time. Turn in the exam papers quickly.

033
언제나

[언제나] 부사 always

[Synonym] 항상 at all times

[Example] 좋아하는 친구를 만나는 일은 언제나 즐거워요.

Meeting friends that I get along with is always fun.

나는 자기 전에 언제나 일기를 쓰는 습관이 있다.

I have a habit of always writing in my diary before I go to sleep.

034
옛날

[옛날] 명사 the old days

[Expression] 먼 옛날 a long time ago

[Example] 아주 먼 옛날 착하고 예쁜 공주가 살았어요.

In the old days, there was a kind and pretty princess.

옛날에는 컴퓨터가 없어서 숙제를 직접 써서 냈다.
A long time ago, there were no computers, so homework needed to written out by hand.

035
요즘

[요즘] 명사 these days

[Expression]   요즘 세상 the world now-a-days

요즘에 these days

[Example]   어머니께서 무슨 걱정이 있나 봐요. 요즘 잘 주무시지 못해요.
Mother must be worrying about something. She hasn't been able to sleep lately.

요즘 날씨가 추워져서 감기에 걸리는 사람들이 많아지고 있어요.
The weather has been getting cold recently, so there are a lot of people catching a cold.

036
이따가

[이따가] 부사 later

[Related word]   나중에 sometime later

[Example]   내가 이따가 바로 전화할게. I will call you back later.

지금 하고 있는 일을 먼저 끝내야 하니까 이따가 얘기하자.
I have to finish something that I'm working on, so let's talk later.

037
이제

[이제] 부사 now

[Related word]   지금 this instant

[Example]   이제 하던 일을 정리하고 퇴근합시다.
Now let's organize everything we've worked on and let's go home.

제 얘기는 다 끝났으니까, 이제부터는 여러분의 이야기를 듣겠습니다.
I have finished talking, so now I will listen to what all of you have to say.

038
자주

[자주] 부사 often

[Related word]   가끔 sometimes

항상 always

[Example]   저는 도서관에 자주 갑니다. I go to the library often.

부모님께 자주 연락을 드립니다. I call my parents often.

039
잠깐

[잠깐] 부사 for a little while

[Expression]   잠깐만 just a minute

[Synonym]   잠시 for a little bit

[Example]   잠깐만 기다려 주세요. 금방 오겠습니다.
Please wait a little bit. I will come quickly.

쉬지 않고 오래 일을 했으니까 이제 잠깐 쉽시다.
We kept working without resting, so let's rest for a little bit.

040
지금

[지금] 부사 right now

[Related word] 이제 now

[Example] 지금 바로 출발하면 늦지 않을 거야.
If we leave right now, we won't be late.

지금 말씀하시는 분이 우리 반 선생님입니다.
The person who is now talking is my teacher.

041
천천히

[천천히] 부사 slowly

[Synonym] 느리게 slowly

[Antonym] 빨리 hurriedly

[Example] 말이 너무 빨라요. 좀 천천히 말씀해 주세요.
You're speaking too quickly. Please talk a bit slower.

경치가 아름다우니까 천천히 걸으면서 구경하자.
The landscape is so beautiful, let's walk slowly and look around.

042
틈틈이

[틈트미] 부사 in one's spare time

[Example] 관심 있는 책들을 틈틈이 사 모으는 게 내 취미예요.
I like to collect books which I am interested in whenever I have time.

학교 수업과 아르바이트로 바쁘지만 틈틈이 공부를 하려고 노력해요.
I am busy with class and work, but I try to make time to study.

043
항상

[항상] 부사 always

[Synonym] 언제나 always

[Example] 항상 웃는 내 친구의 얼굴이 아름답다.
My friend's face is always pretty because she laughs all the time.

저는 힘든 일이 있을 때마다 항상 엄마와 이야기해요.
Whenever I have a hard time, I always talk with my mom about my problem.

[1~15] 다음 단어를 한국어로 바꿔 쓰십시오. Change these words into Korean.

1. the time/moment ( )   2. time ( )
3. a few days ( )   4. a long time ( )
5. week ( )   6. right after ( )
7. a long time ago ( )   8. these days ( )
9. often ( )   10. 10 days ( )
11. to be short ( )   12. sometimes ( )
13. in spare time ( )   14. all of a sudden ( )
15. to rush ( )

[16~20] 그림을 보고 ( )에 알맞은 것을 고르십시오.
Look at the picture and choose the correct word.

16.

가 : 여행은 며칠 동안 하실 거예요?
나 : ( ) 동안 여행할 생각이에요.

❶ 사흘   ❷ 나흘
❸ 보름   ❹ 일주일

17.

가 : 밤이지만 어둡지 않군요.
나 : 네, 오늘이 보름날이어서 ( )이/가 아주 밝아요.

❶ 해   ❷ 날
❸ 월   ❹ 달

18.

가 : 이번 시간이 한국어이지요?

나 : 아니요, 이번 시간은 역사 시간이에요. 한국어
는 (   ) 시간이에요.

❶ 첫째   ❷ 지난

❸ 다음   ❹ 마지막

19.

가 : 집에서 회사까지 얼마나 걸려요?

나 : (   )이오/요.

❶ 한 시 삼십 분   ❷ 한 시간 반

❸ 일곱 시 십 분   ❹ 여덟 시간 사십 분

20.

《 한국에서
한국어를 공부합니다 》

날짜:7월 1일~7월 31일
신청 날짜:6월 11일까지
신청 장소:한국어과 사무실

한국어에 관심 있는
많은 사람들이
참여하길 바랍니다.

가 : 얼마 동안 한국에서 한국어를 공부한다고 해요?

나 : 일 (   ) 동안 공부한다고 해요.

❶ 달   ❷ 월

❸ 해   ❹ 개월

96

[21~30] 다음 문장을 읽고 알맞은 어휘를 골라 쓰십시오. 어휘는 한 번만 쓰십시오.

Read the following sentence and choose the right word. Use the words once.

첫	때	해	개월	요즘
시간	아직	옛날	동안	계속
바로	먼저	갑자기	천천히	서두르다

21. 한국에 얼마 (　　　　) 계실 거예요?

22. 네가 (　　　　) 샤워해. 나는 나중에 할게.

23. 여기가 엄마가 말한 (　　　　) 그 식당이에요?

24. 숙제가 많아서 (　　　　) 다 끝내지 못했다.

25. 영희는 선생님께 모르는 문제들을 (　　　　) 질문했다.

26. 밥을 (　　　　) 먹어야 살도 찌지 않고 건강에도 좋대요.

27. 친구를 처음 만났을 (　　　　) 친구의 첫인상이 참 인상적이었어요.

28. 한국에서는 (　　　　) 월급을 받으면 보통 부모님께 속옷을 선물한다.

29. 그 학생이 공부를 하다가 선생님께 말도 하지 않고 (　　　　) 나가 버렸어요.

30. 옛날에는 공중전화를 많이 썼는데 (　　　　)에는 사람들이 핸드폰을 가지고 다니니까 공중전화를 잘 쓰지 않아요.

[31~35] (　　　　) 안에 알맞은 것을 고르십시오. Choose the correct one.

31. 늦었어요. 빨리 (　　　)어야/아야/여야 해요.

❶ 걸리다　　　❷ 빠르다　　　❸ 지나다　　　❹ 서두르다

32. 지난 시간에 공부한 것을 다 복습했으니까 (　　　) 32쪽부터 공부해 봅시다.

❶ 가끔　　　❷ 계속　　　❸ 이제　　　❹ 갑자기

97

33. 저는 수업이 끝나면 (　　　) 친구들과 점심을 먹습니다.

❶ 언제　　　　　❷ 요즘　　　　　❸ 이제　　　　　❹ 항상

34. 시간이 있을 때마다 (　　　) 한국말을 공부해요.

❶ 어서　　　　　❷ 마지막　　　　❸ 이따가　　　　❹ 틈틈이

35. 지금 좀 바쁜데 (　　　) 다시 연락해 주시겠어요?

❶ 먼저　　　　　❷ 나중에　　　　❸ 언제나　　　　❹ 처음에

[36~40] 밑줄 친 부분과 반대되는 뜻을 가진 것을 고르십시오.
Choose the word that is the opposite of the underlined word.

36. **가 :** 첫째 시간에 영어를 공부해요?
　　나 : 아니요, 오늘은 (　　　) 시간에 영어를 공부해요.

❶ 다음　　　　　❷ 먼저　　　　　❸ 지난　　　　　❹ 마지막

37. **가 :** 여자 친구는 머리가 길어요?
　　나 : 아니요. (　　　)어요/아요/여요.

❶ 작다　　　　　❷ 적다　　　　　❸ 짧다　　　　　❹ 가볍다

38. **가 :** 선생님 말이 좀 빨라요?
　　나 : 아니요, 조금 (　　　)어요/아요/여요.

❶ 늦다　　　　　❷ 느리다　　　　❸ 이르다　　　　❹ 서두르다

39. **가 :** 시간이 없으니까 빨리 합시다.
　　나 : 서두르지 말고 좀 (　　　) 하면 안 돼요?

❶ 곧　　　　　　❷ 금방　　　　　❸ 아직　　　　　❹ 천천히

98

40. **가** : 오래 기다렸어요?

    나 : 아니요, (　　　) 기다렸어요.

    ❶ 못　　　　　　　❷ 가끔　　　　　　❸ 벌써　　　　　　❹ 잠깐

[41~45] 밑줄 친 부분과 의미가 가장 가까운 것을 고르십시오.

Choose the word that is most similar to the underlined section.

41. **가** : 오늘 정말 반가웠어. 나중에 시간 있을 때 한 번 만나자.

    나 : 그래, 내가 (　　　)에 연락할게.

    ❶ 다음　　　　　　❷ 옛날　　　　　　❸ 처음　　　　　　❹ 마지막

42. **가** : 지금 몇 시예요?

    나 : (　　　) 한 시예요.

    ❶ 벌써　　　　　　❷ 요즘　　　　　　❸ 이제　　　　　　❹ 일찍

43. **가** : 정말 금방 오실 거지요?

    나 : 그래, 걱정하지 마. (　　　) 갈게.

    ❶ 곧　　　　　　　❷ 늦게　　　　　　❸ 먼저　　　　　　❹ 천천히

44. **가** : 아침에 일어나면 항상 운동을 하세요?

    나 : 네, 저는 (　　　) 아침 운동을 해요.

    ❶ 계속　　　　　　❷ 물론　　　　　　❸ 언제나　　　　　❹ 열심히

45. **가** : 한국어를 공부한 지 반 년쯤 됐지요?

    나 : 네, 벌써 (　　　)이/가 됐어요.

    ❶ 보름　　　　　　❷ 두 주　　　　　　❸ 육 개월　　　　　❹ 여섯 해

[46~50] 밑줄 친 단어의 쓰임이 잘못된 것을 고르십시오. Choose the one that is incorrectly used.

46.　❶ 영수는 금방 나갔어요.　　　　　　(　　　)

　　❷ 금방 뭐라고 하셨어요?

　　❸ 여기가 금방 경복궁이에요.

　　❹ 금방 나갈 테니까 조금만 기다려 주세요.

47.　❶ 이따가 연락하자. 지금은 조금 바쁘다.　(　　　)

　　❷ 지금 손님이 와 있으니까 이따가 갈게.

　　❸ 이따가 만났는데 친구는 꽤 뚱뚱해졌다.

　　❹ 죄송하지만 이따가 다시 와 주시겠어요?

48.　❶ 추우니까 어서 이쪽으로 들어오세요.　　(　　　)

　　❷ 갑자기 집에 일이 생겨서 학교에 가지 못했다.

　　❸ 저는 시간이 있으면 계속 중국 음식을 만들어 먹습니다.

　　❹ 사장님께서 곧 오실 거예요. 여기서 잠깐 기다려 주세요.

49.　❶ 이 하숙집에서 삼 달 동안 살았습니다.　(　　　)

　　❷ 12월이 되면 지난 한 해를 정리합니다.

　　❸ 약속 장소에서 친구를 한 시간 동안 기다렸어요.

　　❹ 한국에서 한국어를 공부한 지 이 년 되었습니다.

50.　❶ 주말을 재미있게 보냈어요?　　　　　(　　　)

　　❷ 여름이 되니까 밤이 길어졌어요.

　　❸ 집에서 학교까지 걸어서 10분 걸려요.

　　❹ 시간이 참 빨라요. 벌써 고향에 돌아갈 때가 되었어요.

사람 Ⅰ

05

People Ⅰ

001
가족

[가족] 명사 family

[Expression] 가족사진 family photo

가족 모임 family meeting

[Related word] 친척 relative

[Example] 주말에 가족과 함께 여행을 가기로 했다.

This weekend my family and I are going on vacation.

가족이 모두 모였을 때 가족사진을 한 번 찍었으면 좋겠어요.

I would like to take a family picture when we are together.

002
고모

[고모] 명사 aunt

the word used to call the sisters of your father

[Expression] 고모부 uncle (aunt's husband)

[Related word] 이모 aunt (used to call mother's sisters)

[Example] 고모는 우리 아빠를 '오빠'라고 부른다.

My aunt calls my dad 'older brother'.

아빠도 어렸을 때 장난감 때문에 고모와 많이 싸웠다고 해요.

My dad told me that he fought with my aunt over toys when he was younger too.

003
누나

[누나] 명사 older sister

the word used that a younger brother uses to call his older sister

[Synonym] 언니 older sister (used when a girl calls her older sister)

[Example] 누나가 나보다 한 살밖에 많지 않아서 어렸을 때 친구처럼 지냈어요.

My older sister is only a year older, so we were just like friends when we were younger.

엄마가 계시지 않을 때는 누나가 나와 동생을 위해서 식사를 준비했다.

When mom wasn't at home, my older sister prepared the meal for me and my younger sibling.

004
동생

[동생] 명사 younger sibling

the word used to call the younger sibling, male or female

[Expression] 남동생 younger brother

여동생 younger sister

[Example] 저는 동생하고 같이 인형 놀이하는 것을 좋아해요.

I like to play with dolls with my younger sibling.

내가 놀러 나갈 때 동생이 따라 나오면 너무 귀찮다.

It's so irritating whenever my younger sibling follows me when I go out to play.

005
딸

[딸] 명사 daughter

[Expression] 아들딸 son and daughter

[Related word] 아들 son

자녀 children

[Example] 저는 딸만 세 명 있어요. I have only 3 daughters.

어제 제 딸이 자기 남자 친구를 소개해 주었어요.

Yesterday my daughter introduced her boyfriend to me.

006
사촌

[사촌] 명사 cousin

the word used to refer to the children of the parents siblings

[Expression] 사촌 형제 cousins

사촌 오빠 older boy cousin

[Related word] 형제 sibling

[Example] 나는 사촌들과 친형제처럼 친하게 지내요.

My cousins and I are like siblings.

설날에는 친척 분들과 사촌들이 모두 모이니까 참 즐거워요.

During the Lunar New Year, my relatives and cousins get together and have a good time

007
삼촌

[삼촌] 명사 uncle

word used to refer to the father's brothers, especially for the father's unmarried younger brother

[Expression] 외삼촌 uncle (the mother's brother)

[Synonym] 숙부 uncle (father's younger brother)

[Related word] 숙모 aunt (father's younger brother's wife)

[Example] 삼촌은 결혼하기 전까지 우리와 함께 살았다.

My uncle lived with us before he got married.

저는 어렸을 때 삼촌처럼 잘생기고 멋진 사람과 결혼하고 싶었어요.

When I was younger, I wanted to marry someone handsome and cool like my uncle.

008
아내

[아내] 명사 wife

[Synonym]　　부인　wife

　　　　　　　집사람　house wife

[Related word]　남편　husband

[Example]　　　오랜만에 아내와 함께 둘이서만 여행을 다녀왔어요.

　　　　　　　It's been a while, but my wife and I went on vacation together.

　　　　　　　평일에는 회사 일로 바빠서 아내와 함께 지내는 시간이 많지 않다.

　　　　　　　During the week, I have so much office work that I don't have much time to spend with my wife.

009
어머니

[어머니] 명사 mother

[Expression]　　시어머니　mother-in-law (used only for the husband's mother)

[Related word]　아버지　father

[Example]　　　어머니, 아버지! 학교 다녀오겠습니다! Mother, father! I'm off to school!

　　　　　　　내 생일이 되면 어머니는 아침에 미역국을 끓여 놓으신다.

　　　　　　　The morning of my birthday, my mother cooks seaweed soup for me.

010
조카

[조카] 명사 nephew, niece

the children of your siblings

[Example]　　　언니는 일이 있을 때 엄마에게 조카를 맡겼다.

　　　　　　　Whenever my sister is busy, she leaves my niece or nephew with my mother.

　　　　　　　여섯 살짜리 조카의 생일 선물을 사려고 하는데 뭐가 좋을까요?

　　　　　　　I am trying to buy my 6 year old niece/nephew a birthday present, what would be good?

011
친척

[친척] 명사 relative

very close people (blood related)

[Related word]　가족　family

[Example]　　　명절이 되면 가까운 친척들이 모두 할아버지 댁에 모여요.

　　　　　　　During the holidays, all of my close relatives get together at my grandfather's house.

　　　　　　　미국으로 간 후에 오랫동안 한국에 계시는 친척 분들과 연락을 하지 못했어요.

　　　　　　　After moving to the United States, I haven't contacted my relatives in Korea for a long time.

012
큰아버지

[크나버지] 명사 uncle

father's older brother

[Related word] 삼촌 uncle

큰집 house of the eldest son of the family

큰어머니 aunt (father's oldest brother's wife)

작은 아버지 uncle (father's younger brother)

[Example] 설날과 추석에는 큰아버지 댁에 갑니다.

During the lunar new year and thanksgiving, we go to my uncle's house.

큰아버지는 우리 아버지보다 세 살 많다.

My uncle is 3 years older than my father.

013
형

[형] 명사 older brother

the word used to call the male sibling that is older, only used by a younger male sibling

[Synonym] 오빠 older brother (said by a younger girl sibling)

[Related word] 형제 siblings

[Example] 형과 동생이 아주 사이좋게 지낸다.

The older and younger brother get along very well.

저는 모르는 것이 있으면 언제나 형에게 물어봐요.

Whenever I have something I don't know, I ask my older brother.

05-2 | 관계

014
결혼

[결혼] 명사 marriage

the official act of becoming a wife and husband

[Expression] 결혼식 wedding

결혼하다 to get married

[Related word] 약혼 engagement

이혼 divorce

신혼여행 honeymoon vacation

[Example] 결혼하면 부모님과 같이 살 거예요? 따로 살 거예요?
Are you going to live with your parents after you get married? Or live separately?

남편은 결혼 전에 나를 이 세상에서 가장 행복한 여자로 만들어 주겠다고 약속했다.
My husband promised me before we got married that he would make me the happiest woman in the world.

015
너

[너] 대명사 you

the word used to refer to someone who is a friend, or a younger person, used when trying to teach or telling someone to do something

[Expression] 네 you

[Synonym] 당신 you (a bit more formal), darling, dear

[Related word] 나 I

[Example] 어제 너하고 같이 점심을 먹은 사람이 누구야?
Who is the person who had lunch with you yesterday?

미선아, 너 오늘 집에 좀 일찍 와라. 저녁에 손님이 오시니까 네가 나를 좀 도와주었으면 좋겠다.
Mi-sun, come home early today. There are customers coming tonight, so it would be nice if you could help me.

016
누구

[누구] 대명사 1. who 2. whoever

1. (used in a question or statement) referring to someone that you're not too familiar with

[Example] 어제 누구하고 같이 집에 갔어요?
Who did you go home with last night?

2. not someone in particular but used to refer to someone

[Expression] 누구나 whoever
누구든지 anyone

[Synonym] 아무 anyone

[Example] 이 일은 누구든지 할 수 있다. Anyone can do this job.

017
룸메이트

[룸메이트] 명사 roommate

person who shares the same room, also call them 'room friend'

[Related word] 친구 friend
기숙사 dorm

[Example]	나는 일찍 자는데 내 룸메이트는 늦게 잔다.
	I go to sleep early, but my roommate goes to sleep later.
	룸메이트는 방을 같이 쓰니까 친해지기도 쉽지만 사이가 나빠지기
	도 쉽다.
	It is easy to get along with a roommate quickly because people live together, but
	it's easy to have a bad relationship too.

018
부모

[부모] 명사 parent

[Expression]	시부모 parents-in-law
	부모님 parents
[Example]	좋은 부모가 되려면 어떻게 해야 할까?
	What do I have to do become a good parent?
	외롭고 힘들 때 부모님 생각이 많이 나요.
	Whenever I am struggling or lonely, I think of my parents a lot.

019
부부

[부부] 명사 married couple

the word referred to the husband and wife

[Expression]	부부 사이 the couple relationship
[Example]	결혼을 해서 이제 부부가 되었다.
	We got married and now we are a married couple.
	가족 관계 중에서 부부 관계가 가장 중요하다고 합니다.
	In a family the married couple's relationship is the most important.

020
서로

[서로] 부사 with each other, with one another

the word used to refer to 2 people or more in a relationship

[Expression]	서로서로 with each other
[Example]	결혼은 서로 사랑하는 사람들이 하는 거야.
	A marriage is something that people do when they are in love with each other.
	이제 같이 살게 되었으니까 우리 서로 사이좋게 지내자.
	Since we are now living with each other, let's try to get along.

021
소개

[소개] 명사 1. introduce a person   2. introduce new material

1. to introduce people who don't know each other and let them be together to get along with each other

[Expression]	소개하다 to introduce
	소개로 만나다 to be introduced

107

[Example] 아르바이트를 할 사람이 필요하세요? 제가 한 명 소개해 드릴까요?
Do you need someone to work part-time? Shall I introduce you to someone?

2. to introduce new material such as information or truth

[Expression] 책 소개 introduce a book
자기소개 one's introduction
친구 소개 friend's introduction

[Example] 오늘은 제가 다니는 학교를 여러분에게 소개해 드리겠습니다.
Today I will show my school to everyone.

022
아무

[아무] 대명사 no one, anyone
not particularly picking someone in general but referring to someone

[Expression] 아무도 없다 there is no one
아무나 하다 anyone can do it

[Synonym] 누구 whoever, anyone

[Example] 집에 아무도 없어서 무서웠어요.
There was no one at home ,so I was scared.

이 일은 아무나 할 수 있는 쉬운 일이다.
This work is so easy that anyone can do it.

'아무' is usually used in a negative description.
집에 아무도 없어요. There is no one at home.
선생님의 질문에 아무도 대답을 하지 않았다. No one replied to the teacher's question.

If you use '나', '라도' together with this word , it gives a positive meaning.
아무나 한 번 해 보세요. Anyone, please try.
아무라도 저하고 함께 갑시다. Someone should come with me.

023
애인

[애인] 명사 a significant other
two people that love each other

[Synonym] 남자 친구 boyfriend
여자 친구 girlfriend

[Related word] 데이트 date

[Example] 사랑하는 애인이 생겨서 요즘 행복해요.
I have found someone that I love, so I have been really happy these days.

애인과 함께 데이트를 하려고 하는데 어디가 좋을까요?
I want to go on a date with my significant other. Do you have any suggestions for a good place?

024
우리

[우리] 대명사 1. we   2. my, our

1. the speaking person including the person who is listening and other as well

[Synonym] 저희 we

[Example] 우리 이번 주말에 부산으로 놀러가자.
Let's go on a short trip to Busan this weekend.

2. (usually used in front of a noun) when the person who is speaking is making it noticeable that he or she is close to a certain person

[Expression] 우리나라 our country
우리 남편 my husband
우리 엄마 my mom (our mom)

[Example] 오늘 우리 학교에서 운동회를 해요.
There is a sports festival at school today.

025
저

[저] 대명사 I

pronouncing one's presence to an older person or an unfamiliar person and putting oneself at a lower level

[Expression] 제 my

[Synonym] 나 I

[Example] 저는 한국에서 온 김영수라고 합니다.
I am Young-soo Kim from Korea.

이번 주말에 저하고 같이 도서관에서 공부합시다.
Let's study at the library this weekend.

도움말

'저' is used when the speaker is putting him or herself at a lower level and puts the listener at a higher level. When the person is talking to a younger person or a friend we use '나', but when talking to a older or higher person '저' is used.

When the listener is older or higher : 제가 갔다 올게요. I will go.

When the listener is a friend or lower person : 내가 갔다 올게. I will go.

026
친구

[친구] 명사 friend

[Expression]   한국 친구 Korean friend

친한 친구 a close friend

친구가 많다 to have a lot of friends.

친구를 만나다 to meet a friend

친구를 사귀다 to get to know a friend

[Example]   한국에 와서 한국 친구를 많이 사귀었어요.
I made a lot of Korean friends since coming to Korea.

이번 생일에는 친구들을 집에 많이 초대하기로 했어요.
For my birthday this year, I decided to invite a lot of friends to my house.

027
친하다

[친하다] 형용사 to be close
to be very friendly with one another

[Usage]   N과/와 친하다

[Expression]   친한 친구 a close friend

친하게 지내다 to be good friends

[Example]   친한 친구들과 함께 얘기를 하면 기분이 좋아진다.
Whenever I talk to my close friends, I feel really happy.

유학하는 동안 외국 친구들 몇 명하고 친하게 지냈다.
During my study abroad, I was close to a few foreign friends.

028
형제

[형제] 명사 1. sibling between a younger and older brother   2. sibling (girl and boy)
1. referring to younger and older brother

[Expression]   삼형제 3 brothers

형제자매 brothers and sisters

형제가 많다 I have many siblings.

[Related word] 자매 sisters

[Example]   우리 삼형제는 초등학교부터 고등학교까지 모두 같은 학교를 졸업
했다.
Me and my two brothers graduated from the same elementary, middle, and high
school.

2. brothers and sisters

[Example]   형제가 어떻게 되세요? How many siblings do you have?

029
계시다

[계시다/게시다] 동사 be, stay

the formal version of '있다' (to be)

[Usage]　　　N에 계시다

[Related word]　있다 to be

[Example]　　우리 선생님은 지금 교실에 계세요.
My teacher is in the classroom right now.

어머니께서 지금 집에 안 계세요. 금방 나가셨어요.
My mother is not home right now. She just left.

030
나이

[나이] 명사 age

telling the progress of how long a person, plant, or animal has been since it's been born

[Expression]　　나이가 많다 to be old

나이가 들다 to age

나이를 먹다 to get older

[Related word]　살¹ age, years

연세 age (formal-when naming the age of an elder)

[Example]　　언니가 나보다 나이가 5(다섯)살 많아요.
My sister is 5 years older than me.

설날이 되면 아이들은 나이를 한 살 더 먹었다고 좋아한다.
During the Lunar New Year, children are happy because they have grown one year older.

031
남자

[남자] 명사 man

[Expression]　　남자 친구 boyfriend

남자 화장실 men's restroom

[Synonym]　　남성 male

[Antonym]　　여자 woman

[Example]　　남자친구를 사귄 지 3(삼)개월 되었어요.
I've dated my boyfriend for 3 months.

우리 기숙사는 남자는 1(일)층과 2(이)층을 쓰고 여자는 3(삼)층과 4(사)층을 쓴다.
The men use the first and second floor in our dormitory and the women use the third and fourth floor.

032
노인

[노인] 명사 elderly, senior citizens

an older person who has aged

[Synonym] 늙은이 elderly

[Antonym] 청년 youth

[Example] 요즘은 몇 살부터 노인이라고 말합니까?
How old do you have to be now-a-days to be considered an elderly?

이 텔레비전 프로그램은 노인들을 위해서 만든 프로그램이에요.
This television program is made for senior citizens.

033
댁

[댁] 명사 home

the honorific form of '집' (house)

[Related word] 집 home

[Example] 선생님 댁은 학교에서 멀지 않아요.
The teacher's home is not far from school.

오늘 남자 친구의 부모님 댁에 가서 인사하기로 했어요.
I am meeting my boyfriend's parents at their home today.

034
드리다

[드리다] 동사 to give

to give something to someone older, or a person in higher position
honorific form of '주다' (to give)

[Usage] **AV**어/아/여 드리다
N께 **N**을/를 드리다

[Expression] 갖다 드리다 to give
만들어 드리다 to make

[Related word] 주다 to present

[Example] 마지막 수업 때 선생님께 선물을 드렸어요.
After the last lesson I gave my teacher a present.

눈이 잘 안 보이는 어머니를 위해서 책을 읽어 드렸다.
I read the book for my mother because her sight is not very good.

035
드시다

[드시다] 동사 to eat

the honorific form of '먹다' (eat)

[Usage] **N**을/를 드시다

[Expression] 진지를 드시다 to eat the food ('진지' is the honorific form of '밥')

[Related word] 먹다 to eat
마시다 to drink

[Example]	어머니, 이것 좀 드셔 보세요. 아주 맛있어요.
	Mother, try this. It is very delicious.
	할아버지가 드시기 전에 먼저 먹으면 안 된다.
	You cannot eat before grandfather starts to eat.

036
말씀

[말씀] 명사 words

the honorific form of '말' (word)

[Expression]	말씀하시다 he/she is speaking
[Related word]	말 word
[Example]	어른이 말씀하실 때에는 조용히 잘 듣고 있어라.
	Whenever an elder speaks be quiet and listen carefully.
	선생님 말씀을 끝까지 잘 듣고 질문이 있으면 하세요.
	Listen to the teacher until the very end and ask questions in the end.

037
뵙다

[뵙따] 동사 to meet

to meet someone older, or a person in higher position

[Synonym]	뵈다 to see, meet
[Example]	안녕하세요. 처음 뵙겠습니다. Hello. It's nice to meet you.
	직접 찾아가서 뵙고 말씀 드리겠습니다.
	I will go in person and meet and talk to him.

038
부르다¹

[부르다] 동사 to call

to call the name and make sure a person is there, or to sing to the tune, 르 verb

[Usage]	N을/를 부르다
[Expression]	노래를 부르다 to sing the song
	이름을 부르다 to call the name
[Example]	저는 친구들하고 노래방에 가서 노래 부르는 걸 아주 좋아해요.
	I like going to the karaoke and singing with my friends.
	친구가 지나가는 걸 보고 이름을 불렀지만 듣지 못하고 가 버렸다.
	I saw my friend so I called his name, but he didn't hear me and just passed me.

039
분²

[분] 명사 1. person   2. person (counting)

1. the honorific form of '사람' (person)

[Related word]	사람 person, someone
[Example]	어느 분이 중국에서 오셨어요?
	Which person is the one from China?

2. counting unit used when counting people, a proper form

[Usage] **Num**분

[Related word] 명 person

사람 human

[Example] 오늘 손님 몇 분이 집에 오신다고 해요.

There will be a few guests coming home today.

040

살¹

[살] 명사 year

(usually used before the Korean number) counting unit for age

[Usage] **Num**살

[Synonym] 세 year

[Example] 너 나이가 몇 살이니? How old are you?

저는 30(서른) 살에 결혼했어요. I got married when I was thirty.

041

생신

[생신] 명사 birthday

the honorific form of '생일' (birthday)

[Related word] 생일 birthday

[Example] 아버지 생신 때 뭘 선물해 드릴까?

What should I get for father on his birthday?

어머니 생신날에 우리 일찍 일어나서 직접 음식을 만들어 보자.

Let's get up earlier and make food for mother's birthday.

042

아가씨

[아가씨] 명사 a young lady

a woman that's old enough to get married

[Example] 어머, 정말 예쁜 아가씨네요. 여자 친구예요?

Wow, she is a pretty lady. Is she your girlfriend?

빵집에서 아르바이트를 하는 아가씨가 친구의 동생이었다.

The lady working at the bakery was my friends younger sister.

043

아기

[아기] 명사 baby

a very young child

[Expression] 아기가 울다 the baby is crying

아기가 태어나다 the baby is born

아기를 낳다 to give birth

[Synonym] 아이 child

[Example] 우리 아기는 밤에 울지 않고 잘 자요.

My child does not cry at night and sleeps well.

아기가 정말 많이 컸네요. 잘 먹고 잘 놀아요?

Your baby has grown a lot. Is she eating and playing well?

044
아이

[아이] 명사 1. child   2. child

1. a very young person

[Expression]   어린 아이 _a young child_
노는 아이 _the child who is playing_
아이를 돌보다 _to watch over the child_

[Synonym]   아기 _baby_
어린이 _child_

[Antonym]   어른 _adult_

[Example]   공원에서 아이들이 즐겁게 놀고 있다.
The children are playing very happily in the park.

2. when talking to a person the speaker uses this to lower ones child

[Expression]   우리 아이 _my child_

[Synonym]   자식 _children_

[Example]   우리 아이는 올해 대학을 졸업하고 취직했어요.
My child graduated from college and got a job this year.

045
아주머니

[아주머니] 명사 a lady, like an auntie

when an unacquainted person refers to a lady who is married

[Expression]   주인아주머니 _owner lady_
옆집 아주머니 _the lady next door_

[Antonym]   아저씨 _mister, uncle_

[Example]   아주머니, 여기 물 좀 더 주세요.
Mrs. please give us more water.

오늘 저녁에 하숙집 아주머니가 무슨 음식을 해 주실까?
What will the hostel lady give us for dinner tonight?

046
어른

[어른] 명사 adult

a full grown person, a person who has grown and can take responsibility for ones work

[Expression]   어른이 되다 _to become an adult_

[Antonym]   아이 _child_

[Example]   나이가 어린데도 생각은 어른 같아요.
The person is very young, but thinks like an adult.

저도 이제 어른이 되었어요. 제 일은 제가 알아서 하겠습니다.
I am an adult now. I will do my own job for myself.

047
유명하다
[유명하다] 형용사 to be famous
the name is well known by many

[Usage] **N**으로/로 유명하다

DV/**AV**기로 유명하다

[Expression] 유명한 곳 a famous place

유명한 사람 a famous person

[Example] 여기는 경치가 아름답기로 유명하다.
This place is famous for the beautiful scenery.

제 딸은 유명한 연예인이 되고 싶어해요.
My daughter wants to be a celebrity.

048
이름
[이름] 명사 name
the word that is behind the last name and is used to label the
difference between one person to another, the last and first name

[Expression] 이름을 짓다 to give a name

이름을 부르다 to call the name

[Synonym] 성명 full name

[Related word] 성함 family name and last name

[Example] 여기에 이름, 전화번호, 주소를 좀 써 주세요.
Please write your name, phone number, and address here.

이름을 발음하기 어려운데요. 한국 이름을 하나 만들면 어떨까요?
It is hard to pronounce your name. How about if we make a Korean name for you?

049
잡수시다
[잡쑤시다] 동사 to be eating
the honorific form of '먹다'(to eat)

[Usage] **N**을/를 잡수시다

[Synonym] 드시다 to eat (also formal)

[Related word] 먹다 to eat

[Example] 속이 안 좋아도 뭘 좀 잡수셔야지요.
You must eat something even though your stomach feels a little bad.

할아버지께서 저녁을 잡수시지 않았다고 해요. 빨리 준비하세요.
Grandfather says he didn't have dinner. Hurry up and prepare the food.

050
주무시다
[주무시다] 동사 to sleep
the honorific form of '자다'(to sleep)

[Related word] 자다 to sleep

[Example] 할머니께서 주무시니까 조용히 하세요.
Grandmother is sleeping, so please be quiet.

아버지는 점심을 드신 후 2(두)시쯤 항상 낮잠을 주무신다.
Father takes a nap at 2 after eating lunch.

05-4 | 외모 · 성격

051
귀엽다

[귀엽따] 형용사 to be cute
to be pretty and act in a cute and loving way, ㅂverb

[Usage]   **N**이/가 귀엽다
[Expression]   귀여운 아이 a cute child
               귀여운 얼굴 cute face
               강아지가 귀엽다 the puppy is cute.
               귀엽게 웃다 she laughs in a cute way.
[Related word] 예쁘다 to be pretty
[Example]   너 참 귀엽게 생겼구나. 몇 살이니?
               You have a really cute face. How old are you?

               엄마, 귀여운 강아지를 한 마리 사 주세요.
               Mom, please buy me a cute puppy.

052
다정하다

[다정하다] 형용사 to be affectionate
to have a lot of affection

[Usage]   **N**이/가 다정하다
[Expression]   다정한 사람 an affectionate person
               성격이 다정하다 personality is affectionate
               다정하게 말하다 to talk in an affectionate way
[Example]   아버지는 다정한 눈빛으로 아이를 보았다.
               The father looked at his child in an affectionate way.

부부가 저녁을 먹은 후에 다정하게 손을 잡고 산책하는 모습이 아름답다.

The couple ate dinner and they walked together holding hands affectionately. That image was so beautiful.

053

똑똑하다

[똑또카다] 형용사 to be smart, to be bright

to be clever

[Usage] **N**이/가 똑똑하다

[Expression] 머리가 똑똑하다 to be very intelligent

[Example] 부모는 모두 자기 아이들이 똑똑하기를 바란다.

All parents want their children to be bright

머리가 똑똑한 아이가 모두 공부를 잘하는 것은 아니에요.

Just because the child has intelligence doesn't mean the child will do well in studies.

054

마음

[마음] 명사 1. personality   2. a thought or idea

1.the character that one was born with

[Expression] 마음씨 mind, heart

마음이 좋다 to have a good heart/personality

마음이 넓다 to be generous

[Example] 예쁜 여자보다 마음이 착한 여자가 더 좋다.

A kind woman is better than a pretty woman.

2. the positive or negative feeling one gets of a person or object

[Expression] 마음에 들다 to like something

[Example] 새로 이사한 집이 넓고 밝아서 마음에 들어요.

I like the new house we moved into because it is big and bright.

055

멋있다

[머싣따/머딛따] 형용사 to be cool or fabulous

this word is used when something looks awesome

[Usage] **N**이/가 멋있다

[Expression] 멋있는 사람 a cool person

옷이 멋있다 the clothing is cool

멋있게 입다 to wear it in a fabulous way

[Example] 이렇게 멋있는 옷을 입고 어디에 가세요?

Where you going with such fabulous clothes on?

우리 반에서 영수가 제일 멋있어요. 착하고 친절해요.

Young-soo is the coolest in our class. He is kind and generous.

056
부지런하다

[부지런하다] 형용사 to be diligent, to be hard-working

when doing a certain type of work the person does not procrastinate and works hard

[Usage] N이/가 부지런하다

[Expression] 부지런한 사람 a hard-working person
부지런하게 일하다 to work diligently

[Antonym] 게으르다 to be lazy

[Example] 부지런하게 일해야 오늘 끝낼 수 있어요. 서두르세요!
We have to work hard so we finish it today. Hurry!

매일 아침 일찍 일어나서 운동도 하고 방 청소도 하는 걸 보니까 영수 씨는 참 부지런한 것 같아요.
Young-soo seems to be very diligent because he gets up early, exercises and cleans his room everyday.

057
성격

[성격] 명사 personality

the character and attitude that one has

[Expression] 성격이 밝다 personality is positive
성격이 좋다 to have a good personality
성격이 급하다 to be quick tempered

[Example] 영희는 성격이 밝아서 친구들이 많다.
Young-hee has a positive personality, so she has a lot of friends.

이번에 새로 들어온 직원은 일을 참 잘 하더군요. 성격은 어떤 것 같아요?
The new employer works very hard. What do you think his/her personality is?

058
예쁘다

[예쁘다] 형용사 to be pretty

to have a beautiful outer appearance, and one looks good for other people, or when the persons actions are loving and cute, 으 verb

[Usage] N이/가 예쁘다

[Expression] 예쁜 구두 pretty heels
얼굴이 예쁘다 a pretty face

[Related word] 귀엽다 to be cute
아름답다 to be beautiful

[Example] 딸아이가 눈이 참 크고 예쁘네요.
Your daughter has big eyes and is very pretty.

예쁜 여자 친구가 하나 있었으면 정말 좋겠다.
I wish I could have a pretty girlfriend.

059
잘생기다

[잘생기다] 형용사 to be good-looking, to be handsome

when a person's face is good to look at and when one has a great presence

[Usage]	**N**이/가 잘생기다
[Expression]	잘생긴 남자 a handsome man
[Antonym]	못생기다 to be ugly
[Example]	오늘 새로 전학온 남학생이 진짜 잘생겼지?
	Isn't the new male student who transferred handsome?
	요즘 텔레비전에 나오는 연예인들은 다 잘생겼어요.
	The stars that come on television these days are all good looking.

060
착하다

[차카다] 형용사 to be kind

speech, action, and heart is proper and gentle

[Usage]	**N**이/가 착하다
[Expression]	착한 사람 a kind person
	마음이 착하다 heart is kind
	착하게 살다 to live a good life
[Antonym]	못되다 to be mean
[Example]	내 여자 친구는 마음도 착하고 얼굴도 예쁘다.
	My girlfriend has a good heart and has a pretty face.
	착한 마음으로 열심히 살면 언젠가 좋은 날이 올 거예요.
	If you live diligently with a kind heart, then there will be good days.

061
친절하다

[친절하다] 형용사 to be kind and gentle

attitude is soft and nice

[Usage]	**N**이/가 친절하다
[Expression]	친절한 사람 a nice person
	친절하게 대답하다 to answer in a gentle way
[Example]	여기 종업원들이 모두 친절하군요.
	All the workers here are all kind.
	학생이 질문을 하니까 선생님이 친절하게 가르쳐 주셨다.
	The student asked the teacher a question and the teacher answered in a kind way.

[1~15] 다음 단어를 한국어로 바꿔 쓰십시오. Change these words into Korean.

1. older brother ( )   2. aunt (father's sister) ( )

3. who ( )   4. personality ( )

5. anyone ( )   6. woman ( )

7. friend ( )   8. siblings ( )
                                     (between brother and brother and sisters)

9. to be cute ( )   10. to eat (formal) ( )

11. to be cool ( )   12. to be close-to ( )

13. lady ( )   14. older man (like an uncle) ( )
    (old enough to be married)

15. roommate ( )

[16~20] 그림을 보고 ( )에 알맞은 것을 고르십시오.

Look at the picture and choose the correct word.

16.

가 : 학생이 있어요?

나 : 아니요, 선생님만 ( )으세요/세요.

❶ 계시다   ❷ 마시다

❸ 드시다   ❹ 가르치다

17.

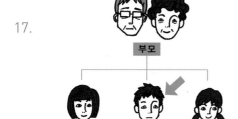

부모

나

가 : 누구예요?

나 : 제 ( )이에요/예요.

❶ 형   ❷ 오빠

❸ 누나   ❹ 아빠

18.

가 : (   )이/가 어떻게 되세요?

나 : 김영수입니다.

❶ 이름   ❷ 나이

❸ 주소   ❹ 전화번호

19.

가 : 참 잘 어울리네요.

나 : 네, 이제 두 사람이 (   )이/가 되었어요.

❶ 부모   ❷ 형제

❸ 부부   ❹ 친척

20.

가 : 할아버지께서 뭘 하세요?

나 : 지금 (   )고 계세요.

❶ 자다   ❷ 드시다

❸ 주무시다   ❹ 말씀하다

[21~30] 다음 문장을 읽고 알맞은 어휘를 골라 쓰십시오. 어휘는 한 번만 쓰십시오.
Read the following sentence and choose the right word. Use the words once.

아기	아이	노인	말씀	서로
생신	남자	멋있다	착하다	계시다
부르다	드리다	유명하다	친절하다	잡수시다

21. 선생님 (　　　　)을/를 잘 들으세요.

22. 두 분 (　　　　) 인사도 하고 얘기도 해 보세요.

23. 아버지의 (　　　　) 선물을 사러 백화점에 갑니다.

24. 할아버지, 저녁을 (　　　　)었어요/았어요/였어요?

25. 우리 (　　　　)이/가 오늘 고등학교를 졸업했어요.

26. 제 한국 친구가 아주 예쁘고 (　　　　)습니다/ㅂ니다.

27. 양복을 입은 모습이 아주 (　　　　)어요/아요/여요.

28. (　　　　)이/가 참 귀엽네요. 태어난 지 몇 개월 됐어요?

29. 정희는 부모님의 말씀을 잘 듣는 (　　　　)은/ㄴ 아이예요.

30. 저도 다 컸어요. 그러니까 이제 엄마하고 같이 여자 목욕탕에 안 갈 거예요. 이제부터 혼자
(　　　　) 목욕탕에 갈 거예요.

[31~35] (　　　) 안에 알맞은 것을 고르십시오. Choose the correct one.

31. 엄마의 여동생을 (　　　)이라고/라고 불러요.

　❶ 이모　　　❷ 고모　　　❸ 숙모　　　❹ 아줌마

32. 아주머니, 좀 도와 (　　　)을까요/ㄹ까요?

　❶ 보다　　　❷ 주시다　　　❸ 시키다　　　❹ 드리다

33. 오늘 우리 처음 만났으니까 서로 자기(   )을/를 해 봅시다.

❶ 말   ❷ 소개   ❸ 운동   ❹ 대답

34. 안녕하세요? 처음 (   )겠습니다. 제 이름은 김미선입니다.

❶ 보다   ❷ 뵙다   ❸ 사귀다   ❹ 만나다

35. 선생님 (   ) 주소를 좀 가르쳐 주세요.

❶ 댁   ❷ 전화   ❸ 연세   ❹ 성함

[36~40] 밑줄 친 부분과 반대되는 뜻을 가진 것을 고르십시오.
Choose the word that is the opposite of the underlined word.

36. **가 :** 영준이가 <u>게을러요</u>?

   나 : 아니요, 아주 (   )어요/아요/여요.

❶ 착하다   ❷ 다정하다   ❸ 아름답다   ❹ 부지런하다

37. **가 :** 영희가 머리가 <u>나빠요</u>?

   나 : 아니요, 아주 (   )어요/아요/여요.

❶ 착하다   ❷ 똑똑하다   ❸ 유명하다   ❹ 친절하다

38. **가 :** 영수의 여자 친구가 <u>못생겼어요</u>?

   나 : 아니요, 아주 (   )어요/아요/여요.

❶ 멋지다   ❷ 예쁘다   ❸ 다정하다   ❹ 친절하다

39. **가 :** 제 딸은 곧 스무 살이 되지만 아직 <u>어린아이</u> 같아요.

   나 : 제가 보기에는 (   )이/가 다 된 것 같은데요.

❶ 부모   ❷ 어른   ❸ 학생   ❹ 할머니

40. **가 :** 우리나라에서 그 가수를 <u>아는 사람이 별로 없어요.</u>

 나 : 그래요? 한국에서는 아주 (   )은데요/ㄴ데요.

 ❶ 비싸다   ❷ 모르다   ❸ 불편하다   ❹ 유명하다

[41~45] 밑줄 친 부분과 의미가 가장 가까운 것을 고르십시오.
Choose the word that is most similar to the underlined section.

41. **가 :** 영수 씨가 오늘도 <u>여자 친구</u>를 만나러 갔어요?

 나 : 네, 요즘 날마다 (   )을/를 만나는 것 같아요.

 ❶ 가족   ❷ 애인   ❸ 학생   ❹ 형제

42. **가 :** 우리 반에서 누구하고 <u>가깝게 지내요?</u>

 나 : 저는 영수하고 가장 (   )어요/아요/여요.

 ❶ 같다   ❷ 친하다   ❸ 똑똑하다   ❹ 다정하다

43. **가 :** 뭘 <u>드릴까요?</u>

 나 : 커피 한 잔 (   )으세요/세요.

 ❶ 주다   ❷ 드시다   ❸ 보이다   ❹ 시키다

44. **가 :** 오늘 아침에 뭘 <u>드셨어요?</u>

 나 : 간단하게 김밥을 (   )었어요/았어요/였어요.

 ❶ 먹다   ❷ 뵙다   ❸ 계시다   ❹ 말씀하시다

45. **가 :** <u>형제</u>가 몇 명 있어요?

 나 : 저는 (   )이/가 한 명 있어요.

 ❶ 삼촌   ❷ 동생   ❸ 친구   ❹ 할머니

[46~50] 밑줄 친 단어의 쓰임이 잘못된 것을 고르십시오. Choose the one that is incorrectly used.

46. ❶ 사람은 <u>착하게</u> 살아야 한다.　　　　(　　　)
　　❷ 내 친구는 참 <u>착한</u> 사람이다.
　　❸ 저 여자는 옷을 <u>착하게</u> 입었다.
　　❹ 그 사람은 <u>착한</u> 일을 많이 했다.

47. ❶ 아버지께 말씀을 <u>드렸어요</u>.　　　　(　　　)
　　❷ 아버지, 뭘 사다 <u>드릴까요</u>?
　　❸ 아버지께서 용돈을 <u>드렸어요</u>.
　　❹ 아버지께 물을 갖다 <u>드렸어요</u>.

48. ❶ 누가 제 이름을 <u>불렀어요</u>?　　　　(　　　)
　　❷ 좀 더 큰 소리로 <u>불러</u> 보세요.
　　❸ 노래방에 가서 노래를 <u>부릅시다</u>.
　　❹ 그 문제는 선생님과 <u>부르는</u> 게 좋겠어요.

49. ❶ 내가 <u>말씀드리겠습니다</u>.　　　　(　　　)
　　❷ 우리 같이 선생님 <u>댁</u>에 갑시다.
　　❸ 선생님, <u>저희</u>가 뭘 잘못했어요?
　　❹ 조금 전에 여기 <u>계셨던 분</u>이 누구세요?

50. ❶ 너 <u>나이</u>가 몇 살이니?　　　　(　　　)
　　❷ 저 <u>아이</u>가 참 잘생겼어요.
　　❸ 선생님 <u>성격</u>이 참 빠른 것 같아요.
　　❹ <u>어른</u>이 말씀하실 때는 조용히 해라.

사람 Ⅱ

06

People Ⅱ

001
감사

[감사] 명사 thanks

an expression of thanks, being grateful

[Expression]
감사 인사 thankful greeting

감사 편지 thank you note

감사하다 thank you(honorific form)

감사를 전하다 to send thanks

[Related word] 고맙다 thank you

[Example] 짐을 여기까지 들어 주셔서 정말 감사합니다.
Thank you for carrying my things all the way here.

선생님께 편지를 써서 감사의 마음을 전했다.
I wrote a letter to my teacher to express my thanks.

002
걱정

[걱쩡] 명사 worry

not being at peace and constantly think about something irritating

[Expression]
걱정이 있다 to have a worry

걱정이 많다 to have many things to worry about

걱정하다 to worry

[Example] 요즘 아이가 아파서 걱정이 많아요. My child is sick, so I am worried.

이번 시험을 또 못 보면 어떻게 하지요? 정말 걱정이에요.
What if I don't do well on this test again? I am so worried.

003
관심

[관심] 명사 interest

being pulled towards an object, place or person

[Expression]
관심이 많다 I am very interested

관심이 없다 I don't have any interest

관심을 갖다 to have interest

[Example] 요즘 학생들은 유명한 연예인들에게 관심이 많다.
These days students are interested in famous celebrities.

우리 아이는 공부에 너무 관심이 없어서 걱정이에요.
My child has no interest in studying, so I am worried.

004
괜찮다

[괜찬타] 형용사 1. to be good or ok   2. there is no worry

1. not bad, average or above

[Usage] N이/가 괜찮다

[Expression] 집이 괜찮다 the house is good

성적이 괜찮다 grades are ok

사람이 괜찮다 the person is good

[Example] 지난 번 시험은 잘 못 봤는데, 이번에는 성적이 괜찮아요.
Last time I didn't do so well on the test, but this time my grades are pretty good.

2. there is no problem or worry

[Usage] DV/AV어도/아도/여도 괜찮다

[Expression] 좁아도 괜찮다 to be ok even though it is very close tight

나가도 괜찮다 to be ok to go out

힘들어도 괜찮다 I am ok even though I am tired

[Example] 시간이 지나면 괜찮아질 거예요. 너무 걱정하지 마세요.
It will get better after time passes. Don't worry.

005
기분

[기분] 명사 mood, feeling

having an object or environment change the mood of someone for a period of time

[Usage] DV은/ㄴ 기분

[Expression] 이상한 기분 a weird mood

기분이 좋다 to be in a good mood

DV은/ㄴ 기분이 들다 to have some feeling

[Example] 오늘 기분이 나빠 보여요. 무슨 안 좋은 일이 있어요?
You look to be in a bad mood today. Did something happen?

오늘 친구들한테서 선물을 많이 받아서 진짜 기분이 좋다.
I received a lot of presents from my friends, so I'm in a good mood.

006
기쁘다

[기쁘다] 형용사 to be happy

when one feels light-hearted, 으 verb

[Usage] N이/가 기쁘다

[Related word] 즐겁다 to feel good

[Example] 대학교에 합격해서 너무 기뻐요.
I am happy because I got accepted to a college.

어머니는 선물을 받고 기뻐하셨다.
Mother became happy after receiving the present.

007
놀라다

[놀라다] 동사 to be surprised

when something happens without planning creating a shock, or when one is scared and his/her heart starts beating quickly

[Usage] N이/가 놀라다

[Expression] 놀란 가슴 a scared heart

깜짝 놀라다 to be surprised

[Example] 갑자기 밖에서 큰 소리가 나서 깜짝 놀랐어요.
I was scared because suddenly there was a really loud sound that came from outside.

여자 친구에게 반지를 선물하니까 여자 친구가 깜짝 놀란 얼굴로 나를 보았다.
I gave my girlfriend a ring for a present and she looked at me in a surprised way.

008
무섭다

[무섭따] 형용사 to be scary

there is something frightening about someone or something , ㅂverb

[Usage] N이/가 무섭다

[Expression] 무서운 영화 a scary movie

개가 무섭다 dogs are scary

무섭게 화내다 to get angry in a scary way

[Example] 늦은 밤 혼자 집으로 걸어갈 때가 제일 무섭다.
It is scary whenever I walk home late at night.

거짓말을 했다고 엄마가 저를 무섭게 야단치셨어요.
My mother scolded me in a frightening way because I lied to her.

009
물론

[물론] 명사 of course

needless to say

[Usage] N은/는 물론이고 N도 DV/AV

[Example] 부모님은 물론이고 친구들도 모두 내 생일을 축하해 주었다.
My friends told me happy birthday and needless to say my parents celebrated my birthday with me.

파티에 올 거냐고? 물론이지. 내 제일 친한 친구인데 당연히 가야지.
Are you coming to the party? Of course. It's my best friends birthday, I will definitely be there.

010
반갑다

[반갑따] 형용사 to be glad, delighted, happy

when meeting someone you've missed, when something is fulfilling because one's work is complete, ㅂverb

[Usage]	N이/가 반갑다
[Expression]	반가운 소식 happy news
	반가운 손님 a welcomed guest
	만나서 반갑다 it's nice to meet you
	반갑게 맞다 to give a joyous welcome
	반갑게 인사하다 to welcome delightfully
[Example]	어머니는 내 친구들을 반갑게 맞아 주셨다.
	My mother greeted my friends happily.
	오랜만에 친구들을 만나서 아주 반가웠어요.
	I met my friends after a long time and it was nice to see them.

011 사랑

[사랑] 명사 love

to like to someone a lot, or when thinking of someone or something in a precious and valuable way

[Expression]	사랑하다 to love
	사랑에 빠지다 to fall in love
[Example]	미선 씨를 진심으로 사랑합니다. 저와 결혼해 주시겠어요?
	Mi-sun, I love you with all of my heart. Will you marry me?
	저는 이 세상에 사랑보다 중요한 것은 없다고 생각합니다.
	I think love is the most important thing in this world.

012 생각

[생각] 명사 1. thinking 2. an idea, notion 3. a purpose 4. an opinion

1. using one's mind to make judgment

[Expression]	생각하다 to think
[Example]	뭐가 맞는지 잘 생각해 보고 대답해라.
	Think about what is right and answer.

2. a memory of someone or something

[Expression]	친구 생각 thinking of a friend
	생각이 나다 to remember
[Example]	엄마가 해 주셨던 맛있는 음식이 생각난다.
	I remember the delicious food that mother used to make for me.

3. wanting to do something

[Usage]	AV을/ㄹ 생각이다
	N을/를 할 생각이 있다
[Example]	너는 졸업하면 뭘 할 생각이니? What do plan to do after you graduate?

4. a personal thought or feeling

[Expression]	생각이 들다 to think of something
[Example]	집에 아무도 없을 때 가끔 외롭다는 생각이 든다.
	When there is no one home, I sometimes feel lonely.

013
슬프다

[슬프다] 형용사 to be sad

when one's heart is hurting or painful, 으 verb

[Usage] **N**이/가 슬프다

[Expression] 슬픈 영화 sad movie

슬프게 울다 to cry painfully

[Example] 시험에 떨어져서 너무 슬프다.
I am sad because I didn't pass the exam.

슬픈 영화를 보니까 눈물이 나요.
Tears are coming down while watching this sad movie.

014
싫다

[실타] 형용사 to dislike

[Usage] **N**이/가 싫다

[Expression] 공부가 싫다 I don't like studying

싫어하다 to dislike

[Antonym] 좋다 to like

[Example] 말이 너무 많은 사람은 시끄러워서 싫다.
I don't like people who talk a lot because they are noisy.

하기 싫은 마음으로 일을 하면 일이 잘 되지 않아요.
If you do the work without wanting to do it, then the final product will not be
that great.

015
싫증

[실쯩] 명사 weariness, being annoyed

a dislike in thought or feeling

[Expression] 싫증이 나다 to be tired

싫증을 느끼다 to feel weary

[Example] 맛있는 음식도 매일 먹으면 싫증이 나요.
Eating delicious food all the time can get annoying .

매일 하는 똑같은 생활에 싫증이 날 때는 새로운 일을 시작해 보세요.
When everyday life seems to the same, try something new.

016
심심하다

[심심하다] 형용사 to be bored

when one has nothing to do and when there is nothing fun to do

[Related word] 지루하다 to feel dull

[Example] 심심한데 우리 비디오나 빌려서 볼까?
I'm bored. Shall we borrow a movie and watch it?

토요일인데 약속도 없고 할 일도 없어서 참 심심하다.
It's Saturday and I have no plans so I am bored.

017
아마

[아마] 부사 perhaps, maybe

(used as a guessing expression) not very sure but when looking back at it, it was probably correct

[Example] 오빠는 아마 지금 도서관에서 공부하고 있을 거예요.
My older brother is probably studying in the library.

지금 출발하면 아마 오후 1(한)시쯤에는 도착할 수 있을 거예요.
If we leave right now, we'll probably arrive around 1pm.

018
외롭다

[외롭따] 형용사 to feel lonely

to feel alone and feel as if there is no one lean on, ㅂverb

[Usage] N이/가 외롭다

[Expression] 외로운 생활 a lonely life

마음이 외롭다 to have lonely heart

[Synonym] 쓸쓸하다 to be alone

[Example] 가족과 함께 살지 않고 혼자 살면 외롭지 않아요?
Doesn't it feel lonely to live alone and not with your family?

유학 생활은 가족과 친한 친구가 옆에 없어서 외로울 때가 많다.
During study abroad I often feel lonely because I am away from my family and close friends.

019
잊다

[읻따] 동사 to forget

something that happened a long time ago and something that was known, something that needs to be remembered but can't seem to recognize

[Usage] N을/를 잊다

[Expression] 깜빡 잊다 to forget a bit

잊어버리다 to forget

약속을 잊다 to forget about the promise

[Example] 어디에 지갑을 두었는지 잊어버렸어요.
I don't know where I put my wallet, I forgot.

오늘이 엄마 생일이라는 것을 깜빡 잊었다.
I forgot that today was mom's birthday.

020
재미있다

[재미읻따] 형용사 to be entertaining, to be fun

to have fun and enjoyable feeling

[Usage] N이/가 재미있다

[Expression] 재미있는 영화 an entertaining movie

133

책이 재미있다 the book is fun

요리가 재미있다 cooking is fun

[Antonym] 재미없다 to not be fun

[Example] 이 영화가 정말 재미있으니까 꼭 보세요.
This movie is really great you should definitely watch the movie.

내가 어렸을 때 어머니는 재미있는 옛날이야기를 많이 해 주셨다.
When I was younger, my mother told us a lot of old stories that were fun.

021
좋아하다

[조아하다] 동사 to like

when someone or a type of work has a good feeling, and wanting to the do the work with the best ability

[Usage] N을/를 좋아하다

[Expression] 좋아하는 사람 someone I like

공부를 좋아하다 to like to study

여행을 좋아하다 to like to travel

[Antonym] 싫어하다 to dislike

[Example] 저는 혼자 산책하는 것을 좋아해요.
I like to take walks alone.

좋아하는 사람이 생겼는데 어떻게 이야기하면 좋을까요?
I have someone that I like, how should I tell that person?

022
죄송하다

[죄송하다] 형용사 to be sorry or regretful

to be uncomfortable with regret

[Usage] DV/AV 어서/아서/여서 죄송하다

[Expression] 늦어서 죄송하다 to be sorry for being late

[Synonym] 미안하다 to feel sorry

[Example] 약속에 늦어서 정말 죄송합니다.
I'm sorry I was late for the promised meeting.

죄송해서 아무 말도 하지 못했다.
I was so sorry that I couldn't even speak.

023
즐겁다

[즐겁따] 형용사 to be cheerful

to feel very delightful and happy, ㅂverb

[Usage] N이/가 즐겁다

[Expression] 즐거운 여행 cheerful vacation

즐거운 마음 happy mood

요리가 즐겁다 cooking is fun

즐겁게 지내다 to be living happily

[Example] 즐거운 마음으로 여행을 떠났다.
I went off to vacation in a very happy mood.

따뜻한 봄날 가족들과 소풍갈 생각으로 마음이 즐겁다.
I feel happy just thinking about going on a picnic with my family on a warm spring day.

024
필요

[피료] 명사 need

having a specific necessity

[Usage] **DV/AV** 을/ㄹ 필요가 있다

[Expression] 필요하다 to need

[Example] 지금 네게 필요한 것은 잠깐의 휴식이다.
What you need right now is a short break.

아이가 스스로 하는 게 중요해요. 도와 줄 필요가 없어요.
It is important for the child to do it on his own. There is no need to help him.

025
행복하다

[행보카다] 형용사 to be blissful

the word used when life is great and everything feels right

[Usage] **N**이/가 행복하다

[Expression] 행복한 삶 a blissful life

행복한 사람 a blissful person

[Antonym] 불행하다 to be unhappy

[Example] 돈이 많으면 행복할까요?
If I have a lot of money, will I be happy?

사랑하는 사람 옆에 서 있는 친구의 얼굴이 행복해 보였다.
My friends face looked blissful as she was looking at the person she loved.

026
화

[화] 명사 anger

getting infuriated and express this anger

[Expression] 화가 나다 to feel angry

화를 내다 to express anger

[Example] 친구가 약속 시간에 늦어서 화가 났다.
My friend was late and I felt angry.

너한테 미안한 일이 하나 있는데, 화내지 말고 끝까지 내 말을 들어줘.
I have something I need to confess, don't get mad and listen to everything I have to say.

135

027
가수

[가수] 명사 singer
[Related word] 가요 song
[Example] 노래를 잘해야 가수가 될 수 있어요.
You have to sing well in order to become a singer.

요즘 학생들이 제일 좋아하는 가수가 누구예요?
Which singer do students like the most these days?

028
간호사

[간호사] 명사 nurse
[Related word] 의사 doctor
환자 patient
[Example] 간호사 선생님이 주사를 놓으려고 올 때가 제일 무서워요.
When the nurse comes to give me shots, it is very scary.

입원했을 때 간호사 선생님이 친절하게 나를 돌봐 주셨다.
When I was hospitalized, the nurse was very kind.

029
경찰

[경찰] 명사 police
[Expression] 경찰관 a police officer
경찰서 police station
[Example] 경찰인 아버지가 아주 자랑스럽다.
I am proud of my father because he is a policeman.

우리 아이는 경찰을 보면 무서워해요.
My child is scared whenever he sees a police.

030
공무원

[공무원] 명사 government employee, civil servant
a person working for the nation or region doing public office work
[Example] 요즘 대학생들에게 인기 있는 직업은 공무원이다.
The favorite job for college students these days is a government employee.

우리 아들은 지난달부터 공무원 시험을 준비하고 있어요.
My son has been preparing for the civil servant exam since last year.

031
교사

[교사] 명사 teacher
a person who is certified to teach at a elementary, middle, or high school
[Synoynm] 선생님 teacher
[Related word] 학교 school

[Example] 저는 나중에 커서 아이를 가르치는 교사가 되고 싶어요.
I want to become a teacher when I grow up.

시골에 있는 초등학교는 학생이 적어서 교사가 한두 명뿐이라고 한다.
There are few elementary students in the country, so there are only one or two teachers.

032
교수

[교수] 명사 professor

someone that teaches at a college and also studies a field specifically

[Expression] 교수님 professor
[Related word] 대학교 college, university
[Example] 교수님께서 이번에 너무 어려운 숙제를 내 주셨다.
My professor gave us a hard assignment this time.

이번 주에 졸업 여행을 가는데 교수님도 저희하고 함께 가실 거지요?
This week we're going on the graduating class trip. Are you going to go with us professor?

033
군인

[구닌] 명사 soldier

[Related word] 군대 armed services
[Example] 초등학교 때 군인 아저씨들에게 편지를 쓰곤 했다.
In elementary school I used to write to men in the armed services.

아버지가 군인이기 때문에 우리 가족은 자주 이사를 가요.
My father is a soldier, so my family and I move a lot.

034
기사¹

[기사] 명사 driver

a person who works by driving vehicles

[Expression] 운전기사 driver
[Related word] 승객 a passenger
[Example] 기사 아저씨, 저 육교 앞에 세워 주세요.
Mister, can you take me in front of the pedestrian overpass.

친절한 운전기사 아저씨가 약속 장소까지 저를 잘 안내해 주었어요.
A kind taxi driver took me to the place I needed to go.

035
기사²

[기사] 명사 technician

a person with a specialized knowledge of a skill

[Synonym] 엔지니어 engineer
[Example] 기사 아저씨, 이 텔레비전이 왜 고장이 났지요?
Mr. technician, why did the television break?

137

우리 집만 불이 나갔네. 전기 기사를 불러야겠다.

Our house seems to be the only one with no lights. I better call the electric technician.

036
기자

[기자] 명사 writer, reporter, journalist

a person that works for the newspaper, magazine, or broadcast station by writing, reporting or investigating

[Example] 글을 잘 쓰는 사람은 기자가 될 수 있어요.

A person who is good at writing can be a good journalist.

대학교를 졸업한 후에 신문사에 기자로 취직했습니다.

After I graduated from college, I started working at the newspaper company as a reporter.

037
농부

[농부] 명사 farmer

[Related word] 농사 farming

농촌 farming village/area

[Example] 농사일이 많은데 일할 농부가 적다.

There are many things to do on the farm but there are very few farmers.

영수는 도시에서 살다가 갑자기 농부가 되겠다고 시골로 내려갔다.

Young-soo lived in the city but he suddenly went down to the country to become a farmer.

038
되다

[되다] 동사 1. to be 2. to become 3. to go well 4. to be becoming

1. to have a new status or to gain power

[Usage] N이/가 되다

[Expression] 의사가 되다 to became a doctor

교사가 되다 to became a teacher

[Example] 대학교 4(사)년 동안 열심히 공부해서 선생님이 되었다.

I studied hard in college for 4 years and became a teacher.

2. to become the moment, the quantity, or number

[Usage] N이/가 되다

[Expression] 봄이 되다 to become spring

열 명이 되다 to become 10 people

[Example] 봄이 되니까 날씨가 따뜻해졌어요.

Now that it is spring, the weather is warm.

3. something is made or some sort of work becomes well done

[Usage] N이/가 되다

[Expression] 밥이 되다 the meal is ready

일이 되다 the work is done well

[Example] 밥이 다 됐다. 어서 와서 먹어라.
The food is ready. Hurry up and eat.

4. (used with '-게') telling the situation or the state of something

[Usage] **DV/AV**게 되다

[Expression] 잘하게 되다 to do better

유학가게 되다 to be able to go to study abroad

[Example] 해외로 유학을 갈 수 있는 장학금을 받게 되었습니다.
I was able to receive a scholarship to go travel abroad.

039
모델

[모델] 명사 model

fashion model, or someone who is the subject of an art project

[Expression] 모델료 model

패션모델 fashion model

[Example] 이번 광고에는 키가 크고 잘 생긴 모델이 필요합니다.
I need a tall and good looking model for this advertisement.

미술 학원에서 모델이 필요하다고 하는데 한 번 해 보시겠어요?
The art institution needs a model for the subject of the art piece. Would you like to be the model?

040
배우

[배우] 명사 actor

a person who acts in plays or movies

[Expression] 영화배우 movie star

신인 배우 new actor

[Related word] 연극 play

영화 movie

연기하다[1] to act

[Example] 나는 좋아하는 배우가 나온 영화 DVD를 모두 모은다.
I collect movies that have some of my favorite actors.

배우는 외모보다 연기를 잘 하는 것이 더 중요하다고 생각해요.
I think it's more important for an actor to be good at acting than be good looking.

041
변호사

[변호사] 명사 lawyer

[Related word] 검사 prosecutor

판사 judge

법원 court

[Example]   변호사와 의논한 후에 이 일을 처리해야겠다.
I better talk to a lawyer and take care of this situation.

변호사가 옆에 없으면 아무 말도 하지 않겠습니다.
I won't speak unless I have a lawyer beside me.

042 비서

[비서] 명사 secretary, personal assistant

[Related word]   회장 president, chairman
사장 CEO

[Example]   김 비서, 오늘 일정은 어떻게 되지?
Secretary Kim, what is today's schedule?

사장님을 만나고 싶으시면 먼저 비서에게 말해야 합니다.
If you want to meet with the CEO, you must talk to the secretary first.

043 선수

[선수] 명사 athlete

a sports representative that is professional and talented in the field and is picked up to play, someone that works as an athlete

[Expression]   운동선수 sports athlete
대표 선수 representative player

[Related word]   운동 exercise
스포츠 sports

[Example]   골프를 참 잘 치시네요. 골프 선수예요?
You are good at golf. Are you a professional golfer?

영수는 축구 국가 대표 선수가 되기 위해서 열심히 훈련을 하고 있다.
Young-soo is training hard to become a representative player for the national team.

044 소설가

[소설가] 명사 novelist

a professional novel writer

[Related word]   책 book
작가 writer

[Example]   한국의 유명한 소설가가 쓴 책을 읽고 있어요.
I am reading a book written by a famous Korean novelist.

이야기를 좋아하고 글 쓰는 것을 좋아하니까 너는 소설가가 되면 좋겠다.
You like stories and like to write, so you should become a novelist.

045
약사

[약싸] 명사 pharmacist

[Related word] 약국 pharmacy

[Example] 약사가 되려고 약학대학에 들어갔다.
I went to the college of pharmacy to become a pharmacist.

약사 선생님께서 이 약을 하루에 세 번 식사한 후에 먹으라고 했어요.
The pharmacist told me to take the medicine three times a day after each meal.

046
연예인

[여녜인] 명사 celebrity

a person who works in the entertainment industry as an actor, singer, comedian or other sort of job in the industry

[Related word] 방송국 broadcasting station

[Example] 많은 청소년들이 커서 연예인이 되고 싶어 한다.
Many young adults want to become a celebrity when they become older.

요즘은 연예인들에 대한 소식을 알려주는 TV 프로그램이 아침에도 있어요.
There are morning programs that tell the news about celebrities.

047
의사

[의사] 명사 doctor

[Related word] 병원 hospital

환자 patient

[Example] 의사 선생님, 우리 아이가 왜 이렇게 아픈 거예요?
Doctor, why is my child so sick?

의사가 되려면 대학에서 6(육)년 동안 열심히 공부해야 한다.
In order to become a doctor, you must study hard for 6 years at the college.

048
주부

[주부] 명사 housewife, homemaker

a person who takes care of the housekeeping items for the family and takes care of the family

[Expression] 가정주부 family homemaker

[Example] 어머니는 일을 하지 않아요. 가정주부예요.
Mother does not work. She is a housewife.

요즘 일을 하려고 하는 주부가 늘고 있다고 한다.
They say there are many housekeepers who want to work.

049
직업

[지겁] 명사 work, occupation

something that one does to keep living and the person chooses this by testing his or her aptitude and ability

[Expression] 직업을 갖다 to get a job

직업을 구하다 to look for a job

[Related word] 직장 occupation

[Example] 제 아버지의 직업은 교사입니다. My father's job is a teacher.

요즘 대학생들은 어떤 직업을 갖고 싶어해요?
What kinds of jobs do college students want now-a-days?

050
화가

[화가] 명사 artist, painter

[Related word] 그림 picture

[Example] 유명한 화가가 그린 그림은 비싸요.
A picture drawn by a famous artist is expensive.

그림을 잘 그리는 미선이는 커서 화가가 되고 싶어한다.
Mi-sun draws great pictures and later wants to become an artist.

051
회사원

[회사원] 명사 office worker

a person who works in the office

[Related word] 직원 employer

[Example] 제 오빠는 무역회사에 다니는 회사원입니다.
My older brother is an office worker at an international trade office.

출근하는 회사원들로 지하철이 아주 복잡하네요.
The office workers all rush to get to the office so the subways are very busy.

052
걷다

[걷따] 동사 to walk

to move by moving your legs alternately, ㄷverb

[Usage] **N**을/를 걷다

[Expression] 걸어서 가다 to go by walking

걸을 걷다 to walk on the streets

[Related word] 뛰다 to run

[Example] 집에서 학교까지 걸어서 가면 10(십)분쯤 걸려요.
It takes 10 minutes to walk from my home to school.

날씨가 따뜻해지니까 공원을 걷는 사람들이 많아졌다.
The weather has gotten warmer, so there are many people walking in the park.

053
나오다

[나오다] 동사 1. to go out   2. to get   3. to bring out (food)

1. to move from inside to out

[Usage] **N**으로/로 나오다

[Example] 뭐하니? 빨리 나오지 않고. 지금 출발해야 된다!
What are you doing? Hurry up and come out, we have to leave now!

2. to manage or receive a result

[Usage] **N**이/가 나오다

[Expression] 결과가 나오다 the result is out

성적이 나오다 to grades are out

[Example] 선생님께서 시험 본 다음날 성적이 나온다고 하셨어요.
My teacher told us that the test results would come out the day after the test.

3. to prepare and lay out the food

[Usage] **N**이/가 나오다

[Expression] 음식이 나오다 the food is out

[Example] 주문한 지 30(삼십)분이나 지났는데 아직도 음식이 나오지 않네요.
We've been waiting for 30 minutes but the food is still not out.

054
눕다

[눕따] 동사 to lay down

to have the whole body lay horizontally on the floor or bed, ㅂverb

[Usage] **N**에 눕다

[Expression] 침대에 눕다 to lay on the bed

[Antonym] 일어나다 to get up

[Related word] 엎드리다 to lay face down

[Example] 누워 계시지 않고 왜 일어나셨어요?
You should lay down, why did you get up?

오늘은 너무 피곤해서 일찍 침대에 누웠다.
I was so tired ,so I laid down in my bed at an early time.

055
들어가다

[들어가다] 동사 1. to go inside   2. to become a member

1. to go from outside to inside

[Usage] <u>N</u>에 들어가다

<u>N</u>으로 들어가다

[Expression] 집에 들어가다 to go inside the house

안으로 들어가다 to go inside

[Example] 밖이 춥구나. 빨리 안으로 들어가자.
It's cold outside. Let's hurry and come inside.

2. to become a member in a group

[Usage] <u>N</u>에 들어가다

[Expression] 학교에 들어가다 to get accepted into a school

회사에 들어가다 to get into an office

[Example] 대학교에 들어간다고 축하하던 때가 엊그제 같은데 네가 벌써 졸업
할 때가 되었구나.
It feels like I congratulated you for getting into college just yesterday, and it's
already time for you to graduate college.

056
뛰다

[뛰다] 동사 to run

to move feet really quickly and move out

[Usage] <u>N</u>을/를 뛰다

[Expression] 뛰어가다 to run out

운동장을 뛰다 to run in the exercise room

[Synonym] 달리다 to dash

[Example] 수업에 늦어서 교실까지 뛰었어요.
I was late for class, so I ran to class.

비가 많이 온다. 버스에서 내려서 집까지 뛰어가자!
It's raining a lot. Let's get off the bus and run home!

057
서다

[서다] 동사 1. to stand   2. to stop, halt

1.to place the foot firmly on the ground, keep the legs apart and
balance the body on the ground

[Usage] <u>N</u>이/가 서다

[Expression] 서 있다 to be standing

줄을 서다 to stand in line

서서 가다 to go standing

[Antonym] 앉다 to sit

[Example] 이 영화가 재미있나 봐요. 표를 사려고 줄을 선 사람들이 많아요.

This movie seems to be really good. There are many people standing in line to buy the tickets.

2. to stop in the middle of moving

[Usage] N이/가 서다

[Expression] 차가 서다 the car has stopped

시계가 서다 the clock has stopped

[Example] 차가 왜 갑자기 섰지요? 앞에 사고가 났나요?

Why did the car suddenly stop? Is there an accident in the front?

058
안다

[안따] 동사 to hug

to open both arms and pull into an embrace

[Usage] N을/를 안다

[Expression] 안고 가다 to take while hugging or carrying

아이를 안다 to hug the child

[Related word] 업다 to carry on one's back

[Example] 아이가 많이 우네요. 빨리 안아 주세요.

The child is crying a lot. Hurry and hold her.

이렇게 무거운 가방은 들고 가는 것보다 안고 가는 게 좋겠어요.

Instead of carrying this heavy bag, just hug the bag.

059
앉다

[안따] 동사 to sit

[Usage] N에 앉다

앉아서 AV

[Expression] 의자에 앉다 to sit on the chair

바닥에 앉다 to sit on the ground

앉아서 듣다 to listen while sitting

앉아서 공부하다 to study while sitting

[Antonym] 서다 to stand

일어나다 to get up

[Example] 다리가 아픈데 우리 여기에 좀 앉아서 쉬었다가 갑시다.

My legs are hurting, let's sit here and take a break.

저기 나무 아래에 앉아서 책을 읽고 있는 사람이 보이세요?

Do you see the person sitting below the tree and reading?

060
올라가다

[올라가다] 동사 1. to go up　2. to go from a region to the middle
3. to have higher status

1. to go from the bottom to top

[Usage] **N**을/를 올라가다

N에 올라가다

N으로 올라가다

[Expression] 계단을 올라가다 to go up the stairs

위로 올라가다 to go above

산에 올라가다 to go up a mountain

[Antonym] 내려가다 to go down

[Example] 친구가 위층에서 기다리고 있으니까 빨리 올라가 보세요.
Your friend is waiting upstairs, so hurry and go see him upstairs.

2. to go from a region to the city

[Usage] **N**에 올라가다

N으로 올라가다

[Expression] 서울에 올라가다 to go up to Seoul

[Antonym] 내려가다 to go south

[Example] 이번 추석에는 아이들을 내려오라고 하지 말고 우리가 서울로 올라
갑시다.
For this thanksgiving, let's go up to Seoul instead of having the kids come
down.

3. to go up in class, status

[Usage] **N**으로/로 올라가다

[Related word] 승급하다 to be promoted

진급하다 to advance

[Example] 우리 반 학생 모두 한국말을 열심히 공부해서 4(사)급으로 올라가게
됐다.
All of the students in my class studied Korean very hard and moved up to level 4.

 도움말

The word means the direction of movement, means the same as the verb.

• to go from inside to outside : 나가다/나오다 to go outside

• to go from outside to inside : 들어가다/들어오다 to come inside

• to go from below to top : 올라가다/올라오다 to go above

• to go from top to bottom : 내려가다/내려오다 to go down

'-가다' is used when the speaker and the listener's relationship becomes distanced or when
the speaker and listener move together.

빨리 들어가자. 비가 올 것 같다.

Let's hurry and go inside. It looks like it's about to rain. (a situation where both are moving together)

빨리 나가 봐라. 친구가 기다리잖니.

Hurry and go outside. Your friend is waiting. (the speaker and listener have distance in this case)

'-오다' shows that the speaker and listener are becoming closer.

정우야! 아버지 들어오신다. 빨리 내려와서 인사 드려라.

Jung-woo! Father is coming inside. Hurry and greet him.

061
잡다

[잡따] 동사 **1. to hold with hands 2. to catch (cab) 3. to take the opportunity**

1. to grasp with the hand

[Usage]   N을/를 잡다

[Expression]   손을 잡다 to hold hands

[Example]   아이는 엄마 손을 꼭 잡고 걸어갔다.
            The child held his mother's hand tightly and walked around.

2. to hail down a taxi

[Usage]   N을/를 잡다

[Expression]   택시를 잡다 to catch a taxi

[Example]   여기는 택시가 별로 다니지 않아서 택시를 잡기가 어려워요.
            There are not many taxis here, so it was hard to grab a cab.

3.to get up and take the opportunity

[Usage]   N을/를 잡다

[Expression]   기회를 잡다 to grab the chance

[Antonym]   놓치다 to lose the chance

[Example]   장학금을 받고 유학갈 수 있는 기회니까 이런 기회는 꼭 잡아야 해.
            You get to receive a scholarship to go study abroad, you should grab this opportunity.

[1~15] 다음 단어를 한국어로 바꿔 쓰십시오. Change these words into Korean.

1. worry ( )　　2. artist ( )

3. professor ( )　　4. secretary ( )

5. model ( )　　6. athlete ( )

7. need ( )　　8. blissful, happy ( )

9. to walk ( )　　10. to forget ( )

11. to be happy, glad ( )　　12. to be lonely ( )

13. to go down ( )　　14. to be bored ( )

15. to be entertaining ( )

[16~20] 그림을 보고 ( )에 알맞은 것을 고르십시오.
Look at the picture and choose the correct word.

16.

가 : 영화가 어때요?

나 : 아주 ( )어요/아요/여요.

❶ 기쁘다　　❷ 슬프다

❸ 아프다　　❹ 재미있다

17.

가 : 누구예요?

나 : ( ) 선생님이에요.

❶ 의사　　❷ 약사

❸ 간호사　　❹ 변호사

18.

가 : 집에서 학교까지 무엇으로 가요?

나 : (   )어서/아서/여서 가요.

❶ 걷다   ❷ 서다

❸ 앉다   ❹ 타다

19.

가 : 엄마, 조금만 기다려 주세요.

나 : 빨리 준비하고 (   )어라/아라/여라.

❶ 나가다   ❷ 나오다

❸ 들어가다   ❹ 들어오다

20.

가 : 한국 생활이 어때요?

나 : 아주 (   )어요/아요/여요.

❶ 놀라다   ❷ 외롭다

❸ 즐겁다   ❹ 심심하다

[21~30] 다음 문장을 읽고 알맞은 어휘를 골라 쓰십시오. 어휘는 한 번만 쓰십시오.
Read the following sentence and choose the right word. Use the words once.

관심	기분	기사	생각	배우
주부	물론	아마	눕다	뛰다
서다	슬프다	사랑하다	감사하다	걱정하다

21. (   ) 이번 시험은 어려울 거예요.

22. 이번 주말에는 뭘 할 (   )이에요/예요?

23. 시험을 잘 보지 못해서 (   )이/가 나빴다.

24. 이 책은 아이들은 (   ) 어른들도 좋아합니다.

25. 좀 피곤해서 잠깐 (   )어서/아서/여서 잤어요.

26. 지금까지 잘 가르쳐 주셔서 (   )습니다/ㅂ니다.

27. (   )은/는 사람이 생기면 꼭 가고 싶은 곳이 있어요.

28. 어머니는 일을 하지 않으세요. 가정(   )이에요/예요.

29. 이번 주말 드라마에 어느 (   )이/가 나온다고 해요?

30. 지각할까 봐 집에서 학교까지 (   )어서/아서/여서 갔어요.

[31~35] (   ) 안에 알맞은 것을 고르십시오. Choose the correct one.

31. 제 남자 친구의 (   )은/는 경찰이에요.

    ❶ 일   ❷ 직장   ❸ 직업   ❹ 공무원

32. 열심히 공부해서 의사가 (   )었어요/았아요/였어요.

    ❶ 되다   ❷ 보다   ❸ 아니다   ❹ 진찰하다

33. (   ) 아저씨, 육교 아래에서 세워 주세요.

    ❶ 기사   ❷ 기자   ❸ 선수   ❹ 의사

34. 늦어서 정말 (   )습니다/ㅂ니다.

    ❶ 괜찮다   ❷ 반갑다   ❸ 감사하다   ❹ 죄송하다

35. 순두부찌개가 맛있어서 날마다 먹었는데 이제는 (   )이/가 나요.

    ❶ 걱정   ❷ 기분   ❸ 싫증   ❹ 짜증

[36~40] 밑줄 친 부분과 반대되는 뜻을 가진 것을 고르십시오.

Choose the word that is the opposite of the underlined word.

36. **가 :** 선생님이 <u>앉아서</u> 말씀하세요?

    나 : 아니요, (   )어서/아서/여서 말씀하세요.

    ❶ 들다   ❷ 놓다   ❸ 서다   ❹ 세우다

37. **가 :** 한국음식을 <u>싫어해요</u>?

    나 : 아니요, 아주 (   )어요/아요/여요.

    ❶ 잊다   ❷ 놀라다   ❸ 걱정하다   ❹ 좋아하다

38. **가 :** 이 책이 <u>필요해요</u>?

    나 : 아니요, (   )어요/아요/여요.

    ❶ 없어지다   ❷ 준비하다   ❸ 필요없다   ❹ 심심하다

39. **가 :** 노래방은 위층으로 <u>올라가야</u> 해요?

    나 : 아니요, 아래층으로 (   )어야/아야/여야 해요.

    ❶ 나오다   ❷ 내려가다   ❸ 들어가다   ❹ 올라오다

40. **가** : 불고기가 <u>좋아</u>?

    나 : 아니, (   )어/아/여.

    ❶ 싫다   ❷ 나쁘다   ❸ 나오다   ❹ 내리다

[41~45] 밑줄 친 부분과 의미가 가장 가까운 것을 고르십시오.
Choose the word that is most similar to the underlined section.

41. **가** : 저 위에서 <u>노래 부르는 사람</u>이 누구예요?

    나 : 저 유명한 (   )도 모르세요?

    ❶ 배우   ❷ 기자   ❸ 가수   ❹ 연예인

42. **가** : <u>선생님</u>이 되고 싶어요?

    나 : 네, 제 꿈은 (   )이에요/예요.

    ❶의사   ❷ 교사   ❸ 화가   ❹ 간호사

43. **가** : 무슨 좋은 일이 있어요? <u>기분이 좋아 보여요.</u>

    나 : 네, 시험 점수가 좋아서 정말 (   )어요/아요/여요.

    ❶ 기쁘다   ❷ 슬프다   ❸ 심심하다   ❹ 재미있다

44. **가** : 집에만 있으니까 <u>심심하지요</u>?

    나 : 네, 좀 (   )어요/아요/여요.

    ❶ 무섭다   ❷ 싫어하다   ❸ 재미없다   ❹ 죄송하다

45. **가** : 이번 기회는 정말 <u>놓치지 마세요.</u>

    나 : 알았어요. 기회를 꼭 (   )을게요/ㄹ게요.

    ❶ 놓다   ❷ 안다   ❸ 입다   ❹ 잡다

[46~50] 밑줄 친 단어의 쓰임이 잘못된 것을 고르십시오. Choose the one that is incorrectly used.

46.   ❶ 시험 결과가 <u>나왔어요</u>?   (   )
   ❷ 올해 대학교에 <u>나왔어요</u>.
   ❸ 준비를 다 했어? 빨리 <u>나와</u>.
   ❹ 왜 이렇게 음식이 안 <u>나오지</u>?

47.   ❶ 기분이 좀 <u>괜찮아졌어요</u>?   (   )
   ❷ 이 요리는 맛이 <u>괜찮은데요</u>.
   ❸ <u>괜찮은</u> 사람이 있으면 소개해 주세요.
   ❹ 친구를 오랜만에 만나니까 정말 <u>괜찮았어요</u>.

48.   ❶ <u>즐거운</u> 영화를 보고 사람들이 울었어요.   (   )
   ❷ 혼자 생활하니까 가끔 <u>외로울</u> 때가 있어요.
   ❸ 제가 약속 시간에 늦어서 친구가 <u>화를</u> 냈어요.
   ❹ 오래 기다려도 친구가 오지 않으니까 <u>짜증이</u> 나요.

49.   ❶ 아이 손을 꼭 <u>잡고</u> 가세요.   (   )
   ❷ 버스에 자리가 없어서 <u>서서</u> 왔어요.
   ❸ 침대에 <u>누워서</u> 텔레비전을 보고 있어요.
   ❹ 오랜만에 친구를 만나서 두 팔로 꼭 <u>앉았다</u>.

50.   ❶ 저는 영화에 관심이 <u>많아요</u>.   (   )
   ❷ 저는 이 일에 관심이 별로 <u>없어요</u>.
   ❸ 이번 대회에 대한 사람들의 관심이 <u>작아요</u>.
   ❹ 학생들이 공부에 대해서 관심을 <u>갖지</u> 않아요.

일상 생활 I

07

Daily Life I

001
가다

[가다] 동사 to go

[Usage]   N에 가다

           N으로/로 가다

[Antonym] 오다 to come

[Example] 수업이 끝난 후에 어디에 가세요?

           Where do you go after you're finished with class?

           이 앞 사거리에서 오른쪽으로 가면 우체국이 있어요.

           If you go to the intersection and take a right there, there is a post office.

002
계획

[계획/계획] 명사 a plan

[Usage]   N 계획

           AV을/ㄹ 계획이다

[Expression] 계획하다 to plan

           계획을 세우다 to make a plan

[Example] 저는 이번 방학에 한국을 여행할 계획이에요.

           I plan on going to vacation to Korea during the break.

           언니는 시험 공부하기 전에 항상 계획을 세워요.

           My older sister always makes a plan before studying for a test.

003
꾸다

[꾸다] 동사 to dream

to see a dream, or to think of the good future that will come

[Usage]   N을/를 꾸다

[Expression] 꿈을 꾸다 to dream

[Example] 어제 무서운 꿈을 꿔서 잠을 잘 자지 못했다.

           Yesterday I had a bad dream so I didn't get much sleep.

           저는 어렸을 때 변호사가 되는 꿈을 꾸었어요.

           I dreamed of becoming a lawyer when I was younger.

004
놀다

[놀다] 동사 to play

to do something enjoyable and be happy spending the time, ㄹverb

[Usage]   N이/가 놀다

           N을/를 가지고 놀다

[Example] 우리 집에 놀러 오세요. Come to our house to play.

           제 동생은 공부는 하지 않고 놀기만 해요.

           My younger sibling does not study, instead he plays all the time.

005
뉴스

[뉴스] 명사 news

programs where they update on the latest news, this information can come from newspapers, broadcast stations and the internet

[Expression] 뉴스를 보다 to watch the news

뉴스를 듣다 to listen to the news

[Example] 요즘 사람들은 경제 뉴스에 관심이 많다.

People are interested in the economic part of the news.

아버지는 저녁 식사 후에 텔레비전 뉴스를 보십니다.

Father watches the news after dinner.

006
듣다

[듣따] 동사 1. to listen 2. to attend

1. people or animals being able to hear through the ear, ▭verb

[Usage] N을/를 듣다

[Expression] 음악을 듣다 to listen to music

소리를 듣다 to listen to the sound

[Example] 저는 학교에 갈 때 MP3(엠피스리)로 음악을 듣습니다.

On my way to school I listen to my MP3.

2. to pick a class and attend, ▭verb

[Usage] N을/를 듣다

[Expression] 수업을 듣다 to attend class

[Example] 김 선생님 수업은 재미있어서 학생들이 많이 듣습니다.

Teacher Kim's class is so fun that a lot of students take her class.

007
마시다

[마시다] 동사 to drink

[Usage] N을/를 마시다

[Expression] 물을 마시다 to drink water

술을 마시다 to drink alcohol

[Related word] 먹다 to eat

[Example] 한국에서는 회식을 할 때 자주 술을 마셔요.

In Korea whenever there is a get-together, there's alcohol.

중국 사람들은 차를 마시는 것을 좋아하지요?

Chinese people like to drink tea, is that correct?

008
만나다

[만나다] 동사 to meet

[Usage] N을/를 만나다

[Antonym] 헤어지다 to part, leave

[Example] 저는 이번 주말에 남자 친구를 만날 거예요.
I am going to meet my boyfriend this weekend.

오늘 저녁에 학교 앞에서 선생님을 만나기로 했다.
I will be meeting my teacher in front of the school tonight.

009
말하다

[말하다] 동사 to speak

[Usage] **N**을/를 말하다

[Synonym] 이야기하다 to tell a story

[Example] 힘든 일이 있으면 언제든지 나한테 말해.
If you ever have a difficult time, just call me.

내 생각을 많은 사람들 앞에서 말하는 것은 어려운 일이에요.
It is difficult to talk about what is on one's mind in front of many people.

010
먹다

[먹따] 동사 to eat

[Usage] **N**을/를 먹다

[Expression] 밥을 먹다 to eat rice

빵을 먹다 to eat bread

[Related word] 식사하다 to eat a meal

[Example] 아침을 먹고 학교에 갔어요. I ate breakfast and went to school.

오늘 점심에는 뭘 먹을까요? What should I eat for lunch?

011
면도

[면도] 명사 shave
to cut away hair on the face or on the body

[Expression] 면도기 razor

면도하다 to shave

[Example] 남편은 아침마다 면도기로 면도를 해요.
My husband shaves with his razor every morning.

면도를 할 때에는 피가 나지 않게 조심해야 해요.
Whenever you shave, you must be careful not to cut yourself.

012
목욕

[모굑] 명사 bathing
washing hair and body

[Expression] 목욕탕 bathing, shower room

목욕하다 to bathe

[Synonym] 샤워 shower

[Example] 목욕을 하니까 기분이 상쾌합니다. I feel refreshed after taking a shower.

우리 할아버지는 겨울에도 찬물로 목욕을 하십니다.
My grandfather washes in cold water even during the winter.

013

바르다

[바르다] 동사 to spread on, rub on

to paste on things such as medication, makeup, jam, butter and other things, 르 verb

[Usage] N을/를 바르다

[Example] 가려운 곳에 이 연고를 바르세요.
Rub the ointment on the itchy area of your body.

빵에 잼을 발라서 먹으면 맛있어요.
It is good if you spread the jam on the bread and eat it like that.

014

벗다

[벋따] 동사 to take off, undress

when one is taking off something from the body such as something one wore, used or placed on the body

[Usage] N을/를 벗다

[Expression] 옷을 벗다 to take off the clothing

신발을 벗다 to take off the shoes

모자를 벗다 to take off the hat

[Antonym] 입다 to put on(clothes)

신다 to put on (shoes)

쓰다¹ to put on(hat, glasses)

[Example] 수업 시간에는 모자를 벗으세요.
Please take off your hat during class.

한국에서는 집에 들어갈 때 신발을 벗습니다.
In Korea we take off our shoes when we go into the house.

015

보다

[보다] 동사 1. to see 2. to watch, look 3. to take 4. to taste

1. to realize or feel something when looking at an object

[Usage] N을/를 보다

[Example] 윗집에서 키우는 강아지를 본 적이 있어요?
Have you seen the puppy that lives in the house above?

2. to use the eye to appreciate, enjoy or read into an object

[Usage] N을/를 보다

[Expression] 책을 보다 to read the book

영화를 보다 to watch the movie

연극을 보다 to watch the play

신문을 보다 to read the newspaper

[Example] 저는 텔레비전을 보면서 밥을 먹어요. I watch television while eating.

3. to take the exam

[Usage]	<u>N</u>을/를 보다
[Expression]	시험을 보다 to take the exam
[Example]	오늘 시험을 잘 봤니? Did you take the exam with your best abilities?

4. to taste a little bit to check out the flavor of the food and to see if the saltiness is reasonable

[Usage]	<u>N</u>을/를 보다
[Expression]	간을 보다 to taste the saltiness
[Example]	간 좀 봐 줘. 맛이 어때? Taste the saltiness of the food. How does it taste?

016
살다

[살다] 동사 1. to be alive 2. to live somewhere

1. to maintain one's life, ㄹverb

[Usage]	<u>N</u>이/가 살다
[Antonym]	죽다 to die
[Example]	우리 할머니는 백 살까지 사셨다. My grandmother lived until she was 100 years old.

2. to live in an area, ㄹverb

[Usage]	<u>N</u>에 살다
	<u>N</u>에서 살다
[Example]	저는 서울에 살아요. I live in Seoul.

017
생활

[생활] 명사 life, living

a human's everyday routine

[Usage]	<u>N</u> 생활
[Expression]	생활비 living expenses
	학교생활 school life
	회사 생활 office life
	유학 생활 study abroad
	생활하다 to live everyday
[Example]	학교생활이 어때요? How's school life?
	유학 생활은 외롭기는 하지만 재미있었다. Studying abroad was lonely but it was a good experience.

018
샤워

[샤워] 명사 shower

[Expression]	샤워하다 to take a shower
[Synonym]	목욕 bath
[Example]	저는 피곤할 때 따뜻한 물로 샤워를 해요. I take a shower in hot water whenever I am tired.

지금 사는 하숙집은 샤워 시설이 잘 되어 있어서 마음에 들어요.
I like the boarding house that I live in because the shower facility is really great.

019
세수

[세수] 명사 face or hand wash

washing one's face or hands with water

[Expression] 세수하다 to wash one's hands or face

[Example] 오늘 아침에 늦게 일어나서 세수도 못 하고 출근했다.
I woke up late this morning and did not even have time to wash my face.

쌀을 씻은 물에 세수를 하면 피부가 좋아진다고 해요.
Apparently is it good to wash your face in water that has been used to rinse rice.

020
세우다

[세우다] 동사 1. to set up 2. to stop or park

1. to make up one's mind or to create a plan

[Usage] N을/를 세우다

[Expression] 계획을 세우다 to set up a plan

[Example] 휴가 계획을 세우셨어요?
Did you make plans for your vacation?

2. to halt something that has been moving

[Usage] N을/를 세우다

[Related word] 서다 to stop

[Example] 아저씨, 횡단보도 앞에서 세워 주세요.
Mister, please stop in front of the crosswalk.

021
쉬다

[쉬다] 동사 1. to rest, relax 2. to take a break

1. to be at a restful state to relieve tiredness

[Usage] N이/가 쉬다

[Example] 피곤하면 좀 쉬세요.
If you are tired, rest for a little bit.

2. to stop work or some sort of movement for a short time

[Usage] N이/가 쉬다

[Expression] 쉬는 날 resting day

쉬는 시간 break time

[Related word] 휴가 vacation

휴일 holiday

[Example] 오늘은 회사가 쉬는 날이어서 가족들과 동물원에 갔다.
My family and I went to the zoo because it was my day off from work.

022
신문
[신문] 명사 newspaper

[Expression]　신문사　newspaper publishing company

신문 기사　newspaper article

신문 한 부　a copy of the newspaper

신문을 보다　to read the newspaper

신문을 읽다　to read the newspaper

[Example]　아버지는 아침마다 신문을 보신다.
My father reads the newspaper every morning.

요즘은 인터넷에서도 신문을 볼 수 있어요.
These days you can view the newspaper through the internet.

023
쓰다²
[쓰다] 동사 to write

to use a brush, pen, pencil, or other writing utensil to write words or express one's thinking and put them into words, ─ verb

[Usage]　N을/를 쓰다

[Expression]　이름을 쓰다　to write one's name

일기를 쓰다　to write in one's diary

소설을 쓰다　to write a novel

편지를 쓰다　to write a letter

[Example]　책에 이름을 썼어요.　I wrote my name in the book.

저는 날마다 일기를 씁니다.　I write in my diary every day.

024
씻다
[씯따] 동사 to wash, cleanse

to wash dirty things with water and make it clean

[Usage]　N을/를 씻다

[Expression]　손을 씻다　to wash one's hand

얼굴을 씻다　to wash one's face

[Related word]　닦다　to cleanse

[Example]　밥을 먹기 전에 손을 씻어라.　Wash your hands before you eat.

과일은 깨끗한 물에 잘 씻어서 먹어야 해요.
You must wash the fruits cleanly before eating them.

025
일기
[일기] 명사 diary, journal

writing that is done every day and used to record one's feeling, thinking and other things that happened throughout the day

[Expression]　일기장　diary

일기를 쓰다　to write about one's day

[Example]	힘든 일이 있을 때 일기를 쓰면 기분이 좀 좋아진다.
	Whenever I have a bad day, I write in my diary and it makes me feel better.
	한국말로 일기를 쓰면 한국어 실력이 좋아질 거예요.
	If you write in Korean whenever you write in your diary, your Korean will improve.

026 일어나다

[이러나다] 동사 1. to get up, stand up 2. to wake up

1. to have laid down but to get up, to be sitting but changed to standing

[Usage]	N이/가 일어나다
[Antonym]	앉다 to sit
	눕다 to lay down
[Related word]	서다 to stand
[Example]	사장님이 오셔서 사람들이 모두 의자에서 일어났어요.
	Everyone stood up from their chair because the boss came inside.

2. to wake up from sleeping

[Usage]	N이/가 일어나다
[Related word]	자다 to sleep
[Example]	저는 아침 일찍 일어나는 것이 너무 힘들어요.
	It's hard for me to get up early.

027 하다

[하다] 동사 to do

this word is used when an animal or human does something

[Usage]	N을/를 하다
[Example]	제 취미는 운동을 하는 것입니다. *Exercising is my hobby.*
	아버지는 신문을 읽으시고 어머니는 요리를 하신다.
	My father reads the newspaper and my mother cooks.

028 화장

[화장] 명사 makeup

cosmetic used to put on the face so that one can become more pretty

[Expression]	화장품 cosmetic
	화장하다 to put on makeup
	화장을 지우다 to take off makeup
[Example]	화장을 지우니까 다른 사람 같아요.
	You look like a different person after taking off your makeup.
	지금 출발했으면 좋겠는데 아내가 아직도 화장을 해요.
	It would be nice to leave now, but my wife is still putting on makeup.

029
공중전화

[공중전화] 명사 phone booth

[Example] 전화를 하고 싶은데 이 근처에 공중전화가 있어요?
Is there a phone booth nearby? I need to make a call.

요즘 사람들이 휴대전화를 가지고 다녀서 공중전화를 쓰는 사람이 별로 없어요.
There are not many people who use phone booths these days because everyone has cell phones.

030
국제전화

[국쩨전화] 명사 international call

[Expression] 국제전화 요금 the fee for the international call

[Related word] 시외전화 call to the countryside

[Example] 중국에서 한국으로 국제전화를 걸면 얼마예요?
How much is it make a call from China to Korea?

인터넷에서 국제전화를 싸게 거는 방법을 찾아 보세요.
Look on the internet to see how we can call internationally for cheaper.

031
끊다

[끈타] 동사 1. to hang up 2. to quit or stop

1. to discontinue a phone call

[Usage] N을/를 끊다

[Expression] 전화를 끊다 to hang up the phone

[Example] 통화가 끝났으면 어서 끊어라.
If you are done talking, then hang up the phone.

2. to stop a habit or an action that has been going on for a while

[Usage] N을/를 끊다

[Expression] 술을 끊다 to stop drinking

담배를 끊다 to stop smoking

[Example] 이제부터 술을 끊기로 했어요. I have decided to stop drinking.

032
누르다

[누르다] 동사 to press or push

to push using pressure or press from top to bottom, or from outside to inside, 르 verb

[Usage] N을/를 누르다

[Example] 버스에서 내리려면 미리 벨을 눌러야 합니다.
If you want to get off the bus, you must press the button ahead of time.

전화번호를 잘못 누르신 것 같아요. 다시 확인해 보세요.
I think you've called the wrong number. Please check again.

033
답장

[답짱] 명사 reply letter
the letter written to reply to the letter that was received

[Expression] 답장하다 to reply
답장이 오다 to receive a reply letter
답장을 쓰다 to write a reply letter
답장을 보내다 to send a reply letter

[Example] 이메일을 받으면 빨리 답장을 보내 주세요.
If you receive an email, please reply quickly.

초등학교 때 친구에게서 편지가 와서 답장을 썼다.
I received a letter from my friend in elementary school so I sent a reply letter.

034
문자 메시지

[문짜메시지] 명사 text message
a short message sent through the cell phone

[Expression] 문자 메시지를 받다 to receive a text message
문자 메시지를 보내다 to send a text message
문자 메시지를 확인하다 to check a text message

[Example] 문자 메시지가 왔나 봐요. 확인해 보세요.
It seems you received a text message. Check to see if you received a message.

전화하지 않고 문자 메시지를 보내는 것이 편할 때가 많다.
There are many times where it is more comfortable to not call but just send a text message.

035
발신자

[발씬자] 명사 person who called or sent something
a person who called, sent a letter, package, or message

[Antonym] 수신자 the person who received the call or object

[Example] 발신자 번호를 보니까 광고 전화인 것 같아서 받지 않았어요.
The person who was calling me seemed to be an advertiser so I did not pick up the phone.

편지에 발신자 이름과 주소가 없어서 누가 보냈는지 모르겠어요.
I'm not sure who sent me this letter because there is no name or address on the letter.

036
버튼

[버튼] 명사 button

[Expression] 버튼을 누르다 to press the button

[Example] 전자사전을 켜려면 이 버튼을 누르세요.
If you want to turn on the electronic dictionary, press this button.

휴대전화 버튼이 고장이 나서 잘 눌러지지 않아요.
The buttons on my cell phone are broken, so it is hard to press.

165

037
번

[번] 명사 1. time   2. number

1. the order or number

[Usage]   **Num** 번

[Expression]   1(한)번 one time

                 10(열)번 ten times

[Example]   오늘 너한테 다섯 번이나 전화했는데 왜 전화를 안 받았어?
                 I called you five times today. Why didn't you pick up the phone?

2. something that corresponds to a number

[Usage]   **Num** 번

[Expression]   1(일)번 one

                 10(십)번 ten

[Related word]   번호 number

[Example]   선생님, 전화번호가 몇 번이에요? Teacher, what is your phone number?

038
별표

[별표] 명사 star, asterisk

the symbol that looks like a star (*)

[Related word]   우물 정자(#)   the pound key

[Example]   저는 공부할 때 중요한 내용에는 별표를 해요.
                 When I am studying, I label the important parts with an asterisk.

                 녹음이 끝난 후에는 별표나 우물정자를 누르십시오.
                 If you are done recording a message, press the star button or pound key.

039
부치다

[부치다] 동사 to send

to send a letter or package

[Usage]   **N**을/를 부치다

[Expression]   편지를 부치다   to send a letter

                 소포를 부치다   to send a package

[Synonym]   보내다 to mail or send

[Example]   편지를 부치려고 우체국에 가고 있어요.
                 I am going to the post office to send my letter.

                 빠른 우편으로 소포를 부치면 얼마나 걸려요?
                 How long does it take to send my package on the fastest post?

040
붙이다

[부치다] 동사 to glue, stick

(something, somewhere)to make it to where it does not come off

[Usage]   **N**에 **N**을/를 붙이다

[Related word]   붙다 to stick

[Example]　편지 봉투에 우표를 붙이세요.
Stick the postage stamp on the envelope of the letter.

한국어 단어를 적은 종이를 벽에 붙여 놓았어요.
I sticked the paper with the Korean vocabularies on the wall.

041
소포

[소포] 명사 package

a small packaged material that is sent through the post

[Expression]　소포를 받다　to receive a package
소포를 보내다　to send a package
소포를 부치다　to mail a package

[Example]　이 소포를 배편으로 보내려고 합니다.
I plan on sending this package by boat.

어머니에게서 겨울에 입을 옷이 들어 있는 소포를 받았다.
I received a package from my mother with clothes for the winter.

042
신호

[신호] 명사 signal

the sound that continuously rings until someone picks up

[Expression]　신호 소리　signal sound
신호가 가다　the signal is sent

[Example]　신호는 가는데 전화를 안 받아요.
The signal is going but no one is picking up.

핸드폰으로 전화를 걸면 신호가 가는 소리는 들리지 않고 음악
소리가 들릴 때도 있어요.
There are times when I hear music while it is sending the signal on the phone.

043
여보세요

[여보세요] 감탄사 hello?

a word used to address a person when picking up the phone or when trying to grab someone's attention, like at a restaurant or on the street

[Example]　여보세요, 전화 바꿨습니다.　Hello, I have picked up the phone.
여보세요, 여기 물 한 잔 좀 갖다 주세요.
Hello, please give me a glass of water.

044
연락

[열락] 명사 contact

being in touch with

[Expression]　연락처　contact information
연락하다　to contact

연락이 오다 to receive contact

연락을 받다 to receive contact

[Example] 어려운 일이 있으면 저에게 연락하세요.

If there is any problem, please call me.

죄송합니다. 요즘 너무 바빠서 자주 연락을 드리지 못했어요.

Sorry, I was so busy that I couldn't able to contact you often.

045
엽서

[엽써] 명사 postcard

[Expression] 그림엽서 picture postcard

엽서를 보내다 to send a postcard

[Related word] 편지 letter

[Example] 고향 친구에게서 엽서를 받았어요.

I received a postcard form my friends back home.

저는 여행을 가면 가족들에게 엽서로 소식을 전해요.

Whenever I go on vacation, I send my family postcards to tell them how I am doing.

046
우표

[우표] 명사 postage stamp

[Expression] 우표 한 장 one postage stamp

우표를 붙이다 to stick on a postage stamp

[Example] 여기에 우표를 붙이세요. Please put the postage stamp here.

제 취미는 우표 수집입니다. My hobby is to collect stamps.

047
인터넷

[인터넫] 명사 internet

[Expression] 인터넷 홈페이지 internet homepage

[Example] 인터넷으로 영화표를 예매했어요.

I reserved a movie ticket through the internet.

저는 집에 들어가면 먼저 컴퓨터를 켜고 인터넷을 합니다.

When I go home the first thing I do is turn on the computer and go on the internet.

048
전화

[전화] 명사 1. speaking through the telephone 2. telephone

1. using the telephone to speak to one another

[Expression] 전화번호 phone number

전화 한 통 one phone call

전화하다 to call

전화가 오다 to have an incoming call

전화를 끊다 to hang up the phone

[Related word] 통화 to call

[Example] 조금 전에 부모님께 전화가 왔어요.
My parents called a little while ago.

2. a machine that allows people to speak to each other

[Expression] 전화 한 대 one phone call

[Synonym] 전화기 telephone

[Related word] 핸드폰 cell phone

휴대전화 mobile phone

[Example] 전화가 고장이 났어요. The phone is broken.

049
전화번호

[전화번호] 명사 telephone number

[Related word] 지역 번호 area code

[Example] 전화번호 좀 가르쳐 주세요. Please tell me your telephone number.
친구의 전화번호가 바뀌어서 통화를 하지 못했어요.
My friends phone number changed so I wasn't able to talk to him.

050
주소

[주소] 명사 address

[Expression] 주소를 적다 to write down the address

주소를 찾다 to look for the address

[Example] 주소가 어떻게 되세요? What is your address?
여기에다가 받으실 분의 주소를 적으세요.
Please write the address of the person who will be receiving the package.

051
진동

[진동] 명사 vibration

one of the signals that a cell phone can give off to signal that there is an incoming call, the phone shakes

[Expression] 진동이 울리다 it is vibrating

진동으로 바꾸다 to change to vibrate

[Example] 휴대전화가 왔나 봐요. 진동이 울려요.
You must have a phone call. The phone is vibrating.

도서관에서는 휴대전화를 진동으로 해 놓아야 합니다.
You must put the phone on vibrate in the library.

052
켜다

[켜다] 동사 to turn on

to make a machine or electricity work

[Usage] N을/를 켜다

[Expression] 불을 켜다 to turn on the light

컴퓨터를 켜다 to turn on the computer

[Antonym] 끄다 to turn off

[Example]　　방이 어두워서 불을 켰다.　The room was dark so I turned on the light.

휴대전화를 켜니까 문자 메시지가 와 있었어요.
When I turned on my cell phone, I had a text message.

053

택배

[택빼] 명사 parcel (delivery) service

a service that delivers mail or postage material to the desired place

[Expression]　　택배 기사　parcel delivery man

택배 서비스　parcel delivery service

택배를 보내다　to send a parcel

[Related word]　배달　delivery

[Example]　　요즘은 우체국에도 택배 서비스가 있어서 편리해요.
These days there are delivery services at the post office, so it is very convenient.

물건을 소포로 보내면 며칠 걸리지만 택배로 보내면 내일 도착할 거예요.
If you send material to a regular delivery service, it will take a few days but if you send it through the parcel delivery service it will arrive by tomorrow.

054

통화

[통화] 명사 talking

talking on the phone

[Expression]　　통화료　phone bill

통화 중　in conversation on the phone

전화 통화　conversation on the phone

화상 통화　video telephone call

통화하다　to talk on the phone

[Example]　　지금 통화 중이니까 조금만 기다려 주세요.
I am talking on the phone right now, please wait a little bit.

요즘은 인터넷으로 화상 통화도 할 수 있어요.
These days you can video call on the internet.

055

편지

[편지] 명사 letter

[Expression]　　편지 한 통　one letter

편지를 쓰다　to write a letter

편지를 보내다　to send a letter

편지를 부치다　to send a letter

[Related word]　이메일　email

[Example]　　고향에 계신 부모님께 편지를 써서 보냈어요.
I wrote a letter and sent it to my parents in my hometown.

요즘 사람들은 편지를 많이 쓰지 않는 것 같아요. 인터넷으로
메일을 보내면 간단하니까요.
These days not many people write letters. It must be because email is simpler.

056
확인

[화긴] 명사 identifying, checking, making sure

checking if something is accurate confirming it

[Expression] 이메일 확인 email check

메시지 확인 message check

확인하다 to check

[Example] 제가 문자 메시지를 보냈는데 확인했어요?

I sent a text message. Did you check it?

출발하기 전에 빠진 물건이 없는지 짐을 다시 한 번 확인해 보세요.

Check all your material and make sure you have everything before we leave.

171

[1~15] 다음 단어를 한국어로 바꿔 쓰십시오. Change these words into Korean.

1. news ( ) 2. reply letter ( )

3. postage stamp ( ) 4. address ( )

5. bath ( ) 6. diary ( )

7. face or hand wash ( ) 8. to rest ( )

9. to write ( ) 10. to wash ( )

11. to turn on ( ) 12. to stop, quit ( )

13. to make stand ( ) 14. to mail ( )

15. to stick ( )

[16~20] 그림을 보고 ( )에 알맞은 것을 고르십시오.

Look at the picture and choose the correct word.

16.

가 : 아침에 일어나면 제일 먼저 뭘 해요?

나 : 제일 먼저 ( )부터 해요.

❶ 목욕 ❷ 면도

❸ 샤워 ❹ 세수

17.

우편창구

가 : 이 ( )을/를 미국에 보내고 싶어요.
   얼마예요?

나 : 2kg이군요. 2만 원입니다.

❶ 소포 ❷ 엽서

❸ 편지 ❹ 문자메시지

18.

가 : 동생이 뭘 해요?

나 : 거실에서 텔레비전을 (   )고 있어요.

❶ 놀다   ❷ 듣다
❸ 보다   ❹ 하다

19.

가 : 지금 뭘 하고 있어요?

나 : (   )을/를 하고 있어요.

❶ 노래   ❷ 전화
❸ 운동   ❹ 인터넷

20.

가 : 뭘 해요?

나 : 한국말을 (   )고 있어요.

❶ 듣다   ❷ 보다
❸ 쓰다   ❹ 하다

[21~30] 다음 문장을 읽고 알맞은 어휘를 골라 쓰십시오. 어휘는 한 번만 쓰십시오.
Read the following sentence and choose the right word. Use the words once.

번	뉴스	진동	생활	인터넷
국제전화	놀다	쉬다	듣다	누르다
바르다	세우다	연락하다	일어나다	여보세요

21. 초등학교 때 친구와 아직도 (   )고 지내요.

22. 아저씨, 저 학교 앞에서 (   )어/아/여 주세요.

23. 저는 아침에 (   )으면/면 제일 먼저 이를 닦아요.

24. 요즘 사람들이 많이 (   )는/은/는 노래가 뭐예요?

25. 한국 아파트에 가려면 몇 (   )버스를 타야 해요?

26. 아이들이 공원에서 공을 가지고 재미있게 (   )고 있어요.

27. 세수를 한 후에 얼굴에 로션을 (   )었어요/았어요/였어요.

28. 전화번호를 잘못 (   )어서/아서/여서 다른 곳으로 전화했어요.

29. 저는 지금 한국에서 공부하고 있어서 중국에 계신 부모님과 일주일에 한 번 (   )
을/를 해요.

30. 그 사람은 한국에 온 지 6개월 되었는데 한국 음식도 좋아하고 한국 친구들도 많이 사귀어서
한국 (   )이/가 아주 재미있다고 해요.

[31~35] (   ) 안에 알맞은 것을 고르십시오. Choose the correct one.

31. 도서관에서는 전화를 하면 안 되니까 휴대전화를 (   )어/아/여 놓으세요.

   ❶ 끄다   ❷ 끊다   ❸ 켜다   ❹ 누르다

32. 편지를 보낼 때에는 우표를 (   )어야/아야/여야 해요.

   ❶ 쓰다   ❷ 보내다   ❸ 부치다   ❹ 붙이다

33. 사람들은 1월 1일이 되면 1년 (   )을/를 세웁니다.

   ❶ 계획   ❷ 생활   ❸ 일기   ❹ 확인

34. 집에 돌아오면 제일 먼저 손을 (   )으세요/세요.

   ❶ 쉬다   ❷ 쓰다   ❸ 씻다   ❹ 바르다

35. 어제 밤에 꿈을 (   )었는데/았는데/였는데 너무 무서웠어요.

   ❶ 놀다   ❷ 꾸다   ❸ 보다   ❹ 살다

[36~40] 밑줄 친 부분과 반대되는 뜻을 가진 것을 고르십시오.
Choose the word that is the opposite of the underlined word.

36. **가** : 휴대전화를 <u>껐어요</u>?
   나 : 아니요, 조금 전에 (   )었는데요/았는데요/였는데요.

   ❶ 꾸다   ❷ 켜다   ❸ 끊다   ❹ 쓰다

37. **가** : 언제 한국에 <u>올</u> 거예요?
   나 : 다음 달에 한국에 (   )을/ㄹ 거예요.

   ❶ 가다   ❷ 보다   ❸ 쉬다   ❹ 하다

38. **가** : 주말에 친구를 <u>만나서</u> 뭘 했어요?
   나 : 영화를 보고 저녁을 먹었어요. 그리고 8시쯤에 (   )었어요/았어요/였어요.

   ❶ 놀다   ❷ 쉬다   ❸ 공부하다   ❹ 헤어지다

39. **가** : 한국에서는 신발을 <u>신고</u> 방에 들어가도 돼요?
   나 : 아니요, (   )어야/아야/여야 해요.

   ❶ 들다   ❷ 먹다   ❸ 벗다   ❹ 씻다

40. **가 :** 그 호랑이는 몇 살까지 살았어요?

    나 : 15살까지요. 작년에 (   )었어요/았어요/였어요.

    ❶ 가다   ❷ 놀다   ❸ 쉬다   ❹ 죽다

[41~45] 밑줄 친 부분과 의미가 가장 가까운 것을 고르십시오.
Choose the word that is most similar to the underlined section.

41. **가 :** 지금 뭘 <u>읽고</u> 있어요?

    나 : 소설책을 (   )고 있어요.

    ❶ 보다   ❷ 듣다   ❸ 놀다   ❹ 하다

42. **가 :** 아침에 뭘 <u>드세요</u>?

    나 : 시간이 없어서 보통 주스를 한 잔 (   )어요/아요/여요.

    ❶ 듣다   ❷ 보다   ❸ 쓰다   ❹ 마시다

43. **가 :** 우체국에 가서 뭘 <u>부쳤어요</u>?

    나 : 유학을 간 동생에게 겨울에 입을 옷을 (   )었어요/았어요/였어요.

    ❶ 누르다   ❷ 바르다   ❸ 보내다   ❹ 세우다

44. **가 :** 이건 비밀이니까 다른 사람에게 <u>이야기하지</u> 마세요.

    나 : 걱정하지 마세요. 다른 사람에게 (   )지 않을게요.

    ❶ 만나다   ❷ 말하다   ❸ 연락하다   ❹ 확인하다

45. **가 :** 누구와 <u>전화했어요</u>?

    나 : 고향에 계신 어머니와 (   )었어요/았어요/였어요.

    ❶ 계획하다   ❷ 생활하다   ❸ 통화하다   ❹ 확인하다

[46~50] 밑줄 친 단어의 쓰임이 잘못된 것을 고르십시오. Choose the one that is incorrectly used.

46. ❶ 문자메시지를 <u>썼어요</u>?   (   )
    ❷ 편지를 받으면 답장을 <u>쓰세요</u>.
    ❸ 저는 자기 전에 항상 일기를 <u>써요</u>.
    ❹ 요즘 사람들은 편지를 많이 <u>쓰지</u> 않아요.

47. ❶ 신발을 <u>벗고</u> 들어가세요.   (   )
    ❷ 손을 씻으려고 반지를 <u>벗었다</u>.
    ❸ 모자를 <u>벗어서</u> 책상 위에 놓았어요.
    ❹ 옷을 <u>벗고</u> 수영복으로 갈아입으세요.

48. ❶ 샤워를 하니까 참 <u>상쾌해요</u>.   (   )
    ❷ 어제 밤에 무슨 꿈을 <u>꿨어요</u>?
    ❸ 초등학생은 화장을 <u>그리면</u> 안 됩니다.
    ❹ 저는 저녁 식사를 하면서 뉴스를 <u>봐요</u>.

49. ❶ 집에 오면 인터넷을 <u>놀아요</u>.   (   )
    ❷ 그 분은 바빠서 통화를 <u>하기가</u> 어려워요.
    ❸ 목욕을 한 후에 문자메시지를 <u>확인했어요</u>.
    ❹ 중학교 때 친구에게서 연락을 <u>받고</u> 정말 반가웠어요.

50. ❶ 샤워를 한 후에 로션을 <u>발랐어요</u>.   (   )
    ❷ 남자들은 아침마다 면도를 <u>벗어요</u>.
    ❸ 건강에 나쁘니까 담배를 <u>끊으세요</u>.
    ❹ 집에 오면 손을 깨끗하게 <u>씻어야지</u>.

일상 생활 Ⅱ

08

Daily Life Ⅱ

001
같이

[가치] 부사 together

[Usage]	**N**하고 같이
	N과/와 같이
[Expression]	친구와 같이 together with friends
	동생하고 같이 with my younger sibling
[Synonym]	함께 along with
[Example]	저는 일요일마다 친구와 같이 등산을 해요.
	Every Sunday my friend and I go hiking together.
	주말에 부산에 가려고 하는데 너도 같이 갈래?
	I plan on going to Busan this weekend. Would you like to go together?

002
기다리다

[기다리다] 동사 to wait

to wait for the right time for a certain job or for a right person

[Usage]	**N**을/를 기다리다
[Expression]	친구를 기다리다 to wait for a friend
	결과를 기다리다 to wait for the results
[Example]	한 시간 동안 기다렸는데 왜 전화하지 않았어요?
	I waited for an hour. Why didn't you call?
	출퇴근 시간에는 지하철역에 지하철을 타려고 기다리는 사람들이 많아요.
	During rush hour there are many people waiting to take the subway.

003
꼭

[꼭] 부사 surely, certainly, always

no matter what happens, it will be done

[Example]	약속은 꼭 지켜야 해요.
	You must always keep your promises.
	힘든 일이 있으면 나한테 꼭 전화해.
	If you ever have trouble, always call me.

004
데이트

[데이트] 명사 date

when two people who like each other meet

[Expression]	데이트를 하다 to date
	데이트를 신청하다 to ask out for date
[Related word]	애인 lover
	남자 친구 boyfriend

여자 친구 girlfriend

[Example] 주말에 남자 친구와 데이트를 했어요.
I went on a date with my boyfriend last weekend.

데이트를 할 때 보통 어디에서 만나요?
When you go on a date where do you usually meet?

005
미루다

[미루다] 동사 to delay

to put back the date for something you are about to do

[Usage] **N**을/를 미루다

[Expression] 일을 미루다 to delay work

약속을 미루다 to delay a promise

[Related word] 연기하다² to postpone

[Example] 오늘 일을 내일로 미루지 마세요. Don't delay today's work for tomorrow.

회의 시간을 한 시간 뒤로 미룰 수 있을까요?
Can we postpone the meeting an hour?

006
생기다

[생기다] 동사 to be formed, or happen

something that wasn't there but is there now

[Usage] **N**이/가 생기다

[Expression] 친구가 생기다 to make a friend

약속이 생기다 to make a promise

[Related word] 나다 to happen, occur

있다 to be

[Example] 학교 근처에 새로 생긴 식당에 가 봤어요?
Have you been to the new restaurant near school?

외국인 친구가 많이 생겨서 유학생활이 재미있어요.
I made a lot of international friends, so I like my time studying abroad.

007
선물

[선물] 명사 present

[Usage] **N** 선물

[Expression] 생일 선물 birthday present

선물하다 to give a present

선물을 받다 to receive a present

선물을 주다 to present a gift

[Example] 남자 친구에게서 꽃다발을 선물로 받았어요.
I received flowers as a present from my boyfriend.

어머니 생신인데 어떤 선물을 드리면 좋을까요?
It's my mother's birthday, so what do you think I should buy her?

008
선약

[서냑] 명사 previous engagement
a promise that was made earlier

[Expression] 선약이 있다 I have a previous engagement

[Example] 죄송합니다. 선약이 있어서 반 모임에 갈 수 없을 것 같아요.
Sorry. I won't be able to attend the class meeting because I have a previous engagement.

내일 반 친구들과 만나려고 했는데 친구 한 명이 선약이 있대요.
다음 주로 미루어야 할 것 같아요.
I was going to meet my friends from class tomorrow, but one of my friends has a previous engagement. I will have to postpone it for next week.

009
송별회

[송별회] 명사 farewell party
a party opened for someone who is leaving, a meeting for other people to say their goodbyes and to hope for a great future for that person

[Expression] 송별회를 열다 to give a farewell party
송별회를 하다 to have a farewell party

[Related word] 환송회 farewell party
환영회 welcoming party

[Example] 오늘 저녁에 고향으로 돌아가는 친구의 송별회가 있습니다.
Tonight there is a farewell party for my friend who is returning to her hometown.

친구들이 저를 위해 송별회를 열어 주어서 정말 고마웠어요.
My friends opened a farewell party for me and I was so thankful.

010
안녕

[안녕] 명사 stability (used to say hello, and bye)
no worries and no problems, everything is peaceful

[Expression] 안녕히 to be peaceful
안녕하다 to be stable

[Example] 선생님, 안녕하세요? Teacher, is everything ok?
안녕! 주말 잘 보냈니? Hello! Did you have a good weekend?

011
약속

[약쏙] 명사 promise

[Expression] 약속이 있다 to have a promise
약속하다 to promise
약속을 지키다 to keep a promise
약속을 취소하다 to cancel a promise

[Example]　약속 시간에 늦으면 안 됩니다. you can't be late for a promised meeting.
친구하고 커피숍에서 만나기로 약속했어요.
I promised my friend I would meet her at the coffee shop.

012
이야기

[이야기] 명사 conversation, story

[Usage]　**DV**은/ㄴ 이야기

[Expression]　슬픈 이야기 a sad story
재미있는 이야기 a fun story
이야기하다 to tell a story
이야기를 나누다 to share a story

[Example]　내가 재미있는 이야기를 해 줄까? Shall I tell you a funny story?
이건 비밀이니까 다른 사람에게 이야기하지 마세요.
This is a secret, so don't tell others this story.

013
인사

[인사] 명사 greeting

a first time meeting that requires one's name and short introduction, or a respectful way of showing respect through words or action when meeting someone or saying goodbye to someone

[Expression]　인사하다 to greet
인사를 받다 to receive greeting
인사를 드리다 to greet an elder

[Example]　1(일)월 1(일)일에는 친척 어른들께 새해 인사를 드리러 다닙니다.
On January 1st we go around and greet the elders for the new year.

한국에서 처음 만나는 사람과 인사할 때에는 "처음 뵙겠습니다."
라고 해요.
Whenever you meet someone for the first time in Korea, you say "how do you do?".

014
지키다

[지키다] 동사 to obey, to follow, to keep

to follow the rules, promises, laws, and etiquettes without changing or forgetting about what they are

[Usage]　**N**을/를 지키다

[Expression]　시간을 지키다 to be on time
약속을 지키다 to keep the promise
예의를 지키다 to follow the etiquette

[Related word]　어기다 to disobey

[Example]　교실에서 지켜야 하는 규칙은 뭐예요?
What are the rules that I need to follow in the classroom?

183

아주 친한 친구 사이에서도 예의를 지켜야 해요.
You must have respect for even your closest friends.

015
초대

[초대] 명사 invitation

to give people an announcement to attend a party or meeting

[Expression] 초대권 invitation ticket

초대장 invitation card

초대하다 to invite

초대를 받다 to get invited

[Example] 생일이어서 친구들을 집에 초대했어요.
It was my birthday, so I invited my friends to my house.

한국에서는 이사를 한 후에 친한 사람들을 집에 초대한다.
In Korea after you have moved, you invite close friends to your new home.

016
축하

[추카] 명사 celebration

to be happy about someone's good work or success

[Expression] 축하하다 to celebrate

[Example] 가족들이 졸업을 축하해 줬어요.
My family congratulated me for my graduation.

저희의 결혼을 축하해 주기 위해 이렇게 와 주셔서 감사합니다.
Thank you for coming and congratulating us for our wedding.

017
취소

[취소] 명사 cancel

to cancel a promise, reservation or something one said

[Expression] 취소하다 to cancel

취소되다 to become cancelled

[Example] 비행기 표를 취소했어요. I canceled my airplane ticket.

비가 와서 공연이 취소되었습니다.
The concert got cancelled because of the rain.

018
파티

[파티] 명사 party

[Expression] 생일 파티 birthday party

파티가 있다 there is a party

파티를 열다 to open a party

파티를 하다 to have a party

[Synonym] 잔치 feast

[Example] 내 생일 파티에 반 친구들을 초대했어요.
I invited my class friends to my birthday party.

졸업 파티에는 선생님들도 오시니까 꼭 오십시오.
Please come to my graduation party. My teachers are coming too, so please come.

019
환영하다

[화녕하다] 동사 to welcome

to greet someone who is new or coming in to do something and doing it with a warm gesture

[Usage] N을/를 환영하다

[Example] 어서 오세요. 환영합니다. Welcome. Please come inside.
입국하는 선수들을 환영하려고 온 사람들 때문에 공항이 아주 복잡하다.
The airport is so crowded because there are many people who want to welcome the athletes on coming back home.

08-2 | 쇼핑

020
값

[갑] 명사 price

[Expression] 값이 싸다 the price is low
값이 비싸다 the price is high
값이 내리다 the price has decreased
값이 오르다 the price has risen
값을 깎다 to take off from the original price

[Synonym] 가격 price

[Example] 요즘 과일 값이 많이 올랐다. The price of fruits has risen a lot.
시장은 값도 싸고 가끔 값을 깎을 수도 있어서 좋아요.
At the market the prices are cheaper and I can also take off from the regular price so I like going there.

021
거스름돈

[거스름똔] 명사 change
the remaining money given to a person after paying the amount

[Related word] 잔돈 change
[Example] 만 원을 내고 이천 원을 거스름돈으로 받았어요.
I paid 10,000won and got back 2,000won for change.

택시 아저씨가 계산을 잘못해서 거스름돈을 조금 줬어요.
The taxi driver calculated the money wrong and gave me a small amount of change.

022
계산하다

[계산하다/계산하다] 동사 1. to calculate 2. to pay
1. to add, subtract, multiply or divide numbers

[Usage] N을/를 계산하다
[Expression] 돈을 계산하다 to count money
[Related word] 계산기 calculator
[Example] 수학 문제를 풀 때에는 정확하게 계산해야 해요.
When you solve math problems, you should calculate exactly.

2. to pay for objects or after you have eaten

[Usage] N을/를 계산하다
N으로/로 계산하다
[Expression] 식사비를 계산하다 to pay the meal
현금으로 계산하다 to pay with cash
[Example] 카드로 계산하시겠어요? 현금으로 계산하시겠어요?
Would you like to pay with card? Or with cash?

023
고르다

[고르다] 동사 to choose
to pick one out of many, 르 verb

[Usage] N을/를 고르다
[Synonym] 선택하다 to make a selection
[Example] 알맞은 대답을 고르십시오. Choose the correct answer.
마음에 드는 것을 하나 골라 봐. Choose one that you like.

024
교환하다

[교환하다] 동사 to exchange
to change for something else

[Usage] (N을/를) N으로/로 교환하다
[Synonym] 바꾸다 to change
[Example] 어제 산 옷이 작아서 큰 치수로 교환했어요.
The clothes I bought yesterday were a bit small, so I exchanged them for bigger ones.

마음에 안 들면 1(일)주일 안에 교환할 수 있습니다.
If you don't like it, you have one week to exchange the clothing.

025
깎다

[깍따] **동사** to cut down the price

to lower the price

[Usage] **N**을/를 깎다

[Expression] 값을 깎다 to cut down the price

[Example] 값이 비싸요. 좀 깎아 주세요.

The price is too high. Please cut the price for me.

어머니는 수박 값을 삼천 원이나 깎으셨다.

My mother cut 3,000 won off of the watermelon.

026
돈

[돈] **명사** money

[Expression] 돈이 많다 to have a lot of money

돈을 벌다 to make money

돈을 쓰다 to spend money

돈을 모으다 to save money

돈을 빌리다 to borrow money

[Related word] 동전 coins

수표 checks

[Example] 아르바이트를 해서 돈을 모았어요.

I worked part time and made money.

돈은 생활에 꼭 필요한 것이지만 가장 중요한 것은 아니다.

Money is very important for everyday life, but it is not the most important thing.

027
무료

[무료] **명사** free of charge

something that doesn't have to be paid for

[Synonym] 공짜 free

[Antonym] 유료 charged

[Example] 오늘은 무료로 박물관을 관람할 수 있다고 합니다.

You can go into the museum for free today and look at everything in the museum.

저쪽에서 무료로 음료수를 주는 행사를 하고 있어요.

There is an event over there and you can get drinks for free.

028
무엇

[무얻] **대명사** something, anything

something that is unknown or asking about something, when speaking we use '뭐'

[Related word] 무슨 what, what sort of

[Example] 이것을 한국말로 뭐라고 해요? What do you call this in Korean?

내 취미는 사진 찍기인데 넌 취미가 뭐야?
My hobby is taking pictures, what is your hobby?

029
바꾸다

[바꾸다] 동사 to switch, change, alter

to change something into something else, or to replace something

[Usage] <u>N</u>을/를 바꾸다

<u>N</u>으로/로 바꾸다

[Expression] 계획을 바꾸다 to change plans

자리를 바꾸다 to change seats

다른 것으로 바꾸다 to change for something else

[Synonym] 교환하다 to exchange

[Example] 습관을 바꾸는 것은 정말 어려운 일이에요.
It is really hard to change your habits.

옷이 마음에 들지 않으면 다른 옷으로 바꿔도 돼요.
If you don't like the clothing, you can change it for something else.

030
보이다

[보이다] 동사 to be seen

to recognize target with the eyes and to recognize it

[Usage] <u>N</u>이/가 보이다

[Expression] 보여 주다 to show

[Related word] 보다 to see

[Example] 우리 집에서 한강이 보여요. Han river can be seen from my house.
뒤에 앉으면 칠판 글씨가 잘 안 보이니까 앞에 앉으세요.
If you sit in the back you won't be able to see the writing on the blackboard, so move to the front.

031
사다

[사다] 동사 to buy

to make something one's own by paying the price of the object

[Usage] <u>N</u>을/를 사다

[Antonym] 팔다 to sell

[Example] 저는 멋있는 자동차를 사고 싶어요. I want to buy a cool car.
슈퍼마켓에서 채소를 세일해서 싸게 샀어요.
The vegetables were on sale at the supermarket so I bought some for cheap.

032
상품

[상품] 명사 product, merchandise

objects that you buy and sell

[Expression] 상품권 gift certificate

신상품 new product

[Example] 신상품이 나왔는데 보여드릴까요?
A new product has come out. Shall I show you?

백화점에는 여러 가지 상품이 있어서 구경하는 것이 재미있어요.
There are many different products in the shopping mall, so it's nice to look around.

033
손님

[손님] 명사 customer, guest

[Related word] 주인 owner

고객 customer

[Example] 식당에 항상 손님이 많네요.
There are always many customers at the restaurant.

오늘 집에 손님이 오시니까 집을 깨끗하게 청소해야 한다.
There will be guests coming to our home so we need to clean the house.

034
쇼핑

[쇼핑] 명사 shopping

[Expression] 인터넷 쇼핑 internet shopping

쇼핑하다 to shop

[Example] 수업이 끝난 후에 친구와 쇼핑을 했어요.
After class I went shopping with my friend.

백화점 세일 기간에는 쇼핑을 하려고 백화점에 오는 사람들이 많습니다.
There are many people coming to shop during the sale season.

035
신용카드

[시뇽카드] 명사 credit card

[Expression] 신용카드로 계산하다 to pay with a credit card

[Example] 신용카드가 있으면 현금이 없어도 물건을 살 수 있어서 아주 편리해요.
Credit card is really convenient because I can pay for things even when I don't have cash.

잃어버린 지갑을 찾았는데 신분증과 신용카드가 그대로 있어서 다행이었다.
I found my wallet that I lost and I was so happy that my ID card and credit card were still in there.

036
싸다

[싸다] 형용사 to be cheap

to have a low price

[Usage] N이/가 싸다

[Expression] 값이 싸다 the price is low

물건이 싸다 the merchandise is cheap

[Antonym] 비싸다 to be expensive

[Example] 어디에 가면 옷을 싸게 살 수 있어요?
Where can I go to buy clothes for cheap?

학생 식당은 음식 값이 싸고 맛있어서 학생들이 좋아해요.
The food at the students restaurant is cheap and delicious, so the students like it a lot.

037
쓰다³

[쓰다] 동사 to use

to use something, 으 verb

[Usage] N을/를 쓰다

[Expression] 물건을 쓰다 to use a product

[Synoynm] 사용하다 to use

[Example] 로봇 청소기를 써 본 적이 있어요?
Have you ever used a robot vacuum cleaner?

한국 사람들은 식사할 때 숟가락과 젓가락을 씁니다.
Korean people use spoon and chopsticks when they eat.

038
어느

[어느] 관형사 which

a word used to pick out one out of many

[Usage] 어느 N

[Related word] 무슨 what, what kind of

[Example] 어느 나라에서 오셨어요? What country are you from?
두 개 중에서 어느 것이 더 마음에 들어요?
Which one do you like more out of the two?

039
어울리다

[어울리다] 동사 to harmonize with, to match, goes well with

things that go well together and look natural

[Usage] N에 어울리다
N에게 어울리다

[Example] 청바지에는 흰 티셔츠가 잘 어울려요.
White t-shirts looks good with jeans.

이 원피스는 제 딸아이에게 잘 어울릴 것 같아요.
This one-piece will look good on my daughter.

040
얼마

[얼마] 명사 how much

a price or amount that one doesn't know of, when wanting to know the degree of something

[Example] 한국어 교과서가 얼마예요? How much is the Korean textbook?

하숙비는 한 달에 얼마입니까?
How much is the boarding expenses per month?

041
점원

[점원] **명사** clerk

a person who works at a store

[Related word] 주인 owner

[Example] 저는 서점에서 점원으로 일한 적이 있어요.
I used to work as a clerk at the bookstore.

가게의 점원이 모두 친절해서 기분이 좋았다.
All the clerks at the store were very friendly, so I felt happy after leaving the store.

042
주다

[주다] **동사** to give

to let someone have something

[Usage] N을/를 주다

[Antonym] 받다 to receive

[Example] 생일 선물로 무엇을 줬어요? What did you give as a birthday present?
동생에게 주려고 CD를 샀다. I bought a CD for my younger sibling.

043
짜리

[짜리] **접미사** worth, value

(used after words that address number of, amount, or price) a suffix that adds value to the amount, number of or price

[Usage] N짜리

[Expression] 세 살짜리 3 years old
두 개짜리 2 piece
천 원짜리 worth 1,000won
오백 원짜리 worth 500won

[Example] 미안한데 백 원짜리 동전이 있어?
I'm sorry but do you have 100 won coin?

선생님에게 열 살짜리 딸이 있는데 귀엽고 똑똑해요.
My teacher has a daughter that is 10 years old and she is cute and intelligent.

044
치수

[치수] **명사** size, measurement

the size of an object

[Usage] N 치수

[Expression] 옷 치수 the measurment on clothing
신발 치수 the size of the shoe
치수가 크다 the size is too big
치수가 맞다 the size is just right

[Related word] 사이즈 size

[Example] 신발 치수가 어떻게 되세요? What is your shoe size?

선물로 받은 옷이 치수가 커서 입을 수 없어요.

The clothing that I received as a present is too big, so I cannot wear the clothing.

045
현금

[현금] 명사 cash

[Expression] 현금영수증 receipt for cash

현금을 쓰다 to use cash

[Related word] 수표 check

신용카드 credit card

[Example] 여행을 갈 때 현금을 많이 가지고 가면 위험해요.

Whenever you go on vacation, it is dangerous to carry a lot of cash.

돈을 얼마나 쓰는지 정확하게 알기 위해서는 현금을 사용하는 것이 좋아요.

In order to know exactly how much you spend, you should use cash.

[1~15] 다음 단어를 한국어로 바꿔 쓰십시오. Change these words into Korean.

1. money ( )   2. surely, certainly ( )

3. product, goods ( )   4. previous engagement ( )

5. customer ( )   6. clerk ( )

7. party ( )   8. cash ( )

9. invitation ( )   10. cancel ( )

11. to welcome ( )   12. story ( )

13. to give ( )   14. to buy ( )

15. to be seen ( )

[16~20] 그림을 보고 ( )에 알맞은 것을 고르십시오.
Look at the picture and choose the correct word.

16.

가 : 주말에 뭘 했어요?

나 : 백화점에서 ( )을/를 했어요.

❶ 쇼핑   ❷ 파티

❸ 데이트   ❹ 송별회

17.

가 : 현금으로 계산하시겠어요?

나 : 아니요, ( )으로/로 계산할게요.

❶ 값   ❷ 돈

❸ 거스름돈   ❹ 신용카드

18.

가 : 뭘 사러 가요?

나 : 친구 생일이어서 (   )을/를 사러 가요.

❶ 상품   ❷ 선물

❸ 점원   ❹ 짜리

19.

가 : 안녕하세요, 아주머니.

나 : 그래, 영수구나! 영수는 (   )을/를
       참 잘하는구나!

❶ 꼭   ❷ 안녕

❸ 인사   ❹ 이야기

20.

가 : 뭘 하고 있어요?

나 : (   )을/를 하고 있어요.

❶ 약속   ❷ 통화

❸ 환영   ❹ 데이트

[21~30] 다음 문장을 읽고 알맞은 어휘를 골라 쓰십시오. 어휘는 한 번만 쓰십시오.
Read the following sentence and choose the right word. Use the words once.

꼭	같이	어느	얼마	무엇
짜리	데이트	송별회	깎다	싸다
쓰다	미루다	바꾸다	어기다	기다리다

21. (　　　　　) 나라에 가 봤어요?

22. 김치는 (　　　　　)으로/로 만들어요?

23. 아주머니, 이 가방 (　　　　　)이에요/예요?

24. 이 볼펜은 500원(　　　　　)인데 아주 좋아요.

25. 주말에 친구와 (　　　　　) 여행을 갔다가 왔다.

26. 아저씨, 너무 비싸요. 조금 (　　　　　)어/아/여 주세요.

27. 유학을 끝내고 고향으로 돌아가는 친구의 (　　　　　)을/를 했다.

28. 색깔이 마음에 안 들어서 다른 색깔로 (　　　　　)었다/았다/였다.

29. 미안해, 약속 시간을 3시에서 7시로 (　　　　　)어야/아야/여야 할 것 같아.

30. 시장 물건은 (　　　　　)어서/아서/여서 좋지만 가끔 질이 나쁜 것도 있어요.

[31~35] (　　　) 안에 알맞은 것을 고르십시오. Choose the correct one.

31. 오랜만에 중학교 동창을 만나서 커피숍에서 재미있게 (　　　　)을/를 했어요.

　❶ 운동　　　❷ 예약　　　❸ 송별회　　　❹ 이야기

32. 옷이 마음에 들지 않아서 다른 것으로 (　　　　)으러/러 왔어요.

　❶ 깎다　　　❷ 사다　　　❸ 교환하다　　　❹ 쇼핑하다

33. 음료수가 1,500원이어서 2,000원을 내고 500원을(   )으로/로 받았어요.

   ❶ 값   ❷ 현금   ❸ 거스름돈   ❹ 신용카드

34. 그 치마와 구두가 잘 (   )어요/아요/여요.

   ❶ 깎다   ❷ 고르다   ❸ 바꾸다   ❹ 어울리다

35. 친구가 약속 시간에 늦어서 1시간 동안 친구를 (   )었어요/았어요/였어요.

   ❶ 미루다   ❷ 보이다   ❸ 어기다   ❹ 기다리다

[36~40] 밑줄 친 부분과 반대되는 뜻을 가진 것을 고르십시오.

Choose the word that is the opposite of the underlined word.

36. **가 :** 이 가게 주인이세요?
   나 : 아니요, 저는 (   )이에요/예요.

   ❶ 상품   ❷ 손님   ❸ 쇼핑   ❹ 신용카드

37. **가 :** 약속을 어기면 안 된다.
   나 : 네, 꼭 (   )을게요/ㄹ게요.

   ❶ 팔다   ❷ 고르다   ❸ 바꾸다   ❹ 지키다

38. **가 :** 값이 싸요?
   나 : 아니요, (   )어요/아요/여요.

   ❶ 넓다   ❷ 나쁘다   ❸ 비싸다   ❹ 깨끗하다

39. **가 :** 꽃을 파는 사람이 많군요.
   나 : 네, 우리도 한 다발 (   )읍시다/ㅂ시다.

   ❶ 사다   ❷ 깎다   ❸ 주다   ❹ 교환하다

40. **가** : 선물을 많이 <u>받았어요?</u>

    나 : 네, 친구들이 선물을 많이 (   )었어요/았어요/였어요.

    ❶ 쓰다   ❷ 팔다   ❸ 주다   ❹ 생기다

[41~45] 밑줄 친 부분과 의미가 가장 가까운 것을 고르십시오.
Choose the word that is most similar to the underlined section.

41. **가** : 숙제를 누구와 <u>함께</u> 했어?

    나 : 언니와 (   ) 했어.

    ❶ 꼭   ❷ 같이   ❸ 안녕   ❹ 환영

42. **가** : 조금 전에 어느 컴퓨터를 <u>사용했어요?</u>

    나 : 이 컴퓨터를 (   )었는데요/았는데요/였는데요.

    ❶ 놓다   ❷ 하다   ❸ 치다   ❹ 쓰다

43. **가** : 서울에서 옷이 많고 <u>가격도</u> 싼 시장이 어디예요?

    나 : 동대문 시장이 옷도 많고 (   )도 싸요. 한번 가 보세요.

    ❶ 값   ❷ 돈   ❸ 얼마   ❹ 현금

44. **가** : 물건을 산 후에 언제까지 <u>교환할</u> 수 있어요?

    나 : 1주일 안에 오시면 언제든지 (   )을/ㄹ 수 있어요.

    ❶ 사다   ❷ 고르다   ❸ 드리다   ❹ 바꾸다

45. **가** : 무슨 영화를 볼지 <u>선택했어?</u>

    나 : 아니, 아직 (   )지 못 했어.

    ❶ 사다   ❷ 쓰다   ❸ 고르다   ❹ 보이다

[46~50] 밑줄 친 단어의 쓰임이 잘못된 것을 고르십시오. Choose the one that is incorrectly used.

46.　❶ <u>안녕</u>! 오랜만이다.　　　　　　　　　　(　　)

　　❷ <u>안녕하게</u> 지냈어요?

　　❸ 그럼 <u>안녕히</u> 계세요.

　　❹ <u>안녕하세요</u>? 그동안 어떻게 지내셨어요?

47.　❶ 윗사람에게는 예의를 <u>지켜야</u> 합니다.　　(　　)

　　❷ 처음 만나는 사람과 인사를 <u>지켰어요</u>.

　　❸ 사회생활을 할 때 시간을 잘 <u>지키는</u> 것은 아주 중요하다.

　　❹ 아침에 늦게 일어나서 약속을 <u>지키지</u> 못했어요. 미안해요.

48.　❶ 친구들에게 인사를 <u>줬다</u>.　　　　　　　(　　)

　　❷ 후배가 선배에게 인사를 <u>했다</u>.

　　❸ 선생님께서 내 인사를 <u>받지</u> 않으셨다.

　　❹ 설날에 친척 어른들께 인사를 <u>드렸습니다</u>.

49.　❶ 요즘 물건 값이 많이 <u>올랐어요</u>.　　　　(　　)

　　❷ 값을 잘 <u>고르는</u> 방법이 뭐예요?

　　❸ 백화점은 시장보다 값이 <u>비싸요</u>.

　　❹ 제가 물건을 많이 사니까 아저씨가 값을 <u>싸게</u> 해 주셨어요.

50.　❶ 저는 약속을 <u>어기는</u> 사람을 싫어해요.　　(　　)

　　❷ 친구와 학교 앞에서 만나기로 약속을 <u>했어요</u>.

　　❸ 죄송합니다. 오늘 약속이 <u>나서</u> 만날 수 없어요.

　　❹ 갑자기 일이 생겨서 약속을 내일로 <u>미뤄야</u> 할 것 같아요.

학교와 직장

09

School and Work

001
동기

[동기] **명사** friend (person who is same grade or level)

a person who enrolled in school or office at the same time

[Related word] 동창 alumni

[Example] 김 과장은 나와 5(오)년 전에 함께 회사에 들어온 입사 동기입니다.

Manager Kim and I entered into this office 5 years ago at the same time.

대학 동기들과 나는 졸업한 지 20(이십)년이 넘었지만 아직도 한 달에 한 번씩 만난다.

I graduated with my college friends over 20 years ago but we still meet each other once a month.

002
동료

[동뇨] **명사** colleague

a person who works at the same work place

[Expression] 직장 동료 work colleague

회사 동료 office colleague

[Example] 오늘은 직장 동료들과 퇴근 후에 회식을 하기로 했어요.

My colleagues from work decided to have an office party after work.

동료 직원이 회사에 나오지 않아서 내가 그 동료의 일까지 모두 했다.

My colleague did not come to the office so I finished all of her work too.

003
동창

[동창] **명사** alumni

a person who studied at the same school

[Expression] 동창회 alumni reunion

[Example] 30(삼십)년 만에 초등학교 동창들과 만나니까 정말 반가웠어요.

I was so happy to meet my elementary alumni after 30 years.

이번 주 토요일에 고등학교 동창회가 있는데 갈 수 있을지 모르겠다.

I don't know if I will be able to go to my high school reunion this Saturday.

004
사귀다

[사귀다] **동사** to make friends, or to date

to get to know each other

[Usage] N을/를 사귀다

[Expression] 친구를 사귀다 to make a friend

여자 친구를 사귀다 to go out with a girlfriend

[Example] 두 사람은 사귄 지 7(칠)년 만에 결혼했다.

Those two married after dating for 7 years.

한국 친구들을 많이 사귀어서 한국 문화에 관심을 갖게 되었어요.
I made a lot of Korean friends and became interested in Korean culture.

005
사장

[사장] 명사 CEO

the person who represents a company and takes responsibility for that company and is the highest person in charge

[Expression] 사장님 CEO

[Example] 그 신문사 사장은 너무 바빠서 만나기가 어렵다.
That CEO from the newspaper company is always busy so it's not easy to meet him.

우리 회사 사장님은 아침에 제일 먼저 출근하십니다.
Our CEO is the first one to come to work in the morning.

006
선배

[선배] 명사 senior

a person who entered school ahead of you or graduated ahead of you, or the person who entered the same work place earlier than you

[Expression] 선후배 senior-junior relationship

[Antonym] 후배 junior

[Example] 선배들이 후배들을 위해서 신입생 환영회를 열었다.
The seniors opened a welcoming party for the incoming juniors.

일을 하다가 모르는 것이 있으면 선배에게 언제든지 물어 보세요.
If you run into something you don't know while working, don't hesitate to ask a senior.

007
선생님

[선생님] 명사 1. teacher 2. used to address someone in a honorific way

1. a person who's job is to teach others, and is a way of formally addressing them

[Usage] N 선생님

[Example] 저는 외국인에게 한국어를 가르치는 한국어 선생님이 되고 싶어요.
I want to be a teacher who teaches Korean to foreigners.

2. a formal address used after the last name, name, or work position

[Usage] N 선생님

[Expression] 김 선생님 Mr. kim, Ms. kim

의사 선생님 doctor (honorific form)

[Example] 의사 선생님, 제가 이제 다 나았습니까? Doctor, am I all well now?

008
싸우다

[싸우다] 동사 to fight

to use words, strength, or objects and with it, in order to get what one wants

[Usage] **N**과/와 싸우다

[Example] 여자 친구와 싸워서 기분이 안 좋아요.
I fought with my girlfriend so I am not very happy.

나는 어렸을 때 동생과 많이 싸웠지만 지금은 사이가 좋다.
When I was younger I fought a lot with my younger sibling but now we get along.

009
직원

[지권] 명사 employee

people who are hired to work at a place

[Example] 회사 직원이 3,000(삼천)명이 넘으면 큰 회사이다.
If the amount of employees is over 3,000, it is a big company.

요즘 일이 많아서 회사의 모든 직원들이 날마다 늦게까지 일을 해요.
There is a lot to do these days so everyone at the office works until late every day.

010
학생

[학쌩] 명사 student

[Expression] 초등학생 elementary students
중학생 middle school students
고등학생 high school students
대학생 college students

[Related word] 학교 school

[Example] 학생이 해야 할 일은 열심히 공부하는 거예요.
A student's work is to study hard.

고등학교 3(삼)학년 학생들은 대학교 입학시험 때문에 스트레스를 받고, 대학교 4(사)학년 학생들은 취직 때문에 스트레스를 받는다.
Third year high school students suffer from stress about the college entrance exams and fourth year college students suffer from stress about getting a job.

09-2 | 학업과 업무

011
가르치다

[가르치다] 동사 to teach

to teach others new knowledge, information, technological skills, and other things

[Usage] **N**을/를 가르치다

[Antonym] 배우다 to learn

[Example] 저는 지금 중학교에서 학생들에게 수학을 가르치고 있습니다.
I am teaching math to middle school students.

제가 사장님과 직접 통화하고 싶은데 전화번호 좀 가르쳐 주시겠습니까?
I have to talk to the CEO personally, can you teach me her number?

012
공부하다

[공부하다] 동사 to study

to gain knowledge about a field of study or skill by reading or doing what is necessary to learn it

[Usage] **N**을/를 공부하다

[Expression] 한국말을 공부하다 to study Korean

[Example] 저는 대학교에서 경영학을 공부했습니다.
I studied business administration at the university.

한국에 오기 전에 고향에서 한국어를 조금 공부했어요.
Before coming to Korea, I studied Korean at my hometown.

013
교과서

[교과서] 명사 textbook

[Example] 과학 교과서를 집에 놓고 와서 선생님께 혼났다.
I left my science textbook at home, so the teacher scolded me.

시험 문제는 우리가 공부한 교과서에서만 나올 거예요.
Test questions will come only from the textbook.

014
교실

[교실] 명사 classroom

[Related word] 강의실 lecture room

[Example] 학생의 수에 비해서 교실이 너무 좁아요.
The classroom is too small compared to the amount of students in the room.

선생님이 교실에 들어오기 전에 자리에 앉아 있어야 해.
We need to sit in our seats before our teacher comes inside.

015
권

[권] 명사 volume, book, copy

used as a counting unit for counting books or notebooks

[Expression] 책 1(한) 권 one book

공책 30(삼십) 권 30 notebooks

[Example] 이 공책은 한 권에 얼마예요? How much is one of these notebooks?

저는 한 달에 책을 두 권쯤 읽어요. I read about 2 books every month.

016
끝나다

[끈나다] 동사 to be finished

to complete something, to mark that it is done

[Usage] N이/가 끝나다

[Antonym] 시작되다 to begin

[Example] 수업이 끝나면 도서관에 갈 거예요.

After class I am going to go to the library.

방학이 끝나고 곧 새 학기가 시작된다.

The new semester will begin after this break.

017
낙제

[낙쩨] 명사 fail

failing a test, or not being able to be promoted

[Related word] 유급 being held back

[Example] 우리 반에서 낙제한 학생은 한 명도 없어요.

There is no one who failed in my class.

모든 과목에서 60(육십)점 이상을 받지 못하면 낙제예요.

If you don't receive more than 60 points for all of the classes, you will fail.

018
노력하다

[노려카다] 동사 to put an effort, to try

to try one's best to achieve some goal, this is done by using body and mind

[Usage] AV으려고/려고 노력하다

[Expression] 열심히 노력하다 to try very hard

[Example] 성공하려고 노력했지만 실패했다. I tried to succeed but I failed.

열심히 노력하면 좋은 결과가 나올 거예요.

If you work really hard and try your best, a good result will follow.

019
단어

[다너] 명사 word, vocabulary

a word that has meaning and can be used in conversation or writing

[Synonym] 낱말 word

[Related word] 어휘 vocabulary

[Example] 외국어를 잘 하려면 단어를 많이 알아야 한다.

In order to know a foreign language, you must know a lot of words.

책을 읽다가 모르는 단어가 나오면 사전에서 찾으세요.

If you read a book and don't know the word, look it up in the dictionary.

020
돕다

[돕따] 동사 to help

to aid someone in trouble or in a bad situation, ㅂverb

[Usage] N을/를 돕다

[Expression] 일을 돕다 to help with work

할머니를 돕다 to help grandmother

[Example] 무엇을 도와 드릴까요? What should I help you with?

형은 날마다 아버지의 일을 돕습니다.

My older brother helps my father with his work.

021
떨어지다

[떠러지다] 동사 1. to fall 2. to fail

1. to go from top to bottom

[Usage] N이/가 N에 떨어지다

[Example] 유리컵이 바닥에 떨어져서 깨졌다.

The glass cup fell on the ground and broke.

2. to not pass a test

[Usage] N에 떨어지다

N에서 떨어지다

[Antonym] 붙다 to pass

합격하다 to get accepted

[Example] 이번 시험에서 떨어지지 않으려면 열심히 공부해야 해.

You must study hard in order to not fail this test.

022
메모하다

[메모하다] 동사 to note

to write a short memo so that one doesn't forget to do something

[Usage] N을/를 메모하다

[Related word] 적다² to write down

[Example] 수첩에 그 남자의 이름과 전화번호를 메모했다.

I wrote down his name and phone number in my planner.

공부하면서 모르는 것은 메모해 놓고 쉬는 시간에 선생님께 질문하세요.

Write down a memo of what you don't understand while studying, and ask the teacher during break time.

205

023
문제

[문제] 명사 problem

a question that is a part of a study or debate that requires an answer

[Usage] **N** 문제

[Expression] 문제가 쉽다 the problem is easy

문제가 생기다 there is a problem

문제를 풀다 to solve a problem

[Example] 이번 대학 입학시험 문제는 작년보다 쉬웠어요.

The problems on this college entrance exam were much easier than last years.

요즘 세계는 주택 문제, 교통 문제, 인구 문제, 환경 문제 등 여러 가지 문제 때문에 살기가 어려워지고 있다.

It's really hard to live these days because there are many problems in housing, transportation, population, and environment.

024
묻다

[묻따] 동사 to ask

to think of a question in something that one has a problem in and wanting an answer from someone who can give an answer or an explanation, ㄷverb

[Usage] **N**을/를 묻다

N에 대해서 묻다

[Expression] 물어보다 to ask

이름을 묻다 to ask one's name

[Synonym] 질문하다 to question

[Antonym] 대답하다 to answer

[Example] 언니에게 언제 만날 수 있는지 물었어요.

I asked my older sister when we could meet.

길을 몰라서 지나가는 사람에게 길을 물었다.

I didn't know the road so I asked a person passing by to show me the right direction.

025
발음

[바름] 명사 pronunciation

making the sound of the word

[Expression] 발음이 좋다 the pronunciation is good

발음이 어렵다 the pronunciation is difficult

발음하다 to pronunciate

[Example] 열심히 연습하면 발음이 좋아질 것이다.

If I keep practicing, my pronunciation will get better.

한국어에서 제일 어려운 발음이 뭐예요?

What is the hardest pronunciation in Korean?

206

026
발전

[발쩐] 명사 progress

being in the process of getting better or moving to a higher status

[Expression] 발전하다 to have progress

[Example] 회사가 발전하려면 직원들의 힘이 필요하다.
If the company wants to become more progressed, the employees must work hard.

과학 기술의 발전을 위해서 더 많이 노력하겠습니다.
We will work hard for the progress of science.

027
배우다

[배우다] 동사 to learn

to gain knowledge or skill

[Usage] N을/를 배우다

[Synonym] 공부하다 to study

[Antonym] 가르치다 to teach

[Example] 나는 어머니께 요리를 배웠다. I learned how to cook from my mother.
저는 한국어를 배우려고 한국에 왔어요. I came to Korea to learn Korean.

028
벌다

[벌다] 동사 to make money

to work and in return get paid, ㄹverb

[Usage] N을/를 벌다

[Expression] 돈을 벌다 to make money
생활비를 벌다 to make money for living expenses

[Example] 돈을 버는 것은 쉬운 일이 아니에요. It is not easy to make money.
영수는 방학마다 아르바이트를 해서 학비를 벌었다.
Young-soo works part-time every vacation to make money to pay for school tuition.

029
복습

[복씁] 명사 review

looking over what was already learned and practicing it

[Expression] 복습하다 to review

[Related word] 예습 preview

[Example] 어제 배운 것을 복습했어? Did you review what you learned yesterday?
수업이 끝난 후에는 꼭 복습을 하세요.
After class always remember to review.

030
분필

[분필] 명사 chalk

a writing tool used to write on a chalkboard

[Related word] 칠판 blackboard

[Example] 선생님은 중요한 내용을 빨간색 분필로 써 주신다.
My teacher writes the important information in red chalk.

학생들이 쉬는 시간이 되면 칠판에 분필로 그림을 그려요.
During break time the kids draw pictures on the chalkboard with the chalk.

031
붙다

[붇따] 동사 1. to attach 2. to pass

1. to put in place so that it does not become unattached

[Usage] N이/가 붙다

[Expression] 붙어 있다 to be attached

[Antonym] 떨어지다 to become unattached

[Example] 기숙사 방 벽에 가족사진이 붙어 있어요.
There is a family picture attached to my wall in my dorm room.

2. to pass a test or get into a school

[Usage] N에 붙다

[Expression] 시험에 붙다 to pass a test
대학교에 붙다 to get into college

[Antonym] 떨어지다 to become unattached or to fail

[Example] 그 사람은 날마다 열심히 공부해서 가고 싶어했던 대학교에 붙었다.
That person studied really hard every day and got into the college that he wanted to got into.

032
빌리다

[빌리다] 동사 to borrow

to use for a while and return whether it be money or an object

[Usage] 빌려서 AV
N을/를 빌려 주다
N에서 N을/를 빌리다
N에게서 N을/를 빌리다

[Synonym] 대여하다 to rent
대출하다 to get a loan

[Antonym] 돌려주다 to return

[Related word] 반납하다 to return

[Example] 친구에게서 볼펜을 빌려서 썼다.
I borrowed and used a pen from my friend.

집을 사려고 은행에서 돈을 빌렸어요.
I borrowed money so that I could buy a house.

208

033
사무실

[사무실] 명사 office room

a room used to organize files at a company or school

[Example] 제가 일하는 사무실은 2(이)층에 있어요.
I work in the office on the second floor.

사무실에 있는 사람들이 모두 열심히 일을 하고 있다.
Everyone in the office is working very hard.

034
사업

[사업] 명사 business

a place organized to make money

[Usage] N 사업

[Expression] 사업가 businessman

환경 사업 environmental business

통신 사업 communication business

사업하다 to do business

[Example] 아버지는 회사를 그만두고 사업을 시작하셨어요.
My father quit his work at the company and started his own business.

대학을 졸업한 후에 의류 사업을 해 보려고 합니다.
After graduating from college I plan on getting into clothing business.

035
사전

[사전] 명사 dictionary

[Expression] 전자사전 electronic dictionary

한국어 사전 Korean dictionary

사전을 찾다 to look up a word in the dictionary

[Example] 모르는 단어가 있으면 선생님께 여쭤 보거나 사전을 찾아요.
If there is a word you don't know, ask the teacher or look it up in the dictionary.

요즘 사람들은 책으로 된 사전보다 전자사전을 더 많이 사용한다.
These days many people use the electronic dictionary rather than the book dictionary.

036
설명

[설명] 명사 explanation, direction

explaining something to someone so that they understand

[Expression] 설명서 directions

설명하다 to explain

[Example] 그럼 지금부터 선생님의 설명을 잘 들으세요.
Starting now listen to the teacher's directions.

친구가 컴퓨터를 어떻게 사용해야 하는지 설명해 주었다.
My friend explained to me how to use the computer.

037
수업

[수업] 명사 class, lesson

a place where teachers teach students knowledge or skill

[Expression] 수업 시간 class time

음악 수업 music class

수업이 있다 to have class

수업하다 to be in class

수업을 듣다 to take class

[Example] 교실에서 학생들이 열심히 수업을 듣고 있어요.

The students are listening intently in class.

김 선생님께서 지금 수업을 하고 계시니까 수업이 끝날 때까지 기다리세요.

Professor Kim is teaching class so please wait until she is done.

038
숙제

[숙쩨] 명사 homework

a study or work given by a teacher so that a student can do it alone

[Expression] 숙제가 있다 to have homework

숙제가 많다 to have a lot of homework

숙제하다 to do homework

숙제를 내다 to give homework

[Synonym] 과제 assignment

[Example] 숙제를 다 하고 놀아라.

Do all of your homework and then play.

아침에 오면 선생님께 숙제부터 내세요.

When you come in the morning, give your homework to the teacher first.

039
스트레스

[스트레스] 명사 stress

being sensitive psychologically and physically to new environments or feeling difficulty in the situation

[Expression] 스트레스가 쌓이다 the stress is piling up

스트레스를 받다 to get stressed

스트레스를 풀다 to relieve stress

[Example] 요즘 시험 때문에 스트레스를 많이 받아요.

I stress so much because I have a test coming up.

스트레스가 많이 쌓였을 때 어떻게 스트레스를 풀어요?

How do you relieve stress that is piling up?

210

040
시험

[시험] **명사** test

a way of grading knowledge, talent, ability, or skill

[Usage] **N** 시험

[Expression] 시험 기간 testing period

시험 성적 test grade

시험이 있다 to have a test

시험을 보다 to take a test

시험에 붙다 to pass a test

[Example] 학생들은 시험 기간이 되면 스트레스를 많이 받는다.
Many students get stressed when testing period comes around.

이번 주에 중요한 시험이 있어서 요즘 열심히 공부하고 있어요.
I have an important test this week so I am studying hard.

041
쌓이다

[싸이다] **동사** to pile

to gain more objects, experience, knowledge, skill, or emotion

[Usage] **N**이/가 쌓이다

[Expression] 빨래가 쌓이다 to have a lot of laundry

숙제가 쌓이다 to have a lot of homework

스트레스가 쌓이다 to have a lot of stress

[Related word] 쌓다 to pile

[Example] 책상 위에 책이 쌓여 있다. There are a lot of books stacked on my desk.
길에 눈이 쌓여 있으니까 조심하세요.
There is a lot of snow piled on the road so be careful.

042
알다

[알다] **동사** to know

to gain information or knowledge through situation and data, ㄹverb

[Usage] **N**을/를 알다

N에 대해서 알다

AV을/ㄹ 줄 알다

DV/**AV**는지/은지 알다

[Antonym] 모르다 to not know

[Example] 형은 기타를 칠 줄 안다. My older brother knows how to play the guitar.
한국 드라마를 보면 한국 문화를 조금 알 수 있어요.

If you watch Korean dramas, you can learn a bit about Korean culture.

043
알리다

[알리다] 동사 to inform

to let people know something they didn't know before

[Usage]	<u>N</u>에게 <u>N</u>을/를 알리다
[Related word]	알다 to know
[Example]	모임 장소가 바뀐 것을 사람들에게 알려 주세요.
	Let everyone know that the meeting place has changed.
	저는 다른 나라 사람들에게 한국의 문화를 알리는 일을 하고 싶어요.
	I want to work in informing other countries about Korean culture.

044
어렵다

[어렵따] 형용사 to be difficult, hard

something that is not easy to do or hard to understand, ㅂverb

[Usage]	<u>N</u>이/가 어렵다
	<u>AV</u>기가 어렵다
[Expression]	발음이 어렵다 the pronunciation is difficult
	이해하기가 어렵다 it is hard to understand
[Antonym]	쉽다 to be easy
[Example]	학생들이 이번 시험이 아주 어려웠다고 해요.
	The students say that this test was really hard.
	외국어를 공부할 때 제일 어려운 것이 뭐예요?
	What is the hardest thing when learning a foreign language?

045
연습

[연습] 명사 practice

repeatedly studing, or practicing a skill to get better at it

[Usage]	<u>N</u> 연습
[Expression]	연습하다 to practice
[Example]	내일의 경기를 위해서 선수들이 열심히 연습하고 있다.
	The athletes are practicing hard for the competition tomorrow.
	외국어를 잘 하려면 연습을 많이 하는 것이 제일 중요해요.
	It is important to practice a lot if you want to be a good at a foreign language.

046
열심히

[열씸히/열씨미] 부사 hard, diligently

working sincerely with mind and body

[Example]	미선 씨는 무슨 일이든지 열심히 한다.
	Misun works hard on everything.
	아직 한국말을 잘 하지 못하지만 열심히 노력하면 잘 하게 될 거예요.
	I can't speak Korean that well as of now but if I work hard then I will able to speak well.

047

외국어

[외구거] **명사** foreign language

another countries lanuage

[Example] 외국어를 전공한 사람을 찾고 있어요.

I am looking for a person who has majored in foreign languages.

여러 가지 외국어를 할 수 있으면 좋은 회사에 취직할 수 있어요.

You can get into a good company if you know a lot of foreign languages.

도움말

'-어' comes after the name of the country to label the language spoken in that country.

한국어, 중국어, 일본어, 영어 , 독일어, 프랑스어, 스페인어, ……

Korean, Chinese, Japanese, English, German, French, Spanish, ……

048

월급

[월급] **명사** salary

money that is given every month after doing work

[Expression] 월급을 받다 to receive salary

월급을 주다 to give salary

[Example] 한 달 월급이 얼마쯤 돼요? How much is one month's salary?

첫 월급을 받으면 친구들에게 한턱낼 거예요.

I'm going to treat my friends after I receive my first pay.

049

유학

[유학] **명사** study abroad

living in a different country and also studying

[Expression] 유학생 study abroad student

유학 생활 studying abroad

유학하다 to study abroad

유학을 가다 to go to study abroad

[Example] 미국으로 유학을 가는 친구를 배웅하러 공항에 갔다.

I went to the airport to send off my friend who is going to study abroad in America.

유학하는 동안 여러 나라 친구들을 사귀고 다양한 나라의 문화를 배울 수 있었다.

I was able to make a lot of friends from different countries and learn about different cultures during my time study abroad.

213

050
일³

[일] 명사 work

thinking or using your body to do something

[Expression] 일하다 to work

일이 쌓이다 to have a lot of work

[Example] 오늘 일이 끝난 후에 회식을 하기로 했어요.
We decided to have an office party after work.

요즘 일이 많아서 날마다 늦게까지 일합니다.
I work late every day because I have so much to do.

051
읽다

[익따] 동사 1. to recite   2. to read

1. to read out loud

[Usage] N을/를 읽다

[Example] 발음 연습을 위해서 교과서를 큰 소리로 3(세)번 읽었어요.
I wanted to practice my pronunciation so I read my textbook out loud 3 times.

2. to read something and know what it means

[Usage] N을/를 읽다

[Related word] 보다 to look

[Example] 어머니는 저녁 식사 준비를 하시고 아버지는 신문을 읽고 계셨다.
My mother was making dinner and my father was reading the newspaper.

052
전공

[전공] 명사 major, specialty

intensely studying one field, or word used to label that field

[Expression] 전공 과목 subject of major study

전공하다 to major in something

[Example] 언니는 대학교에서 무엇을 전공했어요?
What did you major in in college?

전공과 잘 맞는 일을 찾기가 쉽지 않아요.
It's hard to find a job that fits my major.

These are majors in college.

경영학, 경제학, 국어국문학, 법학, 생물학, 수학, 역사학, 영어영문학, 일어일문학, 중어중문학, 컴퓨터공학, ……

business administration, economics, Korean language and literature, law, biology, math, history, English language and literature, Japanese language and literature, Chinese language and literature, computer engineering, ……

053
준비

[준비] **명사** preparation

getting things ready for something

[Usage] **N** 준비

[Expression] 준비하다 to prepare

[Example] 손님이 많이 오실 테니까 음식을 많이 준비하세요.
There will be many guests coming, so prepare a lot of food.

요즘 어머니는 동생의 결혼 준비로 아주 바쁘십니다.
My mother is very busy because of my younger siblings wedding.

054
중요하다

[중요하다] **형용사** to be important

to be precious and valuable

[Usage] 중요한 **N**
N이/가 중요하다

[Expression] 중요한 전화 an important call
건강이 중요하다 health is important

[Example] 중요한 회의가 있으니까 늦지 마세요.
There is an important meeting so don't be late.

시험 점수보다 친구들과 재미있게 공부하는 것이 더 중요해요.
It is important to enjoy studying with your friends than to get a good test grade.

055
직장

[직짱] **명사** job

a place where you work and receive payment in return

[Expression] 직장 생활 work life
직장을 구하다 to look for work
직장에 다니다 to go to work

[Related word] 직업 job, career

[Example] 요즘 직장 생활은 어때요? How is your work life?
일이 너무 힘들어서 다른 직장을 구하고 있어요.
Work is so hard I am looking for another job.

056
진학

[진학] **명사** entering a school of higher level

getting into school of higher level

[Expression] 진학생 student entering a school of higher level
진학하다 to enter school

[Example] 대학원에 진학해서 한국 문학을 공부하고 싶어요.
I want to enter graduate school and study Korean culture.

요즘은 옛날보다 대학교에 진학하는 학생 수가 많아졌다.
There is an increase of people entering college than from the past.

057
질문

[질문] 명사 question

asking something that you don't know, word used to ask

[Expression] 질문이 있다 to have a question

질문하다 to ask

[Related word] 묻다 to ask

[Antonym] 대답 answer

[Example] 선생님, 질문이 있습니다. Teacher, I have a question.

다음 글을 잘 읽고 질문에 답하십시오.
Read the following words and answer the questions.

058
쪽¹

[쪽] 명사 page

the measuring unit used to count pages in books, newspapers, or magazines

[Usage] **Num** 쪽

[Synonym] 페이지 page

[Example] 몇 쪽까지 읽어야 해요? What page do I have to read to?

여러분, 교과서 13(십삼)쪽을 보세요.
Everyone, look at page 13 in the textbook.

059
찾다

[찯따] 동사 1. to look for 2. to search 3. to find

1.something that one doesn't have right now, to look for someone or in search of someone, to gain that person or object

[Usage] **N**을/를 찾다

[Expression] 길을 찾다 to look for the road

일을 찾다 to look for work

[Example] 우리 가게에서 열심히 일할 사람을 찾고 있습니다.
I am looking for someone who will work hard at my store.

2. to search for something one doesn't know by looking in the book or the internet

[Usage] **N**을/를 찾다

[Expression] 사전을 찾다 to look in the dictionary

[Example] 모르는 단어가 있어서 사전을 찾았어요.
I didn't know a word so I looked in the dictionary.

3. to find something that was lost, stolen, left, or borrowed

[Usage] **N**을/를 찾다

[Expression]	돈을 찾다 to find money
	지갑을 찾다 to find the wallet
[Antonym]	잃다 to lose
[Example]	어제 열쇠를 잃어버렸는데 아직 찾지 못했다.
	I lost my key yesterday and I still haven't found the key.

060 책

[책] 명사 book

[Usage]	N책
[Expression]	책장 bookshelf
	소설책 novel
	책 한 권 one book
	책을 보다 to look at the book
	책을 읽다 to read the book
[Example]	한 달에 책을 몇 권 읽으세요? How many books do you read in a month?
	이 책은 초등학생에게 너무 어려워요.
	This book is too difficult for elementary students.

061 처리하다

[처리하다] 동사 to take care of
to organize and finish something

[Usage]	N을/를 처리하다
[Expression]	일을 처리하다 to take care of work
[Example]	남은 일을 다 처리하고 퇴근하세요. Finish the left over work and leave.
	음식물 쓰레기는 어떻게 처리하지요?
	How should I take care of the food and drink waste?

062 출장

[출짱] 명사 business trip
going to another place to do work

[Expression]	지방 출장 regional business trip
	해외 출장 out of country business trip
	출장 중이다 to be on a business trip
	출장을 가다 to go on a business trip
[Example]	아버지는 출장 중이십니다. My father is on a business trip.
	오늘 부산으로 출장을 가게 되었어요.
	Today I am going to Busan for a business trip.

063
틀리다

[틀리다] 동사 to be wrong
to be incorrect

[Usage]	N이/가 틀리다
	N을/를 틀리다
[Expression]	답이 틀리다 the answer is incorrect
	계산을 틀리다 the calculations are wrong
[Antonym]	맞다 to be correct
[Related word]	다르다 to be different
[Example]	잘 읽고 맞으면 O, 틀리면 X 하세요.

Read and if it is correct label O, if it is wrong X.

저는 한국말을 발음할 때 받침 발음을 자주 틀려요.
Whenever I pronounce Korean, I often pronounce the final consonant incorrectly.

064
학기

[학끼] 명사 semester, term
the separation of one year of a school term

[Usage]	N 학기
[Expression]	1(일)학기 one semester
	겨울 학기 winter semester
[Example]	대학교 4(사)학년 2(이)학기에는 학생들이 취업 준비 때문에 바빠요.

Fourth year college students are busy during their second semester because they are getting ready for work.

한국은 보통 3(삼)월부터 8(팔)월까지를 1(일)학기, 9(구)월부터 2(이)월까지를 2(이)학기라고 한다.
In Korea the first semester is from March to August, and the second semester is from September to February.

065
학년

[항년] 명사 grade, year
the way students are labeled every year they are in school

[Usage]	Num학년
[Example]	제 동생은 저보다 한 학년 아래예요.

My younger sibling is one grade lower than me.

고등학교 3(삼)학년 학생들은 대학교 입학을 위해서 학교나 학원에서 밤늦게까지 공부한다.
Third year high school students study at school or at institutions until late in the night to prepare them for college.

066
학비

[학뻬] 명사 tuition

money paid to pay for school or study institution

[Expression] 학비가 들다 to cost tuition

학비를 내다 to pay tuition

[Related word] 등록금 tuition

[Example] 이번 학기에 학비가 많이 올라서 걱정이에요.
I am worried because the tuition has highly increased this semester.

나는 방학마다 아르바이트를 해서 학비와 용돈을 벌었다.
Every vacation I worked part time to pay my tuition and to make my allowance.

067
한국어

[한구거] 명사 Korean

words and spoken language used by Koreans

[Related word] 한글 Korean alphabet

한국말 Korean

[Example] 저는 한국어를 배우려고 한국에 왔어요.
I came to Korea to learn Korean.

우리 오빠는 대학교에서 한국어를 전공하고 한국 회사에 취직했다.
My older brother studied Korean in college and now works in a Korean company.

068
한자

[한짜] 명사 Chinese character

characters used by Chinese people, also used in Korea and Japan

[Expression] 한자어 Sino-Korean word

[Example] 한자는 모두 50,000(오만)자쯤 된다고 해요.
They say that there are about 50,000 Chinese characters.

한국과 일본도 한자를 사용하지만 중국에서 쓰는 한자와 조금 달라요.
Korea and Japan use Chinese characters, but they are a bit different from characters used in China.

069
회의

[회의/훼이] 명사 meeting

getting many people together to discuss something about work, or just a meeting

[Expression] 회의실 meeting room

회의가 있다 to have a meeting

회의하다 to be in a meeting

회의를 열다 to open a meeting

219

회의에 참석하다 to attend a meeting

[Example] 내일 회의는 몇 시에 합니까?

What time do we have the meeting tomorrow?

오늘 오후에 회의가 있으니까 꼭 참석하시기 바랍니다.

There is a meeting this afternoon so I hope you attend.

070
휴게실

[휴게실] 명사 resting area

room used for resting

[Example] 피곤하면 휴게실에서 잠깐 쉬었다가 오세요.

If you are tired, take a short break in the resting room.

회사 휴게실은 좁지만 작은 침대와 냉장고가 있어서 편리해요.

The resting room at our office is a bit small but there is small bed and a

refrigerator so it is convenient.

071
힘들다

[힘들다] 형용사 to be tough, troublesome

to not have much energy in the body and mind because the work is difficult, ㄹverb

[Usage] 힘든 <u>N</u>

<u>N</u>이/가 힘들다

<u>AV</u>기가 힘들다

[Expression] 힘든 일 hard work

생활이 힘들다 the situation is hard

[Example] 힘든 일이 있으면 부모님께 이야기해요.

If there is something troublesome, talk to your parents.

날씨가 너무 더워서 공부하기가 힘들어요.

The weather is so hot that it's hard to study.

072
결석

[결썩] **명사** absence

not coming to school

[Expression] 결석하다 to be absent

[Antonym] 출석 attending

[Related word] 지각 being late

[Example] 감기에 걸려서 수업에 결석했어요.
I caught a cold so I was absent from class.

결석이 많으면 성적이 좋아도 장학금을 받을 수 없습니다.
If you get many absences, you won't be able to receive scholarship even though you have good grades.

073
기숙사

[기숙싸] **명사** dormitory

a place where students or office workers can stay and eat and sleep and live

[Example] 좋은 친구들 덕분에 기숙사 생활에 금방 익숙해졌어요.
I got used to the dormitory life quickly because of my good friends.

우리 학교 기숙사는 시설도 좋고 값도 싸서 학생들에게 인기가 많아요.
Our school dormitory's facilities are nice and the price is cheap so it is popular among the students.

074
도서관

[도서관] **명사** library

[Related word] 책 book

[Example] 요즘 도서관에는 시험 공부를 하는 학생들이 많다.
These days there are many students who study in the library.

학생은 도서관에서 10(십)일 동안 책을 빌릴 수 있습니다.
The students are allowed to borrow books for 10 days.

075
뒤풀이

[뒤푸리] **명사** dinner party, wrap up party

having dinner with people after completing a meeting or work

[Expression] 뒤풀이를 하다 to have a dinner party

[Example] 오늘 음악회 후에 뒤풀이가 있을 예정이니까 모두 참석해 주세요.
After the concert there will be a dinner party, so I hope everyone can attend.

6(육)개월 동안의 연극 공연이 끝난 후에 배우들이 근처 술집에 모여서 뒤풀이를 했다.
After 6 months of working with the play production, the actors had a dinner party at the end in the near bar.

076
방학

[방학] **명사** vacation period

a set break that happens after the end of a school semester

[Expression]   여름 방학 summer vacation

겨울 방학 winter vacation

방학하다 to be on vacation

[Antonym]   개학 beginning of school

[Example]   우리 학교는 다음 주에 방학을 합니다.
Our school goes starts vacation next week.

저는 방학마다 시골에 계신 할머니 댁에 놀러 가요.
During the vacation period I always visit my grandmother who lives in the country.

077
뽑다

[뽑따] **동사** 1. to pull   2. to choose

1. to pull out from the inside by plucking on it, or to pull out food that has been inserted

[Usage]   N을/를 뽑다

[Expression]   돈을 뽑다 to pull out money

커피를 뽑다 to get coffee (from the vending machine)

번호표를 뽑다 to pull out a number from the number slot

[Example]   은행에 가면 먼저 번호표를 뽑아야 해요.
When you go to the bank you should first take out a number from the number slot.

2. to pick one person from many people

[Usage]   N을/를 뽑다

[Expression]   반장을 뽑다 to pick a class president

[Example]   오늘 우리 반의 반장을 뽑을 거예요.
Today we are going to pick the classroom president.

078
소풍

[소풍] **명사** picnic

going outside to somewhere close to rest or to play

[Expression]   소풍날 picnic day

소풍을 가다 to go on a picnic

[Example]   내일이 소풍날이어서 잠이 안 와요.
Tomorrow is the picnic so I can't go to sleep.

소풍을 가서 친구들과 김밥을 먹었어요.
I went to the picnic and ate kim-bab with my friends.

079
수학여행

[수항녀행] **명사** school trip

a small trip with a classroom of students and their teacher going outside to apply what was learned inside the classroom and hearing it and seeing it in the outside world

[Expression] 수학여행을 가다 to go on a school trip

[Example] 2(이)박 3(삼)일 동안 설악산으로 수학여행을 다녀왔어요.
We went on a school trip to Sul-hak mountain for 2 nights and 3 days.

한국 고등학생들은 역사를 공부하기 위해서 보통 경주로 수학여행을 가요.
Usually high school students in Korea go to Kyung-joo for their school trip to learn about history.

080
아르바이트

[아르바이트] **명사** part-time job

it is not a career but a temporary job to make money

[Expression] 아르바이트를 하다 to work part-time

[Example] 학비를 벌기 위해서 아르바이트를 해요.
I work part time to pay for my tuition.

방학에 아르바이트를 하려고 하는데 좋은 곳이 있으면 소개해 주세요.
I plan on working part time during the vacation period, so please let me know if there are any good places to work.

081
졸업하다

[조러파다] **동사** to graduate

to complete all required classes and end the school year

[Usage] N을/를 졸업하다

[Antonym] 입학하다 to begin school

[Example] 저는 2(이)년 전에 고등학교를 졸업했어요.
I graduated from high school 2 years ago.

대학교를 졸업한 후에 외국으로 유학을 갈 계획이에요.
I plan on studying abroad after graduating from college.

082
하숙집

[하숙찝] **명사** boarding home

a house where you pay the owner for housing you and giving you food

[Expression] 하숙집을 구하다 to find a boarding home

[Example] 학교 근처에는 깨끗하고 좋은 하숙집이 많아요.
There are many clean and nice boarding homes near the school.

우리 하숙집 아주머니는 음식을 맛있게 해 주십니다.
Our boarding home owner makes us delicious food.

083
학생증

[학쌩쯩] 명사 student ID

a form of ID that proves that one is a student

[Example] 학생증을 잃어버려서 다시 만들어야 합니다.
I lost my student ID so I need to make another one.

학생증이 있으면 도서관에서 책을 빌릴 수 있어요.
If you have a student ID, you can borrow books from the library.

These words include '-증' and indicate a form of ID or prove that the person is qualified to do something.

학생증, 신분증, 외국인등록증, 운전면허증, 자격증, ······

student ID, ID card, foreign registration card, driver's license, certificate/license, ······

09-4 | 직장 생활

084
다니다

[다니다] 동사 to go

to regularly go to school or work for study or a job

[Usage] **N**에 다니다

[Expression] 학교에 다니다 to go to school

회사에 다니다 to go to the company

[Example] 저와 동생은 같은 대학교에 다녀요.
My younger sibling and I both attend the same college.

좋은 회사에 다니는 사람들이 부럽다.
I am envious of people who go to a good company.

085
바쁘다

[바쁘다] 형용사 to be busy

to have a lot to do or to be in a hurry and have no time, 으 verb

[Usage] **N**이/가 바쁘다

[Antonym] 한가하다 to have free time

[Example] 지금은 바쁘니까 나중에 전화할게요.
I am busy right now so I'll call you later.

요즘 일이 너무 바빠서 날마다 집에 늦게 들어가요.
I have so much work to do these days so I get home late.

086
소식

[소식] 명사 news

writing or word that updates news about a person that is far away

[Usage] **N** 소식

[Expression] 결혼 소식 wedding news
소식을 듣다 to hear the news
소식을 전하다 to send the news

[Example] 앞으로 자주 소식을 전해 드릴게요.
I will update you on the news often

선생님께서 결혼하신다고 하는 소식을 들었어.
I heard the news that our teacher is getting married.

087
실례

[실례/실레] 명사 rude, sorry

talking or acting in a way that is not polite, causing inconvenience

[Expression] 실례지만 excuse me but……, it may be rude but……, I'm sorry but……
실례하다 to feel to excuse, be rude, to be sorry

[Example] 실례지만 박 선생님이 계십니까? Excuse me but is teacher Park there?
실례합니다. 이 근처에 우체국이 어디에 있습니까?
Excuse me. Where is the closest post office?

088
예의

[예의/예이] 명사 manners

talking or acting to keep a good relationship

[Expression] 예의가 없다 to have bad manners
예의를 지키다 to be good mannered

[Related word] 예절 courtesy

[Example] 교실에서는 모자를 벗는 것이 예의입니다.
It is polite to take off your hat in the classroom.

한국에서는 윗사람에게 예의를 지키는 것이 중요하다.
In Korea it is important to be polite to elderly people.

089
지각하다

[지가카다] 동사 to be late

to arrive late to school or to work

[Usage] N에 지각하다

[Example] 지하철이 고장이 나서 회사에 지각했어요.

The subway was broken so I was late to work.

수업에 지각하지 않으려고 아침에 일찍 일어났다.

I woke up early in the morning so that I wouldn't be late for class.

090
지내다

[지내다] 동사 to live, to get along

to live at a place

[Usage] DV게 지내다

[Expression] 잘 지내다 to live well

바쁘게 지내다 to live busily

재미있게 지내다 to live happily

[Example] 저는 요즘 일이 많아서 바쁘게 지내고 있어요.

These days I have a lot of work so I am living busily.

두 사람은 성격이 아주 다르지만 친하게 지내요.

Those two people have very different personalities but get along very well.

091
출근

[출근] 명사 going to work

going to work to do a job

[Expression] 출근 시간 starting work time

출근하다 to go to work

[Antonym] 퇴근 getting off work

[Related word] 결근 being absent from work

[Example] 출근 시간에는 차가 많이 밀려요.

There are a lot of cars during the time everyone has to go to work.

저는 아침 8(여덟)시에 출근합니다.

I go to work at 8 in the morning.

092
취직

[취직] 명사 getting or finding work

getting work

[Expression] 취직하다 to find work

[Antonym] 퇴직 retirement

[Example] 방송국에 기자로 취직했어요.

I got a job as a reporter at a broadcasting station.

대기업에 취직을 하고 싶어하는 사람이 많다.
Many people want to find jobs at a big company.

093
휴가

[휴가] 명사 rest, break, vacation

to have a set time of vacation where no one has to work at the office/
having a short break from the army

[Expression] 휴가철 vacation season

휴가를 가다 to go on vacation

[Example] 작년 여름에 제주도로 휴가를 다녀왔어요.
Last summer I went on a vacation to Jeju island.

이번 여름 휴가에는 바닷가에 가려고 해요.
This vacation I plan on going to the ocean.

227

[1~15] 다음 단어를 한국어로 바꿔 쓰십시오. Change these words into Korean.

1. development, advance ( ) 2. chalk ( )
3. vacation ( ) 4. business ( )
5. CEO ( ) 6. senior ( )
7. picnic ( ) 8. graduation ( )
9. employee ( ) 10. job ( )
11. meeting ( ) 12. boarding house ( )
13. to live ( ) 14. to practice ( )
15. part time job ( )

[16~20] 그림을 보고 ( )에 알맞은 것을 고르십시오.
Look at the picture and choose the correct word.

16.

가 : 학교에서 책을 빌리고 싶은데요.
나 : 그럼 ( )이/가 있어야 해요.

❶ 여권 ❷ 예의
❸ 교과서 ❹ 학생증

17.

가 : 뭐 하고 있어요?
나 : 친구 전화번호를 ( )하고 있어요.

❶ 일 ❷ 노력
❸ 메모 ❹ 뒤풀이

18.

가 : 뭘 하고 있어요?

나 : (   )을/를 보고 있어요.

❶ 책   ❷ 숙제

❸ 시험   ❹ 영화

19.

가 : 어디에서 만날까요?

나 : 제가 일하고 있는 (   )으로/로 오세요.

❶ 식당   ❷ 사무실

❸ 하숙집   ❹ 휴게실

20.

가 : 선생님이 뭘 하고 있어요?

나 : 한국말을 (   )고 있어요.

❶ 가르치다   ❷ 출근하다

❸ 대답하다   ❹ 질문하다

[21~30] 다음 문장을 읽고 알맞은 어휘를 골라 쓰십시오. 어휘는 한 번만 쓰십시오.
Read the following sentence and choose the right word. Use the words once.

동기	소식	퇴근	취직	출장
준비	동창	여행	교과서	벌다
읽다	쌓이다	실례하다	중요하다	지각하다

21. 유학을 갈 (   )은/는 다 끝났니?

22. (   )습니다/ㅂ니다. 김 선생님 계십니까?

23. 이번 학기에 필요한 (   )을/를 사러 가자.

24. 아르바이트를 해서 생활비를 (   )고 있습니다.

25. 회사에 같이 들어온 (   )들과 주말에 모이기로 했다.

26. 아침에 늦게 일어나서 학교 수업에 5분 (   )었다/았다/였다.

27. 아버지께서 중국에 회의가 있어서 1주일 동안 (   )을/를 가셨어요.

28. 한국말 발음을 잘 하려면 교과서를 큰 소리로 많이 (   )어야/아야/여야 한다.

29. 외국에서 생활할 때 가장 (   )은/ㄴ 것은 그 나라의 문화를 이해하는 것입니다.

30. 이번 주 수요일부터 금요일까지 친구들과 함께 경주로 (   )을/를 가기로 했어요.

[31~35] (   ) 안에 알맞은 것을 고르십시오. Choose the correct one.

31. 결혼날짜를 잡으면 바로 (   )어/아/여 주세요.

   ❶ 끝내다　　　❷ 들리다　　　❸ 보이다　　　❹ 알리다

32. 지금은 성적이 좋지 않지만 열심히 (   )을/를 하면 잘 할 수 있을 거예요.

   ❶ 일　　　　❷ 노력　　　　❸ 발전　　　　❹ 예의

33. 나는 3( ) 때 대학을 휴학하고 한국말을 배우러 한국에 갔다.

   ❶ 나이   ❷ 시험   ❸ 학년   ❹ 학비

34. 제 동생은 한국에서 제일 큰 회사에 ( )습니다/ㅂ니다.

   ❶ 끝나다   ❷ 다니다   ❸ 지내다   ❹ 처리하다

35. 친구를 만나러 가는 길에 무거운 짐을 들고 있는 할머니를 ( )어/아/여 드렸어요.

   ❶ 돕다   ❷ 벌다   ❸ 힘들다   ❹ 실례하다

[36~40] 밑줄 친 부분과 반대되는 뜻을 가진 것을 고르십시오.
Choose the word that is the opposite of the underlined word.

36. **가 :** 오늘 학생들이 모두 <u>출석</u>했지요?

   나 : 아니요, 한 명이 ( )었어요/았어요/였어요.

   ❶ 만나다   ❷ 배우다   ❸ 결석하다   ❹ 질문하다

37. **가 :** 이번에 본 입사 시험에 <u>붙</u>었어요?

   나 : 아니요, ( )었어요/았어요/였어요.

   ❶ 바꾸다   ❷ 세우다   ❸ 질문하다   ❹ 떨어지다

38. **가 :** 조금 전에 우체국 앞에서 인사한 사람을 <u>알아요</u>?

   나 : 아니요, 잘 ( )어요/아요/여요.

   ❶ 묻다   ❷ 다니다   ❸ 모르다   ❹ 실례하다

39. **가 :** 한국어 공부가 <u>쉽</u>지요?

   나 : 네, 하지만 발음은 좀 ( )어요/아요/여요.

   ❶ 배우다   ❷ 쌓이다   ❸ 힘들다   ❹ 어렵다

40. **가 :** 요즘 <u>한가하세요?</u>

    나 : 아니요, 좀 (   )어요/아요/여요.

    ❶ 바쁘다   **❷** 지내다   **❸** 실례하다   **❹** 중요하다

[41~45] 밑줄 친 부분과 의미가 가장 가까운 것을 고르십시오.
Choose the word that is most similar to the underlined section.

41. **가 :** 이 책을 다 <u>읽었니?</u>

    나 : 아니요, 아직 다 (   )지 못했어요.

    ❶ 듣다   **❷** 보다   **❸** 쓰다   **❹** 자다

42. **가 :** 뭘 <u>공부하려고</u> 왔어요?

    나 : 한국말을 (   )고 싶어서 왔어요.

    ❶ 배우다   **❷** 바꾸다   **❸** 수업하다   **❹** 시작하다

43. **가 :** 사장님이 시키신 일은 <u>다 됐습니까?</u>

    나 : 네, 조금 전에 (   )었습니다/았습니다/였습니다.

    ❶ 뽑다   **❷** 쌓이다   **❸** 끝나다   **❹** 취직하다

44. **가 :** 어머니, 오늘 퇴근하고 <u>입사 동기</u>들하고 한 잔 하기로 했어요. 집에 늦게 갈 것 같아요.

    나 : 그래, 알았다. (   )들하고 즐거운 시간 보내라.

    ❶ 후배   **❷** 선배   **❸** 동창   **❹** 동료

45. **가 :** 모르는 것이 있으면 누구에게 <u>질문하세요?</u>

    나 : 저는 친구에게 (   )어/아/여 봐요.

    ❶ 묻다   **❷** 배우다   **❸** 시작하다   **❹** 실례하다

[46~50] 밑줄 친 단어의 쓰임이 잘못된 것을 고르십시오. Choose the one that is incorrectly used.

46. ❶ 요즘 <u>사귀는</u> 사람이 있어요?　　　　(　　　)
　　 ❷ 한국친구를 많이 <u>사귀면</u> 좋겠다.
　　 ❸ 오늘 몇 시에 언니를 <u>사귀었어요</u>?
　　 ❹ 여자 친구를 <u>사귄</u> 지 1년 됐습니다.

47. ❶ 가방에서 휴대전화를 <u>뽑았어요</u>.　　　(　　　)
　　 ❷ 오늘 우리 반의 반장을 <u>뽑겠습니다</u>.
　　 ❸ 은행에 가면 먼저 번호표를 <u>뽑으세요</u>.
　　 ❹ 미안한데 커피 한 잔 <u>뽑아</u> 줄 수 있어?

48. ❶ 다음 주에 방학이 <u>끝나요</u>.　　　　(　　　)
　　 ❷ 수업이 <u>끝나고</u> 뭘 할 거예요?
　　 ❸ 비가 <u>끝나고</u> 날씨가 맑아졌어요.
　　 ❹ 시험이 <u>끝났습니다</u>. 시험지를 선생님께 드리세요.

49. ❶ 한국으로 <u>준비할</u> 계획이다.　　　(　　　)
　　 ❷ 이번에도 <u>낙제하면</u> 큰일이다.
　　 ❸ 선생님께서 다시 한 번 <u>설명해</u> 주셨다.
　　 ❹ 많이 <u>연습하면</u> 한국말 실력이 좋아질 거예요.

50. ❶ 스트레스를 <u>만들지</u> 않게 조심하세요.　(　　　)
　　 ❷ 스트레스가 많이 <u>쌓이면</u> 건강이 나빠진다.
　　 ❸ 요즘 회사일 때문에 스트레스를 많이 <u>받아요</u>.
　　 ❹ 저는 힘들 때 노래방에서 노래를 부르면 스트레스가 <u>풀려요</u>.

여가

10

Leisure

001
경기

[경기] **명사** competition

sports competition or rules set up and people are placed to who is better at something

[Usage] N 경기

[Expression] 축구 경기 soccer competition

경기하다 to compete

경기에 지다 to lose at a competition

경기에 이기다 to win at a competition

[Synonym] 시합 tournament

대회 meeting

[Example] 오늘 경기에서 어느 팀이 이겼어요?
Which team won at today's competition?

이번 주 토요일에 브라질과 한국의 축구 경기가 열린다.
This Saturday Brazil and Korea will have a soccer tournament.

002
공

[공] **명사** ball

[Usage] N 공

[Expression] 축구공 soccer ball

공 한 개 one ball

공을 치다 to hit the ball

공을 차다 to kick the ball

공을 던지다 to throw the ball

[Example] 창문 쪽으로 공을 차지 마라. Don't kick the ball near the window.

아이들이 운동장에서 공을 가지고 놀고 있다.
The children are playing with the ball at the playground.

003
던지다

[던지다] **동사** to throw

to use the hand, arm and wrist to fling an object to another place

[Usage] N 을/를 던지다

[Expression] 공을 던지다 to throw the ball

[Example] 강에 돌을 던졌다. I threw the stone into the river.

공을 이쪽으로 빨리 던져! Hurry and throw the ball here!

004
운동

[운동] 명사 exercise

to move the body to become more healthy, or to compete with a team or another person, this competition has a set of rules

[Expression] 운동복 exercise clothing

운동화 tennis shoes

운동회 sports day

운동선수 sports athlete

운동하다 to exercise

[Synonym] 스포츠 sports

[Example] 한국에서 가장 인기 있는 운동은 뭐예요?
What is the most popular sport in Korea?

할아버지께서는 날마다 아침 운동을 하십니다.
Grandfather exercises in the morning everyday.

도움말

These words are example of sports.

골프, 농구, 달리기, 당구, 배구, 배드민턴, 수영, 스케이트, 스키, 야구, 축구, 탁구, 태권도, 테니스, ……

golf, basketball, running, billiards pool, volleyball, badminton, swimming, skate, ski, baseball, soccer, table tennis, tae-kwon-do, tennis, ……

005
차다²

[차다] 동사 to kick

to kick with the foot

[Usage] N을/를 차다

[Expression] 공을 차다 to kick the ball

발로 차다 to kick with the foot

[Example] 화가 나서 의자를 발로 찼다.
I was angry so I kicked the chair with my feet.

아이들이 공원에서 공을 차고 놀고 있어요.
The children are kicking the ball in the playground and playing.

006
치다

[치다] 동사 1. to hit, to play sports   2. to clap, make sound   3. to play an instrument

1. to hit something in your hand or to play sports by hitting an object

[Usage] N을/를 치다

[Expression] 골프를 치다 to play golf

탁구를 치다 to play table tennis

[Example]   주말에 친구들과 볼링을 쳤어요.
I bowled with my friends on the weekend.

2. to hit with hands or an object and make sound

[Usage]   N을/를 치다

[Expression]   손뼉을 치다 to clap one's hand

박수를 치다 to clap with hands

[Example]   공연이 끝나고 사람들이 모두 일어나서 박수를 쳤다.
After the play everyone stood up and clapped their hands.

3. to play and make sound on an instrument

[Usage]   N을/를 치다

[Expression]   북을 치다 to play the drums

장구를 치다 to play the traditional Korean drum (shaped like an hourglass)

기타를 치다 to play the guitar

피아노를 치다 to play the piano

[Example]   오빠는 기타를 치면서 노래를 불렀다.
My older brother played the guitar and sang.

There are many verbs used in exercise.

Sports dealing with the hand, or using the hand with a tool to play the sport use '치다'.

골프, 탁구, 배드민턴, 볼링, 당구, 테니스, ……
golf, table tennis, badminton, bowling, billiard pool, tennis, ……

Sports played with hands but is not played alone but with many people use '하다'.

배구, 농구, 야구, 축구, ……
volleyball, basketball, baseball, soccer, ……

Sports that don't require a ball also use '하다'.

수영, 태권도, 달리기, 요가, ……
swimming, tae-kwon-do, running, yoga, ……

sports where one must get on top of an instrument and play use'타다'.

스케이트, 스키, 스노보드, 썰매, ……
skate, ski, snowboard, sled, ……

007
타다   [타다] 동사 1. to ride (on ice)   2. to ride (moving objects)

1. to ride on top of something on a slippery area

[Usage]   N을/를 타다

[Example]   우리 가족은 겨울이 되면 주말마다 스키를 타러 스키장에 간다.
Our family goes to the ski resort every weekend during the winter.

2. to get on transportation or animal

[Usage] N을/를 타다

[Expression] 말을 타다 to ride a horse

자동차를 타다 to ride a car

[Example] 저는 자전거를 타고 학교에 갑니다. I ride my bicycle and go to school.

008
팀

[팀] 명사 1. sports team 2. team

1. people who are on the same team to play

[Example] 어제 경기에서 우리 학교 축구팀이 이겼어요.
Yesterday at the competition our soccer team won.

2. a meeting of people with the same purpose and people who work together

[Example] 우리 팀에 신입 사원이 새로 들어와서 오늘 회식을 해요.
Today we have a new employee on our team so we will have a dinner party.

10-2 감상 · 관람

009
감상

[감상] 명사 looking and watching, feeling sensitive

being able to understand and feel something after listening or looking at a movie, picture, music and other forms of art

[Usage] N 감상

[Expression] 그림 감상 feeling something from a picture

감상하다 to appreciate

[Example] 제 취미는 영화 감상이에요. My hobby is to watch movies.

주말에 전시회에 가서 미술 작품을 감상했어요.
I went to an art show and looked at the pictures.

010
드라마

[드라마] 명사 drama

a style of drama broadcasted on TV

[Expression] TV 드라마 TV drama

[Example] 요즘 한국에서 인기가 있는 드라마가 뭐예요?
What is the popular Korean drama these days?

한국 역사 드라마는 옛날에 쓰던 한국말이 많아서 이해하기가 어려워요.
Historical Korean dramas use a lot of words used in the olden days that it is hard to understand.

011
매표소

[매표소] 명사 ticketing office

a place where they sell entrance tickets for concerts, museums, and art galleries

[Example] 요즘에는 매표소에 직접 가지 않고 인터넷으로 표를 살 수 있어서 편리하다.
These days you can buy the tickets online rather than going and buying at the ticketing office.

그 전시회는 인기가 많아서 아침부터 사람들이 매표소에 줄을 길게 서 있어요.
That show is very popular so there are many people at the ticketing office waiting to buy the ticket in the morning.

012
미술

[미술] 명사 the fine arts

art that portrays an interpretation of beauty through picture, sculpture, or other arts

[Expression] 미술관 art gallery
미술 작품 art piece

[Related word] 예술 the arts

[Example] 미술관에서 일하고 싶어서 미술을 전공했어요.
I majored in fine arts because I wanted to work in the art museum.

미술을 더 공부하고 싶으면 어느 나라로 유학을 가는 것이 좋을까요?
If I want to study more about the fine arts, what country should I study abroad at?

013
상영

[상영] 명사 screening

showing movies at a theatre

[Expression] 상영 기간 screening length
상영 시간 screening time

상영하다 to show a screening

[Example] 상영 시간이 3(세)시간 10(십)분이면 너무 길지 않아요?
Isn't a 3 hour 10 minute screening too long?

한국의 유명한 배우가 나오는 영화를 상영한다고 합니다.
They say that a movie where a famous Korean actor coming out is screening.

014
연극

[연극] 명사 play

[Expression] 연극배우 theatre actor

연극하다 to act in a play

연극을 보다 to watch a play

연극을 관람하다 to view a play

[Related word] 극장 theatre

관객 audience

[Example] 졸업생들이 연극 공연을 준비하고 있습니다.
The graduating students are preparing a play performance.

지난 주말에 가족들과 함께 연극을 관람했다.
Last week I viewed a play with my family.

015
영화

[영화] 명사 movie

[Expression] 영화관 movie theatre

영화배우 movie actor

영화를 보다 to watch a movie

영화를 찍다 to make a movie

영화를 촬영하다 to shoot a movie

[Example] 인기가 많은 영화는 날마다 영화표가 매진돼요.
A popular movie sells out in tickets all the time.

나는 영화 감상이 취미여서 1(일)주일에 두 번쯤 극장에 간다.
Movie watching is my hobby so I go to the theatre about 2 times a week.

016
예매

[예매] 명사 advance purchase

buying the tickets in advance to watch a movie or go to a museum

[Expression] 예매하다 to purchase in advance

[Related word] 예약 reservation

[Example] 주말인데 영화표를 예매하지 않아도 괜찮을까요?
Is it ok to not reserve the movie ticket even though it's a weekend?

설날과 추석에 고향에 가려면 한 달 전에 기차표를 예매해야 해요.
You need to reserve the tickets a month in advance if you want to go to your hometown during the Lunar new year and thanksgiving.

도움말

The following is different types of movies.

- 가족 영화 family movie: the family is the main character and shows the types of things that happen to the family

- 공상과학영화 Science fiction movie: portraying things that are scientific imagination or things that can happen in space

- 공포 영화 horror movie: telling a scary story

- 만화 영화 animation: a movie that was made through drawing every motion of the character and connecting it together to make it so that the characters look like they are really moving

- 멜로 영화 romantic move: story of a man and woman in love

- 액션 영화 action move: movie about fighting or murder

- 코미디 영화 comedic movie: telling a funny and enjoyable story

017
음악

[으막] 명사 music

[Expression] 음악회 concert
음악을 듣다 to listen to music
음악을 연주하다 to perform music

[Related word] 악기 instrument

[Example] 저는 음악을 들으면서 공부하는 것을 좋아합니다.
I like to listen to music while I study.

우리 학교 음악 선생님은 피아노를 전공해서 피아노를 잘 치신다.
Our school's music teacher majored in piano, so she plays the piano very well.

018
콘서트

[콘서트] 명사 concert

[Expression] 콘서트를 열다 to open a concert
콘서트에 가다 to go to a concert

[Related word] 음악회 music concert
연주회 musical performance

[Example] 인기 가수가 콘서트를 열면 해외 팬들도 와서 공연을 본다.
If popular singers have a concert, international fans come to the concert.

CD로 듣는 것보다 콘서트에 가서 직접 듣는 것이 더 좋아요.
It is much better to go to the concert and listen live than listening to the CD.

019
표

[표] **명사** ticket

[Expression]　기차표 train ticket
　　　　　　　표 한 장 one ticket
　　　　　　　표가 매진되다 all the tickets are sold out
　　　　　　　표를 사다 to buy a ticket
　　　　　　　표를 예매하다 to reserve a ticket

[Synoynm]　티켓 ticket

[Related word]　매표소 ticket selling

[Example]　표를 파는 곳이 어디에 있어요? Where do they sell the tickets?
　　　　　　비행기 표를 잃어버리면 안 되니까 가방에 잘 넣으세요.
　　　　　　You can't lose the airplane ticket so put the tickets inside your bag.

020
필름

[필름] **명사** film

[Example]　디지털 카메라는 필름이 필요 없어서 좋아요.
　　　　　　I like digital cameras because you don't need film.

　　　　　　필름이 다 됐습니다. 새 필름으로 갈아 끼운 후 다시 찍겠습니다.
　　　　　　The film is all used. I will take the picture after I put more film in the camera.

10-3 여행

021
관광

[관광] **명사** sightseeing

going to a different area or a different country to see and experience the landscape or culture

[Expression]　관광객 tourist
　　　　　　　관광지 tour spot
　　　　　　　관광하다 to go on a tour

[Example]　제주도에는 1(일)년 내내 관광객이 많다.
　　　　　　There are many tourists in Jeju island all year long.

이번 휴가에 서울에 가서 관광을 하려고 합니다.
I plan on going to Seoul and sightseeing there during my vacation time.

022
구경

[구경] 명사 tour

watching with interest and appeal

[Usage] N 구경

[Expression] 서울 구경 Seoul tour

구경하다 to tour

구경을 가다 to go on a tour

[Example] 아이와 함께 동물원에 가서 동물들을 구경했어요.
My kid and I went to the zoo and toured the animals.

부모님은 해마다 가을에 설악산으로 단풍 구경을 하러 가십니다.
Every fall my parents tour the leaves on Sorak mountain.

023
기념

[기념] 명사 commemoration

remembering some important event and always keeping it in your heart

[Expression] 기념식 commemoration event

기념일 commemoration day

기념품 souvenir

기념사진 commemorative picture

기념하다 to commemorate

[Example] 저는 여행을 가면 그곳의 대표적인 기념품을 삽니다.
When I go on vacation, I always buy representative souvenir of that place.

우리나라에서 열리는 올림픽을 기념하기 위해 기념우표를 발행한다고 한다.
They say that there will be a commemorative postage stamp that will be made for the olympic that will be opening in our country.

024
떠나다

[떠나다] 동사 to leave

to leave from the place of stay to another place

[Usage] N 을/를 떠나다

[Expression] 집을 떠나다 to leave home

여행을 떠나다 to leave to go on vacation

유학을 떠나다 to leave to go study abroad

[Related word] 돌아오다 to return

[Example] 제 친구는 다음 달에 한국으로 유학을 떠납니다.
My friend leaves next month to go study abroad in Korea.

244

바쁘고 복잡한 도시를 떠나서 시골에서 살고 싶어요.
I want to leave the busy and complicated city and move to the country.

025
묵다

[묵따] 동사 to stay

to stay at a place as a guest

[Expression]   **N**에서 묵다

[Synonym]   숙박하다 to lodge

[Example]   부산에 사는 친구 집에서 며칠 묵었어요.
I stayed at my friend's house in Busan for a few days.

제주도에서 제일 좋은 호텔에서 묵으려고 해요.
I plan on staying at the best hotel in Jeju island.

026
−박 −일

[−박−일] 명사 -night -day

words used to tell the night and days during a vacation

[Usage]   **Num**박 **Num**일

[Example]   이 여행 상품은 19(십구)박 20(이십)일 동안 유럽 10(십)개국을 여행하는 상품입니다.
This travel product is for 19 nights and 20 days for traveling 10 different European countries.

저는 7(칠)월 16(십육)일부터 18(십팔)일까지 2(이)박 3(삼)일 동안 설악산에 놀러갈 거예요.
I am going to go to Sorak mountain on July 16th to the 18th for 2 nights and 3 days.

027
비용

[비용] 명사 cost expense

money that is used to pay for something

[Expression]   여행 비용 cost expense of vacation
비용이 들다 it costs something

[Example]   이번 여행은 비용이 얼마나 들까요?
How much will it cost to go on this vacation?

아버지의 수술 비용이 많이 들어서 나와 동생은 학교를 휴학하고 아르바이트를 시작했다.
Our father's surgery cost was very expensive so my brother and I took time off of school and started to work part time.

028
비자

[비자] 명사 visa

an application that approves a person to enter a foreign country

[Expression]   비자를 받다 to receive a visa
비자를 신청하다 to apply for a visa

비자를 연장하다 to extend a visa

[Related word]　출입국관리사무소 immigration office

[Example]　한국에 가려면 비자가 필요해요?

If I want to go to Korea, do I need a visa?

비자를 신청하기 위해서 대사관에 갔습니다.

I went to the embassy to request a visa.

029
세상

[세상] 명사 the world, society

the whole society of the place where people live

[Expression]　세상 구경 world tour

세상 사람들 people of the world

[Synonym]　세계 the world

[Example]　나는 세상에서 우리 가족이 제일 소중해요.

To me my family is the most precious thing in the world.

이 세상에는 우리가 상상할 수 없는 일들이 아주 많다.

In this world there are many unimaginable things that happen.

030
숙박

[숙빡] 명사 lodge

staying at a hotel or motel to sleep or just stay

[Expression]　숙박비 lodging fee

숙박 시설 lodge facilities

숙박하다 to lodge

[Example]　관광지에는 숙박 시설이 많다.

There are many lodging facilities near tourist areas.

우리는 숙박비를 아끼기 위해서 여관에서 숙박하기로 했다.

We wanted to save on lodging fees so we stayed at the motel.

 도움말

These nouns portray different lodging facilities.

- 민박 private rental room: this is not a hotel but a house where people rent to use during vacation

- 여관 inn/motel: a room that customers can pay and stay in

- 모텔 motel: like a 여관

- 콘도 condo: it is shaped like a apartment and you can make food, and the place is taken care by the office that takes care of the home, kind of like a hotel

- 펜션 pension: western style lodging house, can borrow the whole home and make food and stay

- 호텔 hotel: western style motel that is big and glamorous

031
안내

[안내] 명사 guidance

telling someone of the location, information or other information, going some place with someone who doesn't know the road

[Expression]
안내 방송 guidance broadcast
안내 책자 guidance book
행사 안내 guidance information
안내하다 to guide
안내를 받다 to be guided

[Example]
지하철이나 버스를 타면 내릴 역에 대한 안내 방송이 나옵니다.
When getting off of a subway or bus, there will be guidance broadcast of the station you will be getting off at.

저는 인사동에서 외국인에게 길을 안내하는 봉사활동을 하고 있습니다.
I am volunteering as a guide at Insa-dong for foreigners.

032
여권

[여꿘] 명사 passport

[Expression]
여권이 나오다 the passport is out
여권을 신청하다 to request a passport

[Example]
여권을 신청할 때 필요한 서류가 뭐예요?
What are the needed documents for requesting a passport?

외국에서 여권을 잃어버리면 대사관에 가야 해요.
If you lose your passport in a foreign country, you need to go to the embassy.

033
여행

[여행] 명사 traveling

[Expression]
여행사 traveling agency
여행 경비 vacation expense
여행하다 to travel
여행을 가다 to go on vacation
여행을 떠나다 to leave for vacation

[Example]
나는 휴가 때마다 가족들과 여행을 간다.
During my vacation I always go on vacation with my family.

해마다 해외여행을 가는 사람들이 많아지고 있어요.
Every year there are more people going on vacation in foreign countries.

There are words that show different types of traveling, and these are some.

해외여행, 배낭여행, 신혼여행, 국내 여행, 단체 여행, 세계 여행, ……
foreign country vacation, backpack vacation, honeymoon vacation, in country vacation, group vacation, world vacation, ……

034
예약

[예약] **명사** reservation

reserving a seat in the restaurant, hotel, or airplane in advance, or just reserving in advance

[Expression] 식당 예약 restaurant reservation

호텔 예약 hotel reservation

예약하다 to reserve

예약을 받다 to receive a reservation

예약을 취소하다 to cancel a reservation

[Related word] 예매 advance purchase

[Example] 방학에 고향에 가려고 비행기표를 예약했다.
I reserved an airplane ticket so that I could go to my hometown during the break.

고급 레스토랑은 1(일)주일 전에 미리 예약해야 해요.
You have to reserve a seat at a high class restaurant a week in advance.

'예약' is used when reserving a seat at a hotel, restaurant, or airplane and promising to use it later. '예매' is buying a movie or museum ticket in advance.

035
출국

[출국] **명사** departure of a country

going out of country, going to see other countries

[Expression] 출국 날짜 date of departure

출국하다 to depart

[Antonym] 입국 enter a country

[Example] 한국으로 출국하는 날이 언제예요?
What is the date you depart from Korea?

나는 출국하기 전에 배웅을 나온 친구들과 인사를 했다.
Before I departed the country, I greeted my friends who came to send me off.

036
게임

[게임] 명사 game

[Usage]	<u>N</u> 게임
[Expression]	게임기 portable game
	야구 게임 baseball game
	컴퓨터 게임 computer game
	게임을 하다 to play a game
[Example]	어제 늦게까지 인터넷 게임을 해서 오늘 학교에 지각했다.
	I was late for school today because I played games until late last night.
	여행지에서 여러 사람이 같이 할 수 있는 재미있는 게임을 소개해 주세요.
	Please introduce me to a game we can play at the vacation spot.

037
그리다

[그리다] 동사 to draw

to draw something with lines or colors on paper

[Usage]	<u>N</u>을/를 그리다
[Expression]	풍경을 그리다 to draw the landscape
[Related word]	그림 drawing
	미술 the fine arts
	화가 a painter
[Example]	친구는 나에게 학교에 가는 길을 지도로 그려 주었다.
	My friend drew a map of the road to school.
	제 취미는 주말마다 공원에 가서 사람들의 모습을 그리는 것입니다.
	My hobby is to go to the park during the weekend and draw people's form.

038
낚시

[낚씨] 명사 fishing, fish hook

equipment used for fishing, the end is sharp, pointy and rounded, fishing with the hook

[Expression]	낚시하다 to fish
	낚시를 가다 to go fishing
[Example]	우리는 낚시로 잡은 물고기로 매운탕을 끓였다.
	We made a spicy stew with the fish that we caught.
	아버지는 낚시를 아주 좋아하셔서 쉬는 날마다 낚시를 가십니다.
	Our father really likes to fish. He fishes every time he has a break.

039
노래

[노래] 명사 song

[Expression]   노래방 karaoke

노래 한 곡 one song

노래하다 to sing

노래를 부르다 to sing a song

[Related word]   가수 singer

가요 song

[Example]   동생은 설거지를 하면서 노래를 불렀다.
My younger sibling sang while doing the dishes.

요즘 한국에서 제일 인기가 있는 노래가 뭐예요?
What is the most popular song in Korea these days?

040
독서

[독써] 명사 reading

reading books

[Expression]   독서하다 to read

[Example]   한국 사람들은 가을을 독서의 계절이라고 합니다.
Korean people call autumn the season for reading.

저는 집에서 혼자 조용히 독서하는 것을 좋아합니다.
I like to read quietly at home.

041
등산

[등산] 명사 hiking

walking on a mountain to exercise, or to just enjoy

[Expression]   등산화 hiking shoes

등산객 hiking people

등산로 hiking road

등산하다 to hike

등산을 가다 to go hiking

[Example]   우리 형은 주말마다 서울에 있는 산을 등산한다.
My older brother goes hiking every weekend on mountains in Seoul.

가을에는 단풍을 구경하려고 등산을 가는 사람들이 많습니다.
There are many people who go hiking during the autumn to see the changing leaves.

042
모으다

[모으다] 동사 1. to collect   2. to save

1. to collect a certain item as a hobby, 으 verb

[Usage]   **N**을/를 모으다

[Expression]   우표를 모으다 to collect postage stamps

[Synonym]	수집하다 to gather	
[Example]	제 동생은 외국 돈을 모으는 것이 취미입니다.	
	My younger sibling's hobby is to collect foreign money.	

2. to save money by not using it, 으 verb

[Usage]	<u>N</u>을/를 모으다
[Expression]	돈을 모으다 to save money
[Example]	돈을 모아서 사고 싶었던 오토바이를 샀어요.
	I saved my money and bought a motorbike I wanted to buy.

043
바둑

[바둑] 명사 baduk(Korean chess)

a game where each person gets black and white pieces and uses it to play by placing them on a board

[Expression]	바둑 한 판 a game of Korean chess
	바둑을 두다 to play Korean chess
[Example]	할아버지들이 시원한 나무 아래에서 바둑을 두고 계셨다.
	The grandfathers were sitting under the cool tree and playing Korean chess.

한국에는 바둑이 취미인 사람들이 많아서 24(이십사)시간 바둑 경기만 보여 주는 TV채널도 있습니다.
There are many people in Korea who's hobby is to play Korean chess, so there is a TV channel that only shows Korean chess competitions 24 hours a day.

044
보통

[보통] 부사 mainly, usually

normally

[Related word]	주로 usually
[Example]	보통 몇 시에 출근하세요? When do you usually leave for work?
	너는 보통 수업이 끝난 후에 뭘 하니?
	What do you usually do after you have class?

045
사진

[사진] 명사 photograph

[Usage]	<u>N</u> 사진
[Expression]	사진기 camera
	결혼사진 wedding picture
	여행 사진 vacation picture
	사진 한 장 one picture
	사진을 찍다 to take pictures
[Related word]	카메라 camera
	촬영하다 to photograph

[Example] 가족들이 보고 싶을 때에는 가족사진을 봅니다.
Whenever I want to see my family, I look at my family picture.

오늘은 졸업 사진을 찍는 날이어서 정장을 입은 학생들이 많다.
Today is the day for taking graduating pictures, so there are many students in formal wear.

046
산책

[산책] 명사 a walk

slowly walking somewhere to be healthier or to feel at rest

[Expression] 산책하다 to walk

[Example] 공원에는 산책을 나온 사람들이 많았어요.
There were many people who came to the park to walk.

우리는 날마다 저녁 식사 후에 30(삼십)분씩 집 근처를 산책한다.
Everyday after dinner we go walking near our home for 30 minutes.

047
악기

[악끼] 명사 instrument

an equipment used to play music

[Expression] 악기를 연주하다 to play an instrument

[Related word] 연주회 a performance

[Example] 선배님은 무슨 악기를 연주할 수 있어요?
Senior, what instrument can you play?

음악 선생님은 피아노, 바이올린, 첼로 등 여러 가지 악기를 연주하실 수 있다.
Our music teacher can play the piano, violin, cello and other instruments.

048
야영

[야영] 명사 camping

to set up tents outside for vacation or for training, and stay for some time

[Expression] 야영하다 to camp

[Synonym] 캠핑 camping

[Example] 야영을 가려고 하는데 어디가 좋아요?
I want to go camping. Where is a good place to camp?

여름에 야영을 할 때에는 비가 많이 올 수 있으니까 일기예보를 잘 들어야 한다.
If you go camping during the summer it could rain, you need to listen to the weather news carefully.

These are some western instruments.

- 피아노 : 피아노를 치다 piano: to play the piano
- 기타 : 기타를 치다 guitar: to play the guitar
- 바이올린 : 바이올린을 켜다 violin: to play the violin

049
찍다

[찍따] 동사 to take a picture

to capture an image through a camera film

[Usage] N을/를 찍다

[Expression] 사진을 찍다 to take a picture

영화를 찍다 to shoot a movie

동영상을 찍다 to shoot a short movie

[Synonym] 촬영하다 to film

[Example] 여기가 경치도 아름답고 유명한 곳이니까 여기에서 사진을 찍자!
Let's take a picture here! This place is famous and has a beautiful landscape.

이 섬은 인기 있는 드라마를 많이 찍은 곳이어서 1(일)년 내내 관광객이 많아요.
There are many tourists all year around because this island was used for filming many famous dramas.

050
추다

[추다] 동사 to dance

to move one's body because one feels good or because there is music

[Expression] 춤을 추다 to dance

[Related word] 춤 dance

[Example] 춤은 잘 추지만 노래는 잘 부르지 못하는 가수도 있다.
There are singers that can dance well but can't sing well.

할아버지의 회갑 잔치에서 어른들이 음악에 맞춰서 춤을 추셨다.
At my grandfather's 60th birthday festival, the adults danced to the music.

051
취미

[취미] 명사 hobby

liking something so much that one does it for fun and not for work

[Expression] 취미 생활 hobby life

취미가 있다 to have a hobby

[Example] 제 취미는 독서입니다. My hobby is to read.

나중에 결혼하면 아내와 같이 취미 생활을 할 수 있었으면 좋겠어요.
After marriage I hope I can have a hobby life with my wife.

[1~15] 다음 단어를 한국어로 바꿔 쓰십시오. Change these words into Korean.

1. team	( )	2. touring	( )
3. commemoration	( )	4. visa	( )
5. screening	( )	6. play	( )
7. movie	( )	8. advance purchase	( )
9. lodging	( )	10. walking	( )
11. fine arts	( )	12. music	( )
13. drama	( )	14. to dance	( )
15. to throw	( )		

[16~20] 그림을 보고 (   )에 알맞은 것을 고르십시오.
Look at the picture and choose the correct word.

16.

가 : 어제 뭘 했어요?
나 : 친구들과 운동장에서 (   )을/를 했어요.

❶ 축구　　　　❷ 배구
❸ 농구　　　　❹ 탁구

17.

가 : 보통 주말에 뭘 하세요?
나 : 저는 주말마다 (   )을/를 합니다.

❶ 낚시　　　　❷ 등산
❸ 수영　　　　❹ 달리기

254

18.

가 : 해외 여행을 가려면 뭘 준비해야 해요?

나 : 우선 ( )을/를 준비해야 해요.

❶ 비자 ❷ 안내
❸ 여권 ❹ 필름

19.

가 : 영화표를 사려면 어디로 가야 해요?

나 : 극장 앞에 있는 ( )으로/로 가세요.

❶ 민박 ❷ 여관
❸ 호텔 ❹ 매표소

20.

가 : 이번 주말에 뭘 할 거예요?

나 : 제가 좋아하는 가수의 ( )에 가려고 해요.

❶ 연극 ❷ 영화
❸ 드라마 ❹ 콘서트

[21~30] 다음 문장을 읽고 알맞은 어휘를 골라 쓰십시오. 어휘는 한 번만 쓰십시오.

Read the following sentence and choose the right word. Use the words once.

표	관광	게임	기념	노래
낚시	독서	바둑	보통	비용
사진	악기	취미	예약	그리다

21. 저는 (   ) 아침 7시에 일어납니다.

22. 전시회를 보려면 우선 (   )을/를 사야 합니다.

23. 제 친구는 가수처럼 (   )을/를 아주 잘 불러요.

24. 부모님께서 결혼하신 지 30년이 된 (   )으로/로 여행을 가셨다.

25. 이 건물은 유명한 건물이니까 이 건물 앞에서 (   )을/를 찍읍시다.

26. 제 하숙집 친구는 (   )을/를 좋아해서 책을 한 달에 4권 정도 읽습니다.

27. 그 가수는 피아노, 바이올린, 기타 등 여러 가지 (   )을/를 연주할 수 있어요.

28. 유럽으로 여행을 가고 싶었지만 여행 (   )이/가 너무 많이 들어서 못 갔어요.

29. 제 (   )은/는 볼링입니다. 그래서 주말마다 친구들과 함께 볼링장에 갑니다.

30. 그 식당은 주말에 손님들이 많아서 먼저 (   )을/를 하지 않으면 안 돼요.

[31~35] (   ) 안에 알맞은 것을 고르십시오. Choose the correct one.

31. 저는 영화 (   )이/가 취미여서 주말마다 영화관에 갑니다.

❶ 감상　　　　❷ 상영　　　　❸ 예매　　　　❹ 필름

32. 오늘 축구 (   )에서 독일이 한국을 1:0으로 이겼다.

❶ 팀　　　　❷ 경기　　　　❸ 운동　　　　❹ 스포츠

33. 저는 한국, 일본, 영국, 프랑스 등 세계 여러 나라를 (   )었습니다/았습니다/였습니다.

   ❶ 산책   ❷ 안내   ❸ 야영   ❹ 여행

34. 제 동생은 그림을 잘 (   )습니다/ㅂ니다.

   ❶ 찍다   ❷ 추다   ❸ 그리다   ❹ 모으다

35. 친구가 발로 공을 세게 (   )었다/았다/였다.

   ❶ 묶다   ❷ 차다   ❸ 타다   ❹ 던지다

[36~38] 밑줄 친 부분과 반대되는 뜻을 가진 것을 고르십시오.

Choose the word that is the opposite of the underlined word.

36. **가 :** 여기가 <u>입국하는</u> 사람들이 들어오는 곳이에요?
   나 : 아니요, (   )는 사람들이 나가는 곳이에요.

   ❶ 출국하다   ❷ 여행하다   ❸ 예약하다   ❹ 기념하다

37. **가 :** 영수가 여행을 <u>떠난다고</u> 해요.
   나 : 그래요? 그럼 언제 (   )는다고/ㄴ다고 해요?

   ❶ 묶다   ❷ 타다   ❸ 나가다   ❹ 돌아오다

38. **가 :** 공을 <u>던져</u>!
   나 : 알았어, 던질 테니까 잘 (   )어/아/여.

   ❶ 추다   ❷ 차다   ❸ 받다   ❹ 주다

[39~45] 밑줄 친 부분과 의미가 가장 가까운 것을 고르십시오.
Choose the word that is most similar to the underlined section.

39. **가 :** 제일 좋아하는 <u>스포츠</u>가 뭐예요?

    나 : 저는 모든 (   )을/를 좋아해요.

    ❶ 게임　　　　　❷ 경기　　　　　❸ 산책　　　　　❹ 운동

40. **가 :** <u>세계</u> 여행을 하면 많은 것을 배울 수 있어서 좋아.

    나 : 맞아. 넓은 (   )을/를 구경하면 생각과 마음도 넓어지는 것 같아.

    ❶ 팀　　　　　　❷ 세상　　　　　❸ 비자　　　　　❹ 비용

41. **가 :** 가족들과 <u>캠핑</u>을 간 적이 있어요?

    나 : 네, 아버지께서 여행을 좋아하셔서 초등학교 때에는 주말마다 산에 가서 (   )을/를
    했어요.

    ❶ 관광　　　　　❷ 구경　　　　　❸ 안내　　　　　❹ 야영

42. **가 :** 네가 영화 <u>티켓</u>을 샀어? 이번에는 내가 사려고 했는데 …….

    나 : 그럼 내가 (   )을/를 샀으니까 네가 저녁을 사.

    ❶ 표　　　　　　❷ 감상　　　　　❸ 상영　　　　　❹ 예매

43. **가 :** 오랜만에 가는 가족 여행인데 어디에서 <u>숙박하면</u> 좋을까요?

    나 : 조금 비싸지만 호텔에서 (   )자.

    ❶ 살다　　　　　❷ 묵다　　　　　❸ 차다　　　　　❹ 떠나다

44. **가 :** 요즘 무슨 영화를 <u>촬영하세요</u>?

    나 : 액션 영화를 (   )고 있어요.

    ❶ 찍다　　　　　❷ 추다　　　　　❸ 그리다　　　　　❹ 던지다

45. **가** : 우표를 많이 <u>수집</u>하셨군요.

    나 : 네, 우표를 ( )는 것이 제 취미이니까요.

    ❶ 차다   ❷ 치다   ❸ 하다   ❹ 모으다

[46~50] 밑줄 친 단어의 쓰임이 잘못된 것을 고르십시오. Choose the one that is incorrectly used.

46. ❶ 저는 저녁마다 형과 탁구를 <u>쳐요</u>.   ( )

    ❷ 우리는 생일 축하 노래를 부른 후에 박수를 <u>쳤다</u>.

    ❸ 그 남자는 피아노를 <u>치면서</u> 노래를 부르고 있어요.

    ❹ 우리 반 남학생들은 수업이 끝난 후에 게임방에 가서 게임을 <u>칩니다</u>.

47. ❶ 버스를 <u>타고</u> 학교에 와요.   ( )

    ❷ 코끼리를 <u>타</u> 본 적이 있어요?

    ❸ 비자를 <u>타려면</u> 대사관에 가야 한다.

    ❹ 저는 겨울이 되면 주말마다 스키를 <u>타러</u> 스키장에 갑니다.

48. ❶ 어디에서 표를 <u>살</u> 수 있어요?   ( )

    ❷ 이번 공연은 표가 모두 <u>매진</u>되었습니다.

    ❸ 인기가 많은 영화는 미리 <u>예매</u>해야 해요.

    ❹ 다음 달에 열리는 축구 경기의 표를 <u>하고</u> 싶어요.

49. ❶ 아침 일찍 여행을 <u>출발</u>했어요.   ( )

    ❷ 여행을 가면 어디에서 <u>묵을</u> 거예요?

    ❸ 호텔에서 그 근처 관광지를 <u>안내</u>해 줄 거예요.

    ❹ 8월에 여행을 가려면 우선 비행기표를 <u>예약</u>하세요.

50. ❶ 주말에 서울 구경을 <u>하려고</u> 해요.   ( )

    ❷ 나는 친구들과 같이 동물원 구경을 <u>갔어요</u>.

    ❸ 그 건물은 아주 유명한데 구경을 <u>본</u> 적이 있어요?

    ❹ 제주도는 경치가 아름다워서 구경을 <u>오는</u> 사람이 많다.

음식

11

Food

001
달다

[달다] 형용사 to be sweet

a taste that is like sugar or honey, ㄹverb

[Usage] N이/가 달다

[Expression] 단 맛 sweet taste

사탕이 달다 the candy is sweet

[Example] 설탕을 많이 넣은 것 같아요. 음식이 좀 달아요.

There seems to be a lot of sugar. This food is sweet.

사탕 같이 단 것을 너무 좋아하면 충치가 생길 수 있다.

If you like too many things that are like candy, you can get decayed teeth.

002
맛

[맏] 명사 taste

the sense that can be felt when the tongue touches food

[Expression] 맛이 있다 it has a taste

맛이 좋다 it tastes good

[Example] 음식 맛이 어때요? How is the taste of the food?

맛이 참 좋다. 이 음식을 어떻게 만들었니?

It tastes really good. How did you make this food?

003
맛있다

[마딛따/마싣따] 형용사 to taste good

the taste of the food is good

[Usage] N이/가 맛있다

[Antonym] 맛없다 to not taste good

[Example] 배가 좀 고픈데 뭐 맛있는 음식이 없을까?

I am hungry. Is there any good food?

엄마가 만들어 주신 음식이 제일 맛있어요.

Food that my mom makes tastes the best.

004
맵다

[맵따] 형용사 to be spicy

taste that comes from peppers or wasabe, ㅂverb

[Usage] N이/가 맵다

[Expression] 매운 음식 spicy food

고추가 맵다 the pepper is spicy

[Example] 김치는 맛있지만 좀 매워요. Kimchi is good but a bit spicy.

음식이 너무 매워서 눈물이 나요.

The food is so spicy that tears are coming out.

005
시다

[시다] 형용사 to be sour

to taste like lemon or vinegar

[Usage] N이/가 시다

[Expression] 신 맛 sour taste

굴이 시다 the tangerine is sour

[Example] 식초를 많이 넣어서 음식 맛이 너무 시어요.

The food is too sour because there is too much vinegar.

요즘 파는 굴은 맛이 있기는 하지만 좀 시다.

The tangerines they sell these days are good but a bit sour.

006
싱겁다

[싱겁따] 형용사 to be not salted enough, or bland

it is not salty, but does not have the right amount of salt, ㅂverb

[Usage] N이/가 싱겁다

[Expression] 싱거운 음식 bland food

국이 싱겁다 the soup is bland

싱겁게 먹다 to eat bland

[Example] 국이 좀 싱거워서 소금을 더 넣어야겠어요.

The soup is bland. I should put more salt inside.

음식을 싱겁게 먹는 것이 건강에 좋다고 합니다.

It it healthy to eat food that is less salty.

007
쓰다⁴

[쓰다] 형용사 to be bitter

to have taste like coffee or medicine, 으 verb

[Usage] N이/가 쓰다

[Expression] 쓴 나물 bitter vegetables

한약이 쓰다 herbal medcine

[Example] 한약이 너무 써서 못 먹겠어요.

The herbal medicine is so bitter that I can't drink it.

입에 쓴 음식이 몸에 좋다는 말이 있다.

There is a saying that bitter food is good for your body.

008
짜다

[짜다] 형용사 to be salty

taste similar to salt

[Usage] N이/가 짜다

[Expression] 짠 음식 salty food

찌개가 짜다 the stew is salty

짜게 먹다 to eat it salty

[Example]　저에게 한식은 좀 맵고 짭니다.
Korean food is a bit salty and spicy for me.

설탕을 넣어야 하는데 소금을 넣어서 맛이 너무 짜요.
The food is salty because I was supposed to put sugar in it, but I put salt instead.

11-2 | 음료 · 간식

009
간식

[간식] 명사 snack
food that you eat in between meals

[Example]　배가 좀 고픈데 간식이 있어요?
I'm a bit hungry. Do you have a snack?

간식을 너무 많이 먹으면 밥을 먹기 싫어지니까 조금만 먹어라.
If you eat too many snacks, you will not want to eat the meal so only eat a little bit.

010
과일

[과일] 명사 fruit

[Expression]　과일 주스　fruit juice
과일이 나다　fruit is grown
과일을 따다　to pick fruit

[Example]　무슨 과일을 좋아하세요? 저는 수박을 좋아해요.
What kinds of fruits do you like? I like watermelons.

딸기와 바나나로 만든 과일 주스가 맛있는데 한번 드셔 보세요.
Try the juice made from strawberries and bananas. It is good.

도움말

The following are some fruits.

감, 귤, 딸기, 바나나, 사과, 수박, 오렌지, 포도, ……

persimmon, tangerine, strawberry, banana, apple, watermelon, orange, grape, ……

011
과자

[과자] **명사** cookie

[Expression] 과자 한 봉지 one package of cookies

[Example] 요즘 과자를 많이 먹어서 살이 쪘다.
I ate a lot of cookies these days so I gained a bit of weight.

맛이 단 과자는 쓴 커피와 함께 먹으면 더 좋아요.
It is best to eat sweet cookies with bitter coffee.

012
떡

[떡] **명사** rice cake

food that has been made with grain powder by steaming or baking

[Expression] 떡을 찌다 to steam rice cake

[Example] 요즘 나는 아침에 밥을 먹지 않고 떡을 먹는다.
These days I eat rice cake instead of rice for breakfast.

한국 사람들은 큰 잔치가 있을 때마다 떡을 먹습니다.
Korean people always eat rice cake during big festivals.

013
물

[물] **명사** water

[Expression] 따뜻한 물 warm water
물을 끓이다 to boil water

[Related word] 생수 spring water

[Example] 엄마, 목이 말라요. 물을 좀 주세요.
Mother, I am thirsty. Please give me water.

목감기에 걸렸을 때는 따뜻한 물을 자주 마시는 것이 좋습니다.
If you have a sore throat, it is best to drink warm water.

014
병¹

[병] **명사** bottle

(made out of glass or porcelein) cup used to pour liquid into, counting unit for those cups

[Expression] 물병 water bottle
술 한 병 one bottle of alcohol
병이 깨지다 the bottle is broken

[Example] 맥주를 몇 병쯤 사 놓으면 될까요?
How many bottles of beer should I buy?

냉장고를 열어 보면 문 쪽에 병이 하나 있지? 그게 물이니까 꺼내서 마셔라.
There is a bottle on one side of the refrigerator right? It is water so take it out and drink the bottle.

015

빵

[빵] 명사 bread

a food made from mixing salt and sugar and making it into dough, letting it rise with yeast and then baking it

[Expression] 빵집 bakery shop

빵 한 조각 one slice of bread

빵을 굽다 to bake bread

[Example] 아침에 저는 빵과 우유를 먹어요.
I eat bread and milk for breakfast.

빵집에서 금방 빵을 구워서 좋은 냄새가 나요.
The bakery just baked bread so now it smells good.

016

사탕

[사탕] 명사 candy

[Example] 사탕을 싫어하는 아이는 없어요.
There are no children that don't like candy.

식사 후에 사탕을 서비스로 주는 식당이 있다.
After meals there are restaurants that give candy for free.

017

술

[술] 명사 alcohol

a drink where one gets drunk because there is alcohol in the liquid

[Expression] 술 한 병 one bottle of alcohol

술을 끊다 to stop drinking alcohol

술을 한잔하다 to drink a glass of alcohol

술에 취하다 to get drunk from alcohol

[Example] 퇴근한 후에 동료들과 함께 술을 한잔했다.
I had a drink with my colleagues after work.

저는 술을 잘 마시지 못하지만 술을 마시는 자리는 좋아해요.
I can't drink really well but I like to be at drinking gatherings.

도움말

These words are different types of alcohol.

맥주, 소주, 양주, 포도주, 막걸리, ……
beer, soju, liquor, wine, rice wine, ……

266

018
아이스크림

[아이스크림] **명사** ice cream

[Example] 여름이 되니까 아이스크림을 찾는 손님들이 많아졌다.
It is summer now, so there are many customers that look for ice cream.

우리 식사한 후에 커피를 마실까? 아이스크림을 먹을까?
After eating should we drink coffee? or eat ice cream?

019
요구르트

[요구르트] **명사** yogurt

one type of dairy product made from fermented milk, drank or eaten with a spoon

[Example] 과일샐러드에 요구르트를 부어서 먹으면 맛있어요.
It tastes good if you put yogurt in the fruit salad.

저는 요즘 다이어트를 하려고 아침에는 요구르트만 먹어요.
I am on a diet these days so I eat only yogurt for breakfast.

020
우유

[우유] **명사** milk

[Example] 저는 커피에 우유를 넣어서 마셔요.
I put milk in my coffee and drink the coffee.

우유를 많이 마시면 키가 커질 거야. 많이 마셔.
If you drink a lot of milk, you will grow taller. Drink a lot.

021
음료수

[음뇨수] **명사** drink

something that one can drink to get rid of thirst, water, juice, cola and other drinks

[Example] 손님께 음료수를 한 잔 드리세요. Give the guest something to drink.
아이에게는 음료수보다는 물을 마시게 하는 게 좋아요.
It is better to give children water than other drinks.

022
잔

[잔] **명사** cup, glass

a small cup used to pour tea or coffee in and drinking it out of there, or a counting unit for those kinds of cups

[Expression] 술잔 glass of alcohol
차 한 잔 one cup of tea
한잔하다 to have a glass

[Example] 저는 술을 한 잔만 마셔도 취해요.
I get drunk if I even drink a glass of alcohol.

밥을 먹은 후에 차를 한 잔 할까요?
Should we get a cup of tea after our meal?

023
주스

[주스] **명사** juice

[Expression] 과일 주스 fruit juice

주스 한 잔 a cup of juice

[Example] 어머니는 과일로 직접 주스를 만들어서 우리한테 주신다.
Our mother makes juice by hand and gives it to us.

운전을 해야 하니까 술은 마실 수 없어요. 그냥 주스 한 잔 주세요.
I have to drive so I can't have any alcohol. Please just give me a glass of juice.

024
차¹

[차] **명사** tea

[Expression] 차를 끓이다 to boil tea

[Example] 어머니는 항상 보리차를 끓여서 냉장고에 넣어 놓으신다.
My mother always boils barley tea and puts it in the refrigerator.

선생님은 차를 좋아하셔서 댁에 여러 가지 종류의 차가 많다.
Our teacher likes tea so there are many types of tea at her home.

 도움말

These words are some words that tell the different types of tea.

녹차, 홍차, 인삼차, 보리차, 유자차, 생강차, 대추차, ……
green tea, black tea, ginseng tea, barley tea, citron tea, ginger tea, jujube tea, ……

025
초콜릿

[초콜릳] **명사** chocolate

[Example] 피곤할 때 초콜릿을 먹으면 피로가 좀 풀려요.
If you eat chocolate when you're tired, you will feel less sleepy.

저는 아이스크림 중에서 초콜릿 아이스크림을 제일 좋아해요.
I like chocolate ice cream the best out of all the ice creams.

026
커피

[커피] **명사** coffee

[Expression] 커피숍 coffee shop

[Example] 피곤하면 커피를 한 잔 마시고 계속 공부할까?
If you're tired, should we drink a cup of coffee and start studying again?

저는 커피를 조금만 마셔도 밤에 잠을 자지 못해요.
If I drink even a little bit of coffee, I can't go to sleep at night.

027
케이크

[케이크] **명사** cake

[Expression] 생일 케이크 birthday cake

케이크 한 조각 one piece of cake

[Example] 오늘 언니 생일이니까 우리 케이크를 사러 가자.

It's my older sister's birthday, let's go buy her a cake.

친구 생일이어서 직접 케이크를 만들어서 선물했어요.

It was my friend's birthday so I made her a cake myself and gave it to her as a present.

028
콜라

[콜라] **명사** cola

[Example] 오늘 점심에는 콜라하고 피자를 시켜서 먹었다.

I ordered and ate cola and pizza for lunch.

낮이니까 맥주를 마시지 말고 그냥 콜라를 마시자.

It is early in the afternoon so let's drink cola instead of beer.

11-3 | 재료 · 소스

029
간장

[간장] **명사** soy sauce

a liquid that is black and is made from fermented soybean, it creates flavor for food and is a bit salty

[Example] 나물 맛이 좀 싱거운데요. 간장을 더 넣어야겠어요.

The vegetables are a bit bland. You better put more soy sauce inside.

파전을 간장에 찍어서 드시면 맛이 더 좋을 거예요.

If you dip and eat pajeon in the soy sauce, it will taste better.

030
고기

[고기] **명사** meat

the flesh of animals that is eaten

[Expression] 물고기 fish

닭고기 chicken

고기 한 근 600g of meat

고기가 익다 the meat is cooked

고기를 굽다 to grill the meat

[Example]　고기를 먹을 때에는 채소도 같이 드세요.
Whenever you eat meat, eat vegetables as well.

고기를 좋아해도 너무 많이 먹으면 건강에 좋지 않다.
Even if you like meat, don't eat too much because it's not good for your health.

031
고추

[고추] 명사 pepper

one type of vegetable that has a spicy taste, there are green and red ones

[Expression]　고추장 pepper paste
고춧가루 pepper powder

[Example]　고추는 너무 매워서 못 먹겠어요.
Pepper is so spicy that it's hard for me to eat.

매운 고추를 고추장에 찍어 먹어요?
Do you dip pepper paste on spicy peppers?

032
곡물

[공물] 명사 grain

grain that humans eat that include, rice, barley, beans, millet, sorghum, wheat, corn and others

[Synonym]　곡식 grain or cereal

[Example]　한국 사람들은 여러 가지 곡물 중에서 쌀을 제일 많이 먹는다.
Korean people eat rice mostly out of all the grains.

요즘은 빵을 만들 때 여러 가지 곡물을 넣어서 만들기도 합니다.
These days they put many different types of grains when making bread.

033
달걀

[달걀] 명사 egg

egg laid from a chicken

[Expression]　삶은 달걀 boiled egg
달걀 프라이 fried egg

[Synonym]　계란 egg

[Example]　간식으로 먹으려고 달걀을 삶아 놓았다.
I boiled eggs so that I could eat it as a snack.

라면에 달걀을 넣어서 끓여 보세요. 더 맛있을 거예요.
Put egg when you're cooking ramen. It will taste better.

034
당근

[당근] 명사 carrot

[Example]　당근이 눈에 좋다고 하니까 많이 먹어야 해.
They say carrots are good for your eyes so you should eat a lot.

당근은 그냥 먹는 것보다 볶아서 먹는 것이 더 좋다고 한다.
It is better to eat carrot after it has been stir fried rather than raw.

035 된장

[된장] **명사** fermented soy paste

fermented soy bean that has been put in soy sauce and later taking that soy sauce out and leaving the salty taste

[Expression] 된장찌개 soy bean paste soup

[Example] 고추를 된장에 찍어서 먹어 봐. 진짜 맛있지?
Dip the pepper in the soy bean paste. It's good right?

어머니는 간장, 된장, 고추장을 직접 만들어서 드신다.
My mother makes soy sauce, fermented soy paste and pepper paste by hand and eats them.

036 두부

[두부] **명사** tofu

one type of food made from soy bean

[Expression] 두부 한 모 one block of tofu

두부를 부치다 to grill tofu

[Related word] 콩 soy bean

[Example] 두부는 콩으로 만든 음식이다. Tofu is made from soy bean.

두부를 넣어서 된장찌개를 끓였어요.
I cooked soy bean paste soup with tofu.

037 마늘

[마늘] **명사** garlic

[Example] 한국의 거의 모든 음식에는 마늘이 들어간다.
Most Korean food have garlic in them.

상추에 고기하고 고추장, 마늘을 싸서 먹어 봐라.
Try eating lettuce, meat, pepper paste, and garlic in a wrap.

038 상추

[상추] **명사** lettuce

one type of green vegetable, usually eaten with rice and meat in a wrap

[Expression] 상추쌈 lettuce wrap

[Example] 고기를 먹을 때 상추에 싸서 먹으면 더 맛있습니다.
If you eat meat wrapped in lettuce, it will taste better.

상추는 키우기가 쉬우니까 직접 키워서 드셔 보세요.
Growing lettuce is pretty easy so grow it and eat the lettuce.

271

039
생선

[생선] **명사** fish

[Expression]	생선회 fish sushi
	생선 구이 grilled fish
	생선 한 마리 one fish
[Example]	저는 고기보다 생선을 더 좋아해요. I like fish better than meat.
	겨울이니까 생선회가 아주 싱싱할 거예요. Since it is winter, the fish will be very fresh.

040
소금

[소금] **명사** salt

[Expression]	소금을 넣다 to put salt in
	소금을 뿌리다 to sprinkle salt in
[Related word]	설탕 sugar
[Example]	국이 싱겁네요. 소금을 넣어야겠어요. The soup is bland. I better put some salt inside.
	소금을 넣어야 하는데 설탕을 넣어 버려서 음식 맛이 이상해졌어요. The food tastes weird because I was supposed to put salt inside but I put sugar inside instead.

041
소스

[소스] **명사** sauce

[Expression]	스테이크 소스 steak sauce
	소스를 뿌리다 to sprinkle sauce
[Example]	그 레스토랑의 스테이크는 소스 때문에 더 맛있다. That restaurant is really good because of the steak sauce.
	스파게티 소스를 만들기 귀찮으면 마트에 가서 스파게티 소스를 사서 뿌려 먹으면 됩니다. If it's inconvenient to make spaghetti sauce, then buy it from the grocery store and sprinkle it on and make spaghetti.

042
신선하다

[신선하다] **형용사** 1. to be fresh   2. to be new

1. vegetables, fruit or fish and other foods being fresh

[Usage]	**N**이/가 신선하다
[Expression]	신선한 과일 fresh fruit
	생선이 신선하다 the fish is fresh
[Synonym]	싱싱하다 to be fresh
[Example]	오늘 들어온 과일이 모두 신선해요. The fruits that came in today are all fresh.

2. being clean and new

[Usage]	**N**이/가 신선하다
[Expression]	신선한 공기 clean air
	느낌이 신선하다 the feeling is new
[Example]	영수 씨의 의견에 대해서 동료들이 모두 신선하다고 말했다.
	All of the colleagues said that Young-soo's idea was new.

043
싱싱하다

[싱싱하다] 형용사 to be fresh

something being new and not rotten but lively

[Usage]	**N**이/가 싱싱하다
[Synonym]	신선하다 to be fresh
[Example]	이 생선이 움직이는 것 좀 보세요. 아주 싱싱하네요.
	Look at this fish move. It is very fresh.
	음식을 만들 때는 싱싱한 재료를 쓰는 것이 무엇보다도 중요하다.
	It is most important to use fresh ingredients when cooking.

044
쌀

[쌀] 명사 rice

[Expression]	쌀밥 cooked rice
[Related word]	밥 cooked rice
[Example]	떡은 쌀로 만들어요. Rice cake is made out of rice.
	흰 쌀밥만 드시지 마시고 여러 가지 다른 곡물을 섞어서 드세요.
	Don't just eat white rice but also mix other types of grains.

045
양파

[양파] 명사 onion

[Expression]	양파 껍질 the onion peel
	양파를 썰다 to slice the onion
[Example]	양파를 많이 썰면 눈이 매워서 눈물이 난다.
	If you slice a lot of onions, you will start to cry.
	양파를 너무 많이 먹으면 입 냄새가 나니까 이를 닦아야 해.
	If you eat too many onions, you will have to brush your teeth because they will smell.

046
오이

[오이] 명사 cucumber

[Expression]	오이김치 cucumber kimchi
	오이 마사지 cucumber massage
[Example]	더울 때 오이를 먹으면 속이 시원해져요.
	If you eat cucumber when you are hot, it will cool you down.

273

오이 마사지를 하면 얼굴이 하얘진다고 하니까 한 번 해 보세요.
They say that if you do cucumber massages then your face will become whiter,
so try it out.

047
참기름

[참기름] **명사** sesame oil

oil made out of sesame seeds and has an aromatic smell

[Example]   비빔밥을 비빌 때는 참기름을 넣어야 맛있어요.
When you mix rice with vegetables, it is good to put sesame oil inside the mix.

참기름을 넣고 만들어서 더 맛있는 냄새가 납니다.
I put sesame oil in it, so it smells really good.

048
채소

[채소] **명사** vegetables

[Expression]   채소를 기르다 to grow vegetables

[Example]   싱싱한 채소를 많이 먹어야 건강해진다.
You will become healthier if you eat a lot of vegetables.

나중에 나이가 들면 고추나 상추 같은 채소를 직접 기르고 싶다.
When I grow older, I want to grow my own vegetables such as peppers or
lettuce.

049
치즈

[치즈] **명사** cheese

[Expression]   치즈 한 장 one slice of cheese
치즈 한 조각 one piece of cheese

[Example]   프랑스 사람들은 포도주를 마실 때 치즈를 같이 먹는다고 해요.
They say that French people eat cheese and wine together.

저는 치즈를 아주 좋아해서 피자에 치즈 가루를 꼭 뿌려서 먹어요.
I like cheese a lot so I always put powdered cheese on top of my pizza.

050
토마토

[토마토] **명사** tomato

[Expression]   토마토소스 tomato sauce
토마토케첩 tomato ketchup
토마토 주스 tomato juice

[Example]   토마토가 과일이에요? 채소예요? Is tomato a fruit or a vegetable?
한국 음식 중에서 토마토를 재료로 사용해서 만든 음식이 있어요?
Is there a Korean food that includes tomato inside of it?

051
해산물

[해산물] 명사 marine products

[Expression] 싱싱한 해산물 fresh marine products

[Example] 싱싱한 해산물로 끓인 국이나 찌개는 맛이 참 좋아요.
Soup or stew made with fresh marine products are good.

저는 바닷가에 살아서 어렸을 때부터 여러 가지 해산물을 많이 먹었어요.
I lived near the ocean so I ate a lot of marine products when I was younger.

11-4 요리

052
간

[간] 명사 saltiness

the degree of saltiness, using salt and soy sauce to control the saltiness

[Expression] 간이 맞다 to have the right amount of saltiness

간을 하다 to create the right amount of saltiness

간을 보다 to taste the saltiness

간을 맞추다 to make the right amount of saltiness

[Example] 간장으로 간을 좀 더 해야겠어요.
I better make it better my adjusting the saltiness with the soy sauce.

입맛에 맞는지 안 맞는지 간을 좀 봐 주세요.
Please taste and let me know if there is a right amount of saltiness.

053
굽다

[굽따] 동사 to grill

to cook over fire, ㅂverb

[Usage] N을/를 굽다

[Example] 고기를 굽는 냄새가 집 밖까지 난다.
I can smell the meat being cooked from outside the house.

오늘 저녁에는 생선을 구워서 먹으려고 해요.
I plan on grilling fish and eating it for dinner.

054
끓이다

[끄리다] 동사 to boil

to cook food with water

[Usage] N을/를 끓이다

[Expression] 라면을 끓이다 to boil ramen

[Related word] 끓다 to boil

삶다 to simmer

[Example] 커피를 마시려고 물을 끓이고 있어요.
I am boiling water so that I can drink coffee.

배가 좀 고픈데 라면이나 하나 끓여 먹을까?
Since I am a bit hungry, should I eat some ramen?

055
다지다

[다지다] 동사 to finely chop

to chop meat or vegetables into little pieces

[Usage] N을/를 다지다

[Expression] 다진 고기 finely chopped meat

마늘을 다지다 to finely chop garlic

[Related word] 썰다 to slice

[Example] 이 김밥에는 다진 쇠고기가 들어가서 더 맛있어요.
This kim-bab tastes even better because there is finely chopped beef inside.

음식을 할 때마다 마늘을 다지기가 귀찮으면 마트에서 다진 마늘을 사서 쓰세요.
If it is too inconvenient to finely chop garlic every time you make food, go to the mart and buy already chopped garlic.

056
만들다

[만들다] 동사 1. to make 2. to make

1. to use effort or skill to achieve something, ㄹverb

[Usage] N을/를 만들다

[Expression] 음식을 만들다 to make food

가구를 만들다 to make furniture

[Example] 저는 우리 엄마가 만들어 주시는 음식이 제일 맛있어요.
My mother's hand made food is the best.

2. to create books, movies, songs or writing, ㄹverb

[Usage] N을/를 만들다

[Expression] 노래를 만들다 to make a song

[Example] 영화를 한 편 만들려면 돈이 얼마나 들까요?
How much would it cost me to make a movie?

057
볶다

[복따] 동사 to stir-fry

to stir food with oil and mix together where there is less water and cook until it is done

[Usage] N을/를 볶다

[Expression] 밥을 볶다 to stir-fry rice

음식을 볶다 to stir-fry food

[Related word] 튀기다 to fry

[Example] 김치, 양파, 고기를 볶아서 볶음밥을 해 먹을까?
Should we stir-fry kimchi, onion, and meat and stir it together and make stir-fried rice?

잡채를 만들 때에는 채소를 따로따로 볶아야 해요? 같이 볶아도 돼요?
When I make jap-chae, should I stir-fry the vegetables separately or at the same time?

058
비비다

[비비다] 동사 to mix together

to put many ingredients together and mix

[Usage] N을/를 비비다

[Expression] 밥을 비비다 to mix rice

[Example] 반찬이 없어서 밥에다가 고추장을 넣어서 비벼 먹었다.
There were no side dishes so I put rice with pepper paste and mixed it together and ate the dish.

비빔밥으로 가장 유명한 곳은 전주입니다. 전주에 가면 꼭 비빔밥을 드셔 보세요.
Jun-joo is the most famous place for mixed rice. When you go to Jun-joo, make sure to eat the mixed rice there.

059
삶다

[삼따] 동사 to boil

to put in water and boil

[Usage] N을/를 삶다

[Expression] 국수를 삶다 to boil noodles

[Related word] 찌다 to steam

끓이다 to cook by boiling

[Example] 입맛이 없어서 국수를 삶아서 먹었어요.
I didn't really feel like eating so I boiled some noodles and ate them.

점심에 돼지고기를 삶아서 상추에 싸 먹자.
Let's boil pork and wrap it in lettuce and eat it for lunch.

060
썰다

[썰다] 동사 to slice

to cut with a knife, ㄹverb

[Usage] N을/를 썰다

[Example] 무를 썰다가 칼에 손가락을 베었어요.
I cut my finger while slicing radish.

라면에다가 계란도 넣고, 파도 좀 썰어서 넣어라.
Put egg in your ramen and some sliced green onion.

061
요리

[요리] 명사 cooking

making food, or the food

[Expression] 요리법 cooking recipe
요리사 chef
한국 요리 Korean cooking
요리하다 to cook
요리를 만들다 to make food

[Related word] 음식 food

[Example] 제가 할 줄 아는 요리는 라면뿐이에요.
The only thing I know how to cook is ramen.

저는 외식을 하는 것보다 직접 요리를 해서 먹는 것을 좋아해요.
I like cooking inside rather than going out to eat.

062
젓다

[젇따] 동사 to stir

to use a spoon or other tool to stir liquid and powder, ㅅverb

[Usage] N을/를 젓다

[Related word] 섞다 to mix

[Example] 커피에 설탕하고 우유를 넣고 잘 저으세요.
Put sugar and milk in the coffee and drink it after stirring well.

죽을 끓일 때에는 옆에 서서 계속 저어야 해요.
When cooking porridge, you must be near it and stir it often.

063
튀기다

[튀기다] 동사 to fry

to cook food by putting it in boiling oil

[Usage] N을/를 튀기다

[Expression] 닭을 튀기다 to fry chicken

[Related word] 볶다 to stir-fry

[Example] 탕수육은 돼지고기를 튀겨서 만든 음식이에요.
Sweet and sour pork is made with fried pork.

튀긴 음식은 다이어트에 좋지 않으니까 먹지 마세요.
Fried food is not good for dieting so don't eat fried food.

064
국

[국] **명사** soup

a liquid food cooked with salted water, meat, fish, vegetables and other ingredients

[Expression] 미역국 seaweed soup

국을 끓이다 to cook soup

[Example] 오늘이 내 생일이어서 아침에 엄마가 미역국을 끓여 주셨다.
Today is my birthday so my mom made me seaweed soup for breakfast.

나는 국이 없으면 밥을 잘 먹지 못하기 때문에 어머니는 나를 위해서 꼭 국을 끓여 놓으신다.
I cannot eat if there isn't soup, so my mother always cooks soup for me.

065
김밥

[김밥] **명사** kimbab

food that is made with seaweed and many different types of sides dishes all rolled into a roll

[Example] 김치 김밥 kimchi kimbab

김밥 한 줄 one roll of kimbab

김밥을 말다 to roll a kimbab

김밥을 싸다 to wrap a kimbab

김밥을 썰다 to slice a kimbab

[Example] 소풍을 가는 날 어머니는 아침 일찍 일어나서 김밥을 만드셨다.
Whenever we went on a picnic, my mother would make kimbab early in the morning.

아침을 먹지 못하고 학교에 가면 수업을 시작하기 전에 꼭 김밥을 사서 먹어요.
If I haven't eaten anything for breakfast, I go to school and buy a kimbab and eat it.

066
김치

[김치] **명사** kimchi

fermented cabbage and radish with pepper powder, green onion, garlic

[Expression] 물김치 watery kimchi

김치가 익다 kimchi is ripened

김치를 담다 to make kimchi

[Related word] 김장 kimchi making for the winter

[Example]　요즘은 여러 나라 사람들에게 김치가 유명해졌다.
These days kimchi has become famous to people in many different countries.

저는 김치가 없어도 밥을 잘 먹지만 오빠는 김치가 없으면 밥을 잘 먹지 못해요.
I can eat without kimchi, but my brother can't eat without kimchi.

067
냉면

[냉면] **명사** cold noodles

[Expression]　물냉면　cold soup noodles

비빔냉면　spicy cold noodles

냉면 한 그릇　one bowl of cold noodles

냉면을 말다　to put cold noodles in soup

[Related word]　국수　noodle

[Example]　냉면은 원래 여름에 먹는 음식이 아니라 겨울에 먹는 음식이었다고 해요.
Cold noodles were originally not eaten in the summer but in the winter.

날씨가 더우니까 냉면이 생각나네요. 우리 점심에 시원한 냉면을 먹으러 갈까요?
The weather is hot outside so I want some cold noodles. Should we go eat some cooling cold noodles for lunch?

068
돈가스

[돈까스] **명사** pork cutlet

pork cutlet, pork that has been deep fried

[Example]　돈가스는 일본 사람들이 즐겨 먹는 음식이라고 해요.
Pork cutlet is enjoyed by many Japanese people.

남산에 돈가스로 유명한 음식점이 있는데 값이 싸고 양도 정말 많아요.
There is a famous pork cutlet place in Namsan. The price is cheap and the portion is big.

069
뜨겁다

[뜨겁따] **형용사** to be hot

to be very hot in temperature, or the temperature being so hot that one cannot touch something , ㅂverb

[Usage]　N이/가 뜨겁다

[Expression]　뜨거운 물　hot water

몸이 뜨겁다　the body is hot

[Antonym]　차갑다　to be cold

[Example]　여름 햇빛이 참 뜨겁네요.　The summer sun is very hot.

국물이 뜨거우니까 조심하세요.　The soup is hot so be careful.

070
라면

[라면] 명사 ramen

noodles that have been ripened with hot air and then fried

[Expression] 라면 한 봉지 one bag of ramen

라면을 끓이다 to cook ramen

[Example] 어제 라면을 먹고 자서 얼굴이 부었다.

I ate ramen before I slept so my face is swollen.

음식을 못한다고요? 라면도 끓일 줄 몰라요?

You can't cook? You can't even cook ramen?

071
반찬

[반찬] 명사 side dishes

all the dishes that are eaten with rice

[Expression] 고기 반찬 meat side dishes

반찬을 만들다 to make side dishes

[Example] 제가 제일 좋아하는 반찬은 나물이에요.

My favorite side dishes are the green vegetables.

한국 식당에서는 반찬을 공짜로 계속 줘서 신기했어요.

It was interesting because Korean restaurants give out side dishes for free repeatedly.

072
밥

[밥] 명사 1. rice   2. meal

1. rice or barley that is washed and cooked with water

[Expression] 쌀밥 white rice

보리밥 barley rice

밥 한 그릇 one bowl of rice

밥이 되다 the rice is ready

밥을 하다 to make rice

[Example] 밥이 없으니까 쌀을 씻어서 밥부터 해라.

There is no rice so wash the rice and make the rice first.

2. food that you eat for a meal

[Expression] 밥상 food table

밥을 먹다 to eat food

[Synonym] 식사 meal

[Example] 밥이 다 됐으니까 어서 밥을 먹으러 와라.

The food is ready so come and eat.

281

073
불고기

[불고기] **명사** bulgogi

a beef food that has been sliced thinly and marinated for a long time and then grilled

[Example] 저는 한국 음식 중에서 불고기를 제일 좋아합니다.
I like bulgogi the best out of Korean foods.

불고기에다가 밥을 비벼서 주면 아이가 맛있게 먹을 거예요.
If you mix the bulgogi with rice, your child will like the dish.

074
삼계탕

[삼계탕/삼게탕] **명사** samgyetang

a food that is eaten during the summer because it is known to be healthy, it consists of taking the organs out of the chicken and putting garlic, jujube, sticky rice and cooking it for a long time

[Example] 삼계탕이 싱거우면 소금을 넣어서 드세요.
If the samgyetang is a bit bland, put some salt inside.

한국 사람들은 더운 여름에 건강을 위해서 삼계탕을 먹습니다.
Korean people eat samgyetang during the hot summer to look out for their health.

075
샌드위치

[샌드위치] **명사** sandwich

[Example] 밤에 공부할 때 어머니는 간식으로 샌드위치를 만들어 주셨다.
Whenever I studied during the night, my mother would make sandwiches for me as a snack.

아침에 식사할 시간이 없을 때는 간단하게 샌드위치를 사서 먹어요.
In the morning if I don't have enough time to eat, then I eat a sandwich.

076
샐러드

[샐러드] **명사** salad

[Expression] 과일 샐러드 fruit salad
샐러드 드레싱 salad dressing

[Example] 샐러드를 다 드시면 요리가 나옵니다.
After you eat the salad, your meal will arrive.

저는 과일 샐러드보다 야채 샐러드를 더 좋아해요.
I like vegetable salad more than fruit salad.

077
스테이크

[스테이크] **명사** steak

[Expression] 스테이크를 썰다 to slice a steak
스테이크를 굽다 to grill a steak

[Example] 오랜만에 스테이크를 먹고 싶은데 우리 먹으러 갈까요?
I want to eat steak, should we go eat it today?

집에서 스테이크를 구워서 먹었는데 레스토랑에서 먹는 것처럼 맛있었다.
I grilled a steak at home and it tasted delicious just like at a restaurant.

078
스파게티

[스파게티] 명사 spaghetti

[Example] 스파게티는 이탈리아의 대표적인 요리이다.
Spaghetti is a representative food for Italy.

학교 근처에 스파게티가 아주 맛있는 식당이 있는데 같이 가시겠어요?
There is a good spaghetti restaurant nearby, would you like to go?

079
우동

[우동] 명사 udong
Japanese style noodles

[Example] 우동 국물이 아주 맛있어요. The udong soup is very good.
날씨가 추우니까 따뜻한 우동이 먹고 싶어요.
The weather is cold outside so I want some udong.

080
자장면

[자장면] 명사 black noodles
putting meat and vegetables and mixing it together in black soy sauce, Chinese style food

[Expression] 자장면 한 그릇 one bowl of black noodles

[Related word] 짬뽕 Chinese style seafood noodles
탕수육 sweet and sour pork

[Example] 한국 자장면과 중국 자장면은 좀 달라요.
Korean black noodles and Chinese black noodles are a bit different.

너는 자장면을 먹을 거야? 짬뽕을 먹을 거야?
Are you going to eat black noodles or seafood noodles?

081
죽

[죽] 명사 porridge
food that is made with rice cooked for a long time

[Expression] 호박죽 pumpkin porridge
죽을 쑤다 to cook porridge

[Related word] 밥 rice

[Example] 저는 아침에 입맛이 없으면 죽을 먹어요.
In the morning if I don't feel like eating breakfast, I eat some porridge.

속이 안 좋으니까 밥보다는 죽을 먹는 것이 좋겠어요.
My stomach doesn't feel good so I think I should eat porridge instead of rice.

082
초밥

[초밥] **명사** sushi

Japanese style food that has a slice of fish big enough to fit the mouth and put on top of rice

[Related word] 회 sashimi

[Example] 점심에 일식집에 가서 초밥하고 우동을 시켜서 먹었다.
For lunch we went to a Japanese restaurant and ate sushi and udong for lunch.

밤늦게까지 일하는 직원들을 위해서 사장님께서 초밥을 배달시켜 주셨다.
Our CEO ordered sushi for the employees that were working until very late.

083
카레

[카레] **명사** curry

using ginger, black pepper, garlic and other ingredients to make a spicy and aromatic yellowish colored food

[Expression] 카레가루 curry powder
카레 라이스 curry with rice

[Related word] 인도 음식 Indian food

[Example] 카레 라이스는 만들기가 간단해서 반찬이 없을 때 자주 해서 먹는다.
Curry is simple to make so I make it often when I don't have any side dishes.

저는 카레 냄새를 별로 좋아하지 않아서 카레가 들어간 음식은 잘 먹지 않아요.
I don't like the smell of curry so I can't really eat foods with curry.

084
피자

[피자] **명사** pizza

[Expression] 피자 한 판 one order of pizza
피자 한 조각 one piece of pizza

[Example] 저는 해산물이 들어간 피자를 좋아해요. I like pizza that has seafood.
오늘 점심에는 피자를 한 판 시켜서 먹읍시다.
Let's order pizza for lunch.

085
한식

[한식] **명사** Korean food

Korean style foods

[Expression] 한식집 Korean restaurant

[Example] 한식 중에서 갈비와 불고기를 제일 좋아합니다.
I like kalbi and bulgogi the best out of Korean foods.

학교 근처에 한식집이 하나 생겼는데 점심 때 가 볼까?
There is a new Korean restaurant that has opened near the school, should we try it for lunch?

'-식' is used after the countries name to label the countries food.

한식(한국 음식), 일식(일본 음식), 양식(서양 음식), 중국 음식
Korean food, Japanese food, western food, Chinese food

086
햄버거

[햄버거] **명사** hamburger

[Example]   밥을 해 먹을 시간이 없어서 햄버거를 하나 사서 먹었다.
I didn't have time to eat rice so I bought and ate a hamburger.

가게에서 파는 햄버거보다 엄마가 직접 만들어 주시는 햄버거가 더 맛있다.
I like my mom's hamburger better than the one's they sell at the stores.

11-6 | 식사

087
고프다

[고프다] **형용사** to be hungry

the stomach is empty and you feel hunger, 으 verb

[Usage]   N이/가 고프다

[Expression]   배가 고프다   to have a hungry stomach

[Antonym]   부르다² to be full

[Example]   배가 고프면 배에서 꼬르륵 소리가 납니다.
Whenever I am hungry, my stomach makes a sound.

아침을 안 먹어서 배가 고파요. 뭐 먹을 것이 없어요?
I didn't eat breakfast so I am hungry. Is there anything to eat?

088
덜다

[덜다] **동사** to take a certain amount

to put a certain amount on to the plate, ㄹ verb

[Usage]   N을/를 덜다

[Expression]   밥을 덜다   to take a certain amount of rice

[Example] 아주머니, 밥이 많아요. 좀 덜어 주세요.
Ma'm, I have too much rice. Please take some out.

뷔페에 가면 접시에 음식을 덜어서 먹어요.
At a buffet I take a certain amount on my plate and eat.

089
따로

[따로] 부사 separately

it is alone not mixed together with other things

[Antonym] 같이 together

[Example] 빨래를 할 때 하얀색 옷은 따로 빨아야 한다.
When doing laundry, you have to wash the white clothes separately.

한국 사람들은 찌개를 먹을 때 보통 따로 먹지 않고 같이 먹어요.
When Korean people eat stew, we don't eat separately but together.

090
메뉴

[메뉴] 명사 1. menu   2. different foods

1. the menu book

[Expression] 메뉴판 menu book

[Example] 아주머니, 여기 메뉴 좀 갖다 주세요.
Ma'm, please give us a menu book.

2. the different foods on the menu

[Expression] 세트 메뉴 set menu

저녁 메뉴 dinner menu

오늘의 메뉴 today's menu

[Example] 오늘 저녁 메뉴는 뭐지? 엄마가 무슨 음식을 만들어 놓으셨을까?
What is the dinner menu? What kinds of food do you think mom made?

091
배달

[배달] 명사 delivery

to take an object or a food to the person who ordered it

[Expression] 음식 배달 food delivery

배달하다 to deliver

배달시키다 to order

[Example] 집 앞 슈퍼마켓은 손님이 산 물건들을 집까지 배달해 줍니다.
The supermarket in front of my house delivers grocery to the house.

오늘은 음식하기가 귀찮아서 그냥 중국 음식을 배달시켜서 먹으려고 해요.
I'm too tired to make food so I'm going to order Chinese delivery.

092
붓다

[분따] 동사 to pour

to pour into an object or liquid, ㅅverb

[Usage] N을/를 붓다

[Expression] 물을 붓다 to pour water

[Related word] 담다 to put in

[Example] 국이 좀 짜다. 물을 좀 더 붓고 끓여야겠다.
The soup is a bit salty. I better put more water inside and boil the soup.

국수를 삶을 때 물이 끓으면 찬물을 한 컵 정도 부으세요. 그러면 면이 더 맛있어요.
Whenever you cook noodles, pour a cup of cold water in when the water comes to a boil. The noodles will taste better if you do this.

093
뷔페

[뷔페] 명사 buffet

a buffet restaurant, a place where lots of different foods are placed and the customer can choose what one wants and then take a certain amount of food

[Expression] 뷔페 식당 buffet restaurant

[Example] 결혼식 피로연은 뷔페로 합시다. Let's have buffet food for the wedding.
뷔페는 여러 가지 음식을 다 먹을 수 있어서 좋아요.
I like buffets because I can eat all types of foods.

094
시키다

[시키다] 동사 1. to order   2. to make a person do something

1. to order food, and have it delivered

[Usage] N을/를 시키다

[Synonym] 주문하다 to order

[Example] 음식을 시켜야 하는데 왜 종업원이 안 오지?
I need to order food but why isn't the employer coming?

2. to make someone do an action

[Usage] N에게 AV으라고/라고 시키다

[Example] 설탕이 없어서 아이에게 설탕을 사 오라고 시켰다.
I told to the child to buy some sugar because I had no more sugar.

095
외식하다

[외시카다] 동사 to eat out

to go outside and eat at a restaurant

[Example] 요즘 바빠서 자주 외식을 해서 그런지 건강이 좀 나빠졌다.
These days I've been so busy I've eaten out that my health seems to have gotten worse.

287

오늘은 어머니 생신이어서 부모님을 모시고 외식하려고 해요.
Today is my mother's birthday so I plan on taking my parents out to eat.

096
한식집

[한식찝] **명사** Korean restaurant
a place where they sell Korean food

[Synonym]   한식당 Korean restaurant

[Example]   한식집에 가면 반찬을 많이 줘서 항상 밥을 많이 먹어요.
Whenever I go to a Korean restaurant, they give me a lot of side dishes, so I end up eating a lot.

이번 모임에는 나이가 많은 어른들도 오시니까 한식집에 갑시다.
For this meeting there will be a lot of older people so let's go to a Korean restaurant.

words that end in '-집' that refer to restaurants are the ones below.

한식집, 일식집, 양식집, 중국집
Korean restaurant, Japanese restaurant, western restaurant, Chinese restaurant

[1~15] 다음 단어를 한국어로 바꿔 쓰십시오. Change these words into Korean.

1. grain   (   )   2. cold noodles   (   )

3. tofu   (   )   4. soy bean paste   (   )

5. ramen   (   )   6. cheese   (   )

7. sushi   (   )   8. to grill   (   )

9. pork cutlet   (   )   10. sesame oil   (   )

11. chocolate   (   )   12. hamburger   (   )

13. to chop   (   )   14. sandwich   (   )

15. ice cream   (   )

[16~20] 그림을 보고 (   )에 알맞은 것을 고르십시오.

Look at the picture and choose the correct word.

16.

가 : 맛이 어때요?

나 : 아주 (   )어요/아요/여요.

❶ 달다   ❷ 맵다

❸ 시다   ❹ 짜다

17.

가 : 달걀을 어떻게 했어요?

나 : (   )었어요/았어요/였어요.

❶ 굽다   ❷ 볶다

❸ 삶다   ❹ 비비다

18.

가 : 뭘 샀어요?

나 : (   ) 다섯 마리를 샀어요.

❶ 닭   ❷ 쌀

❸ 고추   ❹ 생선

19.

가 : 맥주를 얼마나 마셨어요?

나 : 두 (   ) 마셨어요.

❶ 잔   ❷ 병

❸ 그릇   ❹ 인분

20.

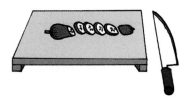

가 : 오이를 어떻게 해야 해요?

나 : (   )어야/아야/여야 해요.

❶ 썰다   ❷ 씻다

❸ 젓다   ❹ 다지다

[21~30] 다음 문장을 읽고 알맞은 어휘를 골라 쓰십시오. 어휘는 한 번만 쓰십시오.
Read the following sentence and choose the right word. Use the words once.

국	술	간식	과일	김치
소금	우유	피자	달다	볶다
삶다	썰다	짜다	뜨겁다	싱싱하다

21. 요구르트는 (　　　　　)으로/로 만든다.

22. 싱거우니까 (　　　　　)을/를 조금 더 넣으세요.

23. 스파게티와 (　　　　　)은/는 이탈리아 음식이다.

24. 당근을 기름에 (　　　　　)었어요/았어요/였어요.

25. 삼계탕은 (　　　　　)을/ㄹ 때 먹어야 맛있습니다.

26. 어제 저녁에 친구들을 만나서 (　　　　　)을/를 한잔했다.

27. (　　　　　)은/ㄴ 음식을 너무 많이 먹으면 충치가 생길 수 있다.

28. 저는 사과, 바나나, 오렌지, 수박 같은 (　　　　　)을/를 좋아합니다.

29. 간장을 많이 넣으면 음식이 (　　　　　)으니까/니까 조금만 넣으세요.

30. 점심과 저녁 사이에 무슨 (　　　　　)을/를 만들어서 아이에게 주는 게 좋을까?

[31~35] (　　) 안에 알맞은 것을 고르십시오. Choose the correct one.

31. 아이들은 기름에 (　　)은/ㄴ 요리를 좋아한다.

❶ 삶다　　❷ 찌다　　❸ 다지다　　❹ 튀기다

32. 바다에서 나는 싱싱한 (　　)을/를 여러 가지 사 왔다.

❶ 과일　　❷ 채소　　❸ 불고기　　❹ 해산물

33. 한국 사람들은 매운 마늘을 매운 (   )에 찍어 먹는다.

❶ 간장   ❷ 소금   ❸ 고추장   ❹ 참기름

34. 한국 사람들의 밥상에는 밥, 국이나 찌개, 그리고 (   )이/가 있다.

❶ 간식   ❷ 과일   ❸ 반찬   ❹ 요리

35. 소화가 잘 되지 않아서 (   )을/를 끓여 먹었다.

❶ 빵   ❷ 죽   ❸ 과일   ❹ 오이

[36~40] 밑줄 친 부분과 반대되는 뜻을 가진 것을 고르십시오.
Choose the word that is the opposite of the underlined word.

36. **가 :** 음식이 맛있어요?

   나 : 아니요, (   )어요/아요/여요.

❶ 맛없다   ❷ 모르다   ❸ 아니다   ❹ 재미없다

37. **가 :** 배가 고파요?

   나 : 아니요, 배가 아주 (   )어요/아요/여요.

❶ 붓다   ❷ 크다   ❸ 부르다   ❹ 아프다

38. **가 :** 밥을 더 담아 드릴까요?

   나 : 아니요, 너무 많으니까 좀 (   )어/아/여 주세요.

❶ 덜다   ❷ 벗다   ❸ 빼다   ❹ 더하다

39. **가 :** 이 음식은 그릇 하나에 같이 먹을까요?

   나 : 아니요, (   ) 먹읍시다.

❶ 바로   ❷ 따로   ❸ 함께   ❹ 혼자

40. **가** : 맛이 <u>짜요?</u>

　　나 : 아니요, (　　　　)어요/아요/여요.

　　❶ 달다　　　　　❷ 맵다　　　　❸ 싱겁다　　　❹ 맛이 없다

[41~45] 밑줄 친 부분과 의미가 가장 가까운 것을 고르십시오.
Choose the word that is most similar to the underlined section.

41. **가** : 음식 재료가 모두 <u>싱싱해요?</u>

　　나 : 그럼요. 얼마나 (　　　　　)은지/ㄴ지 몰라요.

　　❶ 많다　　　　❷ 신선하다　　　❸ 선선하다　　　❹ 깨끗하다

42. **가** : 뭘 <u>주문할까요?</u>

　　나 : 피자하고 콜라를 (　　　　)읍시다/ㅂ시다.

　　❶ 먹다　　　　❷ 마시다　　　　❸ 만들다　　　❹ 시키다

43. **가** : 무슨 <u>음식</u>을 만들까요?

　　나 : 오늘은 중국 (　　　　)을/를 만듭시다.

　　❶ 밥　　　　　❷ 과일　　　　❸ 요리　　　　❹ 찌개

44. **가** : 목이 말라요. <u>마실 것</u> 좀 없어요?

　　나 : 이 (　　　　)을/를 드세요.

　　❶ 간식　　　　❷ 과일　　　　❸ 과자　　　　❹ 음료수

45. **가** : <u>찬 물</u> 좀 주세요.

　　나 : 여기 있어요. 아주 (　　　　)어요/아요/여요.

　　❶ 춥다　　　　❷ 뜨겁다　　　❸ 시원하다　　　❹ 따뜻하다

[46~50] 밑줄 친 단어의 쓰임이 잘못된 것을 고르십시오. Choose the one that is incorrectly used.

46. ❶ 직접 가구를 <u>만드</u>신다고요?　　　　(　　　)

　　❷ 오늘은 뭘 <u>만들</u>어서 먹을까?

　　❸ 이번에 <u>만든</u> 노래는 참 듣기 좋았다.

　　❹ 양파하고 당근을 기름에 같이 <u>만들</u>었다.

47. ❶ 소금으로 <u>간</u>을 해라.　　　　　　(　　　)

　　❷ <u>간</u>을 넣으니까 매워졌어요.

　　❸ 이 음식은 <u>간</u>이 딱 맞네요.

　　❹ <u>간</u>을 좀 봐 주세요. 어때요?

48. ❶ 이 고추는 별로 <u>맵</u>지 않네요.　　　(　　　)

　　❷ 소금을 많이 넣어서 음식이 <u>짜</u>요.

　　❸ 식초가 너무 많이 들어가서 맛이 <u>달</u>다.

　　❹ 약이 <u>쓰</u>니까 아이가 먹으려고 하지 않아요.

49. ❶ 메뉴를 보고 음식을 <u>지켜</u>라.　　　(　　　)

　　❷ <u>배달시킨</u> 음식이 왜 이렇게 안 오지?

　　❸ 이 음식은 따뜻할 때 <u>드셔야</u> 맛있어요.

　　❹ <u>외식</u>하면 음식을 안 해도 되니까 편하다.

50. ❶ 라면을 <u>끓여</u>서 먹었다.　　　　　(　　　)

　　❷ 밥에 고추장을 넣고 <u>비볐</u>다.

　　❸ 고기를 <u>굽</u>는 냄새가 아주 좋다.

　　❹ 물이 적으니까 물을 더 <u>저어</u>라.

교통

12

Transportation

12-1 | 탈것 · 타는 곳

001
공항

[공항] **명사** airport

[Related word] 비행기 airplane

항공사 an airline

[Example] 오늘 친구가 한국에 와서 공항에 마중을 가야 해요.
Today my friend is arriving in Korea so I have to meet him at the airport.

선생님이 타신 비행기가 몇 시에 공항에 도착한다고 해?
What time does our teacher's airplane arrive at the airport?

002
기차

[기차] **명사** train

[Expression] 기차표 train ticket

기차역 train station

기차를 타다 to ride a train

[Example] 서울에서 부산까지 기차로 몇 시간 걸려요?
How long does it take to go from Seoul to Busan by train?

차를 타고 가는 여행도 좋지만 기차를 타고 가는 여행이 더 좋을 것 같아.
Traveling by car is good, but riding a train and taking a trip seems to be more exciting.

003
배¹

[배] **명사** boat, ship

[Expression] 배를 타다 to ride a boat

[Related word] 항구 a harbor

[Example] 부산에서 제주도까지 배를 타고 왔어요.
I took a boat from Busan to Jeju island.

배로 소포를 보내면 비행기로 보내는 것보다 느리지만 값이 싸요.
Sending posts my boat take longer than by airplane but it is less expensive.

004
버스

[버스] **명사** bus

[Expression] 시내버스 city bus

고속버스 express bus

버스 요금 bus fare

버스를 타다 to ride a bus

[Related word] 정류장 a stop

[Example] 아저씨, 이 버스가 신촌으로 갑니까?
Sir, does this bus go to Shinchon?

여기에서 경복궁에 가려면 지하철보다 버스를 타는 것이 더 빨라요.
If you want to go to Kyung-book palace from here, then it's faster to take the bus than to take subway.

005
비행기

[비행기] **명사** airplane

[Expression] 비행기 표 airplane ticket

비행기 한 대 one airplane

비행기가 출발하다 the airplane departs

[Example] 제주도에서 서울까지 비행기로 1(한)시간쯤 걸려요.
Going from Jeju island to Seoul by airplane takes about an hour.

오빠가 탄 비행기는 아직 도착하지 않았어요. 2(두)시간 더 기다려야 한다고 해요.
My older brother's airplane has not arrived yet. They say we have to wait 2 more hours.

006
역

[역] **명사** station

the place where a train leaves or stops at

[Expression] 기차역 train station

지하철역 subway station

[Example] 친구가 기차역으로 마중을 나왔다.
My friend came out to greet me at the train station.

지하철 신촌역 1(일)번 출구에서 기다리기로 했어요.
I decided to wait at the the Shinchon station number one exit in the subway.

007
정류장

[정뉴장] **명사** a stop

a place where a bus or a taxi stops to pick up a person and then drop them off at a certain stop

[Expression] 버스 정류장 bus stop

택시 정류장 taxi stop

[Example] 아저씨, 명동에 가려고 하는데 어느 정류장에서 내려야 해요?
Sir, I want to go to Myung-dong but what stop should I get off at?

이번 정류장은 연세대학교입니다. 다음 정류장은 세브란스 병원입니다.
This stop is Yonsei University. The next stop is Severance hospital.

008
지하철

[지하철] 명사 subway

[Expression] 지하철역 subway station

[Example] 출퇴근 시간에는 지하철을 타는 것이 더 좋습니다.
During the rush hour it's better to ride the subway.

광화문에 가려면 지하철 5(오)호선을 타야 합니다.
If you want to go to Kwang-ha-moon, you should take subway line 5.

009
차²

[차] 명사 automobile

a form of transportation that can carry people or cargo and moves on wheel

[Expression] 차 한 대 one car
차를 타다 to ride a car
차를 수리하다 to fix a car
차에 태우다 to put inside a car

[Related word] 운전 driving
카센터 car repair shop

[Example] 차가 고장이 나서 수리하려고 카센터에 맡겼어요.
My car had some problems so I left it at the car repair shop to get it fixed.

차가 오래 되어서 바꾸려고 하는데 요즘 인기가 있는 차가 뭐예요?
My car is old and I want to change it, what is the popular car these days?

010
택시

[택씨] 명사 taxi

[Expression] 빈 택시 empty taxi
택시 요금 taxi fare
택시 기사 taxi driver
택시를 잡다 to catch a taxi

[Related word] 승객 passenger

[Example] 오늘 늦게 일어나서 택시를 타고 출근했어요.
I woke up late this morning so I took a taxi to work.

여기에서는 택시를 잡기가 어려우니까 좀 더 큰 길로 갑시다.
It is hard to catch a cab here so let's go to the bigger road.

011
터미널

[터미널] 명사 terminal

a place where there are many types of vehicles for travel collected for use, airplane, train, and bus

[Expression] 고속버스 터미널 express bus terminal
시외버스 터미널 suburb bus terminal

[Example]

기차표가 없으면 고속버스 터미널로 가서 고속버스를 타고 가자.

If you don't have a train ticket, let's go to the fast bus terminal and let's take the fast bus.

거기는 시골이어서 여기서 직접 가는 버스는 없어요. 시외버스 터미널에 가야 될 거예요.

This is the country so there are no buses that go directly there. You will have to go to the suburb bus terminal.

12-2 | 승차 · 탑승

012
갈아타다

[가라타다] 동사 to transfer

to get off the vehicle and switch to another vehicle

[Usage]

N을/를 갈아타다

N에서 내려서 **N**으로/로 갈아타다

[Expression]

버스를 갈아타다 to transfer buses

버스에서 내려서 지하철로 갈아타다

to get off the bus and transfer to a subway.

[Example]

서울에서는 버스를 갈아타도 버스 요금을 더 내지 않으니까 참 좋아요.

In Seoul you don't have to pay more for when transferring buses so I like it a lot.

종합운동장으로 가려면 3(삼)호선을 타고 가다가 교대역에서 2(이)호선으로 갈아타세요.

If you want to go to the gym, take the line 3 and transfer at Kyo-dae station line 2.

013
교통카드

[교통카드] 명사 transportation card

a card shaped electronic ticket that allows the public to use transportation after scanning it and then the card takes out the money that is used

[Expression]

후불제 교통카드 transportation card(deferred payment)

교통카드를 충전하다 to charge the transportation card

교통카드를 단말기에 대다

to place the transportation card over the terminal scanner

[Example] 세상이 참 편리해졌다. 교통카드만 있으면 서울 어디든지 갈 수 있구나.

The world is very comfortable these days. If you have a transportation card, you can go anywhere in Seoul.

요금 할인을 받으려면 내리실 때에도 교통카드를 꼭 단말기에 대셔야 합니다.

If you want to get a discount on transportation, you should swipe the card over the terminal scanner.

014
교통편

[교통편] 명사 transportations

the sort of transportation used when traveling to another place, these can be car, train, or airplane

[Expression] 교통편이 나쁘다 the transportations are bad

교통편을 이용하다 to use transportations

[Related word] 차편 car transportations

배편 boat transportations

[Example] 서울에서 부산까지 어떤 교통편을 이용하는 것이 좋을까요?

What kinds of transportations should I use to go from Seoul to Busan?

여기는 교통편이 나빠서 시내에 가려면 버스를 갈아타야 한다.

The transportations are bad here. If you want to go to the city, you will need to go transfer to a bus.

015
내리다

[내리다] 동사 1. to get off   2. to pour or fall

1. to get off of a vehicle, to get off and go somewhere

[Usage] N에 내리다

N에서 내리다

[Expression] 공항에 내리다 to get off at the airport

버스에서 내리다 to get off of the bus

[Example] 버스에서 내리면 빵집이 보일 거예요. 그 건물의 2(이)층에 커피숍이 있어요.

If you get off of the bus, you will see the bakery. Inside that building the second floor is a coffee shop.

2. rain or snow coming down

[Usage] N이/가 내리다

[Expression] 눈이 내리다 the snow is coming down

[Example] 날씨가 많이 흐려요. 곧 비가 내릴 것 같아요.

The weather is very cloudy. It seems like it will rain soon.

016
노선도

[노선도] 명사 transportation route

a picture that shows where the subway or bus will stop

[Expression] 버스 노선도 bus route

지하철 노선도 subway route

[Related word] 환승역 transfer station

[Example] 지하철 노선도를 보면 어디에서 갈아타야 하는지 알 수 있을 것이다.
If you look at the subway transportation route, you will know where to transfer.

버스 정류장에 노선도가 있으니까 동대문쪽으로 가는 버스가 있는지 알아보자.
There is a transportation route at the bus stop. Let's see if there is a bus going to Dong-dae-moon.

017
노약자석

[노약짜석] 명사 priority seating

reserved seating in a bus or subway for elders, disabled, pregnant women, and children

[Example] 버스에 있는 노란색 좌석이 노약자석이에요?
Are the yellow bus seats priority seating?

보통 중고등학생들은 지하철 노약자석에 앉지 않아요.
Usually middle and high school students don't sit on the priority seating in the subway.

018
도착하다

[도차카다] 동사 to arrive

to arrive at a destination

[Usage] N에 도착하다

[Expression] 학교에 도착하다 to arrive at school

[Antonym] 출발하다 to depart

[Example] 비행기가 몇 시에 도착하니? What time does the airplane arrive?
축구 대표팀이 탑승한 비행기가 벌써 도착했다고 해요.
The airplane that the Korean soccer players took has already arrived.

019
방법

[방법] 명사 a plan, method, way

the means or method of achieving a goal

[Expression] 사용 방법 usage method

방법이 없다 there is no way

방법을 찾다 to look for a way

[Example] 영수를 도와줄 방법이 없을까? Is there any way we can help Young-soo?
학교까지 한 시간이나 걸린다고요? 더 빨리 가는 방법은 없을까요?
It will take an hour to get to school? Is there any way I could go faster?

020
불편하다

[불편하다] 형용사 1. to be inconvenient or uncomfortable   2. to feel uncomfortable

1.when using something it is uncomfortable or difficult

[Usage]   <u>N</u>이/가 불편하다

[Expression]   교통이 불편하다 the transportation is inconvenient

의자가 불편하다 the chair is uncomfortable

[Antonym]   편하다 to be comfortable

편리하다 to be convenient

[Example]   집에서 학교까지 거리는 멀지 않은데 직접 가는 버스가 없어서 불편해요.
The distance from my home to school is not far but there isn't a bus that goes directly there so it is inconvenient.

2.when one's health or mental state is not so good, or when a relationship with someone is not comfortable

[Usage]   <u>N</u>이/가 불편하다

[Expression]   불편한 관계 an uncomfortable relationship

다리가 불편하다 my leg is uncomfortable

마음이 불편하다 my mind is uncomfortable

[Antonym]   편하다 to feel comfortable

[Example]   영수하고 싸운 후에는 영수를 만나는 것이 불편하다.
After fighting with Young-soo it is uncomfortable meeting Young-soo.

021
승강장

[승강장] 명사 platform

the place where one gets on and off of a transportation

[Expression]   지하철 승강장 subway platform

[Example]   여자 친구가 기차 승강장까지 나와서 나를 배웅했다.
My girlfriend came to the platform of the train and sent me off.

출퇴근 시간이 아니어서 지하철 승강장에 사람이 별로 없어요.
It is not rush hour so there are not many people at the subway platform.

022
안전선

[안전선] 명사 safety line

the line that draws where it is safe to stand when waiting for a vehicle

[Example]   얘야, 위험하다. 안전선 가까이 가지 마라.
Oh, it is dangerous. Don't go near the safety line.

열차가 들어오고 있으니까 안전선 안으로 한 걸음 물러서시기 바랍니다.
The train is coming near so please step one step behind the safety line.

023
왕복

[왕복] 명사 round trip, going and coming

going and arriving

[Expression] 왕복표 round trip ticket

왕복 요금 round trip fare

[Related word] 편도 one way

[Example] 유학을 갈 때 왕복표를 살 계획이에요.

I plan on buying a round trip ticket when I go study abroad.

산 정상까지 왕복 1(한)시간 반쯤 걸려요.

Going and coming back down from the top of the mountain takes about one and a half hour.

024
요금

[요금] 명사 fare, fee

money that is paid to use something

[Expression] 버스 요금 bus fare

주차 요금 parking fee

전화 요금 calling fee

요금이 나오다 the fare comes out

요금을 내다 to pay a fee

[Example] 한 달에 전화 요금이 얼마나 나와요?

How much is one month's calling fee?

이제 곧 버스 요금이 오를 것 같아요.

I think the bus fare will increase soon.

025
자리

[자리] 명사 seat

a place made for someone to sit

[Expression] 자리를 양보하다 to offer one's seat

[Synonym] 좌석 a seat

[Example] 지하철 안에 자리가 없어서 한 시간 동안 계속 서서 갔다.

There were no seats in the subway so I stood for an hour.

자리에 앉아 있다가 할머니가 버스에 타셔서 자리를 양보해 드렸다.

I was sitting in a seat but a grandmother came in and I offered her my seat.

026
직접

[직쩝] 부사 directly, personally

not through something or someone else but immediately, personally

[Usage] 직접 AV

[Expression] 직접 가다 to go in person

직접 만나다 to meet in person

[Antonym]	간접 indirect
[Example]	여기에서 신촌 기차역까지 직접 가는 버스가 없어요. There are no buses that go from here to the Shin-chon train station.
	우리 전화로만 얘기할 것이 아니라 직접 만나서 이야기하는 것이 어 때요? Let's not only talk on the telephone but how about meeting in person?

027
출구

[출구] 명사 exit

an exit to go out

[Usage]	<u>Num</u>번 출구
[Expression]	출구로 나가다 to go out of the exit
[Example]	세종문화회관에 가려면 1(일)번 출구로 나가세요. Go out of exit 1 if you want to go to the Sejong Center for Performing Arts.
	화장실은 앞쪽 출구로 나가서 왼쪽으로 가시면 됩니다. Go out of the exit and turn to the left to go to the restroom.

028
하차하다

[하차하다] 동사 to get off

to get off the car

[Usage]	<u>N</u>에서 하차하다
[Antonym]	승차하다 to get on
[Example]	명동에서 하차해서 길을 건너세요. Get off at Myung-dong and cross the road.
	이번에 정차할 역은 수원입니다. 하차하실 분은 미리 준비하시기 바 랍니다. The stop that we will be stopping at next is Su-won. Everyone who will get off, please prepare to get off.

029
건너다

[건너다] 동사 to cross

to put something in between and to go to another side

[Usage] **N**을/를 건너다

N으로/로 건너다

[Expression] 건너가다 to cross

길을 건너다 to cross the road

육교를 건너다 to cross the pedestrian overpass

지하도로 건너다 to cross the underground pass

[Example] 쭉 가다가 횡단보도로 건너가면 은행이 있어요.
If you keep going and cross the crosswalk, the bank will be there.

아이들이 한손을 들고 길을 건너는 모습이 참 귀여워요.
The kids who are holding hands and crossing the road are very cute.

030
교통

[교통] 명사 transportation, traffic

[Expression] 교통편 traffic facilities

교통사고 traffic accident

교통이 복잡하다 the traffic is chaotic

교통이 편리하다 the traffic is convenient

[Example] 서울이 복잡하기는 하지만 교통이 편리해서 좋아요.
Seoul is a bit chaotic but the traffic is convenient so it's nice.

교통이 복잡하니까 지하철을 탑시다.
The traffic is a bit chaotic at this time, so let's take the subway.

031
길

[길] 명사 1. road 2. way

1. a path made for people and transportation to travel on

[Expression] 길거리 street

길이 넓다 the street is wide

길이 막히다 the street is blocked

길이 복잡하다 the street is chaotic

[Synonym] 거리 road

[Example] 길이 막혀서 안 되겠어요. 다른 길로 돌아가야겠어요.
The street is blocked so it won't work. I better go another way.

2. in the middle of doing something

[Usage] **AV**는 길에

AV는 길이다

[Example] 친구를 만나러 가는 길에 은행에 잠깐 들렀다.
On the way to meet my friend, I stopped by the bank.

032
돌아가다

[도라가다] **동사** 1. to go back 2. to return

1. there is a shorter way, but taking the longer way and turning around

[Usage] <u>N</u>으로/로 돌아가다

[Expression] 옆길로 돌아가다 to turn around the next street

[Example] 차가 밀리니까 다른 길로 돌아가야겠다.
The cars are really blocked so I should go back the other way.

2. to go back to the original place

[Usage] <u>N</u>으로/로 돌아가다

[Expression] 고향으로 돌아가다 to go back to the hometown

[Example] 이번 방학에는 바빠서 고향으로 돌아가지 않을 생각이에요.
I will be busy this break, so I won't be returning to my hometown.

033
동

[동] **명사** east

the direction of where the sun rises

[Expression] 동쪽 east side
동문 east door
동서남북 east, west, south, north

[Related word] 방향 direction

[Example] 동쪽 하늘에 해가 떠올랐다. The sun rose in the east part of the sky.
제 집은 학교 동문 근처에 있어요.
My house is near the east gate of the school.

034
똑바로

[똑빠로] **부사** straight, upright

not leaning to one side but keeping straight

[Expression] 똑바로 가다 to go straight
똑바로 놓다 to lay straight
똑바로 보다 to look straight

[Synonym] 쭉 straight

[Example] 의자에 똑바로 앉아라 Sit straight in the chair.
이 길로 똑바로 가면 지하철역이 나올 거예요.
If you go straight on this road, the subway station will appear.

035
막히다

[마키다] 동사 to be blocked

to not be able to go through a road, path, or area

[Usage] **N**이/가 막히다

[Expression] 길이 막히다 the road is blocked

코가 막히다 my nose is blocked

[Related word] 막다 to close off

밀리다 to be clogged

[Example] 길이 막힐까 봐 집에서 일찍 출발했다.

I thought the road would be blocked so I left early.

앞에 사고가 났나 봐요. 길이 갑자기 막히네요.

There must be an accident up front. The street suddenly got blocked.

036
맞은편

[마즌편] 명사 opposite side

the direction opposite of one side

[Related word] 건너편 opposite side

[Example] 학교 맞은편에 우리 아파트가 있어요.

My apartment is on the opposite side of the school.

맞은편에 있는 교실에서 노래 소리가 들린다.

I can hear songs from the opposite side of the classroom.

037
멀다

[멀다] 형용사 1. to be far   2. to feel distance

1. the distance is far from one place to another, ㄹverb

[Usage] **N**이/가 멀다

[Expression] 먼 산 far mountain

집이 멀다 the house is far

[Antonym] 가깝다 to be close

[Example] 집에서 학교까지 너무 멀어서 아침마다 힘들어요.

My house is so far from my school so it's very difficult for me to go to school in the morning.

2. to not feel close to a person but some distance, ㄹverb

[Expression] 멀게 느껴지다 to feel distanced

[Antonym] 가깝다 to be close

[Example] 친구가 아무 말도 하지 않고 앉아 있으니까 멀게 느껴진다.

My friend is not saying anything while sitting so I feel a bit of distance.

038
밀리다

[밀리다] 동사 1. to be clogged   2. to be pushed back, delayed

1. to be blocked for some reason

[Usage] **N**이/가 밀리다

[Expression] 차가 밀리다   the car is clogged

[Related word] 막히다   to be blocked

[Example] 차가 많이 밀리니까 가까운 지하철역에서 그냥 내릴게요.
The car seems to be very clogged so I'll get off at the nearest subway station.

2. to be delayed in work

[Usage] **N**이/가 밀리다

[Expression] 밀린 빨래   delayed laundry

일이 밀리다   work is delayed

[Related word] 쌓이다   to be stacked

[Example] 일이 많이 밀려서 오늘은 퇴근이 늦을 것 같아요.
I have a lot of delayed work so I will get off work late today.

039
방향

[방향] 명사 direction

a place of direction

[Expression] 방향 감각   a sense of direction

반대 방향   opposite direction

방향을 잃다   to lose direction

[Example] 지하철역은 이쪽 방향이 아닌 것 같은데요?
This doesn't seem to be the right direction for the subway station.

이 버스는 반대 방향으로 가니까 저쪽으로 가서 버스를 타세요.
This bus goes to the opposite direction so take the bus over there.

040
복잡하다

[복짜파다] 형용사 to be chaotic

to have something be unorganized so one feels flustered

[Usage] **N**이/가 **N**으로/로 복잡하다

[Example] 명동 거리는 언제나 사람들로 복잡하다.
The Myungdong road is always chaotic because there are so many people.

세일기간이라서 백화점이 아주 복잡하군요.
It is the sale season so the shopping malls seem to be very chaotic.

041
비키다

[비키다] 동사 to get out of the way, to move

to get out of the way and move to another area

[Usage] **N**을/를 비키다

N으로/로 비키다

[Expression]　길을 비키다　to get out of the road

옆으로 비키다　to get to the side

[Example]　머리를 좀 비켜 봐. 텔레비전이 안 보인다.

Move your head. I can't see the television.

사진을 찍으려고 하는데요. 옆으로 좀 비켜 주시겠어요?

I am trying to take a picture. Will you move to the side a bit?

042
사거리

[사거리] **명사** four way street

a street that has four directions

[Synonym]　십자로　four way street

[Related word]　삼거리　three way street

교차로　a cross road

[Example]　저기 사거리에서 좌회전해 주세요.

Please take a left at the four way street.

두 번째 사거리를 지나서 바로 세워 주세요.

Please pass the second four way street and let me off there.

043
신호등

[신호등] **명사** stop light

a tool that has red, green, and yellow arrows to signal when automobiles and people can move

[Expression]　신호등이 바뀌다　the stop light has changed

[Example]　신호등이 초록색으로 바뀌었으니까 길을 건너가자.

The stop light has changed to green so let's cross the street.

우회전할 때에는 교차로의 신호등뿐만 아니라 횡단보도의 신호등도 잘 확인해야 해요.

When turning right, check the street lights but also the cross light.

044
약도

[약또] **명사** map

a simple map

[Expression]　약도를 그리다　to draw a map

[Related word]　지도　map

[Example]　약도를 보고 식당을 찾아 갔어요.

I looked at the map and found the restaurant.

집에서부터 학교까지 어떻게 가야 하는지 약도로 그려주세요.

Please draw a map to show me how to get from my house to the school.

045
우회전

[우회전] **명사** right turn

to change and turn to the right

[Expression]   우회전하다   to turn a right

[Antonym]   좌회전   left turn

[Related word]   직진   to go straight

             유턴   u-turn

[Example]   아까 사거리에서 우회전을 해야지. 직진하면 어떻게 하니?
You were supposed to turn a right at the four way street. Why did you go straight?

          우회전할 때에는 오른쪽 횡단보도의 신호등을 잘 확인해야 해요.
When turning to the right, you should check the cross intersection stop light on the right.

046
운전

[운전] **명사** driving

moving a car or a machine

[Expression]   운전석   driving seat

             음주 운전   driving drunk

             운전면허증   diver's license

             운전하다   to drive

[Example]   오늘도 안전 운전하시기 바랍니다.   Please drive safely today.

          음주 운전을 하면 안 돼요. 차는 그냥 두고 택시를 타고 가세요.
You cannot drive drunk. Please leave your car and take a taxi.

047
위험하다

[위험하다] **형용사** to be dangerous

to be harmful to the point of death

[Usage]   <u>N</u>이/가 위험하다

[Antonym]   안전하다   to be safe

[Example]   음주 운전은 아주 위험해요.   Driving drunk is very dangerous.

          공사장 근처는 위험하니까 가까이 가지 마라.
It is dangerous near the construction site so don't go near there.

048
육교

[육교] **명사** overpass

a constructed bridge used to let automobiles and trains cross

[Expression]   육교를 건너다   to cross an overpass

[Example]   아저씨, 앞에 보이는 육교 아래에서 세워 주세요.
Sir, please stop at the overpass in the front.

다리가 아파서 계단을 오르기가 어려운데 여기는 육교밖에 없네요.

My legs hurt so it's hard for me to go up stairs but there are only overpasses here.

049
조심하다

[조심하다] 형용사 to be careful

to be carful not to do anything wrong, to watch what one says or does

[Usage]	N을/를 조심하다
	N에 조심하다
[Expression]	감기를 조심하다 to be careful not to catch a cold
	매사에 조심하다 to be careful in each affair
[Synonym]	주의하다 to be careful
[Example]	다른 사람들과 이야기할 때에는 말을 조심해야 해.

When talking with other people, we need to be careful as to what we say.

아침저녁으로 날씨가 많이 추워졌어요. 감기에 걸리지 않게 조심하세요.

The weather from morning to night time has gotten really cold. Be careful not to catch a cold.

050
주의하다

[주의하다/주이하다] 동사 1. to be cautious   2. to pay attention

1. to put inside one's thoughts and to be cautious

[Usage]	N에 주의하다
[Expression]	건강에 주의하다 to watch one's health
	행동에 주의하다 to be cautious of one's behavior
[Synonym]	조심하다 to be careful
[Example]	길을 건널 때는 항상 주의해야 한다.

Please be cautious every time you cross the road.

2. to pay attention to what one is doing

[Usage]	N에 주의하다
	주의해서 AV
[Expression]	주의해서 듣다 to listen attentively
[Example]	선생님께서 무슨 말씀을 하시는지 주의해서 들어야 한다.

You must listen attentively to what the teacher is saying.

051
주차

[주차] 명사 parking

taking a car and placing it in place

[Expression]	주차장 parking lot
	주차금지 no parking
	주차하다 to park

[Example] 영화관에 주차장이 없으면 어디에 주차하지?

If there are no parking spaces at the movie, where should I park?

여기에는 주차하실 수 없습니다. 다른 곳에다가 주차하세요.

You cannot park here. Please park somewhere else.

052
지도

[지도] **명사** map

a picture telling the road's state and ratio

[Example] 서울 시내 지도를 보면서 서울을 구경했다.

I looked at the Seoul city map and looked around in Seoul.

인터넷에서 지도를 찾아보면 길을 쉽게 찾을 수 있을 거야.

If you look for the map on the internet, you will be able to find the road easily.

053
지하도

[지하도] **명사** underpass

a road underground made to walk on

[Example] 길을 건너려면 지하도로 건너세요.

If you want to cross the road, then cross the underpass.

명동에 있는 지하도에는 상가가 많아서 아주 재미있어요.

There are a lot of underground shopping centers in Myungdong, so it's a lot of fun.

054
직진

[직찐] **명사** going straight

going or driving straight ahead

[Expression] 직진하다 to go straight

[Antonym] 유턴 u-turn

[Example] 여기서부터는 계속 직진해. 그리고 사거리가 나오면 우회전을 해.

Keep going straight from here. When the four intersection comes out, take a right.

이번 사거리에서는 직진해 주시고요, 그 다음 사거리에서 세워 주세요.

Please go straight at this 4 way street and stop the car at the next 4 way street.

055
쪽²

[쪽] **명사** direction

telling the way or direction

[Expression] 이쪽 this way

왼쪽 left

반대쪽 opposite direction

[Example] 어느 쪽으로 가야 해요? Which direction should I go?

이쪽으로 가면 안 되니까 반대쪽으로 가세요.

You can't go this way so go the opposite way.

056
쭉

[쭉] **부사** going straight

going straight down a line

[Expression] 쭉 가다 to go straight

[Synonym] 똑바로 straight

[Example] 여기서 10(십)분쯤 쭉 가면 큰 병원이 보일 거예요.
If you keep going straight for 10 minutes, there will be a big hospital.

횡단보도를 건너서 쭉 가다가 오른쪽 첫 번째 골목으로 가세요.
Cross the crossing way and walk straight and turn right into the first alley way.

057
호선

[호선] **명사** railway line

[Usage] **Num**호선

[Related word] 지하철 subway

[Example] 서울의 지하철은 모두 몇 호선이 있어요?
How many lines are there in the Seoul subway?

우리 집에서 제일 가까운 지하철역은 지하철 2(이)호선 신촌역이에요.
The closest subway stations is subway line 2 Shin-chon station.

058
횡단보도

[횡단보도] **명사** crosswalk

road created for people to walk across

[Expression] 횡단보도를 건너다 to cross the crosswalk

[Example] 초등학교 앞에 횡단보도가 있으니까 천천히 운전해라.
There is a crosswalk in front of the elementary school, so drive slowly.

횡단보도의 신호등이 고장났나 봐요. 빨간불이 계속 켜져 있어요.
The stop light at the crosswalk must be broken. The red light is continuously blinking.

[1~15] 다음 단어를 한국어로 바꿔 쓰십시오. Change these words into Korean.

1. car ( )
2. station ( )
3. to be far ( )
4. direction ( )
5. to travel back and forth ( )
6. exit ( )
7. taxi ( )
8. safety line ( )
9. underpass ( )
10. straight ( )
11. to cross ( )
12. to be pushed back ( )
13. to arrive ( )
14. to return ( )
15. to get off ( )

[16~20] 그림을 보고 ( )에 알맞은 것을 고르십시오.
Look at the picture and choose the correct word.

16.

가 : 뭘 타고 갔어요?

나 : ( )을/를 타고 갔어요.

❶ 배　　　　　　　❷ 기차

❸ 비행기　　　　　❹ 자동차

17.

가 : 이번 사거리에서 어느 쪽으로 갈까요?

나 : ( )으세요/세요.

❶ 유턴하다　　　　　❷ 직진하다

❸ 우회전하다　　　　❹ 좌회전하다

18.

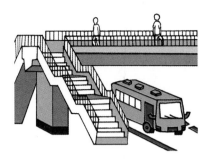

가 : 무엇으로 길을 건널까요?

나 : (　　　　　)으로/로 건너세요.

❶ 육교　　　　　　❷ 사거리

❸ 지하도　　　　　❹ 횡단보도

19.

가 : 길을 모르는데 어떻게 찾아 가지요?

나 : (　　　　　)을/를 보면 돼요.

❶ 책　　　　　　　❷ 거리

❸ 지도　　　　　　❹ 컴퓨터

20.

가 : 어디에서 아빠를 기다렸어요?

나 : (　　　　　)에서 기다렸어요.

❶ 공항　　　　　　❷ 지하철역

❸ 택시 승강장　　　❹ 버스 정류장

[21~30] 다음 문장을 읽고 알맞은 어휘를 골라 쓰십시오. 어휘는 한 번만 쓰십시오.
Read the following sentence and choose the right word. Use the words once.

길	공항	기차	방법	약도
요금	호선	노선도	사거리	승강장
신호등	지하철	위험하다	주의하다	하차하다

21. 이 앞 (   )에서 우회전해 주세요.

22. 저쪽은 물이 깊어서 (   )으니까/니까 가지 마세요.

23. 지하철을 타려고 사람들이 (   )에서 기다리고 있다.

24. 이번에는 서울역에 가서 (   )을/를 타고 부산에 가자.

25. (   )이/가 초록색으로 바뀌었으니까 길을 건너갑시다.

26. 신촌에 가려고 하는데 지하철 몇 (   )을/를 타야 해요?

27. 이 버스가 어디로 가는지 알고 싶으면 (   )을/를 보세요.

28. 우리 집까지 오는 길을 그린 (   )을/를 친구에게 주었다.

29. 이 주차장은 한 시간 주차하면 주차(   )이/가 얼마예요?

30. 핸드폰 문자 메시지를 보내는 (   )을/를 좀 가르쳐 주세요.

[31~35] (   ) 안에 알맞은 것을 고르십시오. Choose the correct one.

31. 지난 주말에 고속버스 (   )에서 고속버스를 타고 설악산에 갔습니다.

   ❶ 역   ❷ 공항   ❸ 정류장   ❹ 터미널

32. 이 길로 (   ) 가세요.

   ❶ 쭉   ❷ 같이   ❸ 보통   ❹ 일찍

33. 젊은 사람들은 보통 (　　)에 앉지 않아요.

　❶ 의자　　　　❷ 자리　　　　❸ 노선도　　　❹ 노약자석

34. 내립니다. 좀 (　　)어/아/여 주세요.

　❶ 앉다　　　　❷ 내리다　　　❸ 비키다　　　❹ 승차하다

35. (　　)을/를 못해서 아직 차를 살 계획이 없어요.

　❶ 돈　　　　　❷ 공부　　　　❸ 방향　　　　❹ 운전

[36~40] 밑줄 친 부분과 반대되는 뜻을 가진 것을 고르십시오.

Choose the word that is the opposite of the underlined word.

36. 가 : 공항에 도착했다고 해요?
　　나 : 아니요, 이제 집에서 (　　)었다고/았다고/였다고 하는데요.

　❶ 오다　　　　　❷ 내려가다　　　　❸ 돌아가다　　　❹ 출발하다

37. 가 : 버스에서 내렸다고 해요?
　　나 : 아니요, 조금 전에 버스를 (　　)었다고/았다고/였다고 해요.

　❶ 타다　　　　　❷ 나오다　　　　　❸ 들어오다　　　❹ 올라가다

38. 가 : 이곳은 교통이 불편해요?
　　나 : 아니요, (　　)어요/아요/여요.

　❶ 쉽다　　　　　❷ 따뜻하다　　　　❸ 편리하다　　　❹ 편안하다

39. 가 : 집이 멀어요?
　　나 : 아니요, (　　)어요/아요/여요.

　❶ 높다　　　　　❷ 좁다　　　　　❸ 가깝다　　　　❹ 두껍다

40. **가 :** <u>위험하지</u> 않아요?

    나 : 아니요, (   )어요/아요/여요.

    ❶ 건너다   ❷ 안전하다   ❸ 주의하다   ❹ 편안하다

[41~45] 밑줄 친 부분과 의미가 가장 가까운 것을 고르십시오.
Choose the word that is most similar to the underlined section.

41. **가 :** 여기에서 신촌으로 <u>직접</u> 가는 버스가 있어요?

    나 : 아니요, (   ) 가는 건 없어요.

    ❶ 곧   ❷ 바로   ❸ 건너서   ❹ 들러서

42. **가 :** 지금 <u>차가 밀려요</u>?

    나 : 네, (   )네요.

    ❶ 바쁘다   ❷ 한가하다   ❸ 길이 넓다   ❹ 길이 막히다

43. **가 :** 학교 <u>맞은편</u>에 병원이 있어요?

    나 : 네, (   )에 있어요.

    ❶ 동쪽   ❷ 저쪽   ❸ 건너편   ❹ 같은 편

44. **가 :** 여기에다가 <u>차를 세울까요</u>?

    나 : 네, 여기에 (   )읍시다/ㅂ시다.

    ❶ 주차하다   ❷ 세차하다   ❸ 유턴하다   ❹ 갈아타다

45. **가 :** 다음부터는 <u>조심하세요</u>!

    나 : 네, (   )겠습니다.

    ❶ 긴장하다   ❷ 소심하다   ❸ 위험하다   ❹ 주의하다

[46~50] 밑줄 친 단어의 쓰임이 잘못된 것을 고르십시오. Choose the one that is incorrectly used.

46.　　❶ 신발이 좀 작아서 <u>불편해요</u>.　　　　　（　　　）

　　　　❷ 지하철역이 좀 멀어서 <u>불편하다</u>.

　　　　❸ 몸은 편하지만 마음은 <u>불편하다</u>.

　　　　❹ 날마다 늦게까지 일해서 건강이 <u>불편해졌다</u>.

47.　　❶ 내일 한국으로 <u>돌아간다</u>.　　　　　（　　　）

　　　　❷ 집에 빨리 <u>돌아가</u> 보세요.

　　　　❸ 갔다가 언제 <u>돌아갈</u> 거예요?

　　　　❹ 이 길은 복잡하니까 옆길로 <u>돌아갑시다</u>.

48.　　❶ 늦었으니까 <u>택시</u>를 탑시다.　　　　　（　　　）

　　　　❷ <u>기차</u> 몇 호선을 타야 해요?

　　　　❸ 집에서 학교까지 <u>버스</u>를 타고 다닙니다.

　　　　❹ <u>비행기</u>가 늦게 도착해서 공항에서 오래 기다렸어요.

49.　　❶ <u>왕복</u> 비행기 표를 샀다.　　　　　（　　　）

　　　　❷ 택시 <u>요금</u>이 모두 얼마예요?

　　　　❸ 버스에 <u>자리</u>가 없어서 서서 갔다.

　　　　❹ 지하철에서 내려서 3번 <u>입구</u>로 나가세요.

50.　　❶ 횡단보도를 <u>걸어서</u> 똑바로 가세요.　　　　　（　　　）

　　　　❷ 시청역에서 1호선으로 <u>갈아타세요</u>.

　　　　❸ 여기는 시골이라서 교통편이 <u>나쁘다</u>.

　　　　❹ 시내에는 사람도 많고 차도 많아서 <u>복잡하다</u>.

자연과 계절

13

Nature and Season

001
강아지

[강아지] 명사 puppy

[Expression] 강아지 한 마리 one puppy

강아지를 키우다 to raise a puppy

[Related word] 개 dog

[Example] 강아지가 작고 참 귀엽네요. The puppy is small and really cute.

엄마, 우리도 강아지를 한 마리 사서 키워요.
Mom, let's buy a puppy and raise him.

002
고래

[고래] 명사 whale

[Expression] 고래 한 마리 one whale

[Example] 한국에서는 고래를 잡아도 돼요? Is it ok to catch whales in Korea?

고래 고기 맛이 소고기 맛과 비슷하다고 해요.
They say that whale meat tastes similar to beef.

003
고양이

[고양이] 명사 cat

[Expression] 고양이 한 마리 one cat

고양이를 기르다 to raise a cat

[Example] 고양이가 쥐를 잡아서 먹었어요. The cat caught the mouse and ate him.

우리 아이는 강아지보다 고양이를 더 기르고 싶어해요.
My child wants to raise a cat more than a dog.

004
꽃

[꼳] 명사 flower

[Expression] 꽃잎 flower leaf

꽃바구니 flower basket

꽃 한 송이 one flower

꽃 한 다발 a bundle of flowers

꽃이 피다 the flower is blooming

[Example] 예쁜 꽃이 많이 피는 봄이 왔어요.
The spring when many flowers bloom is here.

남자친구가 꽃 한 다발을 선물했어요.
My boyfriend gave me a bundle of flowers as a present.

These are some flowers.

개나리, 진달래, 벚꽃, 무궁화, 장미, 카네이션, ……

golden-bell, azalea, cherry blossoms, the rose of Sharon, rose, carnation, ……

005
나무

[나무] **명사** tree

[Usage]	N나무
[Expression]	나뭇잎 tree leaf
	나뭇가지 tree branch
	사과나무 apple tree
	나무 한 그루 one tree
	나무를 심다 to plant a tree
[Related word]	숲 forest
[Example]	우리 집에는 감나무가 한 그루 있다. We have a persimmon tree at home.
	산에 나무가 많아야 공기가 좋아져요.
	There should be a lot of trees in the mountains so that there is good oxygen.

006
단풍

[단풍] **명사** autumn leaves

the leaves changing because of the climate change, the leaves change into red or yellow color, those kinds of leaves

[Example]	단풍 구경 sightseeing autumn leaves
	단풍이 아름답다 the autumn leaves are beautiful
	단풍이 들다 the leaves are changing
[Related word]	가을 autumn
[Example]	단풍이 들어서 산이 아름다워요.
	The autumn leaves make the mountain beautiful.
	가을이 되어서 설악산으로 단풍 구경을 갔다.
	It is autumn so I went to Sorak mountain to sightsee the autumn leaves.

007
닭

[닥] **명사** chicken

[Expression]	닭고기 chicken
	닭 한 마리 one chicken
[Related word]	달걀 egg
	병아리 chick
[Example]	시골에 계신 할머니는 닭을 기르신다.
	My grandmother who lives in the country raises chickens.
	오늘 우리 닭 한 마리를 배달시켜서 먹을까?
	Should we order a chicken for delivery?

008
동물

[동물] **명사** animal

[Expression] 동물원 zoo

동물 병원 animal hospital

[Example] 우리 오빠는 무슨 동물이든지 다 좋아한다.
My brother likes all animals.

어린이날 동물원에 가서 여러 가지 동물들을 구경했다.
I looked at a lot of animals at the zoo on children's day.

009
돼지

[돼지] **명사** pig

[Expression] 돼지고기 pork

돼지 한 마리 one pig

[Example] 어제 돼지꿈을 꿔서 아주 기분이 좋아요.
I dreamt about a pig yesterday so I am very happy.

친구에게 농담으로 돼지라고 했는데 친구가 아주 크게 화를 냈다.
I made a joke by calling my friend a pig and she really got upset.

010
마리

[마리] **명사** one animal

a counting unit for animals and fish

[Expression] 생선 한 마리 one fish

[Example] 오늘은 물고기를 몇 마리 잡았어요?
How many fishes did you catch today?

위층에 사는 사람들은 개를 두 마리 키워요.
The people who live upstairs raise two dogs.

011
새

[새] **명사** bird

[Expression] 새 소리 bird sound

새 한 마리 one bird

새가 날다 a bird can fly

[Example] 새들이 하늘을 날고 있다. The birds are flying in the air.

새 소리가 참 듣기 좋네요. It is good to hear birds chirping.

012
소

[소] **명사** cow

[Expression] 소고기 beef

소 한 마리 one cow

[Example] 불고기는 소고기로 만듭니다. Bulgogi is made out of beef.

오늘 저녁에는 소고기를 사다가 구워 먹어야겠다.
I should buy beef and grill it for dinner.

013
송이

[송이] 명사 a cluster or a bunch

a counting unit for flowers and plants

[Expression]　꽃 한 송이　one flower

　　　　　　　포도 한 송이　a bundle of grapes

　　　　　　　바나나 한 송이　a bundle of bananas

[Example]　바나나 한 송이에 삼천 원입니다. A bundle of bananas is 3,000 won.

　　　　　　여자 친구의 스무 살 생일에 장미꽃 스무 송이를 선물했다.

　　　　　　For my girlfriends 20th birthday, I gave her 20 roses as a present.

014
양

[양] 명사 sheep

[Expression]　양털　wool

　　　　　　　양고기　lamb meat

　　　　　　　양 한 마리　one sheep

[Example]　양고기를 먹어본 적이 있어요? Have you ever eaten lamb meat?

　　　　　　양 한 마리가 길을 잃었나 봐요. 보이지 않아요.

　　　　　　There must be a lost lamb. I don't see him.

015
오리

[오리] 명사 duck

[Expression]　오리고기　duck meat

　　　　　　　오리 한 마리　one duck

[Example]　저는 오리 고기를 정말 좋아해요. I really like duck meat.

　　　　　　저기 호수 위에 오리가 몇 마리 있어요.

　　　　　　There are some ducks on the lake.

016
피다

[피다] 동사 to bloom

the flower part is blooming

[Usage]　N이/가 피다

[Expression]　꽃이 피다 the flower is blooming

[Antonym]　지다 to wither

[Example]　이 나무는 언제쯤 꽃이 피어요? When does this tree bloom flowers?

　　　　　　여자 친구에게 꽃이 많이 피어 있는 화분을 하나 사 주었다.

　　　　　　I bought a plant with many blooming flowers for my girlfriend.

017
호랑이

[호랑이] 명사 tiger

[Expression]　호랑이 한 마리　one tiger

[Example]　동물의 왕은 호랑이라고 생각해요.

　　　　　　I think the king of the animals is the tiger.

옛날에는 산에 호랑이가 많이 살았다고 한다.

They say that there were a lot of tigers living in the mountains in the olden days.

13-2 | 색깔

018
갈색

[갈쌕] **명사** brown

[Example]   우리 집 자동차 색깔은 갈색이다.   Our car at home is brown.

가을이 되면 여자들은 갈색과 까만색 옷을 많이 입는 편이에요.

During the fall women wear a lot of brown and black.

019
까맣다

[까마타] **형용사** to be black or dark

to have no light and be dark like night, ㅎ verb

[Usage]   <u>N</u>이/가 까맣다

[Expression]   까만색   black

까만 눈   black eyes

얼굴이 까맣다   her face is dark or black

까맣게 타다   to burn dark

[Synonym]   검다   to be black

[Example]   그 여자의 머리 색깔과 눈은 밤하늘처럼 까맣다.

That woman's hair and eyes are dark like the night sky.

바닷가에서 재미있게 놀아서 좋았지만 얼굴은 아주 까맣게 탔다.

It was fun to play by the beach but my face got really burnt and dark.

020
노랗다

[노라타] **형용사** to be yellow

the color of chicks or golden-bell tree, ㅎ verb

[Usage]   <u>N</u>이/가 노랗다

[Expression]   노란색   yellow

노란 은행잎   yellow ginko leaf

잎이 노랗다   the leaf is yellow

|[Example]| 노랗고 빨간 단풍이 아름답다.
The changed leaves that are yellow and red are beautiful.

저는 노란색 장미꽃을 제일 좋아해요. I like yellow roses the best.

021
분홍색

[분홍색] **명사** pink

[Example] 여자 아이들은 보통 분홍색을 좋아해요.
Usually girls like the pink color.

결혼식을 한 후에 피로연 드레스는 분홍색으로 하는 것이 어때요?
After the wedding would you like to wear a pink dress for a wedding reception?

022
빨갛다

[빨가타] **형용사** to be red
it is dark and bright red, ㅎ verb

[Usage] N이/가 빨갛다

[Expression] 빨간색 red
얼굴이 빨갛다 the face is red

[Example] 사랑하는 사람에게는 보통 빨간 장미를 선물합니다.
Usually we give red roses to the person we love.

한국 국가대표 축구팀을 응원하려고 빨간색 티셔츠를 입었다.
I wore a red shirt to cheer on the Korean soccer team.

023
색깔

[색깔] **명사** color

[Expression] 밝은 색깔 a bright color
어두운 색깔 a dark color
색깔이 예쁘다 the color is pretty

[Synonym] 색 color

[Example] 디자인은 좋은데 색깔은 마음에 들지 않아요.
The design is pretty but I don't like the color.

봄이 되니까 여자들이 밝은 색 옷을 많이 입었다.
There are many women wearing bright colors because it is spring.

024
주황색

[주황색] **명사** orange
the color made with mixing red and yellow, and it is between those two colors

[Example] 어두운 거리에 주황색 불빛이 보였다.
I saw a orange light on the dark road.

너한테 주황색이 참 잘 어울리는구나.
Orange looks really good on you.

327

025
초록색

[초록쌕] 명사 green

[Example]   초록색 불로 바뀔 때까지 움직이지 말고 기다려라.
Don't move and wait until it changes to a green light.

눈이 아플 때 초록색을 보면 눈의 피로가 풀린다고 해요.
They say that when your eye hurts you should look at the green color and your eyes will feel less tired.

026
파랗다

[파라타] 형용사 blue

the color of a clear sky in autumn or the color of the deep ocean, ㅎ verb

[Usage]   N이/가 파랗다

[Expression]   파란색 blue

하늘이 파랗다 the sky is blue

[Example]   여름이어서 그런지 파란색이 아주 시원해 보인다.
The blue color looks so refreshing. It must be because it's summer.

오랜만에 파란 하늘을 보니까 기분이 아주 좋아집니다.
I feel so good after seeing the blue sky after such a long time.

027
하얗다

[하야타] 형용사 to be white

a very white light, ㅎ verb

[Usage]   N이/가 하얗다

[Expression]   하얀색 white

하얀 피부 white skin

세상이 하얗다 the world is white

[Synonym]   희다 to be white

[Example]   눈이 와서 세상이 하얗게 변했어요.
The world changed to white because it snowed.

어떻게 피부가 이렇게 하얘요? 특별한 피부 관리 방법이 있어요?
How is your skin this white? Is there some special way you take care of your skin?

028
강

[강] **명사** river

[Expression] 한강 Han river

강물 river water

강이 흐르다 the river is flowing

강을 건너다 to cross the river

[Example] 강이 정말 맑고 깨끗하군요. The river is very clear and clean.

옛날부터 사람들은 강 근처에 모여서 살았어요.
Since a long time ago, people lived near the river.

029
경치

[경치] **명사** landscape

mountain, field, river, ocean, and other parts of nature

[Expression] 자연 경치 natural landscape

그림 같은 경치 a picturesque landscape

경치가 아름답다 the landscape is beautiful

[Example] 나중에 경치가 좋은 곳에서 살고 싶어요.
Later I want to live near a nice landscape.

이번 휴가에는 경치가 좋은 곳으로 여행을 갑시다.
For this vacation let's go somewhere with good landscape.

030
공기

[공기] **명사** air

[Expression] 상쾌한 공기 refreshing air

공기가 좋다 the air is nice

공기가 맑다 the air is clear

[Example] 산에 오니까 공기가 정말 상쾌합니다.
The mountain has really refreshing air.

여기는 좀 답답하네요. 맑은 공기를 마시러 밖에 잠깐 나갑시다.
It is stuffy here. Let's go outside to get some fresh air.

031
높다

[놉따] **형용사** 1. to be high 2. to be high (temperature)

1. the length from the bottom to top

[Usage] **N**이/가 높다

[Expression] 높은 산 a high mountain

높은 고층 빌딩 a high storied building

하늘이 높다 the sky is high

[Antonym] 낮다 to be low

[Example]　여기는 시내여서 높은 고층 빌딩이 많아요.
　　　　　Since this is a city, there are many high buildings.

　　　　　2. the numbers are high in temperature and humidity

[Usage]　　N이/가 높다

[Expression]　높은 온도　A high temperature

　　　　　습도가 높다　the humidity is high

[Antonym]　낮다　to be low

[Example]　습도가 높으면 사람들이 쉽게 짜증을 냅니다.
　　　　　When the humidity is high, people get irritated easily.

032
돌

[돌]　**명사**　stone

[Expression]　돌을 던지다　to throw a stone

[Example]　사람들이 다칠 수 있으니까 돌을 던지지 마라.
　　　　　People can get hurt so don't throw stones.

　　　　　삼겹살을 돌 위에다가 구워서 먹는 식당이 있어요.
　　　　　There is a restaurant where you grill pork on a stone.

033
모래

[모래]　**명사**　sand

[Expression]　모래 사장　sand bank

[Related word]　바다　ocean

[Example]　바닷가에 있는 하얀 모래가 참 예뻐요.
　　　　　The white sand on the beach is very pretty.

　　　　　놀이터에서 모래 놀이를 해서 손발이 모두 더러워졌구나.
　　　　　Your hands and feet must be dirty because you played in the sand at the playground.

034
바다

[바다]　**명사**　ocean

the big and wide part of the world that is not part of the land, it has salty water

[Expression]　바닷가　beach

　　　　　시원한 바다　the refreshing ocean

　　　　　바다가 넓다　the ocean is wide

[Related word]　해변　the seashore

　　　　　해수욕장　beach resort

[Example]　이번 여름휴가 때 바다로 놀러 가려고 해요.
　　　　　This summer vacation I plan on going to the ocean to play.

　　　　　설악산으로 여행을 가면 산과 바다를 같이 구경할 수 있어서 좋아요.
　　　　　I like going to Sorak mountain because I get to see both the mountain and the ocean.

035
별

[별] **명사** star

[Expression] 별빛 starlight

별이 빛나다 the star is bright

[Example] 시골에 오니까 별빛이 참 밝아요.
The starlight is very bright in the country.

저기 저 별 좀 봐. 진짜 크고 밝다.
Look at that star. It's very big and bright.

036
산

[산] **명사** mountain

[Expression] 등산 hiking

산이 높다 the mountain is high

산을 오르다 to climb the mountain

[Example] 한국에는 산이 아주 많다. There are many mountains in Korea.

집 근처에 높지 않은 산이 있어서 시간이 있을 때마다 등산을 해요.
There is a mountain that is not too high and it is near my home, so whenever I have time I go hiking.

037
섬

[섬] **명사** island

land that is surrounded by water

[Example] 이 바다 근처에는 크고 작은 섬이 많아서 경치가 참 좋아요.
There are big and small islands near this ocean so the landscape is beautiful.

사람이 살지 않는 섬도 있지만 일본처럼 한 나라가 섬인 곳도 있어요.
There are islands that no people live in, but there are countries like Japan that are islands.

038
아름답다

[아름답따] **형용사** to be beautiful

the beauty of someone's appearance, sound, balance made between eyes and ears and gives happiness to someone, ㅂverb

[Usage] N이/가 아름답다

[Expression] 아름다운 목소리 beautiful voice

경치가 아름답다 the landscape is beautiful

[Related word] 예쁘다 to be pretty

[Example] 노래하는 목소리가 참 아름다워요. 가수를 해도 되겠어요.
Your singing voice is very beautiful. You could become a singer.

집이 아름다울 뿐만 아니라 집 주위의 경치도 참 아름다워요.
The house is beautiful, but the landscape around the house is also very beautiful too.

039
폭포

[폭포] **명사** waterfall

[Expression] 폭포수 a waterfall

[Example] 더운 여름날 폭포 아래에서 수박을 먹으니까 진짜 시원하다.
It is really refreshing eating watermelon at the bottom of the waterfall.

폭포에 가까워질수록 폭포에서 떨어지는 물소리도 점점 커집니다.
The closer I get to the waterfall, I can hear the sound of falling water louder and louder.

040
하늘

[하늘] **명사** sky

[Expression] 하늘색 sky blue

하늘이 맑다 the sky is clear

하늘을 날다 to fly above the sky

[Related word] 구름 cloud

[Example] 가을이 되니까 하늘이 더 높고 더 파래요.
The sky is higher and bluer because it is autumn.

날씨가 아주 맑다. 하늘에 구름이 하나도 없어.
The weather is very clear. There are no clouds in the sky.

041
호수

[호수] **명사** lake

[Expression] 넓은 호수 a wide lake

[Example] 천지는 바다처럼 넓고 깊은 호수이다.
Chunji is a wide and deep lake like the ocean.

우리는 오늘 호수 공원으로 자전거를 타러 가요.
Today we are going to the lake park to ride bicycles.

042
구름

[구름] 명사 cloud

[Expression] 구름이 끼다 to have many clouds

[Related word] 흐리다 to be cloudy

[Example] 하늘에 떠 있는 하얀 구름이 참 예쁘다.
The white clouds in the sky are very pretty.

구름이 많이 낀 걸 보니까 비가 올 것 같아요.
The sky is filled with clouds so it seems like it will rain.

043
끼다²

[끼다] 동사 to fog up, or to be unclear

to block and be unclear because there is fog or smoke

[Usage] N이/가 끼다

[Expression] 구름이 끼다 to have many clouds

안개가 끼다 to be foggy

[Example] 안개가 끼어서 앞이 잘 보이지 않는다.
It is so foggy that I can't really see.

오늘은 낮에 구름이 끼다가 조금씩 개겠습니다.
It will be cloudy in the afternoon but it will get clearer gradually.

044
날씨

[날씨] 명사 weather

the status of the weather, rain, cloudiness, wind, and temperature can affect the weather

[Expression] 맑은 날씨 clear weather

날씨가 좋다 the weather is nice

[Related word] 일기예보 weather forecast

[Example] 아침저녁으로 날씨가 꽤 춥네요.
The weather is pretty cold in the morning and at night.

이번 주말에 날씨가 좋으면 어디로 놀러 갈까요?
Should we go somewhere if the weather is nice this weekend?

045
눈¹

[눈] 명사 snow

[Expression] 첫눈 first snow

눈사람 snowman

눈싸움 snow fight

눈이 오다 the snow is falling

눈이 쌓이다 the snow is piling up

[Related word] 겨울 winter

[Example] 이번 겨울에는 첫눈이 언제쯤 올까요?
When do you think the first snow will come?

어렸을 때 눈이 많이 오면 친구들하고 눈사람도 만들고 눈싸움도 했어요.
When I was young, my friends and I would make snowmen and have snow ball fights.

046
덥다

[덥따] 형용사 to be hot

the temperature is high or for some reason the body feels hot, ㅂverb

[Usage] N이/가 덥다

[Expression] 더운 날씨 hot weather

무덥다 to be hot and humid

몸이 덥다 the body feels hot

[Antonym] 춥다 to be cold

[Related word] 여름 summer

[Example] 밤에도 너무 더워서 잠을 잘 잘 수가 없어요.
It is so hot even during the night that I can't fall asleep.

날씨가 더우니까 시원한 팥빙수를 시켜서 먹을까요?
Should we order and eat refreching iced red bean since it is really hot?

047
따뜻하다

[따뜨타다] 형용사 1. to feel warm 2. to be kind or warm

1. to have temperature that is not hot but just right

[Usage] N이/가 따뜻하다

[Expression] 따뜻한 날씨 warm weather

방이 따뜻하다 the room is warm

손이 따뜻하다 hand is warm

[Related word] 봄 spring

[Example] 오늘은 날씨가 따뜻해서 산책하기가 참 좋아요.
The weather today is warm so it will be nice to take a walk.

2. the feeling or mood is good and friendly

[Usage] N이/가 따뜻하다

[Expression] 따뜻한 분위기 warm feeling

마음이 따뜻하다 heart is warm

[Example] 여자 친구가 직접 만든 목도리를 선물로 받았을 때 여자 친구의 따뜻한 마음을 느낄 수 있었다.
When I received the scarf that my girlfriend made for me, I could feel her warmth.

048
맑다

[막따] 형용사 1. to be clear   2. to be clean

1. the sun is bright and there are no clouds in the sky

[Usage] <u>N</u>이/가 맑다

[Expression] 하늘이 맑다 the sky is clear

[Example] 맑은 하늘을 보고 있으니까 마음도 깨끗해집니다.
My heart feels clear as I'm looking at the clear sky.

2. it is clean and there is nothing mixed with something dirty

[Usage] <u>N</u>이/가 맑다

[Expression] 맑은 물 clear water

공기가 맑다 the air is clear

[Related word] 깨끗하다 to be clean

[Example] 제가 사는 곳은 근처에 큰 산이 있어서 공기가 맑아요.
There is a big mountain near the place I live so the air is very clear.

049
바람

[바람] 명사 wind

[Expression] 차가운 바람 cold wind

바람이 세다 the wind is strong

바람이 불다 the wind is blowing

[Related word] 폭풍 hurricane

태풍 typhoon

황사 yellow sand

[Example] 바람이 차요. 창문을 닫고 자야겠어요.
The wind is cold. I better close the window when I go to sleep.

한국은 봄에 날씨가 따뜻하지만 바람이 많이 불어요.
Korea's spring is warm but there is a lot of wind.

050
비

[비] 명사 rain

[Expression] 비가 오다 it is raining

비를 맞다 to get hit by rain

[Example] 내일 비가 와도 등산을 할 거예요.
I am going to go hiking even if it rains.

오늘 오후에 비가 온다고 하니까 우산을 꼭 가져가라.
They say it will rain today in the afternoon, so take your umbrella.

051
선선하다

[선선하다] 형용사 to be refreshing

the weather is cool enough and refreshing

[Usage] **N**이/가 선선하다

[Related word] 가을 autumn

[Example] 저는 선선한 가을 날씨를 좋아합니다.
I like the refreshing autumn weather.

이제 아침저녁에는 날씨가 꽤 선선해요.
It is refreshing in the morning and night time.

052
습하다

[스파다] 형용사 to be humid

the air has a lot of water

[Usage] **N**이/가 습하다

[Expression] 습한 공기 humid air

날씨가 습하다 the weather is humid

[Antonym] 건조하다 to be dry

[Related word] 무덥다 to be sticky

[Example] 한국의 여름 날씨는 덥고 습해요.
The summers in Korea are hot and humid.

오늘은 날씨가 습해서 빨래가 잘 마르지 않아요.
The laundry is not drying well because the weather is humid.

053
시원하다

[시원하다] 형용사 1. to feel cool   2. to feel refreshed

1. it is not hot and not cold just right

[Usage] **N**이/가 시원하다

[Expression] 시원한 맥주 cool beer

바람이 시원하다 the wind is cool

[Example] 시원한 바람이 부니까 기분이 상쾌해요.
The cool wind is blowing and it makes me feel refreshed.

2. the feeling is light and good after having a stuffy feeling

[Usage] **N**이/가 시원하다

[Expression] 마음이 시원하다 feeling is cool

[Example] 오랫동안 나를 힘들게 했던 일이 끝나서 정말 속이 시원하다.
After completing the work that I worked hard for a long time, I felt refreshed.

054
쌀쌀하다

[쌀쌀하다] 형용사 to feel chilly

the weather or wind is extremely cold

[Usage] N이/가 쌀쌀하다

[Expression] 쌀쌀한 공기 chilly air

바람이 쌀쌀하다 the air is chilly

[Example] 쌀쌀한 바람을 맞으면 감기에 걸리니까 조심해라.

If you stay out in the chilly wind, you will catch a cold so be careful.

아직 날씨가 쌀쌀하니까 겉옷을 하나 가지고 가세요.

The weather is still chilly so take a coat.

055
안개

[안개] 명사 fog

[Expression] 안개가 끼다 it is foggy

[Example] 안개가 껴서 앞이 잘 보이지 않는다.

I can't really see because there is a lot of fog.

오늘은 안개가 낀다고 하니까 운전을 조심해라.

They say that it will be foggy so be careful while driving.

056
장마

[장마] 명사 rainy season

weather during the summer when it keeps raining

[Expression] 장마철 rainy season

장마가 들다 the rainy season is over

[Example] 한국은 6(유)월 말부터 장마가 시작된다.

Korea starts the rainy season at the end of June.

장마가 언제 끝난다고 해요? 맑은 하늘이 정말 그리워요.

When does the rainy season end? I miss the clear sky.

057
흐리다

[흐리다] 형용사 to be unclear, cloudy

the sky is filled with cloud or fog and so the sunlight is not very bright

[Usage] N이/가 흐리다

[Expression] 날씨가 흐리다 the weather is foggy

[Related word] 구름 cloud

[Example] 날씨가 흐리면 기분도 우울해져요.

If the weather is cloudy then my feeling gets depressing too.

하늘이 흐린 걸 보니까 금방 비가 올 것 같아요.

The sky is cloudy so it seems like it will rain soon.

058
가을

[가을] **명사** autumn

[Expression] 선선한 가을 cool autumn

가을이 오다 autumn is coming

가을이 되다 it is autumn

[Example] 가을이 되니까 하늘이 점점 높아집니다.
Since it is fall, the sky is getting higher and higher.

저는 날씨가 선선한 가을을 제일 좋아합니다.
I like the cool autumn weather the best.

059
겨울

[겨울] **명사** winter

[Expression] 겨울방학 winter break

추운 겨울 cold winter

[Related word] 눈¹ snow

스키 ski

[Example] 겨울이 되면 저는 자주 스키를 타러 가요.
When it becomes winter, I go skiing a lot.

이번 겨울은 작년보다 더 추울 거라고 해요.
This year's weather is going to be colder than last year.

060
계절

[계절/계절] **명사** season

[Expression] 사계절 4 seasons

계절이 바뀌다 the season is changing

[Related word] 봄 spring

여름 summer

가을 autumn

겨울 winter

[Example] 계절이 바뀔 때 건강을 조심해야 합니다.
You need to watch your health when the seasons change.

봄, 여름, 가을, 겨울 중에서 어느 계절을 좋아하세요?
Out of spring, summer, autumn and winter, which season do you like the best?

061
봄

[봄] **명사** spring

[Expression]　봄꽃　spring flower
　　　　　　　봄바람　spring wind
　　　　　　　따뜻한 봄　warm spring

[Example]　봄바람이 따뜻해요. The spring wind is warm.
　　　　　우리 할머니는 봄에는 꽃구경을 가시고 가을에는 단풍 구경을 가십니다.

　　　　　My grandmother goes to look at flowers in the spring and look at changing leaves in the fall.

062
얼다

[얼다] **동사** to freeze

the freezing of water or watery liquid because of the cold, body feeling cold, ㄹverb

[Usage]　N이/가 얼다

[Expression]　물이 얼다　the water is frozen
　　　　　　　손이 얼다　the hand is frozen
　　　　　　　몸이 얼다　the body is cold

[Antonym]　녹다　to melt

[Example]　몸이 다 얼었구나. 어서 안으로 들어와라.
　　　　　Your body is frozen. Hurry up and come inside.

　　　　　눈이 온 후에 내린 눈이 얼어서 땅이 미끄러워요.
　　　　　After it snowed, the ground froze and now it is slippery.

063
여름

[여름] **명사** summer

[Expression]　여름휴가　summer break
　　　　　　　여름방학　summer vacation
　　　　　　　무더운 여름　humid summer

[Example]　봄이 가고 여름이 오고 있다.　Spring is passing and summer is coming.
　　　　　여름을 즐기러 온 사람들로 바닷가가 복잡하다.
　　　　　The beach is filled with people who want to enjoy the summer sun.

064
철

[철] **명사** 1. season　2. time

　　　　　1. season

[Expression]　봄철　spring season
　　　　　　　철이 바뀌다　the season is changing

[Example]   여름철에는 모기가 많으니까 물리지 않게 조심해야 한다.

There are a lot of mosquitoes during the summer so you need to be careful not to get bitten.

2. a time during the year when it's perfect to do something, or the right timing

[Expression]   제철   in season

휴가철   vacation season

딸기 철   strawberry season

[Example]   보통 봄학기와 가을학기가 시작될 때쯤이 이사 철이다.

During the beginning of spring semester or autumn semester, it is the time of moving.

065
피서

[피서] 명사 avoiding the heat

going to a cooler place to get out the heat

[Expression]   피서를 가다   to avoid the heat

피서를 떠나다   to go away to avoid the heat

[Related word]   여름   summer

[Example]   이번 여름에 어디로 피서를 갈 계획이에요?

Where are you going this summer to avoid the heat?

피서철에는 사람들이 산이나 바다로 놀러가기 때문에 서울 시내가 복잡하지 않아요.

During the hot season, people go to the mountain or the ocean to avoid the heat, so the city is not so busy.

066
환절기

[환절기] 명사 change of seasons

the time when seasons change

[Related word]   봄   spring

가을   autumn

[Example]   환절기여서 병원에 감기 환자가 많아요.

During the change of seasons, there are a lot of sick people in the hospital.

환절기에는 어떻게 건강을 관리해야 할까요?

How should I look after my health during the seasonal changes?

13 | 연습문제

[1~15] 다음 단어를 한국어로 바꿔 쓰십시오. Change these words into Korean.

1. rock   (   )
2. season   (   )
3. a caunting unit for animals and fish   (   )
4. a caunting unit for flowers and plants   (   )
5. fog   (   )
6. duck   (   )
7. wind   (   )
8. waterfall   (   )
9. ocean   (   )
10. change of seasons   (   )
11. pink   (   )
12. green   (   )
13. to be yellow   (   )
14. to be chilly   (   )
15. to be beautiful   (   )

[16~20] 그림을 보고 ( )에 알맞은 것을 고르십시오.

Look at the picture and choose the correct word.

16.

가 : 뭘 보고 있어요?

나 : 예쁘게 핀 ( )을/를 보고 있어요.

❶ 꽃   ❷ 새

❸ 과일   ❹ 나무

17.

가 : 무슨 계절을 좋아하세요?

나 : 저는 ( )을/를 좋아해요.

❶ 봄   ❷ 여름

❸ 가을   ❹ 겨울

18.

가 : 날씨가 어때요?

나 : (   )이/가 많이 오고 있어요.

❶ 눈　　　　　　❷ 비

❸ 구름　　　　　❹ 안개

19.

가 : 이번 여름에 어디에 놀러 갔다 왔어요?

나 : (   )에 가서 놀았어요.

❶ 산　　　　　　❷ 섬

❸ 강　　　　　　❹ 호수

20.

가 : 무슨 동물을 길러요?

나 : (   )을/를 한 마리 길러요.

❶ 새　　　　　　❷ 소

❸ 강아지　　　　❹ 고양이

[21~30] 다음 문장을 읽고 알맞은 어휘를 골라 쓰십시오. 어휘는 한 번만 쓰십시오.
Read the following sentence and choose the right word. Use the words once.

꽃	고래	겨울	경치	나무
모래	색깔	여름	피서	호수
고양이	맑다	불다	따뜻하다	쌀쌀하다

21. 수박은 (　　　　　)에 먹는 과일이에요.

22. (　　　　　)이/가 바다처럼 크고 넓어요.

23. 엄마, 저 (　　　　　)을/를 한 마리 사고 싶어요.

24. 이번 여름에는 산으로 (　　　　　)을/를 갑시다.

25. 바닷가의 (　　　　　)이/가 하얗고 부드럽습니다.

26. 제가 제일 좋아하는 (　　　　　)은/는 파란색입니다.

27. 날씨가 (　　　　　)으니까/니까 빨리 집으로 들어가자.

28. (　　　　　)이/가 아름다운 곳에 집이 있으면 정말 좋겠다.

29. 우리 하숙집 아주머니는 마음이 아주 (　　　　　)습니다/ㅂ니다.

30. 봄에는 날씨가 따뜻하지만 바람이 많이 (　　　　　)어요/아요/여요.

[31~35] (　　　) 안에 알맞은 것을 고르십시오. Choose the correct one.

31. 봄이 되니까 꽃이 많이 (　　　)는군요/군요.

　❶ 피다　　　❷ 지다　　　❸ 예쁘다　　　❹ 키우다

32. 새 한 마리가 (　　　)을/를 날고 있다.

　❶ 물　　　❷ 공기　　　❸ 바람　　　❹ 하늘

33. 밤하늘에 (   )이/가 빛나고 있다.

   ❶ 강   ❷ 눈   ❸ 별   ❹ 해

34. (   )이/가 시작되면 이제 비가 많이 올 거예요.

   ❶ 철   ❷ 구름   ❸ 습도   ❹ 장마

35. 가을 하늘이 (   )고 파랗습니다.

   ❶ 깊다   ❷ 낮다   ❸ 높다   ❹ 멀다

[36~40] 밑줄 친 부분과 반대되는 뜻을 가진 것을 고르십시오.
Choose the word that is the opposite of the underlined word.

36. **가 :** 집 뒤에 있는 산이 <u>높아요?</u>

   나 : 아니요, (   )어요/아요/여요.

   ❶ 깊다   ❷ 낮다   ❸ 얇다   ❹ 적다

37. **가 :** 그곳 날씨는 <u>더워요?</u>

   나 : 아니요, (   )어요/아요/여요.

   ❶ 춥다   ❷ 흐리다   ❸ 따뜻하다   ❹ 선선하다

38. **가 :** 오늘 날씨가 <u>흐려요?</u>

   나 : 아니요, 아주 (   )어요/아요/여요.

   ❶ 덥다   ❷ 맑다   ❸ 시원하다   ❹ 쌀쌀하다

39. **가 :** 눈이 <u>녹았어요?</u>

   나 : 아니요, 아직도 (   )어/아/여 있어요.

   ❶ 끼다   ❷ 얼다   ❸ 피다   ❹ 내리다

40. **가 :** 오늘은 날씨가 좀 <u>건조하군요</u>.

　　나 : 네, 어제는 비가 와서 좀 (　　　)었는데요/았는데요/였는데요.

　❶ 춥다　　　　　❷ 무덥다　　　　　❸ 습하다　　　　　❹ 흐리다

[41~45] 밑줄 친 부분과 의미가 가장 가까운 것을 고르십시오.
Choose the word that is most similar to the underlined section.

41. **가 :** 경치가 <u>예뻐요</u>?

　　나 : 네, 아주 (　　　　)어요/아요/여요.

　❶ 좋다　　　　　❷ 귀엽다　　　　　❸ 깨끗하다　　　　　❹ 아름답다

42. **가 :** 하늘에 까만 <u>구름</u>이 끼었군요.

　　나 : 네, 날씨가 (　　　　)어요/아요/여요.

　❶ 춥다　　　　　❷ 무덥다　　　　　❸ 흐리다　　　　　❹ 쌀쌀하다

43. **가 :** 강물이 아주 <u>맑군요</u>.

　　나 : 네, 진짜 (　　　　)지요?

　❶ 넓다　　　　　❷ 깨끗하다　　　　　❸ 따뜻하다　　　　　❹ 시원하다

44. **가 :** 바람이 부니까 좀 <u>춥군요</u>.

　　나 : 네, 날씨가 많이 (　　　　)어졌어요/아졌어요/여졌어요.

　❶ 흐리다　　　　　❷ 선선하다　　　　　❸ 쌀쌀하다　　　　　❹ 시원하다

45. **가 :** <u>계절</u>이 바뀌었으니까 집 좀 청소해 볼까?

　　나 : 그래, 우리 (　　　　)이/가 지난 옷부터 정리하자.

　❶ 철　　　　　❷ 날씨　　　　　❸ 시간　　　　　❹ 유행

[46~50] 밑줄 친 단어의 쓰임이 잘못된 것을 고르십시오. Choose the one that is incorrectly used.

46. ❶ 정말 <u>아름다운</u> 분이시군요.　　　　(　　　)
　　 ❷ 단풍이 든 산이 아주 <u>아름답습니다</u>.
　　 ❸ 날씨가 <u>아름다우니까</u> 기분이 상쾌하다.
　　 ❹ 목소리가 <u>아름다워서</u> 가수가 되면 좋겠다.

47. ❶ 샤워를 하니까 참 <u>시원하다</u>.　　　　(　　　)
　　 ❷ <u>시원한</u> 물을 한 잔 마셔야겠다.
　　 ❸ 날씨가 더우니까 <u>시원한</u> 삼계탕을 먹자.
　　 ❹ 머리가 아팠던 일이 잘 끝나서 마음이 <u>시원하다</u>.

48. ❶ 추워서 입술이 <u>노랗다</u>.　　　　(　　　)
　　 ❷ 눈이 오니까 세상이 <u>하얗다</u>.
　　 ❸ 햇빛 때문에 얼굴이 <u>까매졌다</u>.
　　 ❹ 좋아하는 사람을 만나니까 얼굴이 <u>빨개졌다</u>.

49. ❶ 공기가 <u>맑고</u> 시원하다.　　　　(　　　)
　　 ❷ 제 남자 친구는 키가 정말 <u>높아요</u>.
　　 ❸ <u>낮은</u> 신발을 신으면 발이 편하다.
　　 ❹ <u>추우니까</u> 옷을 하나 더 입는 것이 좋겠다.

50. ❶ 꽃이 많이 피어서 <u>아름다워요</u>.　　　　(　　　)
　　 ❷ 비가 <u>오니까</u> 우산을 가지고 가세요.
　　 ❸ 단풍이 <u>든</u> 산을 구경하러 갈 거예요.
　　 ❹ 안개가 <u>내렸으니까</u> 운전을 조심해야 해요.

주거

14

Residence

001
건물

[건물] 명사 building

a home built to store material or used as office space

[Related word] 빌딩 building

[Example] 제 사무실은 은행 옆 건물 2(이)층이에요.
My office is in the second floor building right next to the bank.

서울에서 제일 높은 건물이 뭐예요?
Which building is the tallest building in Seoul?

002
계단

[계단/게단] 명사 stairs

steps created to go up and down

[Expression] 계단으로 올라가다 to go up the stairs
계단으로 내려가다 to do down the stairs

[Example] 다리를 다쳐서 계단으로 올라갈 수 없다.
I hurt my legs so I can't go up the stairs.

계단을 내려가서 왼쪽으로 가면 미용실이 있어요.
If you go down the stairs and turn to the left, the hair salon will be there.

003
빌딩

[빌딩] 명사 building

a western style high rise building

[Expression] 높은 빌딩 a high building

[Related word] 건물 building

[Example] 시내에는 빌딩이 많습니다. There are many buildings in the city.
서울에서 제일 높은 빌딩이 어디에 있어요?
Where is the tallest building in Seoul?

004
아파트

[아파트] 명사 apartment

[Related word] 주택 house

Num동 Num호 apartment building number and room number

[Example] 한강 근처에 있는 아파트는 아주 비싸요.
The apartments near the Han river are very expensive.

아파트는 주택보다 살기 편해서 젊은 사람들에게 인기가 많다.
Apartments are easier to live in than houses so it is popular amongst the young people.

005
엘리베이터

[엘리베이터] 명사 elevator

[Expression] 엘리베이터를 타다 to ride the elevator

[Example] 엘리베이터 안에서 뛰면 안 된다. You can't run in the elevator.

엘리베이터가 고장이 나서 계단으로 올라왔어요.
The elevator was broken so I came up using the stairs.

006
오피스텔

[오피스텔] 명사 studio apartment

an office that is built for people to live inside

[Example] 여기가 사무실로 사용할 오피스텔이에요.
This is the studio apartment that you will use as an office.

오피스텔은 집으로도 쓸 수 있고 사무실로도 쓸 수 있다.
Studio apartments can be used as a house as well as an office.

007
정문

[정문] 명사 main gate

the front door that is used for people and cars

[Related word] 후문 back gate

[Example] 학교 정문 앞에서 친구를 만나기로 했다.
I decided to meet my friend at the front gate.

회사 정문으로 나가서 오른쪽으로 가면 우체국이 있어요.
If you go out the office main gate and turn to the right, there will be a post office.

008
주택

[주택] 명사 house

[Expression] 주택가 residential area

[Related word] 집 house

아파트 apartment

[Example] 노인들은 주택에서 사는 것을 좋아한다.
Elderly people like living in a house.

주택은 아파트보다 관리하기가 어려워요.
Houses are harder to take care of than apartments.

009
지하

[지하] 명사 basement

[Expression] 지하 2(이)층 basement second floor

지하 주차장 basement parking lot

[Antonym] 지상 ground

[Example] 지하 주차장에 차를 주차하세요.
Please park your car in the basement parking lot.

식당은 지하 1(일)층에 있습니다.
The restaurant is in the basement first floor.

010
층

[층] 명사 floor

the counting unit for counting the location of a floor

[Usage] <u>Num</u>층

[Example] 우리 집은 12(십이)층에 있어요. Our house is on the 12th floor.

63(육삼)빌딩은 몇 층 건물일까요?
How many floors does the 63 building have?

011
호

[호] 명사 room number

room number for a house, office, or room

[Usage] <u>Num</u>호

[Example] 우리 교실은 520(오백이십)호입니다. My classroom is 520.

우리 집은 한국 아파트 2(이)동 103(백삼)호입니다.
Our house is Hankuk Apartment building 2 room 103.

14-2 | 집

012
거실

[거실] 명사 living room

[Example] 거실에 있는 창문이 커서 집이 아주 밝군요.
The window in your living room is big so the house looks very bright.

가족들이 모두 거실에서 텔레비전을 보고 있었다.
My family was watching television in the living room.

013
거울

[거울] 명사 mirror

[Expression] 거울을 보다 to look at the mirror

[Example] 옷장 옆에 큰 거울이 있어서 편해요.
There is a large mirror next to my closet so it is convenient.

눈은 마음의 거울이라는 말이 있어요.
There is a saying that eyes are the mirror to the soul.

014
난방

[난방] **명사** heating

the heating system that makes a room warm

[Expression] 난방비 heating cost

난방하다 to heat

난방이 되다 the heater is working

[Example] 온돌은 한국의 난방 시설이에요.
Underground heating system is the Korean heating system.

이 방은 난방이 되지 않아서 아주 춥다.
This room does not have heating so it is very cold.

015
넓다

[널따] **형용사** to be wide, big

to be wide appearance wise or to have a big heart

[Usage] N이/가 넓다

[Expression] 집이 넓다 the house is wide

마음이 넓다 to have a big heart

[Antonym] 좁다 to be cramped

[Example] 우리 학교 운동장은 아주 넓어요. Our school's exercise field is very wide.

아버지는 마음이 넓어서 나를 잘 이해해 주신다.
My father has a big heart so he is very understanding.

016
달력

[달력] **명사** calendar

[Example] 달력을 벽에 걸었어요. I hung the calendar on the wall.

달력에 가족들의 생일을 적어 놓았다.
I wrote my family's birthdays on the calendar.

017
문

[문] **명사** door

[Expression] 문을 열다 to open the door

문을 닫다 to close the door

[Example] 우체국은 몇 시에 문을 열어요? When does the post office open?

밖이 시끄러우니까 문을 닫아 주세요.
It is loud outside so please close the door.

018
방

[방] **명사** room

[Expression] 방 한 개 one room

방이 좁다 the room is very small

[Example] 우리 집은 방이 세 개예요. Our house has 3 rooms.

일주일 동안 청소를 하지 않아서 방이 더럽다.
My room is messy because I haven't cleaned it in a week.

019
베란다

[베란다] 명사 balcony

[Example] 오랜만에 베란다를 청소했어요. I cleaned the balcony after a long time.

우리 집 베란다에서 한강이 보여요.
You can see the Han river from my balcony.

020
벽

[벽] 명사 wall

[Expression] 벽지 wallpaper

벽에 걸다 to hang on the wall

[Example] 아이들이 벽에 그림을 그렸다. The children drew pictures in the wall.

교실 벽에 시계를 걸어 주세요.
Please hang on the clock on the classroom wall.

021
부엌

[부엌] 명사 kitchen

[Synonym] 주방 kitchen

[Example] 냉장고는 부엌에 있어요. The refrigerator is in the kitchen.

어머니는 부엌에서 설거지를 하십니다.
My mother is dishwashing in the kitchen.

022
불

[불] 명사 light

[Expression] 촛불 candle light

전깃불 electric light

불을 켜다 to turn on the light

불을 끄다 to turn off the light

[Example] 이제 불을 끄고 자자. Let's turn off the light and go to sleep.

어두우니까 불을 좀 켜 주세요. It is dark so please turn on the light.

023
서재

[서재] 명사 a study

a room where books are placed and read or just used for writing

[Example] 책이 많아서 큰 방을 서재로 만들었어요.
I have a lot of books so I made the big room into a study.

아버지는 아침마다 서재에서 책을 읽으신다.
Father reads in the study every morning.

024
열다

[열다] 명사 1. to open 2. to start or open

1. to open a closed door, lid, or drawer so it can be seen inside. ㄹverb

[Usage] N을/를 열다

[Antonym] 닫다 to close

[Related word]	열쇠 key
[Example]	창문을 여니까 바람이 들어와서 시원하다.
	After opening the window, it is cooler because there is wind coming inside.

2. to start a business or store, ㄹverb

[Usage]	<u>N</u>을/를 열다
[Antonym]	닫다 to close
[Example]	백화점은 몇 시에 문을 열어요? What time does the shopping mall open?

025 옷걸이

[온꺼리] 명사 hanger

clothing hanger

[Expression]	옷걸이에 걸다 to hang on the hanger
[Related word]	옷장 closet
[Example]	코트는 옷걸이에 걸어 두세요. Please hang the coat on the hanger.
	옷을 옷걸이에 걸어 드릴까요? Should I hang your coat on the hanger?

026 욕실

[욕씰] 명사 shower room

[Related word]	화장실 bathroom
[Example]	욕실에 들어가서 샤워를 했다. I went into the shower and took a shower.
	우리 하숙집에는 방마다 욕실이 있어요.
	Our boarding rooms each have a shower room.

027 창문

[창문] 명사 window

[Example]	비가 와서 창문을 닫았다. It was raining so I closed the window.
	방 안이 답답하니까 창문을 열어라.
	The room is very stuffy so open the window.

028 천장

[천장] 명사 ceiling, roof

[Expression]	천장이 낮다 the ceiling is low
	천장이 높다 the ceiling is high
[Related word]	바닥 floor
[Example]	천장이 낮으니까 조심하세요. The ceiling is low so be careful.
	성당 천장에 그림이 그려져 있다.
	There are pictures drawn on the cathedral's ceiling.

029 커튼

[커튼] 명사 curtain

[Expression]	커튼을 걷다 to open the curtain
	커튼을 치다 to close the curtain
[Example]	집 안이 보이지 않게 커튼을 쳐라.
	Close the curtain so that people can't see the house.

날씨가 좋은데 커튼을 걷고 창문을 열어 놓을까?
The weather is nice so should I open the curtain and open the window?

030
편안하다

[펴난하다] 형용사 to feel comfortable

the body and mind are peaceful and one has no worries

[Usage] <u>N</u>이/가 편안하다

[Expression] 마음이 편안하다 my heart is at peace

의자가 편안하다 my chair is comfortable

[Synonym] 편하다 to feel comfortable

[Antonym] 불편하다 to feel uncomfortable

[Example] 이 의자에 앉아 보세요. 아주 편안해요.
Sit on this chair. It is very comfortable.

요즘은 걱정 없이 편안하게 지내고 있어요.
These days I am comfortable with no worries.

031
편하다

[편하다] 형용사 1. to feel comfortable   2. to be easy

1. body and mind are at peace

[Usage] <u>N</u>이/가 편하다

[Expression] 몸이 편하다 the body is comfortable

집이 편하다 the house is comfortable

마음이 편하다 the mind is comfortable

[Synonym] 편안하다 to feel comfortable

[Antonym] 불편하다 to feel uncomfortable

[Example] 마음이 편하면 몸도 편해요.
If your mind is comfortable, then your body is also comfortable.

2. to be easy and convenient

[Usage] <u>N</u>이/가 편하다

[Snyonym] 편리하다 to be convenient

[Antonym] 불편하다 to feel uncomfortable

[Example] 이 책은 글씨가 커서 읽기가 편하다.
This book has big letters so it is easy to read.

032
화장실

[화장실] 명사 bathroom

[Example] 저는 화장실 청소를 제일 싫어해요. I hate cleaning the bathroom.

죄송하지만 화장실이 어디에 있습니까?
Excuse me, where is the bathroom?

354

033
구하다

[구하다] 동사 to look for

to look for something you need

[Usage] N을/를 구하다

[Related word] 찾다 to find

[Example] 싼 집을 구했어요? Did you find a cheap house?

학교 식당에서 일할 사람을 구하고 있어요.
I am looking for someone who will work in the school restaurant.

034
부동산 소개소

[부동산소개소] 명사 real estate agency

a place where they sell, buy, or borrow buildings or land

[Example] 이 근처에 부동산 소개소가 있나요?
Is there a real estate agency nearby?

하숙집을 구하려면 부동산 소개소에 가세요.
If you are looking for a boarding house, go to the real estate agency.

035
사다리차

[사다리차] 명사 ladder truck

a truck that has a ladder, and it is used to move objects when people move

[Example] 사다리차를 빌리려면 얼마나 필요해요?
If I want to borrow a ladder truck, how much does it cost?

아파트의 높은 층으로 이사할 때에는 사다리차를 이용하세요.
Use the ladder truck when moving objects into a high apartment building.

036
이사

[이사] 명사 moving

moving from one living space to another

[Expression] 포장이사 moving

이사하다 to move

이사를 가다 to go to move

[Example] 내가 내일 이사를 하는데 도와줄 수 있어?
I am moving tomorrow, can you help me?

나는 고등학교를 졸업한 후에 서울로 이사했다.
After graduating from high school, I moved to Seoul.

037
집들이

[집뜨리] 명사 housewarming

after moving, inviting people and helping them look around and cooking for them

[Expression] 집들이 선물 housewarming present

집들이를 하다 to have a housewarming party

[Example]　이번 주말에 집들이를 할 거예요.
I am going to have a housewarming party this weekend.

한국에서는 집들이 선물로 휴지나 비누를 많이 해요.
In Korea people often give napkins and soap as a housewarming present.

14-4 │ 집안일

038
걸레
[걸레] 명사 a floor cloth
　　　　a cloth used to clean dirty places

[Expression]　걸레를 빨다 to wash the floor cloth
　　　　　　걸레로 닦다 to wash with the floor cloth

[Example]　방을 걸레로 닦았다. I washed the room with the floor cloth.
식탁은 걸레로 닦으면 안 돼요.
You can't wash the table with the floor cloth.

039
다림질
[다림질] 명사 ironing

[Expression]　다림질을 하다 to iron

[Related word]　다리미 iron

[Example]　더운 여름에는 다림질을 하기가 힘들어요.
It's hard to iron in the hot summer.

아내는 아침마다 남편의 셔츠를 다림질했다.
The wife ironed her husbands shirt every morning.

040
닦다
[닥따] 동사 to wash, to wipe

[Usage]　N을/를 닦다

[Related word]　씻다 to clean

[Example]　하루에 3(세)번, 3(삼)분 동안 이를 닦아야 해요.
Everyday you need to brush your teeth 3 times for 3 minutes.

미선이는 손수건으로 눈물을 닦으면서 이야기했다.
Misun spoke while wiping her tears with her handkerchief.

041
더럽다

[더럽따] 형용사 to be dirty

to have dirt on something and to not be clean, ㅂverb

[Usage]   N이/가 더럽다

[Antonym]   깨끗하다 to be clean

[Example]   오랫동안 청소를 안 해서 방이 더럽다.
I haven't cleaned for a long time so my room is dirty.

옷이 너무 더러워서 세탁소에 맡겨야겠다.
My clothes are really dirty so I better leave it at the laundry.

042
드라이클리닝

[드라이클리닝] 명사 dry cleaning

[Expression]   드라이클리닝하다 to dry clean

[Related word]   빨래 laundry

세탁소 laundry, dry cleaning

[Example]   이 옷은 드라이클리닝하지 말고 물로 빠세요.
Don't dry clean this clothing just wash it with water.

겨울 코트를 드라이클리닝하려고 세탁소에 맡겼어요.
I left my winter coat at the dry cleaners to get it clean.

043
말리다

[말리다] 동사 to dry

[Usage]   N을/를 말리다

[Related word]   마르다 to be dry

[Example]   고춧가루는 말린 고추로 만들어요.
Pepper powder is made with dried peppers.

비가 오는 날에는 빨래를 잘 말리기가 어려워요.
It is hard to dry laundry when it rains.

044
맡기다

[맏끼다] 동사 to leave

to leave something somewhere

[Usage]   N을/를 N에 맡기다

N을/를 N에게 맡기다

[Related word]   맡다 to handle or manage

[Example]   친구에게 가방을 맡기고 화장실에 갔다.
I left my bag with my friend and went to the restroom.

아이를 언니에게 맡기고 잠깐 외출하려고 해요.
I plan on leaving my child with my older sister and going out for a while.

045
버리다

[버리다] 동사 to throw away

to throw away unwanted things

[Usage] **N**을/를 버리다

[Expression] 쓰레기를 버리다 to throw away trash

[Example] 쓰레기는 쓰레기통에 버려야 합니다.
You need to throw away trash in the trash can.

음식을 남기면 버려야 하니까 남기지 말고 먹는 것이 좋다.
If you leave left over food, you will have to throw it away, so eat all of your food.

046
빨다

[빨다] 동사 to wash in the laundry

to make clothes become clean by rinsing it out in water, ㄹverb

[Usage] **N**을/를 빨다

[Related word] 빨래하다 to wash clothes

세탁하다 to do the laundry

[Example] 운동화를 빠니까 새 운동화 같지?
After washing the tennis shoes, it seems new right?

이 옷은 세탁기로 빨면 안 되고 손으로 빨아야 해요.
This clothing can't be washed in the washing machine, so wash it with your hands.

047
빨래

[빨래] 명사 1. doing laundry   2. laundry

1. washing dirty clothes, socks, or dolls

[Expression] 빨래하다 to wash clothes

[Example] 너무 바빠서 일주일 동안 빨래를 못 했어요.
I was so busy that I wasn't able to do the laundry in a week.

2. things that need to go in the laundry, or things that have already been in the laundry

[Expression] 빨래가 밀리다 the laundry is piled up

[Example] 주말에 밀린 빨래를 해야 해요.
I need to do the piled up laundry during the weekend.

048
설거지

[설거지] 명사 dishwashing

washing and organizing the dishes after eating

[Expression] 설거지가 쌓이다 there are a lot of dishes to wash

설거지를 하다 to do the dishes

[Example] 저는 요리를 하고 남편은 설거지를 해요.
I cook and my husband does the dishes.

밥을 다 먹었으면 남은 반찬은 냉장고에 넣고 그릇은 설거지하세요.
If you're done eating, then put the side dishes in the refrigerator and wash the dishes.

049
세제

[세제] 명사 detergent

a liquid or powder used for washing the face, clothes, or just soap for cleaning

[Expression] 주방 세제 kitchen detergent

세제로 닦다 to clean with the detergent

[Related word] 비누 soap

[Example] 세제를 많이 쓰지 말고 적당히 써라.
Don't use a lot of detergent. Use the right amount.

이 세제는 향도 좋고 빨래도 깨끗하게 돼서 인기가 많아요.
This detergent has a good scent and keeps washed clothes clean, so it is popular.

050
쓰레기

[쓰레기] 명사 trash

[Expression] 쓰레기통 trash can

음식물 쓰레기 food waste

쓰레기를 버리다 to throw away the trash

[Synonym] 휴지 napkin

[Example] 쓰레기는 쓰레기통에 버립시다.
Please throw away the trash in the trash can.

음식물 쓰레기는 따로 버려야 해요.
You need to throw away food waste separately.

051
쓸다

[쓸다] 동사 to sweep

to sweep waste to one side with a broom and throwing it away, ㄹverb

[Usage] N을/를 쓸다

[Expression] 방을 쓸다 to sweep the room

눈을 쓸다 to sweep the snow

빗자루로 쓸다 to sweep with the broom

[Example] 방을 쓰니까 먼지가 아주 많았다.
When I swept the room, there was a lot of dust.

눈이 오면 집 앞의 눈을 쓸어야 한다.
If it snows, you need to sweep the snow in front of the house.

052
얼룩

[얼룩] 명사 stain

[Expression] 얼룩이 생기다 to form a stain

얼룩을 지우다 to get rid of the stain

[Example] 옷에 얼룩이 생겨서 입을 수 없어요.
A stain formed on the clothing so I can't wear it.

여러 번 세탁해도 얼룩이 없어지지 않는다.
Even though I do the laundry several times, the stain will not go away.

053
정리

[정니] **명사** organizing

organizing so that things are in order

[Expression] 책상 정리 organzing the desk
교통 정리 organizing the traffic
정리하다 to organize

[Example] 나는 공부하기 전에 책상 정리부터 한다.
Before I study, I organize my desk.

손님이 오시기 전에 빨리 방을 정리해라.
Organize your room before the guests come.

054
지우다

[지우다] **동사** to erase

to erase writing or a picture with an eraser so that it can't be seen anymore

[Usage] <u>N</u>을/를 지우다
[Related word] 지우개 eraser
[Example] 칠판 좀 지워 주세요. Please erase the chalkboard.
틀린 글씨는 깨끗하게 지우고 다시 써라.
Erase the wrong writing and write it again.

055
집안일

[지반닐] **명사** housework

laundry, cooking, cleaning and other housework

[Expression] 집안일을 하다 to do housework
[Example] 우리 남편은 집안일을 잘 도와 줘요.
My husband helps a lot around the house.

빨래, 청소, 설거지 등 집안일은 끝이 없다.
There is no end to all of the housework. Laundry, cleaning and dishwashing are a lot of work.

056
청소

[청소] **명사** cleaning

[Expression] 청소기 vacuum cleaner
청소하다 to clean

[Example] 저는 집안일 중에서 청소를 제일 싫어해요.
I hate cleaning out of all of the housework.

더러운 방을 청소한 후에 깨끗해진 방을 보면 기분이 좋아진다.
I feel better after looking at the clean room I have cleaned.

057
휴지

[휴지] **명사** 1. wastepaper   2. tissue

1. paper that can' be used

[Expression] 휴지통 waste can

휴지를 버리다 to throw away wastepaper

[Synonym] 쓰레기 trash

[Example] 길에 휴지를 버리지 마십시오.
Don't throw away wastepaper on the street.

2. a soft and thin paper that is used to blow one's nose or to get rid of a dirty area

[Expression] 휴지로 닦다 to wipe with tissue

[Snyonym] 티슈 tissue

[Example] 콧물을 휴지로 닦았다. I wiped my nose with a tissue.

[1~15] 다음 단어를 한국어로 바꿔 쓰십시오. Change these words into Korean.

1. door   (   )   2. room   (   )

3. living room   (   )   4. heating   (   )

5. calendar   (   )   6. detergent   (   )

7. stain   (   )   8. moving   (   )

9. curtain   (   )   10. apartment   (   )

11. hanger   (   )   12. housewarming   (   )

13. elevator   (   )   14. to do laundry   (   )

15. to leave   (   )

[16~20] 그림을 보고 ( )에 알맞은 것을 고르십시오.
Look at the picture and choose the correct word.

16.

가 : 어머니가 뭘 하고 계시니?

나 : 부엌에서 ( )을/를 하고 계십니다.

❶ 빨래   ❷ 다림질

❸ 설거지   ❹ 드라이클리닝

17.

가 : 비가 오는군요.

나 : 비가 방에 들어오지 않게 ( )을/를
닫읍시다.

❶ 창문   ❷ 난방

❸ 천장   ❹ 커튼

18.

가 : 꽃이 어디에 있어요?

나 : (　　　　)에 있어요.

❶ 거실　　　　❷ 서재

❸ 주방　　　　❹ 베란다

19.

가 : 뭘 하고 있어요?

나 : (　　　　)을/를 보면서 화장하고 있어요.

❶ 벽　　　　❷ 거울

❸ 달력　　　　❹ 시계

20.

가 : 수업이 끝난 후에 같이 공부할까요?

나 : 아니요, 저녁에 손님이 오시기 때문에 (　　　　)
　　어야/아야/여야 해요.

❶ 구하다　　　　❷ 버리다

❸ 붙이다　　　　❹ 청소하다

[21~30] 다음 문장을 읽고 알맞은 어휘를 골라 쓰십시오. 어휘는 한 번만 쓰십시오.
Read the following sentence and choose the right word. Use the words once.

벽	불	호	거울	걸레
계단	서재	천장	아파트	닦다
쓸다	열다	버리다	편안하다	정리하다

21. 거실 (   )에 그림을 걸었어요.

22. 먹고 남은 음식을 (   )었다/았다/였다.

23. 바닥을 걸레로 (   )었어요/았어요/였어요.

24. 아버지께서 (   )에서 책을 읽고 계십니다.

25. 열쇠가 없어서 문을 (   )지 못하고 있어요.

26. 우리는 (   )은/ㄴ 의자에 앉아서 차를 마셨다.

27. 엘리베이터가 고장나서 (   )으로/로 올라왔어요.

28. 눈이 오면 집 앞의 눈을 (   )어야/아야/여야 해요.

29. 외출할 때에는 방의 (   )을/를 꼭 끄고 나가야 한다.

30. 외출하기 전에 먼저 방을 깨끗하게 (   )어라/아라/여라.

[31~35] (   ) 안에 알맞은 것을 고르십시오. Choose the correct one.

31. 옷에 생긴 얼룩을 (   )었어요/았어요/였어요.

    ❶ 닫다   ❷ 쓸다   ❸ 버리다   ❹ 지우다

32. 설날이 무슨 요일인지 알고 싶어서 (   )을/를 찾아봤다.

    ❶ 달력   ❷ 사전   ❸ 천장   ❹ 책장

33. 어머니는 날마다 빨래, 설거지, 청소 등 (　　　)을/를 하십니다.

　❶ 이사　　　　❷ 다림질　　　　❸ 집들이　　　　❹ 집안일

34. 사무실은 2(　　　)에 있으니까 옆에 있는 계단으로 올라가세요.

　❶ 방　　　　❷ 층　　　　❸ 호　　　　❹ 지하

35. 빨래는 햇빛에 (　　　)는 것이 좋아요.

　❶ 구하다　　　　❷ 말리다　　　　❸ 맡기다　　　　❹ 붙이다

[36~40] 밑줄 친 부분과 반대되는 뜻을 가진 것을 고르십시오.
Choose the word that is the opposite of the underlined word.

36. **가** : 오늘 학교 후문에서 만날까?
　나 : 아니, 후문은 복잡하니까 (　　　)에서 만나자.

　❶ 정문　　　　❷ 주택　　　　❸ 지하　　　　❹ 창문

37. **가** : 신발이 너무 더러워졌어.
　나 : 응, (　　　)게 빨아야겠다.

　❶ 넓다　　　　❷ 편하다　　　　❸ 깨끗하다　　　　❹ 조용하다

38. **가** : 학생은 많은데 교실은 좀 좁아요.
　나 : 네, 좀 더 (　　　)은/ㄴ 교실에서 공부하면 좋겠어요.

　❶ 밝다　　　　❷ 넓다　　　　❸ 구하다　　　　❹ 말리다

39. **가** : 더워서 문을 열었는데 너무 시끄러워요.
　나 : 그럼 문을 (　　　)고 에어컨을 켭시다.

　❶ 닫다　　　　❷ 붙이다　　　　❸ 지우다　　　　❹ 편안하다

40. **가** : 구두를 신으면 발이 아프고 불편해요.

    나 : 운동화를 신어 보세요. 발이 (   )고 아프지 않을 거예요.

    ❶ 크다   ❷ 맡기다   ❸ 버리다   ❹ 편하다

[41~45] 밑줄 친 부분과 의미가 가장 가까운 것을 고르십시오.
Choose the word that is most similar to the underlined section.

41. **가** : 네가 일하는 회사는 어느 빌딩이야?

    나 : 이 (   ) 2층이야.

    ❶ 방   ❷ 건물   ❸ 계단   ❹ 엘리베이터

42. **가** : 조용하고 깨끗한 하숙집을 찾고 있는데요.

    나 : 부동산 소개소에 가면 (   )을/ㄹ 수 있을 거예요.

    ❶ 살다   ❷ 쓰다   ❸ 구하다   ❹ 소개하다

43. **가** : 이 옷을 세탁했어요?

    나 : 네, 직접 손으로 (   )었어요/았어요/였어요.

    ❶ 빨다   ❷ 닦다   ❸ 쓸다   ❹ 청소하다

44. **가** : 쓰레기는 어디에 버리면 돼요?

    나 : (   )은/는 여기에 있는 봉지에 버리세요.

    ❶ 걸레   ❷ 휴지   ❸ 다림질   ❹ 사다리차

45. **가** : 언니는 주방에 있어요?

    나 : 네, (   )에서 저녁 식사 준비를 하고 있어요.

    ❶ 부엌   ❷ 천장   ❸ 아파트   ❹ 오피스텔

[46~50] 밑줄 친 단어의 쓰임이 잘못된 것을 고르십시오. Choose the one that is incorrectly used.

46. ❶ 집이 넓어서 마음에 들어요.　　　　　(　　　　　)
　　　❷ 이 옷이 좀 넓어서 다른 옷으로 바꾸고 싶어요.
　　　❸ 아버지는 마음이 넓어서 화를 잘 내시지 않아요.
　　　❹ 내 방은 넓지만 물건이 많지 않아서 복잡하지 않다.

47. ❶ 방이 더러우니까 편하지요?　　　　　(　　　　　)
　　　❷ 이 신발을 신으면 발이 편할 겁니다.
　　　❸ 중요한 일을 모두 끝내서 마음이 편하다.
　　　❹ 지금 살고 있는 집은 회사와 가까워서 아주 편해요.

48. ❶ 욕실에서 목욕을 했어요.　　　　　(　　　　　)
　　　❷ 이 집은 천장이 아주 높군요.
　　　❸ 창문에 가족 사진을 걸어 놓았어요.
　　　❹ 가족들이 모두 거실에 모여서 TV를 보고 있어요.

49. ❶ 이 셔츠를 다림질해야겠어요.　　　　　(　　　　　)
　　　❷ 바닥이 더러우니까 편하세요.
　　　❸ 손님이 오시니까 방을 정리해라.
　　　❹ 저녁 식사를 한 후에 설거지했다.

50. ❶ 여기에 휴지를 버리지 마세요.　　　　　(　　　　　)
　　　❷ 너무 시끄러워서 이사가려고 합니다.
　　　❸ 드라이클리닝을 할 옷을 세탁소에 빨았어요.
　　　❹ 하숙집이 학교에서 멀어서 새 하숙집을 구하고 있어요.

건강

15

Health

001
가슴

[가슴] 명사 1. the chest   2. feeling

1. the front part of the body that is between the neck and stomach

[Expression]   가슴이 넓다 the chest is big

[Example]   아이는 인형을 가슴에 꼭 안았다.
The child held the doll close to her chest.

2. thinking, mind, feeling

[Expression]   가슴이 아프다 feeling is hurt

가슴이 답답하다 the chest feels stuffy

가슴이 따뜻하다 to be warm hearted

[Example]   슬픈 영화를 보고 가슴이 아파서 눈물이 났어요.
After watching the sad movie, I felt so sad that I cried.

002
건강

[건강] 명사 health

body and mind are not sick but healthy

[Expression]   건강 상태 the state of health

건강이 좋다 health is good

건강에 좋다 it is good for your health

건강하다 to be healthy

[Example]   담배를 많이 피우면 건강이 나빠져요.
If you smoke a lot, it is bad for your health.

규칙적으로 운동을 하면 건강이 좋아질 거야.
If you exercise consistently, your health will get better.

003
굵다

[국따] 형용사 to be thick

[Usage]   굵은 **N**

N이/가 굵다

[Expression]   굵은 손가락 thick fingers

다리가 굵다 the legs are thick

[Antonym]   가늘다 to be thin

[Example]   어머니는 일을 많이 하셔서 손가락이 굵어졌다.
My mother has worked so much, so her fingers are thicker.

나는 다리가 굵어서 고민이야. 치마를 입어도 예쁘지 않아.
I am concerned because my legs are thicker. Even though I wear skirts, it is not pretty.

004
귀

[귀] **명사** ears

[Example] 요즘은 귀에 귀걸이를 한 남자들이 많아요.
These days there are many guys that wear earrings in their ear.

음악 소리가 너무 시끄러워서 손으로 귀를 막았다.
The sound of the music was so loud that I covered my ears with my hand.

005
눈²

[눈] **명사** eyes

[Expression] 눈물 tears

[Example] 눈을 감고 이야기를 들어 보세요. Close your eyes and listen to the story.
어제 밤에 울다가 자서 눈이 부었어요.
Yesterday night I slept after crying, so my eyes are swollen.

006
다리

[다리] **명사** legs

[Example] 모델들은 다리가 길고 예뻐요. Models have long and pretty legs.
영수는 축구 경기를 하다가 넘어져서 다리를 다쳤다.
Young-soo fell and hurt his legs after competing in a soccer game.

007
등

[등] **명사** back

the back side of a person or animal and it is the opposite of the stomach

[Example] 할머니는 손주를 등에 업고 가게에 가셨다.
The grandmother carried her grandchild on her back and went to the store.

군인들이 등에 배낭을 메고 걸어가고 있습니다.
The soldiers are carrying backpacks on their back and are walking away.

008
땀

[땀] **명사** sweat

[Expression] 땀이 나다 to sweat
땀을 흘리다 to spill sweat

[Example] 날씨가 더워서 땀이 많이 납니다.
The weather is hot so I am sweating a lot.

학생들이 땀을 흘리면서 운동장을 뛰고 있어요.
The students are sweating and running on the sports field.

009
머리

[머리] **명사** 1. head 2. hair 3. thinking

1. the part of the body that is on top of the neck and includes the eyes, nose, mouth, ears, and hair

[Expression] 머리가 아프다 my head hurts

머리를 다치다 to hurt one's head

[Example] 머리가 아파서 공부를 할 수 없어요. My head hurts so I can't study.

2. the hair on one's head

[Expression] 머리카락 hair

머리가 길다 the hair is long

머리를 감다 to wash one's hair

[Example] 머리를 자르려고 미용실에 가요.
I go to the hair salon to cut my hair.

3. the ability to think and make decisions

[Expression] 머리가 좋다 to be smart

[Example] 그 사람은 머리가 좋아서 한 번 들으면 잊어버리지 않아요.
That person is smart so she doesn't forget after listening to something once.

010
목

[목] **명사** 1. neck 2. throat

1. the part of a human or animal that connects the head with the body

[Expression] 목이 길다 the neck is long

[Example] 미선이는 목이 가늘고 길어서 목걸이가 잘 어울려요.
Misun's neck is thin and long so she looks good when she wears necklaces.

2. throat

[Expression] 목감기 sore throat

[Example] 목이 말라서 물을 마셨어요. I was thirsty so I drank water.

011
몸

[몸] **명사** body

the state of the body, the head and whole body of an animal or human

[Expression] 몸이 좋다 to have a healthy body

몸이 약하다 to have a weak body

몸이 건강하다 to have a healthy body

몸에 좋다 it is good for your body

[Example] 제 친구는 몸이 약해서 병원에 자주 갑니다.
My friend's body is very weak so she goes to the hospital often.

지금 입은 양복이 아까 입은 양복보다 몸에 더 잘 맞네요.
The suit that I'm wearing right now fits better than the other one I wore.

012
무릎

[무릎] **명사** knee

[Expression] 무릎을 꿇다 to kneel

[Example] 아이가 놀다가 넘어져서 무릎을 다쳤어요.
The child fell down while playing and hurt his knee.

무릎을 꿇고 앉아서 할아버지 말씀을 들었다.
I kneeled and listened to my grandfather.

013
발

[발] 명사 feet

[Expression]　발등　the instep of the foot
　　　　　　발목　ankle
　　　　　　발가락　toes
　　　　　　발바닥　the sole of the foot
　　　　　　발이 크다　to have big feet

[Example]　새 구두를 신어서 발이 아파요.
　　　　　My feet hurt because I wore my new shoes.

지하철에 사람이 너무 많아서 다른 사람의 발을 밟았다.
There were so many people in the subway that I stepped on people's feet.

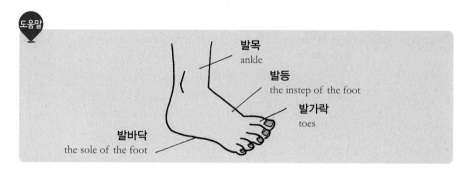

014
배²

[배] 명사 belly, stomach

[Expression]　배가 고프다　to be hungry
　　　　　　배가 부르다　to be full
　　　　　　배가 아프다　the stomach hurts
　　　　　　배가 나오다　to have a big belly

[Example]　아침을 못 먹어서 배가 고파요.　I didn't eat breakfast so I am hungry.
　　　　　나이가 들면 점점 배가 나오니까 운동을 해야 한다.
　　　　　When you get older, your stomach starts to come out, so you need to exercise.

015
뼈

[뼈] 명사 bone

[Expression]　뼈가 굵다　to have thick bone
　　　　　　뼈가 약하다　to have weak bone
　　　　　　뼈가 부러지다　the bone is broken

[Example]　우유를 많이 먹어야 뼈가 튼튼해진다.
　　　　　You must drink a lot of milk to have strong bones.

형이 계단에서 떨어져서 **뼈**가 부러졌어요.

My older brother fell off the stairs and broke his bone.

016
살²

[살] 명사 flesh

the soft part of the human or animal body that covers the bone

[Expression] 살이 찌다 to gain weight

살이 빠지다 to have lost weight

살을 빼다 to lose weight

[Example] 저는 스트레스를 받으면 음식을 많이 먹어서 살이 쪄요.

When I get stressed I eat a lot and gain weight.

기숙사 방 친구는 살을 빼려고 저녁마다 30(삼십)분씩 운동장을 뛴다.

My roommate is trying to lose weight, so she runs in the sports field for 30 minutes every night.

017
속²

[속] 명사 stomach

[Expression] 속이 아프다 the stomach hurts

속이 안 좋다 the stomach doesn't feel good

[Example] 매운 음식을 먹은 후에는 속이 아프다.

After I eat spicy food, my stomach hurts.

어제 술을 많이 마셔서 속이 안 좋아요.

Yesterday I drank a lot, so my stomach doesn't feel good.

018
손

[손] 명사 hands

[Expression] 손을 들다 to raise a hand

[Example] 밥을 먹기 전에 손을 씻어야 한다.

You need to wash your hand before you eat.

데이트하는 커플들이 손을 잡고 걸어간다.

The couples that are on a date are holding hands and walking.

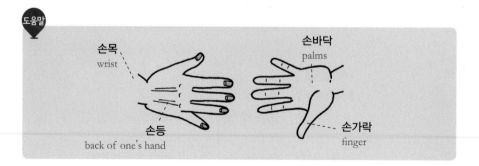

019
신체

[신체] 명사 body

a human body

[Expression] 신체검사 body examination

[Synonym] 몸 body

[Example] 이 일은 신체가 건강한 사람은 누구든지 할 수 있는 일입니다.
This job can be done by anyone who has a healthy body.

초등학교, 중학교, 고등학교에서는 1(일)년에 한 번씩 신체검사를 합니다.
In elementary, middle and high school everyone must do a body examination once a year.

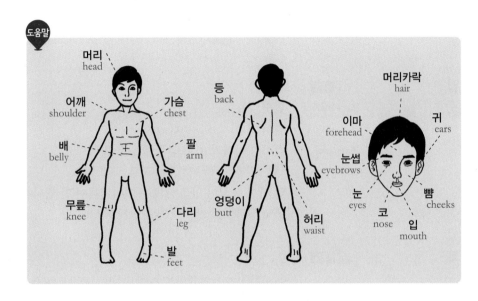

020
어깨

[어깨] 명사 shoulder

[Expression] 어깨가 넓다 the shoulders are wide

어깨가 좁다 the shoulders are narrow

어깨를 펴다 to straighten one's shoulders

[Example] 가방을 어깨에 메고 학교에 갔다.
I carried my bag on my shoulder and went to school.

요즘에는 어깨가 넓어 보이는 옷이 유행이에요.
These days the trend is to wear clothes that make you look like you have wider shoulders.

021
얼굴

[얼굴] 명사 face

the front part of a head, the eyes, nose, and lips

[Expression] 예쁜 얼굴 pretty face

잘생긴 얼굴 handsome face

얼굴이 예쁘다 the face is pretty

얼굴을 씻다 to wash the face

[Example] 미선이는 얼굴이 아주 작아서 인형 같다.
Misun has such a small face that she looks like a doll.

같은 반에서 공부하는 제 친구는 항상 얼굴이 밝아요.
My classroom friend who I study with always has a happy face.

022
엉덩이

[엉덩이] 명사 butt

[Example] 엉덩이에 주사를 맞았어요. I got a shot on my butt.

눈길을 걷다가 넘어져서 엉덩이가 너무 아파요.
I fell while walking in the snow and now my butt hurts.

023
입

[입] 명사 mouth

[Expression] 입맛 appetite

입이 크다 to have a big mouth

[Example] 엄마와 아빠가 아이 얼굴에 입을 맞췄어요.
The mom and dad kissed the child on the face.

입 안에 음식이 있을 때에는 이야기하면 안 됩니다.
Do not speak when you have food in your mouth.

024
코

[코] 명사 nose

a part of the face that is used to smell and breath

[Expression] 콧물 snot

코감기 sinus cold

코를 풀다 to blow one's nose

[Example] 서양 사람들은 코가 높아요. Western people have high noses.

감기 때문에 코가 막혀서 숨을 잘 쉴 수 없어요.
My nose is stuffy because of my cold so it's hard to breathe.

025
키

[키] 명사 height

the height of the body from the feet to the head

[Expression] 키가 크다 to be tall

키가 작다 to be short

[Example] 키가 몇 cm(센티미터)예요? How tall are you in centimeters?

아버지는 키가 크신데 저는 키가 작아요.
My father is tall but I am short.

026
튼튼하다

[튼튼하다] 형용사 to be strong

an object is sturdy and strong, a person's body, teeth, and bones are not weak, and one does not get sick often

[Usage]   N이/가 튼튼하다

[Example]   이 가방은 튼튼해서 물건을 많이 넣어도 괜찮아요.
This bag is strong so you can put a lot of stuff in this.

몸이 튼튼해야 공부도 열심히 할 수 있으니까 공부만 하지 말고 운동도 해야 한다.
Your body needs to be strong so that you can study hard. Don't just study, but also exercise.

027
팔¹

[팔] 명사 arm

[Example]   무거운 짐을 들어서 팔이 아프다.
My arm hurts after carrying the heavy thing.

한국에서는 식사할 때 식탁 위에 팔을 올리면 안 됩니다.
In Korea you should not put your arm on the table when eating.

028
허리

[허리] 명사 waist

[Expression]   허리띠 waist band
허리가 가늘다 the waist is thin

[Example]   한 달 전부터 다이어트를 해서 허리가 가늘어졌어요.
My waist got thinner after going on a diet for a month.

무거운 것을 들면 허리를 다칠 수 있으니까 조심하세요.
If you carry heavy things, it could hurt your back, so be careful.

029
힘

[힘] 명사 strength

the muscle movement of the body used to move objects or one's body

[Expression]   힘이 세다 to have a lot of strength
힘이 들다 to take much energy
힘을 내다 to make strength

[Example]   우리 집에서 가장 힘이 센 사람은 아빠입니다.
My father is the strongest in my family.

응원을 하면 우리 팀이 더 잘할 거예요. 우리 열심히 응원합시다!
If we cheer, our team will do better. Let's all cheer enthusiastically!

030
가래

[가래] 명사 mucus

secretion that forms when one has a sore throat and comes up when coughing

[Expression] 가래를 뱉다 to spit out the mucus

[Example] 담배를 피우면 가래가 많이 생긴다.
If you smoke, you will form a lot of mucus.

목감기에 걸려서 기침을 하면 가래가 나와요.
Mucus will come out of the throat when you cough because I have a sore throat.

031
가렵다

[가렵따] 형용사 to be itchy

to feel like scratching, ㅂverb

[Usage] N이/가 가렵다

[Expression] 머리가 가렵다 the head is itchy

피부가 가렵다 the skin is itchy

[Related word] 긁다 to scratch

[Example] 모기에 물려서 가려워요. I got bit by a mosquito so I am itchy.

배낭여행을 하는 동안 샤워를 자주 하지 못해서 머리가 가려웠다.
During my backpacking trip, I didn't get to shower often. so my head itches.

032
감기

[감기] 명사 a cold

a sickness caused by a virus. coughing, runny nose, headache and fever are some symptoms

[Expression] 감기약 cold medicine

감기가 낫다 to get better from a cold

감기에 걸리다 to catch a cold

[Example] 약국에서 약을 사 먹고 감기가 나았어요.
I bought medicine from the pharmacy and the medicine got rid of the cold.

날씨가 추워져서 감기에 걸린 사람들이 많다.
The weather got colder, so there are a lot of people with a cold.

033
기침

[기침] 명사 cough

[Expression] 기침이 심하다 the cough is heavy

기침이 나다 to have cough

기침을 하다 to cough

[Example] 기침이 심해서 밤에 잠을 잘 자지 못했어요.
My coughing was so heavy that I couldn't stay asleep.

다른 사람 앞에서는 입을 가리고 기침해야 한다.
You should cover your mouth when you cough in front of other people.

034
나다

[나다] 동사 1. to have 2. to grow or form 3. to have or form a feeling

4. to have a smell 5. to form

1. to form a sickness

[Usage]   N이/가 나다

[Expression] 병이 나다 to have a sickness

몸살이 나다 to have body ache

배탈이 나다 to have a stomach ache

[Example]   아기가 열이 많이 나요. 39(삼십구)도예요.
My child has a high fever. It is 39 degrees Celsius.

2. something from inside the body appears

[Usage]   N이/가 나다

[Expression] 수염이 나다 to grow facial hair

여드름이 나다 to have acne

[Example]   사춘기가 되면 남자들은 턱에 수염이 난다.
When guys hit puberty, men start to grow facial hair.

3. feelings such as interest, irritation, courage and other emotions form

[Usage]   N이/가 나다

[Expression] 겁이 나다 to be scared

화가 나다 to be angry

용기가 나다 to be courageous

짜증이 나다 to be irritated

신경질이 나다 to be agitated

[Example]   거짓말하는 사람을 보면 화가 난다.
When I see people who are dishonest, it makes me mad.

4. a sound or smell come out from inside

[Usage]   N이/가 나다

[Expression] 냄새가 나다 to smell

향기가 나다 to smell a fragrance

연기가 나다 the smoke is forming

소리가 나다 a sound comes out

[Example]   방에서 이상한 소리가 나는데 무슨 소리예요?
There is some weird sound coming from the room. What is the sound?

5. sweat, blood, or tears coming out from the body

[Usage]   N이/가 나다

[Expression] 피가 나다 blood drips out

땀이 나다 sweat falls

눈물이 나다 tears fall

[Example] 급하게 뛰어가다가 넘어져서 무릎에 피가 났다.

I was in a hurry and I ran and fell, and my knee started to bleed.

035
다치다

[다치다] 동사 to get hurt

to get injured after running into something or getting hit

[Usage] N을/를 다치다

[Expression] 사람들이 다치다 the people are hurt

다리를 다치다 to hurt one's leg

[Example] 축구를 하다가 다리를 다쳤다. While playing soccer, I hurt my leg.

교통사고가 나서 많은 사람들이 다쳤습니다.

There was an accident and many people got hurt.

036
두통

[두통] 명사 headache, migraine

symptom that one's head hurts

[Expression] 두통약 headache medicine

두통이 심하다 the headache is serious

두통이 나다 the headache formed

[Example] 두통이 심해서 책을 읽을 수 없다.

My headache is severe so I can't read the book.

아버지가 두통이 난다고 하셔서 두통약을 드렸어요.

My father said he was having a headache so I gave him headache medicine.

037
따갑다

[따갑따] 형용사 to sting

the feeling of something pinching or stinging, ㅂverb

[Usage] N이/가 따갑다

[Example] 앗! 따가워! 바늘에 손이 찔렸어! Oh! It stings! The needle stung my hand!

눈병에 걸리면 눈이 아주 따갑다.

If you get an eye infection, your eyes will sting a lot.

038
몸살

[몸살] 명사 body ache

the body is very tired, doesn't have energy, the arm, legs hurt and forms a fever

[Expression] 감기몸살 body ache cold

몸살이 심하다 the body ache is severe

몸살이 나다 to have a body ache

[Example]	몸살이 나서 출근하지 못했어요. I had body ache so I couldn't go to work.
	몸살이 심하면 병원에 가 보세요.
	If you have a serious body ache, go to the hospital.

039
배탈

[배탈] **명사** stomach ache

having indigestion, diarrhea, or stomach pain

[Expression]	배탈약 stomach ache medicine
	배탈이 나다 to have a stomach ache
[Related word]	설사 diarrhea
[Example]	상한 음식을 먹고 배탈이 났어요.
	I ate rotten food and had a stomach ache.
	여름에 찬 음식을 많이 먹으면 배탈이 나니까 조심하세요.
	If you eat a lot of cold food in the summer, you will get a stomach ache, so be careful.

040
변비

[변비] **명사** constipation

an illness when poop does not come out or one has a hard time letting it out

[Expression]	변비약 constipation medicine
	변비가 있다 to have constipation
	변비가 심하다 the constipation is serious
	변비가 생기다 to have constipation
[Example]	저는 스트레스가 쌓이면 변비가 심해져요.
	Whenever I have a lot of stress, I get severe constipation.
	물을 많이 마시는 것이 변비에 좋다고 한다.
	Drinking a lot of water is good for constipation.

041
병²

[병] **명사** illness, disease

[Usage]	N병
[Expression]	심장병 heart disease
	병이 낫다 to be rid of the illness
	병이 나다 to form an illness
	병을 고치다 to cure an illness
	병에 걸리다 to catch an illness
[Example]	일을 너무 많이 해서 병이 났다. I worked so much that I formed an illness.
	병원에서 수술을 받고 병이 다 나았어요.
	I received surgery and it got rid of my illness.

042
부러지다

[부러지다] 동사 to break

something strong becomes broken

[Usage] **N**이/가 부러지다

[Expression] 다리가 부러지다 to break one's legs

[Example] 나뭇가지가 부러져서 떨어졌다. The tree branch broke and fell.

다리가 부러져서 병원에서 치료를 받았어요.
My leg broke so I received treatment at the hospital.

043
빠지다

[빠지다] 동사 to lose

to become less in strength, to be weaker in mind, to get rid of fat, or when hair falls out

[Usage] **N**이/가 빠지다

[Expression] 살이 빠지다 to lose weight

힘이 빠지다 to lose strength

머리카락이 빠지다 to lose hair

[Related word] 빼다 to lose

[Example] 요즘 아버지께서 머리카락이 빠져서 걱정을 많이 하십니다.
These days my father's hair keeps falling out so he is worrying a lot.

1(일)층부터 6(육)층까지 계단으로 올라오니까 다리의 힘이 빠져서 걸을 수가 없다.
I walked from the first floor to the sixth floor up the stairs and lost all of my leg strength, so I can't walk anymore.

044
상처

[상처] 명사 scar, injury, wound

[Expression] 상처가 깊다 the scar is deep

상처가 나다 to form a scar

상처를 치료하다 to treat the injury

[Example] 상처가 깊어서 피가 많이 나니까 빨리 병원에 갑시다.
The wound is deep and it is bleeding a lot, so we must hurry and go to the hospital.

팔에 있는 상처는 어렸을 때 친구와 놀다가 넘어져서 생긴 상처예요.
The scar on my arm formed after I fell from playing with my friend.

045
소화

[소화] 명사 digestion

[Expression] 소화제 digestive medicine

소화하다 to digest

소화가 되다 to be able to digest

[Example] 그저께부터 소화가 잘 되지 않아요. 소화제 좀 주세요.
I haven't been able to digest since the day before yesterday. Please give me digestive medicine.

점심을 먹은 후에 먹은 것을 소화시키기 위해서 산책을 했어요.
After eating lunch, I took a walk so I could digest.

046
식중독

[식쭝독] **명사** food poisoning

illness formed after eating rotten food, the stomach hurts. diarrhea, and vomit are some symptoms

[Expression] 식중독에 걸리다 to get food poisoning

[Example] 여름에는 식중독에 걸리기 쉬우니까 음식을 조심해서 먹어야 합니다.
It is easy to get food poisoning in the summer, so you need to be careful when you eat.

음식이 상했군요. 상한 음식을 먹으면 식중독에 걸리니까 이 음식을 버립시다.
The food is rotten. If you eat rotten food, you will get food poisoning, so let's throw away the food.

047
심하다

[심하다] **형용사** to be harsh, severe

to be worse than normal

[Expression] N이/가 심하다

심하게 **AV/DV**

[Usage] 병이 심하다 the illness is harsh

말이 심하다 the words are harsh

[Example] 어제 컴퓨터 게임 때문에 형과 심하게 싸웠다.
I fought severely with my brother over the computer game yesterday.

친구와 싸우다가 제가 심한 말을 해서 친구가 화가 많이 났어요.
While arguing with my friend, I said something harsh so my friend was very angry.

048
쓰리다

[쓰리다] **형용사** to feel burn (not in a hot way but stinging)

when the eye, skin, or stomach feels like there is something sharp poking, or when it is itchy and uncomfortable

[Usage] N이/가 쓰리다

[Example] 눈에 비눗물이 들어가서 쓰려요.
Soap water went into my eye and now my eye burns.

어제 회식에서 술을 많이 마셔서 속이 쓰리다.
Yesterday I drank too much at the dinner party and now my stomach burns.

049
아프다

[아프다] 형용사 to hurt

body and mind are not healthy and has some sort of illness, 으 verb

[Usage] N이/가 아프다

[Expression] 다리가 아프다 my leg hurts

마음이 아프다 my feelings are hurt

[Example] 몸이 아파서 일찍 퇴근했다. My body hurt so I left early from work.

컴퓨터를 오래 해서 머리도 아프고 눈도 아파요.

I was on the computer too long, so now my head and eyes hurt.

050
알레르기

[알레르기] 명사 allergy

some sort of substance goes into the body and the body reacts to that and forms an antibody, when the same substance goes into the body the substance and the antibody react and the body hurts

[Usage] N 알레르기

[Expression] 꽃가루 알레르기 flower pollen allergy

알레르기가 있다 to have allergies

[Example] 저는 매년 봄이 되면 꽃가루 알레르기 때문에 너무 힘들어요.

Every year during the spring, I suffer from allergies from the flower pollen.

환경이 나빠져서 한두 가지의 알레르기가 있는 사람들이 많다.

The environment has become so bad that there are many types of allergies that people have.

051
여드름

[여드름] 명사 acne

a small sore that appears on the face or the body

[Expression] 여드름이 나다 to have acne

[Example] 여드름에 좋은 약이 있어요?

Is there medicine that gets rid of acne effectively?

얼굴에 여드름이 많이 나서 고민이에요.

I am worrying because I have a lot of acne.

052
열¹

[열] 명사 fever

the temperature of the body is hotter than normal because of sickness

[Example] 열이 있다 to have fever

열이 높다 to have high fever

열이 나다 to get a fever

열이 내리다 to have lower fever

열이 떨어지다 the fever is dropping

[Example] 열이 많이 나는데 해열제가 있어요?
I have a high fever. Do you have a fever reducer?

이번 감기는 열이 높고 몸살이 심한 것이 특징입니다.
The feature of this cold is that you have a high fever and severe body ache.

053
충혈되다

[충혈되다] 동사 to have blood congestion

the symptom or having one part of your body to have collected blood in an abnormal way

[Expression] 눈이 충혈되다 to have bloodshot eyes

[Example] 눈이 충혈된 걸 보니까 눈병이 난 것 같아요.
I've noticed that my eyes are bloodshot. I think I have an eye infection.

밤을 새워서 일을 한 후에 거울을 보니까 두 눈이 빨갛게 충혈되어 있었다.
I looked at my eyes in the mirror after I had worked all night and they were bloodshot.

054
코피

[코피] 명사 nosebleed

[Expression] 코피가 나다 to get a bloody nose
코피가 멈추다 the nose blood stops
코피를 흘리다 the nose blood is running

[Example] 앗, 코피가 나요. 휴지 좀 주세요.
Oh, I have a bloody nose. Please give me a tissue.

제 하숙집 친구는 요즘 시험공부 때문에 잠을 많이 못 자서 코피를 자주 흘려요.
My boarding room friend has been getting bloody noses often because she's been studying for exams.

055
토하다

[토하다] 동사 to vomit

to not digest the food but to regurgitate it

[Usage] N을/를 토하다

[Example] 저녁에 먹은 음식이 소화가 잘 되지 않아서 다 토했어요.
The food that I ate for dinner didn't digest well, so I vomited.

의사 선생님, 아기가 자꾸 우유를 토해요. 왜 그런 거예요?
Doctor, my baby keeps vomiting milk. Why is he doing this?

056
통증

[통쯩] **명사** pain

symptom of pain

[Expression] 통증이 있다 to have pain

통증이 심하다 to have severe pain

통증을 느끼다 to feel pain

[Related word] 진통제 pain reliever

[Example] 허리 통증 때문에 진통제를 먹었어요.
I had lower back pains so I took some pain reliever.

낮에는 괜찮은데 밤이 되면 통증이 심해져서 잠을 잘 수 없다.
During the day I am fine but during the night the pain is so sever that I can't sleep.

057
피

[피] **명사** blood

[Expression] 피 한 방울 one drop of blood

피가 나다 to bleed

피가 멈추다 to stop bleeding

피를 흘리다 to bleed

[Synonym] 혈액 blood

[Example] 바늘에 찔려서 피가 났다. The needle poked me so I bled.

영수 씨, 코피를 너무 많이 흘렸어요. 빨리 병원에 가야겠어요.
Youngsoo, your nose bled too much. You better go to the hospital.

058
피곤하다

[피곤하다] **형용사** to be tired

to not have energy and be tired because one's body and mind are not well

[Usage] N이/가 피곤하다

[Example] 사장님, 피곤해 보이시는데 좀 쉬세요.
Boss, you look tired you should rest.

오랜만에 운동을 하니까 피곤해서 일찍 잤다.
I exercised after a long time of not exercising and was tired, so I slept early.

059
금연

[그면] **명사** 1. stop smoking   2. No smoking sign

1. stopping the habit of smoking

[Expression] 금연하다 to stop smoking
[Related word] 담배 cigarette
[Example] 아버지는 1(일)월 1(일)일부터 금연하기로 하셨어요.
My father decided to stop smoking on January the first.

2. not allowing one to smoke

[Expression] 금연석 non-smoking section
금연 구역 non-smoking area
[Antonym] 흡연 smoking
[Related word] 담배 cigarette
[Example] 이곳에는 어린 아이들이 많기 때문에 금연하셔야 합니다.
This place has a lot of children, so you need to stop smoking.

060
깁스

[깁스] **명사** cast

a plaster bandage that is wrapped around the injured area of the body

[Expression] 깁스하다 to have a cast on
깁스를 풀다 to take off a cast
[Example] 다리를 깁스해서 혼자 걸을 수 없어요.
I have casts on my legs so I can't walk alone.

팔을 깁스하니까 공부하기가 불편하다.
It is uncomfortable to study because I have a cast on my arm.

061
낫다

[낟따] **동사** to feel better

the injury or sickness on one's body becomes better or goes away,
ㅅverb

[Usage] N이/가 낫다
[Expression] 병이 낫다 the sickness get better
감기가 낫다 the cold is better
[Example] 병이 나으면 우리 같이 여행을 가자.
After you feel better, let's go on a trip together.

감기가 나으려면 무리하지 말고 푹 쉬어야 한다.
If you want the cold to go away, don't work too much and rest.

062
내과

[내꽈] 명사 internal medicine

medicine that gets rid of illness, it does not require surgery, or the department

[Expression] 내과 의사 internal medicine doctor

내과에 가다 to go to the department of internal medicine

[Example] 감기에 걸려서 내과에 갔습니다.
I had a cold so I went to the internal medicine department.

배가 아프면 내과에 가야 해. 빨리 가 봐.
If your stomach hurts, you need to go to the internal medicine department. Hurry and go.

🎈 도움말

These are some different departments of hospitals.

내과, 산부인과, 소아과, 안과, 외과, 이비인후과, 피부과, 치과, 성형외과, ……

internal medicine, gynecology, pediatrics, ophthalmology, surgery, otolaryngology, dermatology, dentistry, plastic surgery, ……

063
다이어트

[다이어트] 명사 diet

dieting to become healthier by selecting the right amount of food and exercising

[Expression] 다이어트하다 to diet

[Example] 음식의 양만 줄이고 운동을 하지 않으면 다이어트가 되지 않는다.
The diet does not work if you only decrease the amount of food and don't exercise.

저는 요즘 다이어트 중이어서 저녁 6(여섯)시가 지나면 아무것도 먹지 않아요.
I am dieting these days, so I don't eat anything after 6 pm.

064
문병

[문병] 명사 visiting the sick

going to the hospital to console a person who is sick

[Expression] 문병하다 to go to see the sick

문병을 가다 to go to visit the sick

[Related word] 병문안 visiting the sick

[Example] 병원에 문병을 갈 때 뭘 사 가지고 가면 좋을까요?
What should I buy when I go to the hospital to visit the sick person?

문병을 가서 너무 오랫동안 있으면 환자의 건강에 좋지 않습니다.
If you stay too long with the patient who is sick, it is not good for his or her health.

065
붕대

[붕대] 명사 bandage

a sanitary cloth that is wrapped or placed on the body if it is injured or scratched, the cloth allows air to be flown inside

[Expression]
붕대를 하다 to put a bandage on
붕대를 감다 to wrap a bandage
붕대를 풀다 to unravel a bandage
붕대로 감다 to wrap with the bandage

[Example]
간호사들은 피가 나는 동생의 머리를 붕대로 감았다.
The nurse wrapped a bandage around the bleeding part of my younger siblings head.

다친 다리에 붕대를 감기 전에 우선 소독을 하고 약을 바르세요.
Before you wrap the bandage around the leg, you should sanitize it and put some ointment on the wound.

066
비타민

[비타민] 명사 vitamin

one of the nutrients that people need for health and growth

[Example]
오렌지 주스와 귤에는 비타민C가 많다.
Orange juice has a lot of vitamin C from the tangerine.

과일과 채소에 비타민이 많으니까 고기만 먹지 말고 과일과 채소도 많이 먹어야 해요.
Fruits and vegetables have a lot of vitamin, so don't just eat meat but eat a lot of fruit and vegetables too.

067
수술

[수술] 명사 surgery

getting rid of an illness by cutting a part of the body and taking out the bad, and sewing the wound

[Usage]
<u>N</u> 수술

[Expression]
수술실 surgery room
심장 수술 heart surgery
수술하다 to get surgery
수술을 받다 to receive surgery

[Example]
그 여배우는 코를 수술한 것 같아. 예전보다 코가 높아졌어.
That actress looks like she got nose surgery. Her nose is higher than before.

할아버지는 8(여덟)시간 동안 수술을 받고 수술실에서 나오셨다.
My grandfather was in surgery for 8 hours and now he is out of the surgery room.

068
약

[약] 명사 medicine

drugs used to get rid of illness or prevent illness, it can be eaten, rubbed on, or used inside a shot

[Expression]   약국 pharmacy

약사 pharmacist

약을 짓다 to prepare medicine

약을 먹다 to take medicine

약을 바르다 to rub medicine on

[Example]   이 약은 하루 세 번 식후 30(삼십)분에 드세요.
Take this medicine 3 times a day 30 minutes after eating.

쓴 약이 몸에 좋으니까 맛이 없어도 다 먹어라.
Bitter medicine is good for your body, so eat it even though it doesn't taste good.

These are different types of medication.

• −제 : 소화제, 수면제, 진통제
digestive medicine, sleep medicine, pain reliever

• −약 : 감기약, 두통약, 소독약, 한약, 알약, 물약
cold medicine, headache pill, disinfecting medicine, herbal medicine, tablet, water based

• 연고
ointment

069
입원하다

[이붠하다] 동사 to be hospitalized

[Usage]   **N**에 입원하다

[Antonym]   퇴원하다 to be released from the hospital

[Example]   할머니가 몇 호실에 입원하셨어요?
What room is grandmother hospitalized in?

선생님께서 교통사고가 나서 2(이)주일 동안 병원에 입원하셔야 한다고 해요.
I heard that my teacher was in an accident and she has to be hospitalized for 2 weeks.

070
주사

[주사] 명사 shot

the shot, a needle inserted into the body to insert a liquid medicine

[Expression]   주사 한 대 one shot

주사를 놓다 to put in a shot

주사를 맞다 to take a shot

[Example] 아기가 주사를 맞고 아파서 울었다.
The child took the shot and started crying because it hurt.

주사를 한 대 맞으면 약만 먹는 것보다 더 빨리 나을 거예요.
If you get a shot, it will work better than only taking medication.

071 진단서

[진단서] 명사 medical certificate

a doctor's certificate that is written listing the sickness and result of the illness

[Example] 회사에 입사하려면 건강진단서를 제출해야 합니다.
If you want to enter a company, you must give a medical certificate to the office.

아파서 휴직하는 경우에는 병원 진단서를 내야 한다.
If you are sick and don't come to work, you must give the office the medical certificate.

072 진찰

[진찰] 명사 examination

a doctor looking over a patients illness by listening to the patient and using instruments to tell what the symptoms are

[Expression] 진찰실 examination room
진찰하다 to examine
진찰을 받다 to get examined

[Example] 몸이 안 좋아서 병원에 진찰을 받으러 갔다.
I wasn't feeling good so I went to the hospital to get an examination.

집에서 며칠 쉬어도 나을 것 같지 않아요. 병원에 가서 꼭 진찰을 받으셔야겠어요.
I don't think you'll get better even if you rest for a few days at home. You need to go to the hospital and get an examination.

073 처방

[처방] 명사 prescription

prescribing medication according to the symptoms or to heal the illness

[Expression] 처방전 prescription
처방하다 to prescribe
처방을 받다 to receive a prescription

[Example] 처방전을 가지고 가야 약국에서 약을 살 수 있습니다.
You must take the prescription to the pharmacy so that you can buy the medication.

의사 선생님이 어머니를 진찰한 후에 처방을 해 주었다.
The doctor examined my mother and gave her the prescription afterward.

074
한약

[하냑] 명사 herbal medicine

medicine made from the oriental medicine clinic that has been prescribed and made

[Expression] 한약을 먹다 to take the herbal medicine

한약을 짓다 to prescribe herbal medicine

[Related word] 한의원 oriental medicine clinic

한의사 oriental medicine doctor

[Example] 한의원에 가서 2(두)달 동안 먹을 한약을 지었다.
I went to the oriental medicine hospital and prescribed for 2 months worth of herbal medicine.

한약이 써서 저는 한약을 먹은 후에 꼭 사탕을 먹어요.
Herbal medicine is so bitter that I always eat candy after I take the medication.

075
환자

[환자] 명사 patient

a person who must receive treatment for an illness or injury

[Usage] N 환자

[Example] 오늘은 수술할 환자가 많아서 하루 종일 바쁠 것 같다.
There are a lot of patients needing surgery today so I will be busy all day.

병원에 가니까 요즘 환절기여서 그런지 감기 환자가 많았어요.
The seasons are changing these days so there seems to be a lot of patients who caught cold in the hospital.

[1~15] 다음 단어를 한국어로 바꿔 쓰십시오. Change these words into Korean.

1. back	(	)	2. face	(	)
3. arm	(	)	4. chest	(	)
5. body ache	(	)	6. constipation	(	)
7. digestion	(	)	8. shoulders	(	)
9. face	(	)	10. vitamin	(	)
11. allergy	(	)	12. to sting	(	)
13. to feel burn	(	)	14. to vomit	(	)
15. to be tired	(	)			

[16~20] 그림을 보고 (   )에 알맞은 것을 고르십시오.

Look at the picture and choose the correct word.

16.

가 : 남자 친구와 제 사진이에요.

나 : 남자 친구가 (   )이/가 크고 잘생겼군요!

❶ 배   ❷ 뼈

❸ 키   ❹ 다리

17.

가 : 어디가 아파서 오셨어요?

나 : (   )이/가 아파요.

❶ 발   ❷ 손

❸ 어깨   ❹ 허리

18.

가 : 아이가 아파요?

나 : 네, (   )이/가 많이 나요.

❶ 열   ❷ 두통

❸ 머리   ❹ 여드름

19.

가 : 어디가 아프세요?

나 : (   )이/가 너무 아파요.

❶ 귀   ❷ 눈

❸ 입   ❹ 코

20.

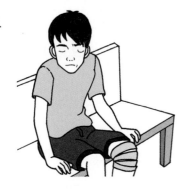

가 : 다리가 왜 그래요? 다쳤어요?

나 : 네, 운동을 하다가 (   )을/를 다쳤어요.

❶ 목   ❷ 발

❸ 팔   ❹ 무릎

[21~30] 다음 문장을 읽고 알맞은 어휘를 골라 쓰십시오. 어휘는 한 번만 쓰십시오.
Read the following sentence and choose the right word. Use the words once.

손	약	피	감기	건강
깁스	상처	몸살	배탈	소화
통증	비타민	다치다	빠지다	심하다

21. (   )에 걸려서 기침이 나요.

22. 질문이 있으면 (   )을/를 드세요.

23. 칼에 손을 베어서 (   )이/가 난다.

24. 진통제를 먹어도 (   )이/가 심해요.

25. 요즘 할아버지는 (   )이/가 어떠세요?

26. (   )이/가 났을 때에는 잘 쉬어야 합니다.

27. 얼굴에 (   )이/가 있어서 보기에 안 좋아요.

28. 머리가 아파서 약국에 (   )을/를 사러 갑니다.

29. 여름에 찬 음식을 많이 먹으면 (   )이/가 나요.

30. 교통사고가 나서 많은 사람들이 (   )었어요/았어요/였어요.

[31~35] (   ) 안에 알맞은 것을 고르십시오. Choose the correct one.

31. 등이 가려우면 이 약을 (   )어/아/여 보세요.

   ❶ 서다   ❷ 쉬다   ❸ 씻다   ❹ 바르다

32. 진찰을 받은 후에 (   )을/를 맞았다.

   ❶ 깁스   ❷ 주사   ❸ 붕대   ❹ 처방

33. 운동을 하니까 이마에서 (   )이/가 납니다.

❶ 땀　　　　　❷ 가래　　　　　❸ 비타민　　　　❹ 알레르기

34. 계단에서 넘어져서 다리가 (   )었어요/았어요/였어요.

❶ 낫다　　　　❷ 다치다　　　　❸ 토하다　　　　❹ 부러지다

35. 중학생이 되니까 얼굴에 (   )이/가 나기 시작했다.

❶ 배탈　　　　❷ 상처　　　　　❸ 여드름　　　　❹ 알레르기

[36~40] 밑줄 친 부분과 반대되는 뜻을 가진 것을 고르십시오.
Choose the word that is the opposite of the underlined word.

36. **가 :** 손가락이 <u>가늘</u>어요?

　　나 : 아니요, (   )어요/아요/여요.

❶ 굵다　　　　❷ 얇다　　　　　❸ 두껍다　　　　❹ 튼튼하다

37. **가 :** 요즘 <u>아픈</u> 사람이 많은 것 같아요.

　　나 : 네, 몸이 (   )어야/아야/여야 일도 잘 할 수 있지요.

❶ 크다　　　　❷ 마르다　　　　❸ 건강하다　　　❹ 뚱뚱하다

38. **가 :** 감기에 <u>걸렸</u>어요?

　　나 : 네, 하지만 거의 (   )었어요/았어요/였어요.

❶ 걸다　　　　❷ 낫다　　　　　❸ 하다　　　　　❹ 내리다

39. **가 :** 건물 안에서는 <u>담배를 피우면</u> 안 됩니다.

　　나 : 화장실에서도 (   )어야/아야/여야 되지요?

❶ 닦다　　　　❷ 앉다　　　　　❸ 금연하다　　　❹ 청소하다

40. **가** : 영수 씨가 지난달에 <u>퇴원했지요</u>?

    나 : 네, 그런데 건강이 안 좋아지셔서 어제 다시 (   )었어요/았어요/였어요.

    ❶ 입원하다   ❷ 수술하다   ❸ 진찰하다   ❹ 처방하다

[41~45] 밑줄 친 부분과 의미가 가장 가까운 것을 고르십시오.
Choose the word that is most similar to the underlined section.

41. **가** : <u>신체</u>가 건강하지요?

    나 : 그럼요. 제 (   )은/는 아주 건강해요.

    ❶ 목   ❷ 몸   ❸ 뼈   ❹ 속

42. **가** : 요즘 감기 때문에 <u>아픈 사람</u>이 많은 것 같아요.

    나 : 네, 그래서 병원에 (   )이/가 많아서 복잡해요.

    ❶ 상처   ❷ 한약   ❸ 환자   ❹ 비타민

43. **가** : 선생님, <u>머리가 아파서</u> 집에 일찍 가고 싶어요.

    나 : (   )이/가 심해요? 그럼 집에 가서 약을 먹고 쉬세요.

    ❶ 열   ❷ 두통   ❸ 얼굴   ❹ 충혈

44. **가** : 나는 뚱뚱해서 <u>살을 빼야</u> 해. 오늘부터 저녁을 안 먹을 거야.

    나 : (   )을/를 할 때 밥을 안 먹는 것보다 조금 먹고 운동을 하는 것이 더 좋다고 해.

    ❶ 변비   ❷ 소화   ❸ 식중독   ❹ 다이어트

45. **가** : 요즘 <u>건강해진</u> 것 같아요.

    나 : 네, 운동을 열심히 해서 (   )었어요/았어요/였어요.

    ❶ 빠지다   ❷ 커지다   ❸ 떨어지다   ❹ 튼튼해지다

[46~50] 밑줄 친 단어의 쓰임이 잘못된 것을 고르십시오. Choose the one that is incorrectly used.

46. ❶ 옆집에서 이상한 소리가 <u>나요</u>.　　　　　(　　)
　　❷ 오늘 갑자기 약속이 <u>났습니다</u>.
　　❸ 이 소설책을 읽고 슬퍼서 눈물이 <u>났어요</u>.
　　❹ 남자 친구가 계속 거짓말을 해서 화가 <u>났다</u>.

47. ❶ 지난 밤에 열이 <u>심하게</u> 났다.　　　　　(　　)
　　❷ 통증이 <u>심하면</u> 진통제를 드리겠습니다.
　　❸ 시험이 있어서 공부를 아주 <u>심하게</u> 했다.
　　❹ 말이 좀 <u>심한</u> 것 같아요. 다음부터 말조심하세요.

48. ❶ 이 병은 <u>진찰해야</u> 나을 수 있습니다.　　　　　(　　)
　　❷ 병원에 입원한 친구를 <u>문병하러</u> 갔다.
　　❸ 할머니는 병이 다 <u>나으셔서</u> 퇴원하셨어요.
　　❹ 강아지가 병에 <u>걸려서</u> 동물 병원에 데리고 갔다.

49. ❶ 다리가 <u>굵어서</u> 치마를 잘 입지 않아요.　　　　　(　　)
　　❷ 일주일 동안 샤워를 못해서 몸이 <u>가늘어요</u>.
　　❸ 우유를 먹었는데 속이 <u>쓰려요</u>. 왜 그럴까요?
　　❹ 발바닥이 <u>따가워요</u>. 신발 안에 뭐가 있는 것 같아요.

50. ❶ 팔이 <u>상해서</u> 깁스를 했어요.　　　　　(　　)
　　❷ 운동을 하다가 다리를 <u>다쳤어요</u>.
　　❸ 저녁에 먹은 음식을 모두 <u>토했어요</u>.
　　❹ 운동을 열심히 해서 살이 <u>빠졌어요</u>.

정답 · 색인

Answers
Index

01 · 위치와 장소

1. 옆
2. 밑
3. 근처
4. 빵집
5. 병원
6. 백화점
7. 박물관
8. 수영장
9. 대사관
10. 걸다
11. 두다
12. 밝다
13. 조용하다
14. 올려놓다
15. 시끄럽다
16. ❹
17. ❸
18. ❶
19. ❹
20. ❶
21. 놓으세요
22. 근처에
23. 밑으로
24. 있으면
25. 넣으세요
26. 걸어
27. 앞에
28. 시끄러운
29. 어두워요
30. 밝군요
31. ❶
32. ❹
33. ❹
34. ❷
35. ❸
36. ❸
37. ❹
38. ❶
39. ❹
40. ❶
41. ❸
42. ❷
43. ❶
44. ❷
45. ❷
46. ❷
47. ❷
48. ❹
49. ❶
50. ❸

02 · 물건

1. 옷
2. 칼
3. 컵
4. 공책
5. 속옷
6. 연필
7. 의자
8. 책상
9. 침대
10. 칫솔
11. 에어컨
12. 컴퓨터
13. 크다
14. 다르다
15. 무겁다
16. ❷
17. ❹
18. ❷
19. ❶
20. ❸
21. 가위로
22. 냄비에
23. 매고
24. 들어
25. 물건도
26. 가지고
27. 메고
28. 봉투에
29. 고치려고
30. 멋져요
31. ❸
32. ❸
33. ❶
34. ❶
35. ❹
36. ❷
37. ❶
38. ❷
39. ❸
40. ❶
41. ❸
42. ❹
43. ❷
44. ❸
45. ❷
46. ❶
47. ❹
48. ❸
49. ❷
50. ❸

03 · 시간 I

1. 밤
2. 백
3. 분
4. 날짜
5. 내년
6. 시월
7. 어제
8. 언제
9. 연휴
10. 오전
11. 일곱
12. 일억
13. 하나
14. 금요일
15. 수요일
16. ❷
17. ❹
18. ❸
19. ❹
20. ❷
21. 아침에
22. 밤마다
23. 올해가
24. 많네요
25. 늦었다
26. 오전에는
27. 지났네요
28. 낮이
29. 주말에
30. 내일
31. ❸
32. ❶
33. ❷
34. ❶
35. ❹
36. ❷
37. ❶
38. ❹
39. ❶
40. ❶
41. ❷
42. ❷
43. ❹
44. ❶
45. ❶
46. ❷
47. ❸
48. ❸
49. ❷
50. ❶

04 · 시간 Ⅱ

1. 때
2. 시간
3. 며칠
4. 오래
5. 주일
6. 바로
7. 옛날
8. 요즘
9. 자주
10. 열흘
11. 짧다
12. 가끔
13. 틈틈이
14. 갑자기
15. 서두르다
16. ❶
17. ❹
18. ❸
19. ❷
20. ❹
21. 동안
22. 먼저
23. 바로
24. 아직
25. 계속
26. 천천히
27. 때
28. 첫
29. 갑자기
30. 요즘에는
31. ❹
32. ❸
33. ❹
34. ❹
35. ❷
36. ❹
37. ❸
38. ❷
39. ❹
40. ❹
41. ❶
42. ❸
43. ❶
44. ❸
45. ❸
46. ❸
47. ❸
48. ❸
49. ❶
50. ❷

05 · 사람 Ⅰ

1. 형
2. 고모
3. 누구
4. 성격
5. 아무
6. 여자
7. 친구
8. 형제
9. 귀엽다
10. 드시다
11. 멋있다
12. 친하다
13. 아가씨
14. 아저씨
15. 룸메이트
16. ❶
17. ❷
18. ❶
19. ❸
20. ❸
21. 말씀을
22. 서로
23. 생신
24. 잡수셨어요
25. 아이가
26. 친절합니다
27. 멋있어요
28. 아기가
29. 착한
30. 남자
31. ❶
32. ❹
33. ❷
34. ❷
35. ❶
36. ❹
37. ❷
38. ❷
39. ❷
40. ❹
41. ❷
42. ❷
43. ❶
44. ❶
45. ❷
46. ❸
47. ❸
48. ❹
49. ❶
50. ❸

06 · 사람 Ⅱ

1. 걱정
2. 화가
3. 교수
4. 비서
5. 모델
6. 선수
7. 필요
8. 행복
9. 걷다
10. 잊다
11. 기쁘다
12. 외롭다
13. 내려가다
14. 심심하다
15. 재미있다
16. ❷
17. ❸
18. ❶
19. ❷
20. ❸
21. 아마
22. 생각이에요
23. 기분이
24. 물론
25. 누워서
26. 감사합니다
27. 사랑하는
28. 주부예요
29. 배우가
30. 뛰어서
31. ❸
32. ❶
33. ❶
34. ❹
35. ❸
36. ❸
37. ❹
38. ❸
39. ❷
40. ❶
41. ❸
42. ❷
43. ❶
44. ❸
45. ❹
46. ❷
47. ❹
48. ❶
49. ❹
50. ❸

07 · 일상 생활 Ⅰ

1. 뉴스
2. 답장
3. 우표
4. 주소
5. 목욕
6. 일기
7. 세수
8. 쉬다
9. 쓰다
10. 씻다
11. 켜다

12. 끊다
13. 세우다
14. 부치다
15. 붙이다
16. ❹
17. ❶
18. ❸
19. ❷
20. ❸
21. 연락하고
22. 세워
23. 일어나면
24. 듣는
25. 번
26. 놀고
27. 발랐어요
28. 눌러서
29. 국제전화를
30. 생활이
31. ❶
32. ❹
33. ❶
34. ❸
35. ❷
36. ❷
37. ❶
38. ❹
39. ❸
40. ❹
41. ❶
42. ❹
43. ❸
44. ❷
45. ❸
46. ❶
47. ❷
48. ❸
49. ❶
50. ❷

08 · 일상 생활 Ⅱ

1. 돈
2. 꼭
3. 상품
4. 선약
5. 손님
6. 점원
7. 파티
8. 현금
9. 초대
10. 취소
11. 환영하다
12. 이야기
13. 주다
14. 사다
15. 보이다
16. ❶
17. ❹
18. ❷
19. ❸
20. ❹
21. 어느
22. 무엇으로
23. 얼마예요
24. 짜리
25. 같이
26. 깎아
27. 송별회를
28. 바꿨다
29. 미뤄야
30. 싸서
31. ❹
32. ❸
33. ❸
34. ❹
35. ❹
36. ❷
37. ❹
38. ❸
39. ❶
40. ❸

41. ❷
42. ❹
43. ❶
44. ❹
45. ❸
46. ❷
47. ❷
48. ❶
49. ❷
50. ❸

09 · 학교와 직장

1. 발전
2. 분필
3. 방학
4. 사업
5. 사장
6. 선배
7. 소풍
8. 졸업
9. 직원
10. 직장
11. 회의
12. 하숙집
13. 지내다
14. 연습하다
15. 아르바이트
16. ❹
17. ❸
18. ❸
19. ❷
20. ❶
21. 준비는
22. 실례합니다
23. 교과서를
24. 벌고
25. 동기들과
26. 지각했다
27. 출장을
28. 읽어야
29. 중요한

30. 여행을
31. ❹
32. ❷
33. ❸
34. ❷
35. ❶
36. ❸
37. ❹
38. ❸
39. ❹
40. ❶
41. ❷
42. ❶
43. ❸
44. ❹
45. ❶
46. ❸
47. ❶
48. ❸
49. ❶
50. ❶

10 · 여가

1. 팀
2. 관광
3. 기념
4. 비자
5. 상영
6. 연극
7. 영화
8. 예매
9. 숙박
10. 산책
11. 미술
12. 음악
13. 드라마
14. 추다
15. 던지다
16. ❶
17. ❷
18. ❸

19. ④
20. ④
21. 보통
22. 표를
23. 노래를
24. 기념으로
25. 사진을
26. 독서를
27. 악기를
28. 비용이
29. 취미는
30. 예약을
31. ①
32. ②
33. ④
34. ③
35. ②
36. ①
37. ④
38. ③
39. ④
40. ②
41. ④
42. ①
43. ②
44. ①
45. ④
46. ④
47. ③
48. ④
49. ①
50. ③

11 · 음식

1. 곡물
2. 냉면
3. 두부
4. 된장
5. 라면
6. 치즈
7. 초밥

8. 굽다
9. 돈가스
10. 참기름
11. 초콜릿
12. 햄버거
13. 다지다
14. 샌드위치
15. 아이스크림
16. ①
17. ③
18. ④
19. ②
20. ①
21. 우유로
22. 소금을
23. 피자는
24. 볶았어요
25. 뜨거울
26. 술을
27. 단
28. 과일을
29. 짜니까
30. 간식을
31. ④
32. ④
33. ③
34. ③
35. ②
36. ①
37. ③
38. ①
39. ②
40. ③
41. ②
42. ④
43. ③
44. ④
45. ③
46. ④
47. ②
48. ③
49. ①

50. ④

12 · 교통

1. 차
2. 역
3. 멀다
4. 방향
5. 왕복
6. 출구
7. 택시
8. 안전선
9. 지하도
10. 똑바로
11. 건너다
12. 밀리다
13. 도착하다
14. 돌아가다
15. 하차하다, 내리다
16. ①
17. ②
18. ①
19. ③
20. ④
21. 사거리에서
22. 위험하니까
23. 승강장에서
24. 기차를
25. 신호등이
26. 호선을
27. 노선도를
28. 약도를
29. 요금이
30. 방법을
31. ④
32. ①
33. ④
34. ③
35. ④
36. ④
37. ①
38. ③

39. ③
40. ②
41. ②
42. ④
43. ③
44. ①
45. ④
46. ④
47. ③
48. ②
49. ④
50. ①

13 · 자연과 계절

1. 돌
2. 철
3. 마리
4. 송이
5. 안개
6. 오리
7. 바람
8. 폭포
9. 바다
10. 환절기
11. 분홍색
12. 초록색
13. 노랗다
14. 쌀쌀하다
15. 아름답다
16. ①
17. ④
18. ②
19. ②
20. ③
21. 여름에
22. 호수가
23. 고양이를
24. 피서를
25. 모래가
26. 색깔은
27. 쌀쌀하니까

28. 경치가
29. 따뜻합니다
30. 불어요
31. ❶
32. ❹
33. ❸
34. ❹
35. ❸
36. ❷
37. ❶
38. ❷
39. ❷
40. ❸
41. ❹
42. ❸
43. ❷
44. ❸
45. ❶
46. ❸
47. ❸
48. ❶
49. ❷
50. ❹

14 · 주거

1. 문
2. 방
3. 거실
4. 난방
5. 달력
6. 세제
7. 얼룩

8. 이사
9. 커튼
10. 아파트
11. 옷걸이
12. 집들이
13. 엘리베이터
14. 빨다
15. 맡기다
16. ❸
17. ❶
18. ❹
19. ❷
20. ❹
21. 벽에
22. 버렸다
23. 닦았어요
24. 서재에서
25. 열지
26. 편안한
27. 계단으로
28. 쓸어야
29. 불을
30. 정리해라
31. ❹
32. ❶
33. ❹
34. ❷
35. ❷
36. ❶
37. ❸
38. ❷
39. ❶
40. ❹

41. ❷
42. ❸
43. ❶
44. ❷
45. ❶
46. ❷
47. ❶
48. ❸
49. ❷
50. ❸

15 · 건강

1. 등
2. 얼굴
3. 팔
4. 가슴
5. 몸살
6. 변비
7. 소화
8. 어깨
9. 얼굴
10. 비타민
11. 알레르기
12. 따갑다
13. 쓰리다
14. 토하다
15. 피곤하다
16. ❸
17. ❶
18. ❶
19. ❷
20. ❹

21. 감기에
22. 손을
23. 피가
24. 통증이
25. 건강이
26. 몸살이
27. 상처가
28. 약을
29. 배탈이
30. 다쳤어요
31. ❹
32. ❷
33. ❶
34. ❹
35. ❸
36. ❶
37. ❸
38. ❷
39. ❸
40. ❶
41. ❷
42. ❸
43. ❷
44. ❹
45. ❹
46. ❷
47. ❸
48. ❶
49. ❷
50. ❶

표: 표제어(headwords), **유**: 유의어(synonyms), **반**: 반의어(antonyms), **관**: 관련어(related words)

416

외국인을 위한 **한국어 어휘 연습 (초급)**

편저자 연세대학교 한국어학당 교재편찬위원회
집필진 전나영 · 김지혜 · 이선영 · 이은지
펴낸곳 연세대학교 출판문화원

주소 서울시 서대문구 연세로 50
전화 2123-3380~2
팩스 2123-8673
　　　 ysup@yonsei.ac.kr
　　　 http://www.yonsei.ac.kr/press
등록 1955년 10월 13일 제9-60호
인쇄 (주)네오프린텍

2011년 12월 9일 1판 1쇄　　　2012년 5월 25일 1판 2쇄
ISBN 978-89-7141-970-0(03710)

값 **25,000원**